Theory of
Computation and Application
(Automata Theory and Formal Languages)

By

Dr. Anil Kumar Malviya
Associate Professor
Department of Computer Science & Engineering,
Kamla Nehru Institute of Technology,
Sultanpur

Dr. Malabika Datta
Associate Professor (Retired)
Department of Mathematics, Agra College,
Agra

BPB PUBLICATIONS
B-14 Connaught Place, New Delhi-110 001

FIRST EDITION 2015

Copyright © BPB Publications, India

ISBN : 978-81-8333-528-7

Distributors:

COMPUTER BOOK CENTRE
12, Shrungar Shopping Centre,
M.G. Road, BENGALURU-560001
Ph: 25587923, 25584641

MICRO BOOKS
Shanti Niketan Building,
8, Camac Street, KOLKATA-700017
Ph: 22826518/22826519

MICRO MEDIA
Shop No. 5, Mahendra Chambers,
150 DN Rd. Next to Capital Cinema,
V.T. (C.S.T.) Station, MUMBAI-400 001
Ph: 22078296/22078297

DECCAN AGENCIES
4-3-329, Bank Street,
HYDERABAD-500195
Ph: 24756967/24756400

BPB PUBLICATIONS
B-14, Connaught Place,
NEW DELHI-110001
Ph:23325760/43526249

BPB BOOK CENTRE
376, Old Lajpat Rai Market,
DELHI-110 006,
Ph: 23861747

INFOTECH
G-2, Sidhartha Building,
96 Nehru Place,
NEW DELHI-110 019
Ph: 26438245

BPB PUBLICATIONS
20, Ansari Road, Darya Ganj,
NEW DELHI-110002
Ph: 23254990/23254991

Published by Manish Jain for BPB Publications, B-14, Connaught Place, New Delhi – 110001 and Printed by him at Akash Press.

Dedicated to
My Parent, My Wife Archana
and
My Daughters Anshita and Arohi
Dr. Anil Kumar Malviya

Preface

This book is designed as a text book for the first course in Theory of Computation and Application (Automata Theory and Formal Languages) for the students of B.Tech Computer Science and Engineering, B.Tech Information Technology and Master in Computer Application (MCA) programs of Uttar Pradesh Technical University, Lucknow, as well as other Indian Universities.

Theory of Computation is a scientific discipline, concerned with the fundamental capabilities and limitations of computers. Being a major foundation of computer science, it forms the part of syllabi of almost all undergraduate and postgraduate courses in computer science. However, many computer science undergraduates lack the mathematical maturity to be able to appreciate the subject.

The overall objective of this book is to provide a reasonable level of understanding of Theory of Automata and Formal languages, the major areas of theory of computation. The book intends to serve as a guide and a motivator even for the average student to follow the subject. The proofs are written with a level of detail that facilitates easy understanding. Each Chapter includes solved examples, wherever felt necessary, to clarify a concept. An extensive variety of exercises, including objective questions, review questions and programming problems, have been added at the end of each Chapter. Answers to objective questions and solutions/hints to solutions of selected review questions have been provided. These features, we hope, will make this book useful for both students and faculty members.

Organization of the book

Chapter 1 introduces theory of computation. We also present an overview of some of the important basic concepts essential for an understanding of the rest of the text.

Chapter 2 introduces the concept of a finite automaton, the simplest abstract model of a computing device. We discuss DFA, NFA with and without ε-transition, Moore and Mealy machines and the equivalence and conversion between them. Chapter 2 also contains Myhill-Nerode theorem and optimization of Finite Automata.

Chapter 3 discusses regular expression, which is one of the ways to represent the regular languages. We present an in-depth discussion of Transition Graph, Kleene's theorem and Arden's theorem. We then explore the relationship between regular expression and Finite Automaton and vice-versa.

Chapter 4 provides full discussion of regular languages and their closure properties. It covers Pigeonhole principle and Pumping lemma theorem which are used to show that some of the languages are non-regular. Decidability of finite automata and regular languages are explored. We end with a discussion on the relationship between computers and regular languages.

Chapter 5 presents context-free grammar (CFG) and regular grammar. We discuss derivation, parse tree and ambiguity in grammars. We demonstrate how to simplify the context-free grammar. Chomsky and Greibach normal forms, useful in proving many theorems, are considered next. The method of converting a context-free grammar into these normal forms concludes the Chapter.

Chapter 6 deals with Pushdown Automata (PDA), which describes context-free grammar. Methods of converting CFG to PDA and vice-versa are discussed next. PDA is a non-deterministic device and deterministic version describes deterministic context-free language, a subset of a context-free language. The Chapter ends with a description of two stack pushdown automata.

Chapter 7 is on pumping lemma that is used to prove that certain languages are not context-free languages. This Chapter also addresses closure and decision properties of context-free languages and grammars.

Chapter 8 is devoted to Turing machine, the ultimate mathematical model of a computer. The Chapter considers basic Turing model, the different ways to represent the Turing machine and the modifications of Turing machine. We then present a thorough discussion of use of Turing machine as a computer of integer functions. The Chapter also includes Linear Bounded Automata, a special Turing machine. Church's thesis concludes the chapter.

Recursively enumerable languages and decidability are introduced in Chapter 9. The language defined by a Turing machine is recursively enumerable language. We discuss Types of grammars and Chomsky Hierarchy of grammar. We then present Decidable and undecidable problems. The Chapter also covers Turing halting problem, PCP, and modified PCP. Finally, we end with recursive function theory.

We heartily welcome comments and suggestions from our students and faculty members for further improvement of the contents of this book.

Authors

Uttar Pradesh Technical University, Lucknow
(Effective from the Session: 2014-2015)
B.Tech (CS/IT), Semester IV
NCS 402: Theory of Automata and Formal Languages

UNIT-1 (Covered in Chapters 1, 2 and Chapter 3)

Introduction: Alphabets, Strings, and Languages; Automata and Grammars, Deterministic finite Automata (DFA) - Formal Definition, Simplified notation: State Transition Graph, Transition Table, Language of DFA, Non-Deterministic Finite Automata (NFA) - NFA with ε-Transitions, Equivalence of NFA and DFA, Minimization of Finite Automata, Distingushing one string from other, Myhill-Nerode Theorem.

UNIT-2 (Covered in Chapters 2, 3 and Chapter 4)

Regular Expression(RE), Definition, Operators of regular expression and their precedence, Algebraic laws for Regular expressions, Kleen's Theorem, Regular expression to FA, DFA to Regular Expression, Arden Theorem, Non-Regular Languages, Pumping Lemma for regular languages, Application of Pumping Lemma, Closure properties of Regular Languages, Decision properties of Regular Languages, Finite Automata with Output: Moore Machine and Mealy Machine, Equivalence of Moore and Mealy Machine, Applications and Limitation of FA.

UNIT-3 (Covered in Chapter 5 and Chapter 7)

Context-Free Grammar(CFG) and Context-Free Languages (CFL): Definition, Examples, Derivation, Derivation Trees, Ambiguity in Grammer, Inherent ambiguity, Ambiguous to Unambiguous CFG, Useless symbols, Simplification of CFGs, Normal Forms of CFGs: CNF and GNF, Closure properties of CFLs, Decision Properties of CFLs: Emptiness, Finiteness and Membership, Pumping Lemma for CFLs.

Unit-4 (Covered in Chapter 6)

Pushdown Down Automata(PDA): Definition and Description, Instantaneous Description, Language of PDA, Acceptance by Final state, Acceptance by empty stack, Deterministic PDA, Equivalence of PDA and CFG, CFG to PDA and PDA to CFG, Two Stack PDA.

UNIT-5 (Covered in Chapter 8 and Chapter 9)

Turing Machines(TM): Basic Model, definition and representation, Instantaneous Description, Language acceptance by TM, Variants of Turing Machine, Turing Machine as Computer of Integer Functions, Universal Turing Machine, Church Thesis, Recursive and recursively enumerable languages, Halting Problem, Introduction to Undecidability, Undeciable problems about TMs, Post Correspondence Problem (PCP), Modified PCP, Introduction to Recursive Function Theory.

Uttar Pradesh Technical University, Lucknow
MCA (II Semester)
(Effective from the Session: 2013-2014)

NMCA-214: Introduction to Automata Theory and Languages

UNIT-1 (Covered in Chapter 1 and Chapter 2)

Basic Concepts of Automata Theory: Alphabets, Strings, and Languages, Deterministic Finite Automata(DFA) and Non-Deterministic Finite Automata (NFA)-Definition, Representation using Transition Tables and State Diagrams, NFA with ε-Transitions, Equivalence of NFA and DFA.

UNIT-2 (Covered in Chapters 2, 3 and Chapter 4)

Regular Expressions and Languages: Introduction, Definition of regular expressions, Kleen's Theorem, Equivalence of regular expression and Finite Automata, Pumping Lemma for regular languages, Closure properties of Regular Languages, Decision properties of Regular Languages, Finite Automata with Output: Moore Machine, Mealy Machine, Equivalence of Moore and Mealy Machines.

UNIT-3 (Covered in Chapters 5, 6, 7 and Chapter 9)

Non-Regular Grammars: Definition of Grammar, Classification of Grammars, Chomsky Hierarchy, Context-Free Grammar(CFG) and Context-Free Languages (CFL)-Definition, Examples, Derivation Trees, Ambiguous Grammars, Simplification of Grammars, Normal Forms of CFGs: CNF, GNF, Closure properties of CFLs, Decision Properties of CFLs, Pumping Lemma for CFL, Pushdown Automata (PDA): Definition and Description, Language of PDA and its applications.

UNIT-4 (Covered in Chapter 8 and Chapter 9)

Turing Machines : Introduction, Basic Features of Turing Machine, Language of Turing Machine, Varients of Turing Machine: Multitapes, Non-deterministic Turing Machine, Universal Turing machine, Turing Machine as Computer of Integer Functions, Halting Problem, Linear Bounded Automata, Church-Turing Thesis.

UNIT-5

Undecidability: Introduction, Undecidable problems about Turing Machines, Rice's Theorem, Post's Correspondance Problem(PCP) and modified PCP, Tractable and Intractable Problems: P and NP, NP-Complete Problems, Introduction to Recursive Function Theory.

Contents

Chapter 1

Introduction and Basic Concepts

The present Chapter begins with a discussion on the theory of computation. This is followed by a review of some of the basic mathematical concepts used in this book and by an introduction to formal languages. Much of the notation used in the subsequent Chapters is also presented here.

Objectives

The purpose of this Chapter is to introduce the theory of computation and provide the basis for understanding the rest of the text. After learning the contents of this Chapter, you will be able to:

1.   Understand what the theory of computation is and how it is different from other computing discipline in computer science,
2.   Define some basic mathematical concepts,
3.   Explain three proofing techniques viz. proof by contradiction, proof by construction and proof by induction,
4.   Describe symbols, alphabet and strings, and
5.   Understand formal languages.

1.1   Introduction to Theory of Computation

Computer science can be classified into two main groups: one that focuses on fundamental ideas and models for underlying computing systems and the other that focuses on engineering techniques for the design of computing systems, both hardware and software, especially on the application of theory to design. The theory of computation deals with the first group.

The theory of computation is a scientific discipline concerned with the fundamental capabilities and limitations of computers. It aims at providing an insight into what can be computed and how efficiently it can be done. The field is divided into three major subfields: automata theory, computability theory and computational complexity theory.

In the beginning, the theory of computation had a number of diverse fields. At that time biologists were studying models for neuron nets, electrical engineers developing switching theory as a tool to hardware design, mathematicians working on the foundation of logic and linguists investigating grammars for natural languages. Out of these studies came models that are central to the theory of computation.

Models of computation are abstract specifications of how it can proceed. In other words, they are the mathematical abstraction of computers. The various models that are in use differ in computing power. The theory of computation can be considered the creation of models that describe with varying degree of accuracy parts of computers, different types of computers and similar machines. The models of the theory of computation are used, not to discuss the practical engineering details of computer hardware but to answer the more abstract questions about the capability of these mechanical devices.

Algorithm, Data Structure, Operating System, Compiler, Computer Architecture, Circuits and Switching theory, etc., are computing disciplines in computer science. These disciplines, in general, have a theoretical component. However, they differ from the theory of computation mostly in two ways - they deal with computers that already exist while models in the theory of computation encompass all computers that do exist, will exist, and that can ever be dreamed of, and secondly they are interested in how best to do the things while the theory of computation is concerned with the question of possibility - what can and cannot be done - rather than optimality.

Godel, Alonzo Church, Alan Turing, Stephen Keene, John von Neumann and Claude Shannon were some of the pioneers in the field of the theory of computation.

1.1.1 Automata, Computability and Complexity

In this section, we will briefly introduce the Automata, Computability and Complexity theory - the three traditional central areas of the theory of computation.

Automata Theory

Automata theory is the study of abstract mathematical models of computer with discrete input and output and the computational problems that can be solved using these models. These models play an important role in various applied areas of computer science. Finite Automata, Pushdown Automata and Turing Machine are three important models in Automata theory. Finite Automaton is used in lexical analysis, text processing, hardware design, etc. Pushdown automaton, a more powerful computing device than a finite automaton, provides a natural way to approach the problem of parsing in high-level programming languages. It determines the syntax of the statement by reconstructing the sequence of rules by which it is derived in the context-free grammar. The Turing machine, introduced in 1936 by Alan Turing to give a formal definition of an algorithm, is the ultimate mathematical model of a computer. In principle, any problem that can be solved by a Turing machine can be solved by a computer with bounded amount of memory.

Computability Theory

Computability theory is primarily concerned with the question of the extent to which the problem is solved by a computer program. It turns out that some problems are not solvable algorithmically, in principle. Halting problem, which cannot be solved by a Turing machine, is one of the most important results in computability theory. Much of computability theory is based on the Halting problem result. Computability theory is closely related to recursion theory, a branch of mathematical logic, which removes the restriction of studying only models of computation that are reducible to the Turing model.

Complexity Theory

In complexity theory, the objective is to classify computational problems according to their inherent difficulty. It is concerned with the question of which problems can be solved efficiently, the two major measures of efficiency being the time and memory space a given algorithm require. In complexity theory, we thus ask the question "what makes some problems computationally hard and others easy?"

1.2   Mathematical Preliminaries and Notations

In this section we review set theory, relations, functions, graphs and trees, propositional logic and proof techniques.

1.2.1   Set Theory

Basic Concepts

A collection of distinct objects is called a *set* and is represented by a pair of curly braces ({ }) enclosing its objects separated by commas. For instance

{1, 2, 3, 4, 5} is the set of all positive integers less than 6.

A set consisting of no objects is called the *empty set*, represented by the symbol ϕ or { }. The empty set is also called *null* or *void set*.

Sets are 'inordered' which means that the objects in the set do not have to be listed in any particular order. The set above could also be written as {5, 2, 1, 3, 4}.

We use capital letters $A, B, C...$ and so forth to denote a set and small letters $a, b, c....$ etc., to denote an object of the set.

An object of a set is called an *element* or a *member* of the set. If x is an element of a set A then we say that 'x belongs to A', denoted by $x \in A$. If x is not in A or does not belong to A then we denote that $x \notin A$.

A set is *finite* if it has finite number of elements and is *infinite* otherwise. The number of elements in a finite set A is called the *cardinality* or *cardinal number* of A and is denoted by $|A|$. A set of cardinality 1 is known as the *singleton set*.

Set Builder Notation

Set builder notation is used to describe a set without listing its elements. If A contains all values of 'x' for which the property P holds, we write

$$A = \{x \mid P(x)\}$$

It is easier to refer to the set $A = \{ 2, 3, 5, 7, 9, 11, 13, 17\ldots\ldots\ldots\}$ using set builder notation as follows:

$$A = \{x \mid x \text{ is prime}\}$$

Subsets of a set

A set A is a *subset* of a set B, written as $A \subseteq B$, if each element of A is also an element of B. The empty set is a subset of every set. When A is a subset of B, we also say B is a *superset* of A. A set is a subset of itself and also a superset of itself. Any set which is the superset of all the sets under consideration is called the *universal set* denoted by U.

Set A is *equal* to set B, denoted by $A = B$ if A and B contain exactly the same elements. Thus two sets A and B are equal if and only if $A \subseteq B$ and $B \subseteq A$.

A is called a *proper subset* of B written as $A \subset B$ if $A \subseteq B$ and $A \neq B$.

The *power set* of a finite set A, denoted by 2^A, is the set consisting of all subsets of A (including A itself and the empty set ϕ). For instance if $A = \{1, 2, 3\}$, then $2^A = \{\phi, \{1\}, \{2\}, \{3\}, \{1, 2\}, \{1, 3\}, \{2, 3\}, \{1, 2, 3\}\}$. If the set A has n elements, then power set of A has 2^n elements, i.e., $|2^A| = 2^{|A|} = 2^n$.

Set Operations

The *union* of sets A and B, denoted by $A \cup B$ is the set consisting of all elements in A or B (or both), i.e.,

$$AB = \{x \cup x \in A \text{ or } x \in B\}.$$

The *intersection* of two sets A and B, written as $A \cap B$, is the set consisting of all elements in both A and B, i.e.,

$$A \cap B = \{x \mid x \in A \text{ and } x \in B\}$$

Sets A and B are said to be *disjoint* if $A \cap B = \phi$

The *set difference* of sets A and B, written as $A - B$, is the set of those elements of A that are not in B, i.e.,

$$A - B = \{x \mid x \in A \text{ and } x \notin B\}$$

The *symmetric difference* of two sets A and B, written as $A \oplus B$, is the set of elements that are in A or in B, but not in both, i.e.,

$$A \oplus B = (A - B) \cup (B - A)$$

The *complement* of a set A, written as A' or A^C, is the set of all elements of the universal set which are not in A, i.e.,

$$A^C = \{x \mid x \in U, x \notin A \text{ where U is a Universal set}\}.$$

The *Cartesian product* or *cross product* of sets A and B, written as $A \times B$, is the set of ordered pairs (x, y) such that x is in A and y is in B, i.e.,

$$A \times B = \{(x, y) \mid x \in A, y \in B\}$$

Example 1.1: Let $A = \{1, 2, 3, 4\}$, $B = \{3, 4, 5, 6\}$ and $U = \{1, 2, 3, 4, 5, 6, 7, 8, 9\}$. Find out (i) $A \cup B$ (ii) $A \cap B$ (iii) $A - B$ (iv) $A \oplus B$, (v) $A \times B$, (vi) A^C and (vii) B^C.

Solution:

(i) $A \cup B = \{x \mid x \in A \text{ or } x \in B\} = \{1, 2, 3, 4, 5, 6\}$

(ii) $A \cap B = \{x \mid x \in A \text{ and } x \in B\} = \{3, 4\}$

(iii) $A - B = \{x \mid x \in A \text{ and } x \notin B\} = \{1, 2\}$

(iv) $A \oplus B = \{x \mid x \text{ is in } A \text{ but } x \text{ is in } B \text{ but not in both}\} = \{1, 2, 5, 6\}$

(v) $A \times B = \{(x, y) \mid x \in A, y \in B\}$
$$= \{(1, 3), (1, 4), (1, 5), (1, 6), (2, 3), (2, 4), (2, 5), (2, 6), (3, 3), (3, 4), (3, 5), (3, 6), (4, 3), (4, 4), (4, 5), (4, 6)\}$$

(vi) $A^C = \{x \mid x \in U, x \notin A\} = \{5, 6, 7, 8, 9\}$

(vii) $B^C = \{x \mid x \in U, x \notin B\} = \{1, 2, 7, 8, 9\}$

Laws of Algebra of Sets

If A, B, C are any sets, then

1. $A \cup A = A$, $A \cap A = A$ (Idempotent Laws)

2. $A \cup U = U$, $A \cap \phi = \phi$ (Boundedness Laws)

3. $A \cup \phi = A$, $A \cap U = A$ (Identity Laws)

4. $A - A = \phi$, $\phi - A = \phi$, $A - \phi = A$

5. $A \cup B = B \cup A$ (Commutative Law of union)

6. $A \cap B = B \cap A$ (Commutative Law of intersection)

7. $A \cup (B \cup C) = (A \cup B) \cup C$ (Associative Law for union)

8. $A \cap (B \cap C) = (A \cap B) \cap C$ (Associative Law for intersection)

9. $A \cup (B \cup C) = (A \cup B) \cup (A \cup C)$ (Distributive Laws)

10. $A \cap (B \cap C) = (A \cap B) \cup (A \cap C)$

11. $(A \cup B)' = A' \cap B'$ (De Morgan's Laws)

12. $(A \cap B)' = A' \cup B'$

1.2.2 Relations

A relation from a set A to a set B is a subset of $A \times B$. If $(a, b) \in A \times B$, we write aRb. If $(a, b) \notin R$ we write $a\overline{R}b$. If $A = B$, we say R is a relation on A.

The domain of a relation is the set of all first components of the ordered pairs in R. The range of the relation is the set of all second components of the ordered pairs in R.

Special Properties of Relations

Relation R on a set A is

(i)   *reflexive* if aRa for each $a \in A$

(ii)   *symmetric* if aRb implies bRa for $a, b \in A$

(iii) *anti-symmetric* if and only if both aRb and bRa implies $a = b$ for $a, b \in A$

(iv)   *transitive* if and only if aRb and bRc imply aRc for $a, b, c \in A$

An *equivalence relation* is a relation that is reflexive, symmetric and transitive. For instance, the familiar relation of equality " = " is an equivalence relation since it is reflexive as $a = a$, symmetric as $a = b$ implies $b = a$ and transitive as $a = b, b = c$ implies $a = c$. However, the relation "<" is not an equivalence relation; while it is transitive, it is neither reflexive since nor symmetric since $a \not< b$ does not imply $b < a$.

If R is an equivalence relation on set A, then the *equivalence class* of $a \in A$, denoted by $[a]$, is the set $\{x \in A \mid xRa\}$.

Equivalence Classes and Set Partition

A partition on a set A is a set of some subsets of A such that the union of the subsets is equal to A and every two distinct subsets are disjoint. The distinct equivalence classes of an equivalence relation on set A constitute a partition of A.

1.2.3 Functions

A function f from a set A to a set B, denoted by $f: A \to B$, is a special kind of relation in which each $a \in A$ is paired with exactly one $b \in B$. The unique element b is called the image of a and we write $b = f(a)$.

A function $f: A \to B$ is *onto* B or *surjective* if each $b \in B$ is the image of at least one $a \in A$. A function $f: A \to B$ is *one-to-one* or *injective* if each $b \in B$ is the image of at most one $a \in A$ and is many-to-one otherwise. A function is a *bijection* if it is one-to-one and onto.

1.2.4 Graphs and Trees

Graphs

A graph or an *undirected graph* G is an ordered pair (V, E) where V is a finite non-empty set of elements called *vertices* or *nodes* and E is a finite set of unordered pairs of vertices called *edges* or *arcs*.

A *directed graph* or *digraph* D is an ordered pair (V, E') where V is finite non-empty set of elements called vertices and E' is a finite set of ordered pairs of vertices called edges. For an edge (u, v), vertex v is called the head and u is called the tail of the edge.

Typically a graph is depicted diagrammatically as a set of dots (the vertices) connected by lines (the edges). In an undirected graph an edge $\{u, v\}$ is a line joining dots u and v. In a digraph, the edge (u, v) is a directed line from dot u to v.

Given an undirected or a directed graph G, a *loop* is an edge that connects a vertex to itself. Two vertices are said to be *adjacent* if they are connected by an edge. The number of edges connected to a vertex is called the *degree* of that vertex with self loop counted twice. Figure 1.1 depicts the graph (V, E)

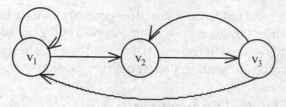

Fig. 1.1: Undirected graph

where $V = \{1, 2, 3\}$, $E = \{(1, 2), (2, 3), (3, 2), (3, 1)\}$.

The directed graph with vertices $\{v_1, v_2, v_3\}$ and arcs $\{(v_1, v_1), (v_1, v_2), (v_2, v_3), (v_3, v_2),$ $(v_3, v_1)\}$ is depicted in Figure 1.2.

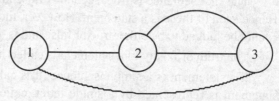

Fig. 1.2: Directed graph

Path and Connectivity

A *path* in a graph is a sequence of vertices $v_1, v_2, \ldots v_k, k >= 1$, such that (v_i, v_{i-1}) for each i, $1 \le i < k$ is an edge . A path that begins and ends at the same vertex is called a *circuit* or *cycle*. A graph is called *acyclic* if it contains no cycles and is called *cyclic* otherwise.

An undirected graph is said to be *connected* or a directed graph is said to be *strongly connected* if every pair of its vertices is connected by a path. A directed graph is said to be connected if the associated undirected graph (obtained by ignoring the directions of all edges) is connected. A Root has no incoming edge. There is exactly one path from root to every other vertex. Graph which is not connected is said to be *disconnected*.

Trees

A connected graph that contains no cycles is called a *tree*. A *rooted tree* is a directed graph whose associated undirected graph is a tree. A specific vertex is designated as the *root* which determines the direction on edges, edges point away from the root. The vertex that the edge points from is called the *parent* and the vertex that the edge points to is called the *child*. All vertices in a tree, except the root, have precisely one parent while all nodes can have an arbitrary number of children. A vertex with no child is called a *leaf*.

1.2.5 Propositional Logic

A statement is a sentence which is either true or false but not both. Consider the following sentences:

(i)   New Delhi is the capital of India.

(ii) 8 is less than 5.

(iii) Mohan is honest.

The first sentence is true, second is false and the third is either true or false. Hence each of these is a statement. However, the sentence "children are naughty" cannot be judged to be either true or false and is, therefore, not a statement.

The truth or falsity of a statement is called its truth value.

If a statement is a simple sentence, it is called a simple statement. A simple statement is represented by a single letter, called a statement letter. A statement composed of two or more simple statements using various connectives is called a compound statement.

The logical connectives generally used for building a compound statement are 'not' (denoted by ~), 'and' (denoted by $\wedge$), 'or' (denoted by $\vee$),'if ... then' (denoted by $\rightarrow$) and 'if and only if' (denoted by $\leftrightarrow$). The truth value of a compound statement depends exclusively on the truth values of its component statements and the connectives used.

Logical Connectives

The *negation* or *denial* of a statement is formed by the use of the word 'not'. For instance the negation of 'Ram is hard working' is 'Ram is not hard working'. If p is a statement then so is its negation $\sim p$. $\sim p$ is true when p is false and $\sim p$ is false when p is true.

The *conjunction* of statements p and q, denoted by $p \wedge q$, is a compound statement obtained by combining p and q by the connective 'and'. The conjunction of 'Ram is honest' and 'Ram is hard working' is 'Ram is honest and hard working'. The compound statement $p \wedge q$ is true only when both p and q are true and is false otherwise.

The *disjunction* of statements p and q, denoted by $p \vee q$, is a compound statement obtained by combining p and q using the connective 'or'. For instance, the statement 'I shall purchase a pen and a pencil' is the disjunction of the statement 'I shall purchase a pen' and the statement 'I shall purchase a pencil'. The statement $p \vee q$ is false if both p and q are false and is true in every other case.

The compound statement denoted by $p \rightarrow q$ is called a *conditional* statement and is read as 'p implies q' or 'if p then q'. In mathematics, statement $p \rightarrow q$ is false only when p is true and q is false. It is true for every other assignment of truth value to p and q.

The statements $q \rightarrow p$, $\sim p \rightarrow \sim q$ and $\sim q \rightarrow \sim p$ are called the converse, inverse and contrapositive of the conditional statement $\sim p \rightarrow \sim q$, respectively.

The statement of the form '*p* if and only if *q*', denoted by $p \leftrightarrow q$ is called a biconditional statement. $p \leftrightarrow q$ is true when *p* and *q* have the same truth values and is false otherwise.

Propositions

A proposition is an expression built up from the statement letters by a finite number of applications of the connectives ~, ∧, ∨, →, ↔.

Specifically

(i)   All statement letters are propositions.

(ii) If *P* and *Q* are propositions, so are ~*P*, $P \wedge Q, P \vee Q, P \to Q, P \leftrightarrow Q$.

Tautologies and Contradictions

A proposition is a *tautology* or a *contradiction* according as its truth value is true or false, irrespective of the truth values of its statement letters.

1.2.6 Proof Techniques

The word "proof" comes from the Latin word Probare ("to test"). A proof is a convincing way of demonstrating that a proposition is true. Proofs employ logic (a sequence of steps or statements that establishes the truth of the proposition) but normally include some amount of natural language which usually admits some ambiguity. In logic, a formal proof is not written in a natural language, but instead uses a formal language consisting of certain strings of symbols from a specific alphabet.

There are several types of proof techniques. The most popular technique is natural deduction or direct proof. In direct proof the conclusion is established by logically combining axioms, definitions and existing theorems. More difficult mathematical hypothesis can be proved or disproved using other powerful techniques. Three techniques, proof by contradiction, proof by induction and proof by construction used in later Chapters, are discussed here.

Proof by Contradiction

In a proof by contradiction, to prove that a statement is true, we assume that it is false and then reach a contradiction. Since a proposition must be either true or false, its falsity being established, the proposition must be true.

Example 1.2: A familiar example of application of proof by contradiction is to prove $\sqrt{3}$ is an irrational number.

Solution:

Assume on the contrary that $\sqrt{3}$ is a rational number so $\sqrt{3} = \dfrac{p}{q}$ where *p* and *q* are non-zero integers with no common factor.

$$\Rightarrow 3 = \frac{p^2}{q^2} \qquad \text{[by squaring both sides]}$$

$$\Rightarrow 3q^2 = p^2$$
$$\Rightarrow 3|p^2$$
$$\Rightarrow 3|p \qquad\qquad\qquad\qquad\qquad\qquad\qquad \dots (1)$$
$$\Rightarrow p = 3c \qquad \text{for some integer c}$$
$$\Rightarrow p^2 = 9c^2$$
$$\Rightarrow 3q^2 = 9c^2$$
$$\Rightarrow q^2 = 3c^2$$
$$\Rightarrow 3|q^2$$
$$\Rightarrow 3|q \qquad\qquad\qquad\qquad\qquad\qquad\qquad \dots (2)$$

From (1) and (2), we obtain that 3 is a common factor of p and q. But this contradicts the fact that p and q have no common factor other than 1. This contradicts our assumption, so we conclude that $\sqrt{3}$ is an irrational number.

Proof by Induction

Proof by induction is a very powerful technique for demonstrating the truth of statements that can be related to natural numbers, i.e., 1, 2, 3, 4,... or a subset of the natural numbers... The technique consists of two steps. If a mathematical statement $P(n)$, involving the natural number n, is to be proved then:

Step 1: Demonstrate that the statement $P(n)$ is true for some particular integer n_0 (usually $n_0 = 0$ or $n_0 = 1$)

Step 2: Demonstrate that if statement $P(n)$ is true for an integer k, $k \geq n_0$ then $P(n)$ is true for the next integer $k + 1$.

Then $P(n)$ is true for all natural numbers n. The Step 1 is called the basis (base case) and Step 2 is called inductive step. In inductive step, the assumption that P is true for some particular integer is known as inductive hypothesis (induction hypothesis). To perform the inductive step, one assumes the inductive hypothesis and then this assumption is used to prove the statement for $n + 1$.

Example 1.3: Prove that $\sum_{i=1}^{n} (2n-1) = n^2$

Solution:

Basis: When we put $n_0 = 1$ in the left hand side of equation, we get

$$\sum_{i=1}^{n} (2i-1) = 2 \times 1 - 1$$
$$= 2 - 1$$
$$= 1$$

When we put $n_0 = 1$ in the right hand side of equation, we get
$$n^2 = (1)^2$$
$$= 1$$

We can observe that the value of left hand and right hand side of equation is same. Therefore it means that the statement is true for $n_0 = 1$.

Inductive Hypothesis: Suppose k is an integer, $k \geq 1$ and the statement is true for $n = k$ that is

$$1 + 3 + 5 + \dots (2k - 1) = k^2$$

Inductive Step: We must show that the statement is true for the next integer, $n = k + 1$ that is we must show that

$$1 + 3 + 5 + \dots (2k + 1) = (k + 1)^2$$

Let us take the left hand side of the above statement, i.e.,

$$1 + 3 + 5 + \dots (2k + 1) = [1 + 3 + 5 + \dots (2k - 1)] + (2k + 1)$$
$$= k^2 + (2k + 1) \text{ [by the inductive hypothesis]}$$
$$= \text{RHS}$$

which is just what we wanted to show. Thus, by the principle of Mathematical Induction, the statement is true for all integers $n \geq 1$.

Proof by Construction

A proof by construction is a technique of proof that demonstrates the existence of object with specific properties by constructing a method for constructing or creating such an object.

Example 1.4: There exist irrational numbers a and b such a^b is rational.

Solution:

Let a and b be any irrational numbers. Construct a^b as follows by taking $a = \sqrt{2}$ (irrational number) and $b = \log_2 9$ (irrational number).

$$a^b = (\sqrt{2})^{\log_2^9}$$

$$= 2^{\frac{1}{2}*2\log_2^3}$$

$$= 2^{\log_2^3}$$

$$= 3 \text{ (rational number)}$$

1.3   Alphabet, Symbol and String

An *alphabet*, denoted by Σ (Sigma), is a (non-empty) finite set of symbols. A *symbol* is an abstract entity and cannot be defined formally just like a "point" and a "line" are not defined in geometry. However, symbols are usually letters and digits.

A *string* or a *word* over an alphabet is a sequence of symbols from the alphabet. For instance, over $\Sigma = \{a, b, c\}$ a, ab, aaa, acb and $aabc$ are strings. The length of a string w, denoted by $|w|$, is the number of symbols in it. If $w = aabc$ then $|w| = 4$. The string with no symbols is called the *empty string* and is denoted by ε(Epsilon). If w is an empty string then $|w| = 0$.

Prefix of a string is a string of any number of leading symbols of that string. A *suffix* is a string of any number of trailing symbols of that string. For example, if $w = abcd$ then ε, a, ab, abc and $abcd$ are the prefixes and ε, d, cd, bcd and $abcd$ are the suffixes of w. A prefix or suffix of a string, other than the string itself, is called a *proper prefix* or *suffix*.

The *reversal* (*reverse*) of a string w, denoted by w^R, is the string obtained by writing w in opposite order For instance if w = reverse then w^R = esrever.

The *concatenation* of two strings w_1 and w_2 is the string w_1w_2, the symbols of w_1 followed by the symbols of w_2 in that order. For instance, w_1 = ab, w_2 = xyz then w_1w_2 = $abxyz$. The concatenation of the empty string ε with any other string w gives the string w itself, i.e., $w\varepsilon = w = \varepsilon w$. The concatenation of a string w with itself k times is denoted by w^k, i.e.,

$ww = w^2$

$www = w^3$, etc.

Given the alphabet Σ, the set of all strings of length k is denoted by Σ^k, i.e.,

$\Sigma^k = \{w | w$ is a string over Σ and $|w| = k\}$

Example 1.5: If $\Sigma = \{0, 1\}$,

Then

$\Sigma^0 = \{\varepsilon\}$

$\Sigma^1 = \{0, 1\}$

$\Sigma^2 = \{00, 01, 10, 11\}$ and so on.

The *Kleene star* or *Kleene Closure* of an alphabet Σ, denoted by Σ^*, is the set of all strings over the symbols in Σ, including the empty string. Hence

$$\Sigma^* = \Sigma^0 \cup \Sigma^1 \cup \Sigma^2 \cup \ldots\ldots$$

The set $\Sigma^+ = \Sigma^* - \{\varepsilon\}$ is called *positive closure* of the alphabet Σ.

For instance if $\Sigma = \{0, 1\}$ then

$\Sigma^* = \{\varepsilon, 0, 1, 00, 01, 10, 11, 000, 001, 010, 011, 100, 101, ...\}$

$\Sigma^+ = \{0, 1, 00, 01, 10, 11, 000, 001, 010, 011, 100, 101, ...\}$

Σ^* is an infinite set. However, each string in Σ^* is of finite length. The members of Σ^* are enumerated lexicographically. The *lexicographic ordering* of strings is the same as the familiar dictionary ordering, except that shorter strings precede longer strings. For instance, the lexicographic ordering of all strings over the alphabet $\Sigma = \{a_1, a_2\}$ is $\{\varepsilon, a_1, a_2, a_1a_1, a_1a_2, a_2a_1, a_2a_2, a_1a_1a_1, a_1a_1a_2, a_1a_2a_1, a_1a_2a_2, a_2a_1a_1, ...\}$.

1.4 Formal Languages

A formal language is a set of strings over some alphabet. A language L over the alphabet Σ is, then, a subset of Σ^*. Since $L \subseteq \Sigma^*$, L may be finite or infinite. A finite language contains a finite number of strings of finite length. An infinite language contains infinite number of strings of finite length. The empty set (ϕ) and the set consisting of the empty string $\{\varepsilon\}$ both are languages.

Languages are sets. Therefore, any operation that can be performed on sets can also be performed on languages. The complement of a language is defined with respect to Σ^* that is, the complement of L is

$L^C = \Sigma^* - L$.

The reverse of a language is the set of all string reversals, i.e.,

$L^R = \{w^R \mid w \in L\}$

The concatenation of two languages L_1 and L_2 is the set of all strings obtained by concatenating any element of L_1 with any element of L_2. We can define it as,

$L_1 L_2 = \{xy \mid x \in L_1, y \in L_2\}$

If the concatenation of L with itself k times is given by L^k then the Kleene closure or star closure of L, denoted L^*, is defined as

$$L^* = L^0 \cup L^1 \cup L^2 ... \bigcup_{i=0}^{\infty} L^i$$

and the positive closure of L, denoted by L^+ is defined as

$$L^+ = L^1 \cup L^2 \cup L^3 ... = \bigcup_{i=0}^{\infty} L^i$$

For instance if $L = \{a, b\}$, then

$$L^* = L^0 \cup L^1 \cup L^2 ... = \bigcup_{i=0}^{\infty} L^i$$

$$= \{\varepsilon, a, b, aa, ab, ba, bb, ...\}$$

> **Note:** *The word "formal" in "formal language" emphasizes that what is significant is the form of the string and not its meaning. In other words, we can say a formal language is an abstraction of the general characteristics of programming languages.*

Example 1.6: If $\Sigma = \{0, 1\}$. Then

$L_1 = \{0, 00, 10, 000, 010, 100, 110, ...\}$

$L_2 = \{1, 01, 11, 001, 010, 011, 101, 111, ...\}$

are two different languages over the same alphabet.

Example 1.7: Let $\Sigma = \{x, y\}$. Then

$\Sigma^* = \{\varepsilon, x, y, xx, xy, yx, yy, xxx, ...\}$

The set

$\{x, xy, yy\}$

is a *finite language* because it has a finite number of strings.

But the set

$\{x^n y^n : n >= 0\}$

is an *infinite language* because it has an infinite number of strings.

1.5   Summary

1. Automata theory is the study of abstract mathematical models of computer with discrete input and output and the computational problems that can be solved using these models.

2. Sets are used to define the concepts of relations and functions. The theory of sets was developed by German mathematician George Cantor (1845-1918).

3. A collection of distinct objects is called a set and is represented by a pair of curly braces ({ }) enclosing its objects separated by commas.

4. A relation from a set A to a set B is a subset of $A \times B$. If $(a, b) \in A \times B$, we write aRb. If $(a, b) \notin R$ we write aRb.

5. A function f from a set A to a set B, denoted by $f: A \to B$, is a special kind of relation in which each $a \in A$ is paired with exactly one $b \in B$. The unique element b is called the image of a and we write $b = f(a)$.

6. A graph or an undirected graph G is an ordered pair (V, E) where V is a finite non-empty set of elements called vertices or nodes and E is a finite set of unordered pairs of vertices called edges or arcs.

7. A connected graph that contains no cycles is called a tree. A rooted tree is a directed graph whose associated undirected graph is a tree.

8. A proposition is an expression built up from the statement letters by a finite number of applications of the connectives $\sim$, $\wedge$, $\vee$, $\to$, $\leftrightarrow$.

9. A proof is a convincing way of demonstrating that a proposition is true. Proofs employ logic (a sequence of steps or statements that establishes the truth of the proposition) but normally include some amount of natural language which usually admits some ambiguity.

10. An alphabet, denoted by Σ (Sigma), is a (non-empty) finite set of symbols. A symbol is an abstract entity.

1.6   Exercises

Objective Questions

1. Theory of Computation deals primarily with:
    (a) The hardware design of computers
    (b) The software design of computers
    (c) The capabilities and limitations of computers
    (d) None of these

2. Which of the following is not the central area of the theory of computation?
    (a) Automata theory   (b) Computability theory
    (c) Complexity theory   (d) Graph theory

3. Computability theory is also called:
    (a) Recursion theory   (b) Switching theory
    (c) Chaos theory   (d) Set theory

4. In computability theory, the objective is to classify problems as:
   (a) Easy ones and hard ones
   (b) Those that are solvable and those that are not solvable
   (c) Decidable and undecidable
   (d) None of these

5. In Complexity theory, the objective is to classify problems:
   (a) According to their inherent difficulty
   (b) As those that are solvable and those that are not solvable
   (c) As decidable and undecidable
   (d) None of these

6. Theory of computation deals with computers that:
   (a) Already exist
   (b) Already exist and also will exist
   (c) Already exist and will exist and that can ever be dreamed of
   (d) None of these

7. A symbol is:
   (a) A finite set of alphabets   (b) An infinite set of alphabets
   (c) An abstract entity   (d) None of these

8. An alphabet is:
   (a) A finite set of symbols   (b) An infinite set of symbols
   (c) Not a set of symbols   (d) An abstract entity

9. Lexicographic ordering of strings is same as:
   (a) Dictionary ordering
   (b) Dictionary ordering except that shorter strings precede longer string
   (c) Size-alphabetical ordering
   (d) None of these

10. The members of Σ^* are enumerated:
    (a) In increasing order of length   (b) In decreasing order of length
    (c) lexicographically   (d) None of these

11. If $\Sigma = \{0\}$, then Σ^+:
    (a) $\{0, 00, 000, ...\}$ (b) $\{\varepsilon, 0, 00, 000, ...\}$
    (c) $\{\varepsilon, 00, 000, 0000, ...\}$ (d) None of these

12. If an alphabet is denoted by Σ, then Σ^* is called the:
    (a) Closure of the alphabet   (b) Kleene star
    (c) Both (a) and (b)   (d) Positive closure of the alphabet

13. If an alphabet is denoted by Σ, then:
    (a) $\Sigma^* = \Sigma^{**}$ (b) $\Sigma^{**} \subseteq \Sigma^+$

(c) $\Sigma^+ = \Sigma^*$ (d) None of these

14. If $\Sigma = \phi$ then Σ^* is:
    (a) $\{\varepsilon\}$ (b) ϕ
    (c) $\{\varepsilon, \phi\}$ (d) None of these

15. Which one of them is not pioneer of theory of computation?
    (a) Von Neumann   (b) Claude Shannon
    (c) Alonzo Church   (d) Charles Babbage

16. The proof technique in which the proof of the statement is initiated by an assumption that the statement is false, is called:
    (a) Proof by contradiction   (b) Direct proof
    (c) Proof by construction   (d) Proof by induction

17. The number of equivalence relations of the set:
    (a) 4   (b) 15
    (c) 16   (d) 24

18. The complement of language L with respect to Σ^* is:
    (a) $\{x \mid x \in (L - \Sigma^*)\}$ (b) $\{x \mid x \in (\Sigma^* - L)\}$
    (c) $\{x \mid x \in (\Sigma^* \cup L)\}$ (d) None of these

19. The word 'formal' in formal language refers to:
    (a) The form as well as the meaning of strings of symbols
    (b) The form of strings of symbols without meaning
    (c) Both (a) or (b)
    (d) None of these

20. If L is a language, then:
    (a) $L^+ = L^* - \varepsilon$ (b) $L^+ = L^* L$
    (c) $L^+ = \bigcup_{i=1}^{\infty} L^i$ (d) None of these

21. The number of elements in the power set 2^A of the set $A = \{ \{\phi\}, 1, \{2,3\}\}$ is:
    (a) 2   (b) 4
    (c) 8   (d) None of these

22. The number of elements in the power set of $A \times A$, where A is a finite set of size n, is:
    (a) 2^{2n} (b) 2^{n^2}
    (c) square of (2^n) (d) None of these

23. Which of the following is null sets?
    (a) $\{0\}$ (b) $\{\phi\}$
    (c) $\{\ \}$ (d) ϕ

24. Which of the following sets is empty:
    (a) $\{ x: x = x \}$ (b) $\{x: \neq xx\}$

(c) $\{x: x = x^2\}$ (d) $\{x: \neq xx^2\}$

25. A set of strings of symbols from an alphabet is called:

(a) Kleene star   (b) Words

(c) Positive closure of the alphabet   (d) Language

26. If Σ is an alphabet, then:

(a) $\Sigma^* = (\Sigma^*)^*$ (b) $(\Sigma^+)^* = (\Sigma^*)^*$

(c) $\Sigma^+ \subseteq (\Sigma^*)^*$ (d) All of these

27. A language is infinite when it has:

(a) Infinite number of words

(b) Infinite number of words each of finite length

(c) Infinite number of words each of infinite length

(d) None of these

28. If $A = \{1, 2\}$, then the power set of A is:

(a) $\{\{1\}, \{2\}\}$ (b) $\{\{\phi\}, \{1,2\}\}$

(c) $\{\phi, \{1\}, \{2\})$ (d) None of these

29. The number of elements in the power set of the set $\{\{1,2\},\{3\}\}$ is:

(a) 8   (b) 4

(c) 3   (d) 7

30. Order of the power set of a set A of order n is:

(a) n (b) $2n$

(c) n^2 (d) 2^n

31. If $w = abc$ is a word, then its prefixes are:

(a) ε, a, ab, abc (b) a, ab, abc

(c) ε, c, bc, abc (d) None of these

32. If $w = abc$ is a word, then its suffixes are:

(a) ε, a, ab, abc (b) c, bc, abc

(c) ε, c, bc, abc (d) None of these

33. If the sets A and B have 3 and 6 elements respectively, then minimum number of elements in $A \cup B$ is:

(a) 6   (b) 3

(c) 9   (d) 18

34. The concatenation of languages L_1 and L_2 is:

(a) $\{ xy \mid x \in L_1, y \in L_2\}$ (b) $\{ xy \mid x \in L_2, y \in L_1\}$

(c) $\{ xx \mid x \in L_1 \}$ (d) $\{ yy \mid y \in L_2\}$

35. If $A = \{4, 5, 7\}$ and the universal set $U = \{1, 4, 5, 6, 7, 8\}$ then:

(a) $A^C = \{1, 6, 8\}$ (b) $A^C = \{1, 5, 7\}$

(c) $A^C = \{1, 4, 5, 6, 7, 8\}$ (d) None of these

36. Let A be an infinite set and $A_1, A_2 \ldots A_n$ be sets such that $A_1 \cup A_2 \cup \ldots \cup A_n = A$, then:
    (a) At least one of the sets A_i is finite
    (b) Not more than one of the sets A_i is finite
    (c) At least one of the sets A_i is an infinite set
    (d) Not more than one of the sets A_i can be infinite

37. If L be set of strings over some alphabet, then Kleene closure of L is given as:
    (a) $L^* = \bigcup_{i=0}^{\infty} L_i$
    (b) $L^+ = \bigcup_{i=0}^{\infty} L_i$
    (c) $L^* = \bigcup_{i=0}^{\infty} L^i$
    (d) $L^+ = \bigcup_{i=1}^{\infty} L^i$

38. A formal language is:
    (a) A set of strings of symbols from some one alphabet
    (b) An abstraction of the general characteristics of programming languages
    (c) Defined as a subset of Σ^*
    (d) All of these

39. If alphabet is denoted by Σ, then Σ^* is called:
    (a) Closure of the alphabet
    (b) Star closure
    (c) Kleene star
    (d) All of these

40. Proper prefix of a string is:
    (a) Number of leading symbols of string
    (b) Number of leading symbols of string except ε
    (c) Number of leading symbols of string except string itself
    (d) None of these

41. Proper suffix of a string is:
    (a) Suffix of a string except ε
    (b) Suffix of a string except string itself
    (c) Number of trailing symbols of string
    (d) None of these

42. The smallest language over any alphabet is:
    (a) ε
    (b) ϕ
    (c) Individual member of alphabet Σ (d) None of these

43. The largest language over any alphabet Σ is:
    (a) Σ^*
    (b) Σ^+
    (c) Power set of Σ
    (d) None of these

Answers to Objective Questions

01.	(c)	02.	(d)	03.	(a)	04.	(b)	05.	(a)	06.	(c)
07.	(d)	08.	(b)	09.	(b)	10.	(c)	11.	(a)	12.	(c)

13.	(a)	14.	(a)	15.	(d)	16.	(a)	17.	(b)	18.	(b)
19.	(b)	20.	(d)	21.	(c)	22.	(b)	23.	(c), (d)	24.	(b)
25.	(d)	26.	(d)	27.	(b)	28.	(d)	29.	(b)	30.	(d)
31.	(a)	32.	(c)	33.	(a)	34.	(a)	35.	(a)	36.	(c)
37.	(a)	38.	(d)	39.	(d)	40.	(c)	41.	(b)	42.	(b)
43.	(a)										

Review Questions

1. What do you mean by theory of computation?
2. Give a major difference between theory of computation and other computer science disciplines.
3. What are the major areas in theory of computation? Discuss them briefly.
A 4. Use Induction to show that, for any natural number $n \geq 1$,

$$1^2 + 2^2 + ... + n^2 = \frac{n(n+1)(2n+1)}{6}$$

5. Use induction to prove that, for $n \geq 1$, $2^{2n} - 1$ is divisible by 3.
A6. A binary tree is a tree in which no parent can have more than two children. Use Mathematical Induction to show that a binary tree of height n has at most 2^n leaves.
A7. Use contradiction to show that $2 - \sqrt{2}$ is irrational.
A8. Use proof by construction technique to show that for any integers x and y, if x and y are odd, then xy is odd.
9. Use proof by contradiction to prove that there is no string x in $\{a, b\}^*$ such that $ax = xb$.
10. Use Mathematical Induction to establish each of the following formulae:

(i) $\sum_{i=1}^{n}(i+1)2^i = n2^{n+1}$

(ii) $\sum_{i=1}^{n}\frac{i*i}{(2i-1)(2i+1)} = \frac{n(n+1)}{2(2n+1)}$

(iii) $\sum_{i=1}^{n}((2i-1)(2i)) = \frac{n(n+1)(4n-1)}{3}$

A11. Use proof by induction technique on the length of v to show that for any strings u and $v \in \Sigma^*$, $(uv)^R = v^R u^R$.
12. What is proof by contradiction? Explain with example.
13. Give the difference between proof by construction and proof by contradiction techniques.
14. What do you mean by proof by construction? Explain with example.

15. What is lexicographic ordering of string? Enumerate the lexicographic ordering of all strings over the alphabet $\Sigma = \{0, 1\}$.

A16. For $a, b \in Z$, define $a \equiv b$ if and only if $a^2 - b^2$ is divisible by 3. Prove that $\equiv$ defines an equivalence relation on z.

17. What is Σ^*? How members of Σ^* are enumerated? Explain with example.

18. If $\Sigma = \{aa, b\}$ then find Σ^*.

19. If $\Sigma = \{a, ab\}$ then find Σ^*.

20. If $\Sigma = \{a, b, c)$ then find Σ^*.

21. For (x, y) and (u, v) in R^2, define $(x, y) \sim (u, v)$ if $x^2 + y^2 = u^2 + v^2$. Prove that $\sim$ defines an equivalence relation on R^2 and interpret the equivalence classes geometrically. Assume that R is the set of real numbers.

A22. If $L = \{a, b\}$ then find L^0, L^1 and L^2.

23. If $L_1 = \{a, ab, a^2\}$ and $L_2 = \{b^2, aba\}$ be languages over $\Sigma = \{a, b\}$ then find $L_1 L_2$ and $L_2 L_1$.

Answers/Hints for Selected Review Questions

4. **Basis:** For $n = 1$, we get

    L.H.S = the sum of the integers from 1^2 to 1^2

    $$= 1$$

    $$\text{R.H.S.} = \frac{1(1+1)(2*1+1)}{6}$$

    $$= \frac{1*2*3}{6}$$

    $$= 1$$

    So the statement is true for $n = 1$.

    Inductive Hypothesis: Assume that the statement is true for $n = k, k \geq 1$. Then

    $$1^2 + 2^2 + ... + k^2 = \frac{k(k+1)(2k+1)}{6}$$

    Inductive Step: We need to prove that the statement is true for $n = k + 1$, i.e.,

    $$1^2 + 2^2 + ... + (k+1)^2 = \frac{(k+1)(k+2)(2k+3)}{6}$$

    Now $1^2 + 2^2 + ... + (k+1)^2 = 1^2 + 2^2 + ... k^2 + (k+1)^2$

    $$= \frac{k(k+1)(2k+1)}{6} + (k+1)^2$$

    [by the inductive hypothesis]

    $$= \frac{k(k+1)(2k+1) + 6(k+1)(k+1)}{6}$$

$$= \frac{(k+1)([k(2k+1)+6(k+1)]}{6}$$

$$= \frac{(k+1)}{6}(2k^2+7k+6)$$

$$= \frac{(k+1)(2k+3)(k+2)}{6}$$

Thus, by the principle of mathematical induction, the statement is true for all integers $n \geq 1$.

>. Let the maximum number of leaves of a binary tree of height n be $l(n)$. Then we need to prove that $l(n) \leq 2^n$.

Basis: Obviously $l(0) = 1 = 2^0$ since a tree of height 0 can have no nodes other than the root, that is, it has only one leaf.

Inductive Step: To get a binary tree of height $n + 1$ from one of height n, we can create at the most two leaves in place of each previous one. Therefore

$l(n + 1) \leq 2l(n)$

Now, using the **inductive hypothesis** we get

$l(n + 1) \leq 2 \times 2^n = 2^{n+1}$

The statement is therefore true for $n + 1$. Since n was an arbitrary positive integer, the statement is therefore for every natural number n.

. Assume that $2 - \sqrt{2}$ is a rational number. Then

$$2 - \sqrt{2} = \frac{p}{q}$$

$$\Rightarrow 2 - \frac{p}{q} = \sqrt{2}$$

$$\Rightarrow \sqrt{2} = \frac{2q - p}{q} = \text{a rational number which is a contradiction.}$$

. Let $x = 2a + 1$, $y = 2b + 1$

where a & b are integers. Then

$xy = (2a + 1)(2b + 1)$

$= 4ab + 2a + 2b + 1$

$= 2(2ab + a + b) + 1$

$= 2z + 1$, $z = 2ab + a + b$, an integer

Hence xy is odd.

11. We can show that for any strings u and $v \in \Sigma^*$, $(uv)^R = v^R u^R$ by induction technique on the length of v.

Basis: Let us take $|v| = 0$. Then $v = \varepsilon$ and $(uv)^R = (u\varepsilon)^R = u^R$

$$= \varepsilon u^R$$
$$= \varepsilon^R u^R$$
$$= v^R u^R$$

Inductive Hypothesis: If $|v| \leq n$, then $(uv)^R = v^R u^R$

Induction Step: Let $|v| = n+1$, then $v = xa$ for some $x \in \Sigma^*$ and $a \in \Sigma$ such that $|x| = n$

$(uv)^R = (u(v))^R$

$= (u(xa))^R \qquad$ [since $v = xa$]

$= ((ux)a)^R \qquad$ [since concatenation is associative]

$= a(ux)^R \qquad$ [by definition of the reversal of $(ux)a$]

$= ax^R u^R \qquad$ [by inductive hypothesis]

$= (xa)^R u^R \qquad$ [by definition of the reversal of (xa)]

$= v^R u^R \qquad$ [since $v = xa$]

which is just we wanted to show.

16. **Reflexive:** For any $a \in Z$, $a \equiv a$ since $a^2 - a^2 = 0$ is divisible by 3.

Symmetric: If $a \equiv b$, then $a^2 - b^2$ is divisible by 3. Clearly $b^2 - a^2 = -(a^2 - b^2$ is also divisible by 3. Hence $b \equiv a$.

Transitive: If $a \equiv b$ and $b \equiv c$, then both $(a^2 - b^2)$ and $(b^2 - c^2)$ are divisible by 3. Clearly $a^2 - c^2 = (a^2 - b^2) + (b^2 - c^2)$ is also divisible by 3. Hence $a \equiv c$.

22. $L^0 = \varepsilon$

$L^1 = \{a, b\}$

$L^2 = LL$

$\quad = \{a, b\} \{a, b\}$

$\quad = \{aa, ab, ba, bb\}$

Chapter 2

Finite Automata

This Chapter introduces the concept of a finite automaton, the simplest abstract model of a computing device. We will define Deterministic Finite Automaton (DFA), Non-Deterministic Finite Automaton (NFA) with and without ε-transition, Moore and Mealy Machines and discuss the equivalence and conversions between them. Myhill-Nerode Theorem and optimization of Finite Automata will be discussed with the help of examples to facilitate thorough understanding of the concepts.

Objectives: The objective of this Chapter is to introduce Finite Automata. After learning the contents of this Chapter, you will be able to:

1. Explain the need of studying Automata,
2. Classify different types of Automata,
3. Define and convert NFA to DFA,
4. Define NFA and convert NFA with ε-transition to NFA without ε-transition,
5. Design DFA and NFA,
6. Describe Automata with output capability,
7. Convert Moore machine to Mealy machine and vice-versa and
8. Optimize an FA.

2.1　Finite Automata (FA)

The term "Finite Automata" describes a class of mathematical models (imaginary machines) that are characterized by having a finite number of states. At any given time, an automaton can be in any of these states (internal configurations). In response to external "inputs", it can switch to another state. This is called a *transition*.

Automata originate from the Greek word $\alpha \cup \tau o\mu\alpha\tau\alpha$ which means something is doing something by itself (or self-acting). The change of state of the system is totally governed by the input. Systems which could transition between finite number of states have been around for a long time. However, a formal description of these appeared in 1943 in McCulloch-Pitts neural network models. Intensive study of finite automata during 1950s established many important basic properties.

Finite Automata are simple computational models for computers with extremely limited memory, the memory being limited by the number of states. Of what use is such a computer? To answer this question, we are only to look around us to observe the *control mechanism* of elevators, vending machines, automatic doors, train track switches, traffic lights, and clock machines, etc. These devices need to remember only a finite set of states and a finite set of inputs. The *Theory of Automata* plays an important role in the design of such devices. Other important non-computer applications for finite automata can be found in various household appliances like dishwashers, washing machines, electronic thermostats (refrigerators) as well as parts of digital watches and calculators. To understand the concept of a finite automaton in depth, let us consider the example of how automatic doors at the entrance and the exit of a supermarket work.

The automatic doors swing open or close according as a person is approaching or exiting the door. The doors have two sensing pads, front and rear, to detect the presence of a person. At any given time, the doors can be in only one of the two states "open" or "closed". Depending upon the input situations (i) Person standing on the front pad "front", (ii) Person standing on the rear pad "rear", (iii) Persons standing on both pads "both" and (iv) No one standing on either pad "neither", the possible movements of the doors are from the state closed to open, open to closed, closed to closed (to remain in the same state) and open to open (to remain in the same state). The supermarket doors, therefore, perform a predetermined sequence of actions depending on a sequence of events they encounter.

In computer science, finite automata theory is successfully applied in various design problems like design of switching circuits, design of lexical analyzers, design of editors and other text processing programs, etc.

We can classify Finite Automata (FA) into Deterministic Finite Automata (DFA) and Non-Deterministic Finite Automata (NDFA). In the next section we will discuss the Deterministic Finite Automata.

2.2　Deterministic Finite Automata (DFA)

A *Deterministic Finite Automaton* has a set of states and a set of transitions.

The inputs are symbols from an alphabet, called the input alphabet. Every state has exactly one transition for each possible input. It has one start (or initial) state and a set of final (accept) states. When the automaton starts working, it is in the start state. If the automaton is in one of the final states when it stops working, the input is said to be accepted by the automaton. If it stops in some other state, the input is said to be rejected.

2.2.1 Formal Definition

Formally, we define a *Deterministic Finite Automaton* as follows:

A *Deterministic Finite Automaton* is a 5-tuple $(Q, \Sigma, \delta, q_0, F)$ where

Q is a finite non-empty set, called the set of states.

Σ is an input alphabet (a finite, non-empty set of symbols).

$q_0 \in Q$ is a fixed element, called the initial state.

F is a subset of Q (possibly empty), called the set of final states.

δ is a function : $\delta : Q \times \Sigma \rightarrow Q$, called the transition function. That is, for each state q and each input symbol a, $\delta(q, a)$ is a state in Q to which the automaton moves if it receives the input a while in state q.

By Finite Automaton (FA), we actually mean Deterministic Finite Automaton (DFA). The word "Deterministic" in the phrase "Deterministic Finite Automaton" originates from the fact that there is a unique transition for each state on each input alphabet which completely determines the next configuration of the automaton. The word "Finite" in the phrase is due to the finite number of possible states of the automaton and the finite number of input symbols in the alphabet.

We can view a finite automaton as a *finite control system*. Input tape, Read head and Finite control are the main ingredients of the system as shown in Figure 2.1.

Input tape

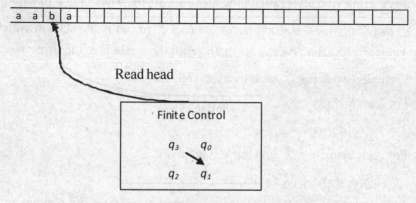

Fig. 2.1: Block Diagram of Finite Automaton

Words are fed into the system by means of an input tape. The tape is divided into squares, each square containing a single symbol from the input alphabet. The finite control can access the information written at any position on the tape with the help of a read head. The head reads one symbol at a time. After reading the input symbol, the read head moves one square to the right on the input tape so that on the next move it will read the symbol in the next tape square. Initially, the read head is placed at the leftmost square of the tape. Finite Automaton, thus, "reads" one letter at a time from the input string (stored on the tape), going from left to right. Each successive symbol in the string causes a transition from the present state to another state in the machine. Eventually, as the head reaches the end on the input string, processing stops and the automaton indicates acceptance or rejection of the string.

Let us take an example to see the working of the Finite Automaton which is described in Figure 2.1. From the Figure 2.1, you can see that $Q = \{q_0, q_1, q_2, q_3\}$, $\Sigma = \{a, b\}$. Let us assume that q_0 is the start state and q_2 is the only final state, i.e., $F = \{q_2\}$ and $\delta(q_0, a) = q_1$, $\delta(q_0, b) = q_3$, $\delta(q_1, a) = q_0$, $\delta(q_1, b) = q_1$, $\delta(q_2, a) = q_2$, $\delta(q_2, b) = q_2$, $\delta(q_3, a) = q_2$ and $\delta(q_3, b) = q_3$. Starting in state q_0 and with the first letter of the input string being a, the machine moves to the state q_1 since $\delta(q_0, a) = q_1$. While in state q_1, it reads the next letter a and moves to the state q_0 (as $\delta(q_1, a) = q_0$). Now machine is again in state q_0. Reading the next letter b, it moves to state q_3 (as $\delta(q_0, b) = q_3$). The next letter, i.e., fourth letter is an a and that takes the machine to the state q_2. Once in state q_2, machine must stay in state q_2, and since that is the final state the string is accepted by the machine.

Extended Transition Function

The extended transition function, usually denoted by $\hat{\delta}$, extends the δ function from single letters to words. Whereas with δ, we can specify the state FA reaches after processing a single symbol, with $\hat{\delta}$ we will be able to describe the state at which FA will arrive after processing an entire string. Thus $\hat{\delta}$ is a function from $Q \times \Sigma^*$ to Q, in which, starting in the state q, $\hat{\delta}(q, w)$ is the state at which the automaton arrives after processing, in order, all the symbols of the string w.

Formally, we define $\hat{\delta}$ recursively as follows:

For each $q \in Q$

$$\hat{\delta}(q, \varepsilon) = q \qquad \qquad \qquad \text{... (1) and}$$

For each string $w \in \Sigma^*$ and input symbol $a \in \Sigma$

$$\hat{\delta}(q, wa) = \delta(\hat{\delta}(q, w), a) \qquad \qquad \text{... (2)}$$

Equation (1) shows that FA cannot change its state without reading an input symbol. Equation (2) shows that if the input string is of the form 'wa', i.e., a is the last symbol of the string and 'w' is the string consisting of all but the last symbol, then to compute $\hat{\delta}(q, wa)$, first compute $\hat{\delta}(q, w)$. Suppose $\hat{\delta}(q, w) = p$, then $\hat{\delta}(q, wa) = \delta(p, a)$. The recursion stops when the remainder of the string is the empty string ε.

Assuming $w = \varepsilon$, we have

$$\hat{\delta}(q, a) = \delta(\hat{\delta}(q, \varepsilon), a) = \delta(q, a)$$

We, therefore, observe that there is no disagreement between δ to $\hat{\delta}$ on the arguments for which both are defined.

2.3 Simplified Notation of Finite Automata

We can describe a Finite Automaton employing (i) Graphical representation and (ii) Tabular representation.

2.3.1 State Transition Graph

A finite automaton is often represented by a directed labeled graph, called a *Transition Diagram/State Diagram/State Transition Graph*. States of the automaton are represented by the vertices (nodes) of the graph (denoted by circles). A transition from a state q to a state p on an input a, i.e., $\delta(q, a) = p$, is represented by an arc (q, p) labeled by a. The start state is indicated by an inward pointing arrow and final states are indicated by double circles. Sometimes we can indicate the start state of FA by labeling it with the word "start" or by a minus sign also and the final states by labeling them with the word "final" or plus sign. The algorithm for construction of the transition diagram is defined in Algorithm 2.1.

Algorithm 2.1: Algorithm for drawing a Transition Diagram

Algorithm (Construction of Transition Diagram): Let $M = (Q, \Sigma, \delta, q_0, F)$ be a finite automaton. Following steps are used to construct the Transition Diagram.

Step 1: Draw small circles for each state with the name of the state written inside the circle.

Step 2: Draw an arc labeled with a from circle q to circle p if there is a transition from state q to state p on input a, i.e., $\delta(q, a) = p$.

Step 3: Repeat the Step 2 for each transition.

Step 4: Indicate start state by an incoming arrow or labeling with word "start" or "−".

Step 5: Indicate final states by double circles or labeling by the word "Final" or "+".

Figure 2.2 shows various ways of drawing the Transition Diagram of the same automata.

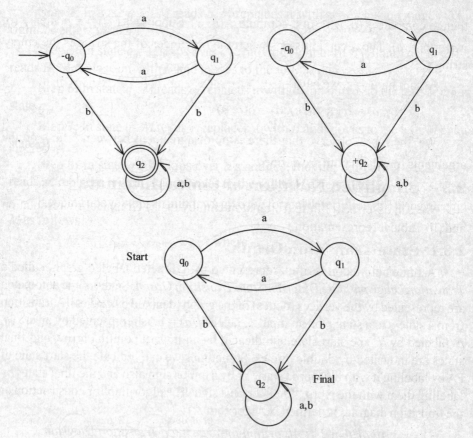

Fig. 2.2: Transition Diagram of a Finite Automation

2.3.2 Transition Table

The *Transition Table* describes the transition function of a Finite Automaton in tabular form. The rows of the table are labeled by the states of the automata and the columns are labeled by the input letters. A row label proceeded by a minus (–) sign indicates the start state and the column labels preceded by plus (+) sign represent the final states. The entry in the cell (q, a), i.e., the cell at the cross section of row q and column a, indicates the transition $\delta(q, a)$. *Transition table* is also known as *state table* or *transition function table* or *transition system table*.

Table 2.1 shows the transition table for the automaton given in Figure 2.2.

This table represents the following transitions:

$\delta(q_0, a) = q_1$, $\delta(q_0, b) = q_2$, $\delta(q_1, a) = q_0$, $\delta(q_1, b) = q_2$, $\delta(q_2, a) = q_2$, $\delta(q_2, b) = q_2$.

The algorithm for construction of a transition table is given in Algorithm 2.2.

Table 2.1: Transition Table

Input States	a	b
$-q_0$	q_1	q_2
q_1	q_0	q_2
$+q_2$	q_2	q_2

Algorithm 2.2: Algorithm for constructing a Transition Table

Algorithm (Construction of Transition Table): Let $M = (Q, \Sigma, \delta, q_0, F)$ be a finite automaton. Following steps are used to construct the Transition Table:

Step 1: Draw a table in which number of rows indicates the number of states in FA and number of columns indicates the number of symbols in Σ.

Step 2: Label the rows with the state names and the columns with the symbols in Σ.

Step 3: For each transition function $\delta(q, a) = p$, put p in the cell (q, a).

Step 4: Start state is preceded by "–" and final states are preceded by " + ".

2.4   Language of DFA

Let $M = (Q, \Sigma, \delta, q_0, F)$ be a DFA. A word (string) $x \in \Sigma^*$ is said to be accepted or recognized by M if and only if

$$\delta(q_0, x) = p$$

for some p in F. M rejects x if and only if $\delta(q_0, x) \notin F$.

Every DFA defines a language in the sense that it differentiates between the words it accepts and the words it rejects. The language accepted (or defined) by M, denoted by $L(M)$, is the set of all strings in Σ^* that are accepted by M. Formally,

$$L(M) = \{x | \delta(q_0, x) \in F\}.$$

The language accepted by a FA is called *regular language*. In other words, a language is a regular language, if it is accepted or defined by a FA.

Example 2.1: Consider the Deterministic Finite Automaton $M = (Q, \Sigma, \delta, q_0, F)$ where

$Q = \{q_0, q_1, q_2, q_3\}$
$\Sigma = \{a, b\}$
$q_0 = \{q_0\}$
$F = \{q_3\}$

and δ is defined by the transition table given in Table 2.2.

Table 2.2: Transition Table

Input States	a	b
$-q_0$	q_1	q_2
q_1	q_3	q_2
q_2	q_1	q_3
$+q_3$	q_3	q_3

(a)   Draw the transition diagram.

(b)   Determine the entire sequence of states for the input string *ababa*.

(c)   Determine whether the word *ababa* is accepted by the machine.

(d)   Determine what will happen if the word *babbb* is fed into the machine.

(e)   Determine the language defined by the machine.

Solution:

(a)   The transition table has four rows labeled q_0, q_1, q_2, and q_3. So, the transition diagram will have four nodes labeled q_0, q_1, q_2, and q_3. We observe that q_0 is the initial state and q_3 is the only final state and represent them accordingly in the diagram. The entry in the cell (q_0, a) is q_1, i.e., $\delta(q_0, a) = q_1$. So, we draw an arch, labeled by a, from state q_0 to state q_1. Repeating this process for each entry of the table, i.e., for each transition, we get the transition diagram as shown in Figure 2.3.

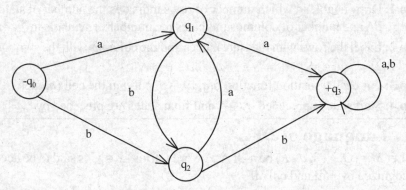

Fig. 2.3: Transition Diagram of DFA for Table 2.2

(b) If M is given the input *ababa*, it starts with its initial configuration $(q_0, ababa)$. Then

$$\delta(q_0, ababa) = \delta(q_1, baba)$$
$$= \delta(q_2, aba)$$
$$= \delta(q_1, ba)$$
$$= \delta(q_2, a)$$
$$= q_1$$

Hence, the sequence of states is given as follows:

$$q_0 \to q_1 \to q_2 \to q_1 \to q_2 \to q_1$$

(c) In (b), we can see that machine begins with initial state q_0 and stops at the state q_1, which is not a final state. Therefore, *ababa* is not accepted by the machine.

(d) If M is given the input *babbb*, then

$$\delta(q_0, babbb) = \delta(q_2, abbb)$$
$$= \delta(q_1, bbb)$$
$$= \delta(q_2, bb)$$
$$= \delta(q_3, b)$$
$$= q_3$$

Beginning with initial state q_0, the machine stops at state q_3, which is a final state. Therefore, *babbb* is accepted by the machine.

(e) Figure 2.5 shows the two possible ways to reach the final state q_3 one through the state q_1 and the other through q_2. The machine enters the state q_1, in case the current input letter is a and the current state is either q_0 or q_2. While in state q_1, if the machine reads an a, it enters the final state q_3. Hence any string that contains at least two consecutive a's is recognized by the machine. Again, the machine enters the state q_2 after reading the letter b for the first time. Once in state q_2, it moves to state q_3 on input b. Clearly, then, any string having at least two consecutive b's is recognized by the machine. Therefore, the language defined/accepted by the FA is the set of all strings that have either aa or bb as a substring.

2.5   Non-Deterministic Finite Automata (NFA)

The Deterministic Finite Automata are restricted to having exactly one transition from a state for each input symbol. By allowing zero, one or more transitions from a state on the same input symbol, we can introduce the feature of unpredictability into the model. The resulting machine, introduced in 1959 by Michael. O. Rabin and Dana Scott, is called *Non-Deterministic Finite Automaton* (NFA). The non-determinism arises from the fact that there are several choices for the possible next state for the same input and by knowing the current state and the current input symbol; we can only partially determine the next state.

Formally, we define a *Non-Deterministic Finite Automaton* as follows:

A *Non-Deterministic Finite Automaton* is a 5-tuple $(Q, \Sigma, \delta, q_0, F)$, where

Q is a finite, non-empty set of states,

Σ is an input alphabet,

$q_0 \in Q$ is the initial state,

$F \subseteq Q$ is the set of final states (possibly empty) and

$\delta : Q \times \Sigma \rightarrow 2^Q$ (2^Q is the power set of Q) is the state transition function. $\delta(q, a)$ is the set of all states p such that there is a transition from state q to state p on input a.

Extended Transition Function

To examine the behavior of NFA on an input string, the transition function δ is extended to $\delta^\wedge$ as in the case of DFA. $\hat{\delta}$, called the *Extended Transition Function*, then, maps $Q \times \Sigma^*$ to 2^Q.

We define $\delta^\wedge$ recursively as follows:

$$\hat{\delta}(q, \varepsilon) = \{q\} \qquad \qquad \dots (1)$$

$$\hat{\delta}(q, wa) = \{p \mid \text{for some state } r \text{ in } \hat{\delta}(q, w), p \text{ is in } \delta(r, a)\} \qquad \dots (2)$$

Equation (1) states that the machine cannot change state without reading an input symbol. As explained earlier, Equation (2) states that to compute $\hat{\delta}(q, wa)$, first compute $\hat{\delta}(q, w)$. In case $r \in \hat{\delta}(q, w)$, then compute $\hat{\delta}(r, a)$. As $\hat{\delta}(r, a) = \delta(r, a)$, δ is used in place of $\hat{\delta}$.

An NFA is typically described by a directed graph in which, from a node, there may be any number of outgoing edges (including zero) that represent the transitions on a single input symbol. The graph, thus, can exhibit several different paths for the same string. All these paths need not to terminate in either accepting or rejecting states. An input string is accepted if and only if at least one of these paths ends in an accepting state.

The language L accepted by an NFA $M = (Q, \Sigma, \delta, q_0, F)$ and denoted by $L(M)$, is the set of all strings accepted by M.

Formally, $L(M) = \{w \mid \delta(q_0, w) \subseteq F\}$.

Example 2.2: Consider the Non-Deterministic Finite Automaton $M = (Q, \Sigma, \delta, q_0, F)$ where

$Q = \{q_0, q_1, q_2, q_3, q_4\}$

$\Sigma = \{0, 1\}$

$q_0 = \{q_0\}$

$F = \{q_2, q_4\}$

and transition function δ is defined by the transition table given in Table 2.3.

(a) Draw the transition diagram.

(b) Determine the entire sequence of states for the input string 01001.

Table 2.3: Transition Table

Input States	0	1
$-q_0$	$\{q_0, q_3\}$	$\{q_0, q_1\}$
q_1	Φ	$\{q_2\}$
$+q_2$	$\{q_2\}$	$\{q_2\}$
q_3	$\{q_4\}$	Φ
$+q_4$	$\{q_4\}$	$\{q_4\}$

(c) Determine whether the word 01001 is accepted by the machine.

Solution:

(a) Draw 5 small circles, labeled with q_0, q_1, q_2, q_3 and q_4 respectively, to denote the five different states in NFA. The start state q_0 and final states q_2 and q_4 are marked as per convention. The entry in the cell $(q_0, 0)$ gives $\delta(q_0, 0) = \{q_0, q_3\}$. It means the machine, while in state q_0, will move either to state q_0 or state q_3 on the same input symbol 0. Therefore, there will be two arcs, each labeled with 0, one from node q_0 to q_0 and the other from q_0 to q_3. Repeating this process for every state on each input symbol, we get the transition diagram as shown in Figure 2.4.

(b) To determine the entire sequence of states for the input string 01001, we calculate $\delta(q_0, 01001) = ?$

$$\delta(q_0, 0) = \{q_0, q_3\} \qquad \text{[from the transition table] ... (1)}$$

$$\delta(q_0, 01) = \delta(\delta(q_0, 0), 1)$$

$$= \delta(\{q_0, q_3\}, 1) \qquad \text{[by eq. (1)]}$$

$$= \delta(q_0, 1) \cup \delta(q_3, 1)$$

$$= \{q_0, q_1\} \cup \Phi \qquad \text{[from the transition table]}$$

$$= \{q_0, q_1\} \qquad \qquad ...(2)$$

$$\delta(q_0, 010) = \delta(\delta(q_0, 01), 0)$$

$$= \delta(\{q_0, q_1\}, 0) \qquad \text{[by eq. (2)]}$$

$$= \delta(q_0, 0) \cup \delta(q_1, 0)$$

$$= \{q_0, q_3\} \cup \Phi \qquad \text{[from the transition table]}$$

$$= \{q_0, q_3\} \qquad \qquad \qquad \dots (3)$$

$$\delta(q_0, 0100) = \delta(\delta(q_0, 010), 0)$$

$$= \delta(\{q_0, q_3\}, 0) \qquad \qquad \text{[by eq. (3)]}$$

$$= \delta(q_0, 0) \cup \delta(q_3, 0)$$

$$= \{q_0, q_3\} \cup \{q_4\} \qquad \text{[by eq. (1) \& the transition table]}$$

$$= \{q_0, q_3, q_4\} \qquad \qquad \dots (4)$$

Thus, $\delta(q_0, 01001) = \delta(\delta(q_0, 0100), 1)$

$$= \delta(\{q_0, q_3, q_4\}, 1) \qquad \qquad \text{[by eq. (4)]}$$

$$= \delta(q_0, 1) \cup \delta(q_3, 1) \cup \delta(q_4, 1)$$

$$\text{[from the transition table]}$$

$$= \{q_0, q_1\} \cup \Phi \cup \{q_4\}$$

$$= \{q_0, q_1, q_4\}$$

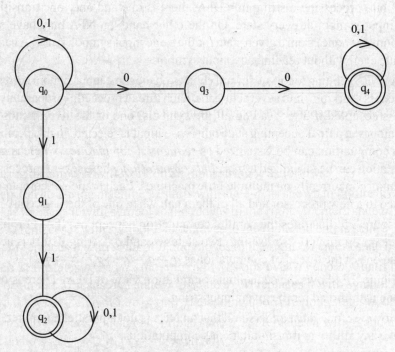

Fig. 2.4: Transition Diagram for Non-Deterministic Finite Automaton

The sequence of states for the input string 01001 is given in Figure 2.5.

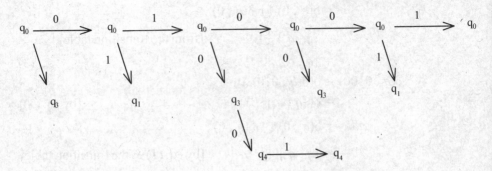

Fig. 2.5: States reached while processing 01001

(c) We know that a string is accepted by a non-deterministic finite automaton if and only if there is at least one sequence of moves leading to a final state. Since $\delta(q_0, 01001) = \{q_0, q_1, q_4\}$ contains a final state. Therefore the word is accepted by the machine.

DFA Computing vs. NFA Computing

The only difference between a DFA and an NFA lies in the transition function.

While processing a string in a DFA, there is one and only one transition for every input symbol at every state. On the other hand, an NFA may have several transitions (or none) from a given state for the same input symbol. An NFA can move to a state even without reading any input symbol.

An NFA splitting to follow several choices on the same input symbol corresponds to a process "forking" into several threads, each thread proceeding separately. Input string is accepted if after reading all the symbols, one of the live threads of the automaton is in a final/accepting state otherwise input is rejected. In this perspective, a DFA computation can be visualized as *sequential computation* whereas an NFA computation can be visualized as *parallel computation* where several processes can be running concurrently on multiple little machines. Each branch of computation is assigned to a new processor and all of them halt when one of them accepts.

Figure 2.5 illustrates the parallel computation concept of NFA. For instance, the state q_0, on input 0, "forks" into two states q_0 and q_3. String 01001 is accepted because one of the thread of computation is $q_0 \rightarrow q_0 \rightarrow q_0 \rightarrow q_3 \rightarrow q_4 \rightarrow q_4$.

Figure 2.3 shows the sequential computation view of DFA. There is one and only one path/thread for the given input string.

However, one must understand that an NFA is not a parallel computer. It does not have any ability to run simultaneous computations.

2.6   The Equivalence of NFA and DFA

Any finite automaton will satisfy the definition of a non-deterministic finite automaton with certain restrictions. In other words, a non-deterministic automaton is a generalization of the deterministic finite automata. It might be thought that because of the additional flexibility, non-deterministic automata might be able to recognize languages that deterministic ones could not. However, this is not so. In fact, the class of languages accepted by NFAs is exactly same as the class of languages accepted by DFAs, that is to say, they are equivalent. However, NFAs are defined because certain properties can be more easily proved on them as compared to their DFA counterpart. The concept of NFA plays a central role in both theory of languages and theory of computation.

Theorem 2.1: For each NFA, there is an equivalent DFA.

Proof: Let us assume $M = (Q, \Sigma, \delta, q_0, F)$ be an NFA accepting the language L. Now, we define DFA, M' as $M' = (Q', \Sigma, \delta', q_0', F')$ where

(i) $Q' = 2^Q$ (power set of Q). We see that $\{q_i : q_i \in Q\}$, a subset of Q, is a single state of the DFA .

(ii) $q_0' = \{q_0\}$

(iii) $F' = \{S \in 2^Q, S \cap F \neq \phi\}$, i.e., F' is the set of all those states in Q' that contain a final state of M.

(iv) $\delta'(\{q_1, q_2, ...q_i\}, a) = \delta(q_1, a) \bigcup \delta(q_2, a) ...... \bigcup \delta(q_i, a)$

i.e. $\delta'(\{q_1, q_2, ...q_i\}, a) = \{p_1, p_2, ...p_j\}$ if and only if

$\delta(\{q_1, q_2.....q_i\}, a) = \{p_1, p_2, ...p_j\}$.

Applying induction on the length of the input string x we will now prove that

$$\delta'(q_0', x) = \{q_1, q_2, ...q_i\} \quad\quad ..... (1)$$

if and only if

$$\delta(q_0, x) = \{q_1, q_2, ...q_i\}$$

Basis: When $|x| = 0$, $\delta'(q_0', \varepsilon) = \{q_0\}$ and $\delta(q_0, \varepsilon) = \{q_0\}$. So, Equation (1) is true for x with $|x| = 0$.

Induction: Suppose that the hypothesis (1) is true for inputs of length m or less. Let xa be a string of length $m + 1$ where $a \in \Sigma$. Then

$$\delta'(q_0, xa) = \delta'(\delta'(q_0', x), a)$$

By the inductive hypothesis,

$$\delta(q_0', x) = \{p_1, p_2, ...p_j\}$$

if and only if

$$\delta(q_0, x) = \{p_1, p_2, ...p_j\}$$

But by the definition of δ'

$$\delta'(\{p_1, p_2, ...p_j\}, a) = \{r_1, r_2, ... r_k\}$$

if and only if

$$\delta(\{p_1, p_2, ...p_j\}, a) = \{r_1, r_2, ...r_k\}$$

Thus

$$\delta' (\delta' (q_0', x), a) = \delta' (\delta' (q_0', x), a)$$

$$= \delta' (\{p_1, p_2, ...p_j\}, a) \quad \text{(since } \delta(q_0', x) = [p_1, p_2, ...p_j])$$

$$= \{r_1, r_2, ... r_k\}$$

$$\text{(since } \delta' ([p_1, p_2, ...p_j], a) = [r_1, r_2, ...r_k])$$

i.e., $\delta'(q_0, xa) = \{r_1, r_2, ... r_k\}$

if and only if

$$\delta(q_0, xa) = \{r_1, r_2, ...r_k\}$$

which establishes the inductive hypothesis.

$\delta'(q_0', x)$ is in F' only when $\delta (q_0, x)$ contains a state of Q that is in F. Thus $L(M)$ = $L(M')$.

Note: *Due to its less restrictive transition function, an NFA may seem more powerful than DFA but this is not so. Both NFA and DFA have the same capability and an NFA can always be reduced into an equivalent DFA. The only disadvantage with DFA is that it will often be much larger than the equivalent NFA. For an n state NFA, the equivalent DFA has 2^n states, an exponentially larger number. In case n is large, the construction of equivalent DFA becomes impractical. However, often a large number of states are not reachable from the start state and therefore we do not need them. The algorithm that uses this concept to construct DFA from NFA is called Subset construction or Rabin-Scott power set construction. The Subset construction algorithm for converting NFA to DFA is given in Algorithm 2.3.*

Algorithm 2.3: Algorithm for conversion of NFA to DFA

Algorithm (Conversion from NFA to DFA): Let $M = (Q, \Sigma, \delta, q_0, F)$ be an NFA that recognizes a language L. The following steps are used to construct the equivalent DFA $M' = (Q', \Sigma', \delta', q_0', F')$.

Step 1: Determine the power set of Q. The elements of the power set will be the states of the DFA, i.e., $Q' = 2^Q$.

Step 2: The input alphabet and the starting state of the DFA will be same as the input alphabet and the starting state of the NFA. Therefore, $q_0' = \{q_0\}$ and $\Sigma' = \Sigma$.

Step 3: Final states of the DFA will be those states of Q' that contain final states of the NFA.

Step 4: Compute δ'. For this we begin with the start state of the DFA, i.e., $\{q_0\}$ and compute $\delta'(\{q_0\}, a) = \delta(\{q_0\}, a)$ for each input alphabet.

Step 5: Repeat the Step 4 for those states only which are the results of a transition from a previous state.

Example 2.3: Consider the Non-Deterministic Finite Automaton $M = (Q, \Sigma, \delta, q_0, F)$ where

$Q = \{q_0, q_1\}$

$\Sigma = \{0, 1\}$

$q_0 = \{q_0\}$

$F = \{q_1\}$

and the transition function δ given in Table 2.4. Construct the equivalent Deterministic Automaton and draw its transition graph.

Table 2.4: Transition Table of NFA

Input States	0	1
$-q_0$	$\{q_0, q_1\}$	$\{q_1\}$
$+q_1$	Φ	$\{q_0, q_1\}$

Solution:

We construct DFA, $M' = (Q', \Sigma', \delta', q_0', F')$ as follows:

Step 1: Q' = Set of all subsets of $\{q_0, q_1\}$

$\qquad = \{\Phi, \{q_0\}, \{q_1\}, \{q_0, q_1\}\}$

Step 2: $\Sigma' = \{0, 1\}$

$\qquad q_0' = \{q_0\}$

Step 3: $F' = \{\{q_1\}, \{q_0, q_1\}\}$ \qquad [the only states in Q' containing q_1]

Step 4: To construct δ', begin with the start state $\{q_0\}$ of the DFA and compute δ' transition on each input symbol as follows.

$\delta'(\{q_0\}, 0) = \{q_0, q_1\}$ \qquad since $\delta(q_0, 0) = \{q_0, q_1\}$ \qquad ... (1)

$\delta'(\{q_0\}, 1) = q_1$ \qquad since $\delta(q_0, 1) = \{q_1\}$ \qquad ... (2)

The transition produces two new states $\{q_1\}$ and $\{q_0, q_1\}$.

Now compute δ' for the state $\{q_1\}$ and the state $\{q_0, q_1\}$ on inputs 0 and 1.

$\delta'(\{q_1\}, 0) = \Phi$ \qquad since $\delta(q_1, 0) = \Phi$ \qquad ...(3)

$\delta'(\{q_1\}, 1) = \{q_0, q_1\}$ \qquad since $\delta(q_1, 1) = \{q_0, q_1\}$ \qquad ...(4)

$\delta'(\{q_0, q_1\}, 0) = \delta'(\{q_0\}, 0) \cup \delta'(\{q_1\}, 0)$

$\qquad\qquad = \{q_0, q_1\} \cup \{\Phi\}$ \qquad [from (1) & (3)]

$\qquad\qquad = \{q_0, q_1\}$

$\delta'(\{q_0, q_1\}, 1) = \delta'(\{q_0\}, 1) \cup \delta'(\{q_1\}, 1)$

$\qquad\qquad = \{q_1\} \cup [q_0, q_1]$ \qquad [from (2) & (4)]

$\qquad\qquad = \{q_0, q_1\}$

Compute δ' on the next new state Φ for inputs 0 and 1.

$$\delta'(\Phi, 0) = \Phi$$
$$\delta'(\Phi, 1) = \Phi$$

The process stops here since no new state is generated from the previous transition.

Table 2.5. gives the Transition Table for the transition function δ' of the DFA M'.

We get the transition diagram as shown in Figure 2.6:

Table 2.5: Transition table of the DFA M'

Input States	0	1
$-\{q_0\}$	$\{q_0, q_1\}$	$\{q_1\}$
$+\{q_0, q_1\}$	$\{q_0, q_1\}$	$\{q_0, q_1\}$
$+\{q_1\}$	Φ	$\{q_0, q_1\}$
Φ	Φ	Φ

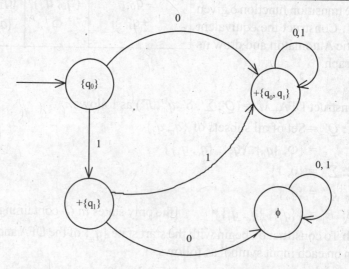

Fig. 2.6: Transition Diagram of the equivalent DFA

2.7   NFA with ε-Transitions

Researchers introduced more flexibility in the computational model by extending the NFA to include transitions on the empty string ε and thus allowing the machine to make a state transition spontaneously, without reading a symbol at all. The resulting machine is called *Non-Deterministic Finite Automaton* with ε-*transition* (ε-*move*).

From any state that has a ε-transition, the machine may move to a new state or may choose to remain in the original state.

Formally, we define NFA with ε–transition as follows:

A *Non-Deterministic Finite Automaton with* ε-*transition* is a 5-tuple $(Q, \Sigma, \delta, q_0, F)$ where

Q is a finite non-empty set of states,

Σ is an input alphabet,

$q_0 \in Q$ is the initial state,

$F \subseteq Q$ is the set of final states and

$\delta : Q \times (\Sigma \cup \{\varepsilon\}) \to 2^Q$ (the power set of Q) is the state transition function, $\delta(q, a)$ is the set consisting of all states p such that there is a transition labeled a from q to p, where a is either ε or a symbol in Σ.

Extended Transition Function

For an NFA with ε-transition to read an input string w, we have to extend the transition function δ to $\hat{\delta}$ that maps $Q \times \Sigma^*$ to 2^Q. $\hat{\delta}(q, w)$ is the set of all states p for which there is a path, beginning at q, ending at p and labeled by components of w (path may include edges labeled ε).

Now we define $\hat{\delta}$ as follows:

$$\hat{\delta}(q, \varepsilon) = \varepsilon\text{-closure } (q) \qquad \qquad \ldots(1)$$

where ε–closure (q) is the set of all states p for which there is a path, beginning at q, ending at p and labeled by ε.

For w in Σ^* and a in Σ, $\hat{\delta}(q, wa) = \varepsilon\text{-closure } (P)$, where $P = \{p | \text{for some } r \text{ in}$

$\hat{\delta}(q, w), p$ is in $\delta(r, a)\}$ $\qquad \qquad \ldots(2)$

The language L accepted by an *NFA* with ε-*transition* $M = (Q, \Sigma, \delta, q_0, F)$ is the set of all strings accepted by M. Formally,

$$L(M) = \{w \mid \hat{\delta}(q_0, w) \text{ contains a state in } F\}.$$

2.8 Equivalence of NFA and NFA with ε-Transitions

Although NFA with ε-transition appears to have more power than the NFA without ε-transition, we shall see that as language recognizer devices both are equivalent. Any language accepted by an NFA with ε -transition can also be accepted by an NFA without ε-transition. However, NFAs with ε-transition are often more convenient to use.

An NFA with ε-transition can always be converted into an NFA without ε-transition as we will see later.

Theorem 2.2: For each NFA with ε-transition, there is an equivalent NFA without ε-transition.

Proof: Let $M = (Q, \Sigma, \delta, q_0, F)$ be an NFA with ε -transition. Construct NFA without ε-transition $M' = (Q, \Sigma, \delta', q_0, F')$ where

$$F' = \begin{cases} F \cup \{q_0\} & \text{if } \varepsilon\text{-closure}(q_0) \text{ contains a state of } F, q \in Q \\ F & \text{otherwise} \end{cases}$$

and $\delta'(q, a)$ is $\hat{\delta}(q, a)$ for q in Q and a in $\cup$.

We will prove $\delta'(q_0, x) = \hat{\delta}(q_0, x)$ by the method of induction on the length of string x. The length of x cannot be zero, i.e., $x \neq \varepsilon$ because $\delta'(q_0, \varepsilon) = q_0$ but $\hat{\delta}(q_0, \varepsilon)$ = ε-closure(q_0). Hence

Basis: $|x| = 1$. Then x is a symbol a, and $\delta'(q_0, a) = \hat{\delta}(q_0, a)$ by definition of δ'.

Induction: $|x| > 1$ Let $x = wa$ for $a \in \Sigma$. Then $\delta'(q_0, wa) = \delta'(\delta'(q_0, w), a)$

By inductive hypothesis,

$$\delta'(q_0, w) = \hat{\delta}(q_0, w).$$

Let $\hat{\delta}(q_0, w) = P$. We must show that $\delta'(P, a) = \hat{\delta}(q_0, wa)$.

Now $\delta'(P, a) \bigcup_{q \text{ in } p} \delta'(q, a) = \bigcup_{q \text{ in } p} \hat{\delta}(q, a)$

Then as $P = \hat{\delta}(q_0, w)$ we have

$$\bigcup_{q \text{ in } p} \hat{\delta}(q, a) = \hat{\delta}(q_0, wa) \text{ by definition of } \hat{\delta}.$$

Thus

$$\delta'(q_0, wa) = \hat{\delta}(q_0, wa).$$

Example 2.4: For the Non-Deterministic Finite Automaton with ε- transition displayed in Figure 2.7.

(i)   Draw the transition table.

(ii) Determine ε-closure (q_0) and

(iii) Determine $\hat{\delta}(q_0, 01)$.

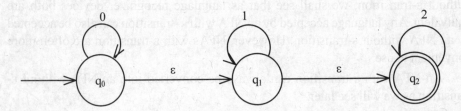

Fig. 2.7: NFA with ε-transition

Solution:

(i) From the Figure 2.7, $Q = \{q_0, q_1, q_2\}$ and $\Sigma = \{0, 1, 2\}$. Therefore, the transition table will have three rows and four columns corresponding to three states and four possible inputs (the symbols 0, 1, 2 and ε), respectively. We also observe that while in state q_0, the machine on inputs 0, 1, 2 and ε will move to states q_0, Φ, Φ and q_1, respectively. Clearly, these states become the entries of the first row of the table. Repeating this process with states q_1, q_2, we get the transition table as shown in Table 2.6:

Table 2.6: Transition Table of NFA with ε-transition

States \ Input	0	1	2	ε
$-q_0$	$\{q_0\}$	Φ	Φ	$\{q_1\}$
q_1	Φ	$\{q_1\}$	Φ	$\{q_2\}$
$+q_2$	Φ	Φ	$\{q_2\}$	Φ

(ii) As we know, ε-closure(q) is the set of all states p such that there is a path from q to p labeled ε. Clearly, the paths from q_0, labeled by ε are $q_0 \rightarrow q_0$ (machine remains in the original state), $q_0 \rightarrow q_1$, and $q_0 \rightarrow q_1 \rightarrow q_2$.

Therefore, ε-closure(q_0) = $\{q_0, q_1, q_2\}$ ... (1)

(iii) First, we compute

$$\hat{\delta}(q_0, 0) = \varepsilon\text{-closure}(\delta(\hat{\delta}(q_0, \varepsilon), 0))$$

$$= \varepsilon\text{-closure}(\delta(\{q_0, q_1, q_2\}, 0))$$

$$[\hat{\delta}(q_0, \varepsilon) = \varepsilon\text{-closure}(q_0) = \{q_0, q_1, q_2\}]$$

$$= \varepsilon\text{-closure}(\delta(q_0, 0) \cup \delta(q_1, 0) \cup \delta(q_2, 0))$$

$$= \varepsilon\text{-closure}(q_0 \cup \Phi \cup \Phi)$$

$$= \varepsilon\text{-closure}(q_0)$$

$$= \{q_0, q_1, q_2\} \qquad [\text{by (1)}] \qquad \text{... (2)}$$

Then $\hat{\delta}(q_0, 01) = \varepsilon\text{-closure}(\delta(\hat{\delta}(q_0, 0), 1))$

$$= \varepsilon\text{-closure}(\delta(\{q_0, q_1, q_2\}, 1)) \, [\text{by (2)}]$$

$$= \varepsilon\text{-closure}(\delta(q_0, 1) \cup \delta(q_1, 1) \cup \delta(q_2, 1))$$

$$= \varepsilon\text{-closure}(\Phi \cup q_1 \cup \Phi)$$

$$= \varepsilon\text{-closure}(q_1)$$

$$= \{q_1, q_2\} \qquad [\text{from the Figure 2.7}]$$

2.8.1 Conversion of NFA with ε-Transition to NFA without ε-Transitions

In this section, we will discuss two different methods of converting a given automaton with ε-transition to an equivalent automaton without ε-transition as given in Algorithm 2.4 and Algorithm 2.5.

Algorithm 2.4: Algorithm for conversion of NFA with ε-transition to NFA without ε-transition

First Algorithm (Conversion of an NFA with ε-Transition to an NFA without ε-Transition): Let $M = (Q, \Sigma, \delta, q_0, F)$ be an NFA without ε-Transition.

Step 1: The input alphabet and states of NFA without ε-transition will be same as those of NFA with ε-transition.

Step 2: Determine ε-closure (q_i) where for each state $q_i \in Q$.

Step 3: Compute $\hat{\delta}$ for each state for each input symbol.

Step 4: Final states of NFA without ε-transition will include the final states of NFA with ε-transition and those states q whose ε-closure(q) contain final states of NFA with ε-transition.

Step 5: Construct the transition table for the transition function computed in Step 2.

Example 2.5: Construct an NFA without ε-transition equivalent to the NFA with ε-transition given in Example 2.4.

Solution:

Let $M = (Q, \Sigma, \delta, q_0, F)$ be the NFA without ε-transition.

Step 1: From Figure 2.7, we observe

$$Q = \{q_0, q_1, q_2\}$$
$$\Sigma = \{0, 1, 2\}$$
$$q_0 = \{q_0\}$$

Step 2: We determine ε–closures of q_0, q_1, and q_2.

As we know that ε-closure(q) is the set of all vertices p such that there is a path from q to p labeled ε. Therefore, from Figure 2.7, we get

$$\varepsilon\text{-closure}(q_0) = \{q_0, q_1, q_2\}$$
$$\varepsilon\text{-closure}(q_1) = \{q_1, q_2\}$$
$$\varepsilon\text{-closure}(q_2) = \{q_2\}$$

Step 3: Now, we compute $\hat{\delta}$ for each state on each input symbol.

As we know $\delta(q_0, x) = \hat{\delta}(q_0, x)$

$$\hat{\delta}(q_0, 0) = \varepsilon\text{-closure}(\delta(\hat{\delta}(q_0, \varepsilon), 0))$$

$$= \varepsilon\text{-closure}(\delta(\{q_0, q_1, q_2\}, 0))$$

$$\text{[since } \hat{\delta}(q_0, \varepsilon) = \varepsilon\text{-closure}(q_0) = \{q_0, q_1, q_2\}]$$

$$= \varepsilon\text{-closure}(\delta(q_0, 0) \cup \delta(q_1, 0) \cup \delta(q_2, 0))$$

$$= \varepsilon\text{-closure}(q_0 \cup \Phi \cup \Phi)$$

$$= \varepsilon\text{-closure}(q_0)$$

$$= \{q_0, q_1, q_2\}$$

$$\hat{\delta}(q_0, 1) = \varepsilon\text{-closure}(\delta(\hat{\delta}(q_0, \varepsilon), 1))$$

$$= \varepsilon\text{-closure}(\delta(\{q_0, q_1, q_2\}, 1))$$

$$\text{[since } \hat{\delta}(q_0, \varepsilon) = \varepsilon\text{-closure}(q_0) = \{q_0, q_1, q_2\}]$$

$$= \varepsilon\text{-closure}(\delta(q_0, 1) \cup \delta(q_1, 1) \cup \delta(q_2, 1))$$

$$= \varepsilon\text{-closure}(\Phi \cup q_1 \cup \Phi)$$

$$= \varepsilon\text{-closure}(q_1)$$

$$= \{q_1, q_2\} \qquad\qquad [\text{since } \varepsilon\text{-closure}(q_1) = \{q_1, q_2\}]$$

$$\hat{\delta}(q_0, 2) = \varepsilon\text{-closure}(\delta(\hat{\delta}(q_0, \varepsilon), 2))$$

$$= \varepsilon\text{-closure}(\delta(\{q_0, q_1, q_2\}, 2))$$

$$[\text{since } \hat{\delta}(q_0, \varepsilon) = \varepsilon\text{-closure}(q_0) = \{q_0, q_1, q_2\}]$$

$$= \varepsilon\text{-closure}(\delta(q_0, 2) \cup \delta(q_1, 2) \cup \delta(q_2, 2))$$

$$= \varepsilon\text{-closure}(\Phi \cup \Phi \cup q_2)$$

$$= \varepsilon\text{-closure}(q_2) \qquad\qquad [\text{since } \varepsilon\text{-closure}(q_2) = \{q_2\}]$$

$$= \{q_2\}$$

Next, we compute $\hat{\delta}$ for q_1 on each input symbol.

$$\hat{\delta}(q_1, 0) = \varepsilon\text{-closure}(\delta(\hat{\delta}(q_1, \varepsilon), 0))$$

$$= \varepsilon\text{-closure}(\delta(\{q_1, q_2\}, 0))$$

$$[\text{since } \hat{\delta}(q_1, \varepsilon) = \varepsilon\text{-closure}(q_1) = \{q_1, q_2\}]$$

$$= \varepsilon\text{-closure}(\delta(q_1, 0) \cup \delta(q_2, 0)$$

$$= \varepsilon\text{-closure}(\Phi \cup \Phi)$$

$$= \varepsilon\text{-closure}(\Phi)$$

$$= \Phi$$

$$\hat{\delta}(q_1, 1) = \varepsilon\text{-closure}(\delta(\hat{\delta}(q_1, '\varepsilon), 1))$$

$$= \varepsilon\text{-closure}(\delta(\{q_1, q_2\}, 1))$$

$$[\text{since } \hat{\delta}(q_1, \varepsilon) = \varepsilon\text{-closure}(q_1) = \{q_1, q_2\}]$$

$$= \varepsilon\text{-closure}(\delta(q_1, 1) \cup \delta(q_2, 1)$$

$$= \varepsilon\text{-closure}(q_1 \cup \Phi)$$

$$= \varepsilon\text{-closure}(q_1)$$

$$= \{q_1, q_2\}$$

$$\hat{\delta}(q_1, 2) = \varepsilon\text{-closure}(\delta(\hat{\delta}(q_1, \varepsilon), 2))$$

$$= \varepsilon\text{-closure}(\delta(\{q_1, q_2\}, 2))$$

$$[\text{since } \hat{\delta}(q_1, \varepsilon) = \varepsilon\text{-closure}(q_1) = \{q_1, q_2\}]$$

$$= \varepsilon\text{-closure}(\delta(q_1, 2) \cup \delta(q_2, 2)$$

$$= \varepsilon\text{-closure}(\Phi \cup q_2)$$

$$= \varepsilon\text{-closure}(q_2)$$
$$= \{q_2\}$$

Next, we compute $\hat{\delta}$ for state q_2 on each input symbol.

$$\hat{\delta}(q_2, 0) = \varepsilon\text{-closure}(\delta(\hat{\delta}(q_2, \varepsilon), 0))$$

$$= \varepsilon\text{-closure}(\delta(\{q_2\}, 0)) \quad [\text{since } \hat{\delta}(q_2, \varepsilon) = \varepsilon\text{-closure}(q_2) = \{q_2\}]$$

$$= \varepsilon\text{-closure}(\Phi)$$

$$= \Phi$$

$$\hat{\delta}(q_2, 1) = \varepsilon\text{-closure}(\delta(\hat{\delta}(q_2, \varepsilon), 1))$$

$$= \varepsilon\text{-closure}(\delta(\{q_2\}, 1)) \quad [\text{since } \hat{\delta}(q_2, \varepsilon) = \varepsilon\text{-closure}(q_2) = \{q_2\}]$$

$$= \varepsilon\text{-closure}(\Phi)$$

$$= \Phi$$

$$\hat{\delta}(q_2, 2) = \varepsilon\text{-closure}(\delta(\hat{\delta}(q_2, \varepsilon), 2))$$

$$= \varepsilon\text{-closure}(\delta(\{q_2\}, 2)) \quad [\text{since } \hat{\delta}(q_2, \varepsilon) = \varepsilon\text{-closure}(q_2) = \{q_2\}]$$

$$= \varepsilon\text{-closure}(\delta(q_2, 2))$$

$$= \varepsilon\text{-closure}(q_2)$$

$$= \{q_2\}$$

Now, we compute F.

As we know, final states of NFA without ε-transition will include the final states of NFA with ε-transition and those states q of it whose ε-closure(q) contain any final state of NFA with ε-transition. Therefore,

$$F = \{q_0, q_1, q_2\}.$$

Transition table of NFA without ε-transition is given in Table 2.7.

The transition diagram of NFA without ε-transition is given by Figure 2.8.

Table 2.7: Transition Table of NFA without ε-transition

Input States	0	1	2
$-+q_0$	$\{q_0, q_1, q_2\}$	$\{q_1, q_2\}$	$\{q_2\}$
$+q_1$	Φ	$\{q_1, q_2\}$	$\{q_2\}$
$+q_2$	Φ	Φ	$\{q_2\}$

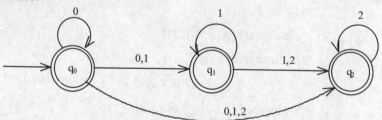

Fig. 2.8: Transition Diagram of NFA without ε-transition

There is another method which is also used to convert finite automaton with ε-transition to finite automaton without ε-transition. The algorithm for said conversion method is given in Algorithm 2.5.

Algorithm 2.5: Algorithm for conversion of automaton with ε-transition to automaton without ε-transition

---

Second Algorithm(Conversion of automaton with ε-transition to automaton without ε-transition):

Step1: Draw the transition diagram of given NFA with ε-transition if the transition diagram is not given.

Step2: If there is an ε-transition from state q_i to q_j, do the Steps 3 to 6 .

Step3: Identify the edges originating at node q_j.

Step4: If an identified edge terminates at state q_k, and has the label a then add a new edge from node q_i to q_k labeled with a . Repeat the process with every identified edge. Remove the ε-transition from state q_i to q_j.

Step5: Designate q_j as initial state if q_i is the initial state of the given machine.

Step6: Designate q_i a final state if q_j is a final state of the given machine,

Step7: Repeat Step 2 to remove all ε-transition arcs.

Example 2.6: Construct a finite automaton without ε-transition equivalent to finite automaton with ε-transition as given in Example 2.4.

Solution:

Step 1: Transition diagram is already given.

Step 2: First, we eliminate the ε-transition between state q_0 and q_1 by introducing new transitions.

Step 3: There are two edges originating at q_1, edge labeled 1 that q_1 and edge labeled ε that terminating at q_2.

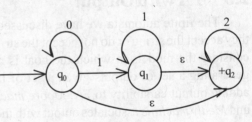

Fig. 2.9

Step 4: So, we draw a new edge from q_0 to q_1 labeled 1 and another from q_0 to q_2 with label ε. We get the transition diagram as given in Figure 2.9:

Step 5: Here q_0 is the initial state so mark q_1 also as initial state.

Step 6: q_1 is not a final state. Now we get the transition diagram as given in Figure 2.10.

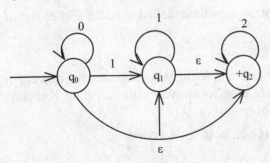

Fig. 2.10

Step 7: Next we eliminating ε-Transition between q_0 and q_2, we get the TD as given in Figure 2.11:

Since q_0 is initial so made q_2 as initial. q_2 is final so made q_0 as a final state. Finally, we eliminate the ε-Transition from q_1 to q_2. Finally, we get the Transition diagram as given in Figure 2.12.

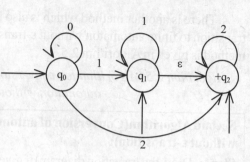

Fig. 2.11

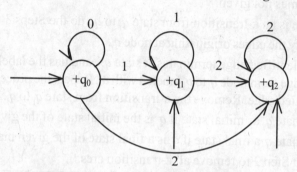

Fig. 2.12

2.9   FA with Output

The finite automata we have discussed so far have binary output, i.e., either they accept the string or do not accept the string. Now we remove this restriction and consider the models in which the goal is not accepting or rejecting strings, but generating a set of outputs given a set of inputs. There are two distinct ways of adding output capability to FA. *Moore machine* associates output with each state and *Mealy machine* associates output with the transition function. Both the concepts proved valuable in sequential circuit design. Although sequential circuits are only a component of a computer, it is nevertheless an important component and acts as a machine.

Automata with input and output are sometimes called *transducers* because of their connection with electronics.

2.9.1 Moore Machine

The *Moore machine*, named after E. F. Moore, who presented the concept in 1956, is a finite automaton that outputs a symbol on every state transition. Formally, we define the Moore machine as follows:

A *Moore Machine* is a 6-tuple $(Q, \Sigma, \Delta, \delta, \lambda, q_0)$ where

    Q is a finite set of states,

    Σ is an input alphabet (finite set of symbols),

    Δ is an output alphabet (finite set of symbols),

$q_0 \in Q$ is the initial state,

$\delta : Q \times \Sigma \rightarrow Q$ is the transition function. That is, for each $q \in Q$, and for each $a \in \Sigma$, $\delta(q, a) \in Q$,

$\lambda: Q \rightarrow \Delta$ is the output function giving the output associated with each state.

When input $a_1 a_2 a_3 .... a_n$, $n \geq 0$ (length of input string) is fed to the machine, it gives the output $\lambda(q_0) (q_1) ... \lambda(q_n)$, where $q_0, q_1, ... q_n$ is the sequence of states such that $\delta(q_{i-1}, a_i) = q_i$ for $1 \leq i \leq n$. Since the machine always starts in the state q_0, it produces the output $\lambda(q_0)$ without processing any input or in other words on input $\in$. Clearly the length of the output string is one greater than that of the input string. There are no final states in a Moore machine. When the last input letter is read and the last output character is printed, the machine terminates processing.

The DFA is a special case of a Moore machine where Δ is $\{0, 1\}$ and λ' maps final states to 1 and other states to 0. The state labeled q is an "accepting state" if and only if $\lambda(q) = 1$.

A Moore machine generally does not define a language. When an input string is fed into Moore machine, it gives an output string. Moore machine can also be represented graphically. The transition diagram of the Moore machine is constructed using the algorithm defined in Algorithm 2.6.

Algorithm 2.6: Algorithm for constructing Transition Diagram of Moore machine.

Algorithm (Construction of Transition Diagram of a Moore Machine):

Let $(Q, \Sigma, \Delta, \delta, \lambda, q_0)$ be a Moore machine.

Step 1: Draw small circles corresponding to each state and inside each circle write the name of the state that it represents.

Step 2: If there is a transition from state q to state p on input a, i.e., $\delta(q, a) = p$, then draw an arc from state q to state p labeled with a.

Step 3: Repeat Step 2 for each transition.

Step 4: Indicate start state by an inward pointing arrow.

Step 5: Write the output character associated with each state inside the circle that represents the state, in a way that the name of the state is followed by the output character, two being separated by a slash '/'.

Example 2.7: Consider the Moore Machine $M = (Q, \Sigma, \Delta, \delta, \lambda, q_0)$ where

$Q = \{q_0, q_1, q_2, q_3\}$

$\Sigma = \{a, b\}$

$\Delta = \{0, 1\}$

$q_0 = \{q_0\}$

and the transition function δ and the output are defined by the transition table given in Table 2.8.

Table 2.8: Transition Table

Old State	New State		Output
	Input a	Input b	(λ)
$-q_0$	q_1	q_3	1
q_1	q_3	q_1	0
q_2	q_0	q_3	0
q_3	q_3	q_2	1

(a) Draw transition diagram of the Moore Machine.

(b) Determine the entire sequence of states and the output string for the input string *abab.*

Solution:

(a) The transition table, given in Table 2.8, has four rows labeled q_0, q_1, q_2, and q_3, respectively. The machine, therefore, has four states q_0, q_1, q_2, and q_3. Draw four small circles, each representing one state. Label each circle by the corresponding state name. In the table, the row, labeled q_0 preceded by – sign, indicates q_0 is the start state. Therefore, draw an incoming arrow to the circle representing the state q_0. Corresponding to each cell entry, draw the appropriate arc labeled by the appropriate symbol. For example, the entry in the cell (q_0, a) is q_1. So draw an arc, labeled *a,* from state q_0 to q_1. Similarly draw all the other

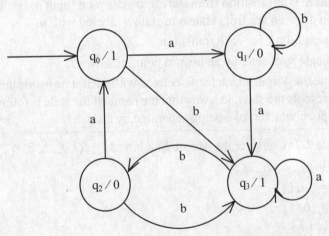

Fig. 2.13: Transition Diagram of the Moore Machine

arcs. Now, according to the given table, the output character associated with the state q_0 is 1. So, inside the circle, after the state name q_0, write 1, the two being separated by a "/". Repeat this process for each state. Finally, we obtain the transition diagram of the Moore machine as given in Figure 2.13.

(b) Machine always starts from start state q_0, which automatically prints out the character 1. After reading the first letter of the input string, i.e., a, the machine moves to state q_1 and prints a 0, the output character associated with the state q_1. With the next input letter b, the machine remains in state q_1 as depicted in the figure. Being in q_1 again, machine prints another 0. The machine, next, reads an a, goes to state q_3 and prints 1. Processing the next symbol, which is b, the machine goes to state q_2, and prints a 0. Thus for the input string $abab$, the transition of states (sequence of states) is given as follows:

$$q_0 \longrightarrow q_1 \longrightarrow q_1 \longrightarrow q_3 \longrightarrow q_2 .$$

The output string will be 10010.

Example 2.8: The Figure 2.14 depicts the Moore machine that determines how many times the substring aab appears in a long input string.

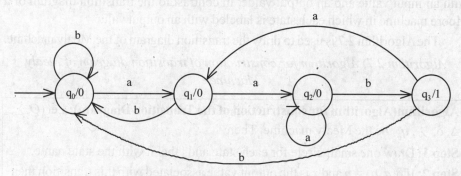

Fig. 2.14: Transition Diagram of the Moore Machine

Every state of this machine prints out the character 0 except state q_3, which prints 1. The machine reaches state q_3 only when it reads a b while in state q_2 whereas it can reach state q_2 from any other state by reading at least two consecutive a's. Therefore, 1 is printed if and only if the machine reads the substring aab. In case the machine encounters the substring aab again, another 1 will be printed. Thus the number of times the substring aab appears in the input string will be exactly equal to the number of 1's in the output string. The example shows one of the useful applications of Moore machine.

2.9.2 Mealy Machine

The *Mealy machine* is named after G.H. Mealy who presented the concept in 1955. Mealy machine differs from the Moore machine in the output function only. In a Mealy machine output values are determined both by its present state and the present input rather than solely by the current state. We formally define a *Mealy machine* as follows:

A *Mealy Machine* is a 6-tuple $(Q, \Sigma, \Delta, \delta, \lambda, q_0)$ where

Q is a finite set of states,

Σ is an input alphabet (finite set of symbols),

Δ is an output alphabet,

$q_0 \in Q$ is the initial state,

$\delta : Q \times \Sigma \rightarrow Q$ is the transition function. That is, for each state $q \in Q$ and each input symbol $a \in \Sigma$, $\delta(q, a) \in Q$,

$\lambda : Q \times \Sigma \rightarrow \Delta$ is the output function That is, (q, a) gives the output associated with the transition from state q on input a.

When input string $a_1 a_2 a_3, \ldots a_n$ is fed to the machine, the output sequence obtained is $\lambda'(q_0, a_1) \lambda'(q_1, a_2) \lambda (q_2, a_3) \ldots \lambda (q_{n-1}, a_n)$ where $q_0, q_1, \ldots q_n$ is the sequence of states such that $\delta(q_{i-1}, a_i) = q_i$ for $1 \le i \le n$. In a Mealy machine the length of the output string is exactly equal to that of the input string.

In the transition diagram of a Mealy machine, each transition edge is labeled with an input value and an output value, in contrast to the transition diagram of a Moore machine in which each state is labeled with an output value.

The Algorithm 2.7 is used to draw the transition diagram of the Mealy machine.

Algorithm 2.7: Algorithm for construction of transition diagram of Mealy Machine

---

Algorithm(Algorithm for construction of the Transition Diagram): Let $(Q, \Sigma, \Delta, \delta, \lambda, q_0)$ be the Mealy machine. Then

Step 1: Draw one small circle for each state and label it with the state name.

Step 2: If $\delta(q, a) = p$ and x is the output value associated with this transition then draw an arc from state q to state p labeled with input symbol a and the output symbol x, the two being separated by a /.

Step 3: Repeat Step 2 for each transition.

Step 4: Indicate the start state by an incoming arrow.

Example 2.9: Consider the Mealy Machine $M = (Q, \Sigma, \Delta, \delta, \lambda, q_0)$ where

$Q = \{q_0, q_1, q_2, q_3\}$

$\Sigma = \{a, b\}$

$\Delta = \{0, 1\}$

$q_0 = \{q_0\}$

and transition function δ and the output function λ are defined by the transition table given in Table 2.9.

Table 2.9: Transition Table of Mealy Machine

Old State	New State				
	Input a		Input b		
	state	output(λ)	state	output(λ)	
$-q_0$	q_1	0	q_3	0	
q_1	q_3	1	q_2	1	
q_2	q_3	0	q_3	1	
q_3	q_3	1	q_0	1	

i)   Draw the Mealy Machine.

ii) Determine the sequence of states and the output string for the input string *aaabb*.

Solution:

Using Algorithm 2.7, we can easily obtain the Transition Diagram as given in Figure 2.15.

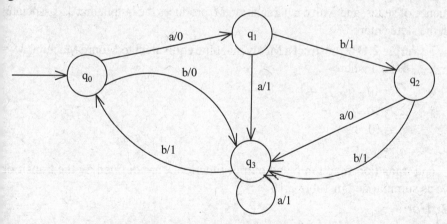

Fig. 2.15: Transition Diagram of Mealy Machine

i)   The machine starts in state q_0. Upon processing the first letter of the input string, an *a*, the machine moves to state q_1 and produces the output 0. On processing the next *a*, the machine moves to state q_3 and produces the output 1. On processing the third *a*, the machine loops back to q_3 and produces the output 1. The fourth letter is a *b*, which takes the machine back to q_0 and produces the output 1. Machine then reads the next letter, again a *b* , moves to state q_3 and outputs a 0. Thus for the input string *aaabb*, the sequence of states is given by

$$q_0 \rightarrow q_1 \rightarrow q_3 \rightarrow q_3 \rightarrow q_0 \rightarrow q_3$$

and the output string is 01110.

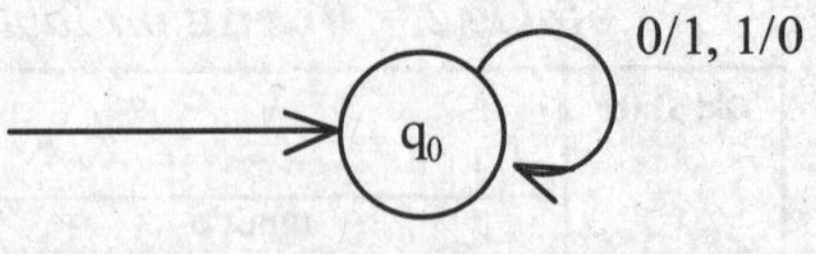

0/1, 1/0

q_0

Fig. 2.16: Transition Diagram of Mealy Machine

Example 2.10: Figure 2.16 depicts a mealy machine that computes the 1's complement of an input bit string.

If the input is 0100110 the output is 1011001. This is the simplest application of a Mealy machine.

2.9.3 Equivalence of Moore and Mealy Machine

As discussed in the earlier sections, the length of output string from a Moore machine is one greater than that from the Mealy machine on the same input. However, in case we ignore the response of the Moore machine to input ε, the two machines are said to be equivalent if for every input string, they will both produce the same output string.

2.9.4 Conversion from Moore to Mealy Machine

Theorem 2.3: If $M_o = (Q, \Sigma, \Delta, \delta, \lambda, q_0)$ is a Moore machine, then there is a Mealy machine M_e equivalent to M_o.

Proof: We know Moore machines are different than Mealy machines in the output function only. Hence let $M_e = (Q, \Sigma, \Delta, \delta, \lambda', q_0)$ where $\lambda'(q, a) = \lambda(\delta(q, a))$ for each $q \in Q$ and each $a \in \Sigma$. Then, on the same input M_o and M_e enter the same sequence of states, and with each transition M_e produces the output that M_o associates with the state entered.

Example 2.11: Construct a Mealy machine equivalent to Moore Machine $M_o = (Q, \Sigma, \Delta, \delta, , q_0)$ where

$$Q = \{q_0, q_1, q_2, q_3\}$$
$$\Sigma = \{a, b\}$$
$$\Delta = \{0, 1\}$$
$$q_0 = \{q_0\}$$

and transition function δ and output function λ are defined by the transition table as summarized in Table 2.10 .

Solution:

Let us assume the equivalent Mealy machine is $M_e = (Q, \Sigma, \Delta, \delta, \lambda', q_0)$ where

$$Q = \{q_0, q_1, q_2, q_3\}$$
$$\Sigma = \{a, b\}$$
$$\Delta = \{0, 1\}$$
$$q_0 = \{q_0\}$$

For converting Moore machine to equivalent Mealy machine, we have to compute the output function λ' of Mealy machine.

Table 2.10: Transition Table of Moore Machine

Old State	New State		Output(λ)
	Input a	Input b	
$-q_0$	q_1	q_2	0
q_1	q_3	q_2	1
q_2	q_2	q_3	0
q_3	q_3	q_3	1

We know that

$\lambda'(q, a) = \lambda\ (\delta(q, a))$ where λ is the output function and δ is the transition function of Moore machine. For the state q_0 and inputs a and b

$$\lambda'(q_0, a) = \lambda(\delta(q_0, a))$$
$$= \lambda\ (q_1) \qquad \text{[from the transition table } \delta(q_0, a) = v\ (q_1)]$$
$$= 1 \qquad \text{[from the transition table } \lambda\ (q_1)\ 1]$$
$$\lambda'\ (q_0, b) = \lambda\ (\ \delta(q_0, b))$$
$$= \lambda\ (q_2) \qquad \text{[from the table } \delta(q_0, b) = q_2]$$
$$= 0 \qquad \text{[from the table } \lambda\ (q_2) = 0\ ]$$

For the state q_1 and inputs a and b

$$\lambda'\ (q_1, a) = \lambda\ (\ \delta(q_1, a))$$
$$= \lambda(q_3) \qquad \text{[from the table } \delta(q_1, a) = q_3]$$
$$= 1 \qquad \text{[from the table } \lambda'(q_3) = 1]$$
$$\lambda'(q_1, b) = \lambda\ (\delta(q_1, b))$$
$$= \lambda\ (q_2)$$
$$= 0$$

For the state q_2 and inputs a and b

$$\lambda'\ (q_2, a) = \lambda\ (\ \delta(q_2, a))$$
$$= \lambda\ (q_2) \qquad \text{[from the table } \delta(q_2, a) = q_2]$$
$$= 0 \qquad \text{[from the table } \lambda\ (q_2) = 0]$$
$$\lambda'\ (q_2, b) = \lambda\ (\ \delta(q_2, b))$$
$$= \lambda\ (q_3) \qquad \text{[from the table } \delta(q_2, b) = q_3]$$
$$= 1 \qquad \text{[from the table } \lambda\ (q_3) = 1]$$

For the state q_3 and inputs a and b

$$\lambda'\ (q_3, a) = \lambda\ (\ \delta(q_3, a)\ )$$
$$= \lambda\ (q_3) \qquad \text{[from the table } \delta(q_3, a) = q_3]$$

$$= 1 \qquad \text{[from the table } \lambda\,(q_3) = 1]$$

$$\lambda'\,(q_3, b) = \lambda\,(\,\delta(q_3, b)\,)$$

$$= \lambda\,(q_3) \qquad \text{[from the table } \delta(q_3, b) = q_3]$$

$$= 1 \qquad \text{[from the table } \lambda\,(q_3) = 1]$$

Now, we easily construct the transition diagram and transition table of the Mealy machine as given in Figure 2.17 and Table 2.11, respectively.

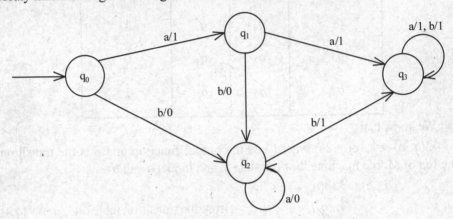

Fig. 2.17: Transition Diagram of Mealy Machine

Table 2.11: Transition Table of Mealy Machine

Old State	New State			
	Input *a*		Input *b*	
	state	output (λ)	state	output (λ)
$-q_0$	q_1	1	q_2	0
q_1	q_3	1	q_2	0
q_2	q_2	0	q_3	1
q_3	q_3	1	q_3	1

2.9.5 Conversion from Mealy to Moore Machine

Theorem 2.4: Let $M_e = (Q, \Sigma, \Delta, \delta, \lambda, q_0)$ be a mealy machine. Then there is a Moore machine M_o equivalent to M_e.

Proof: Let Moore machine be $M_o = (Q \times \Delta, \Sigma, \Delta, \delta', \lambda', [q_0, b_0])$, where b_0 is an arbitrarily selected member of Δ. The states of M_o are of the form (q, b) where $q \in Q$

and $b \in \Delta$. A new transition function δ' is defined for the Moore machine which is given by $\delta'([q, b], a) = (\delta(q, a), \lambda(q, a))$ where $a \in \Sigma$ and $\lambda'([q, b]) = b$. The second component of a state $[q, b]$ of M_o is the output produced by M_e on some transition into state q. Only the first components of M_o's states determine the moves made by M_o. We can easily prove this by induction on n. This shows that if M_e enters states q_0, $q_1, \ldots q_n$ on input $a_1, a_2, a_3, \ldots a_n$, and produces outputs $b_1 b_2 \ldots b_n$ then M_o enters states $[q_0, b_0], [q_1, b_1] \ldots [q_n, b_n]$ and produces outputs $b_0, b_1, b_2 \ldots b_n$ on the same input.

Example 2.12: Consider the Mealy machine $M_e = (Q, \Sigma, \Delta, \delta, \lambda, q_0)$ where

$Q = \{q_0, p_0, p_1\}$
$\Sigma = \{0,1\}$
$\Delta = \{n, y\}$
$q_0 = \{q_0\}$

and transition function δ and output function λ are defined by the transition table shown in Table 2.12.

Table 2.12: Transition Table of Mealy Machine

Old State	New State			
	Input 0		Input 1	
	state	output	state	output
$-q_0$	p_0	n	p_1	n
p_0	p_0	y	p_1	n
p_1	p_0	n	p_1	y

(i)   Draw the transition diagram of Mealy machine.
(ii) Convert Mealy machine into equivalent Moore machine
(iii) Draw the transition diagram of Moore machine.

Solution:

(i) From the algorithm given in Algorithm 2.7, we get the transition diagram of the Mealy machine as shown in Figure 2.18

(ii) Let the equivalent Moore Machine be $M_o = (Q', \Sigma', \Delta', \delta', \lambda', q_0'))$ where
$Q' = Q \times \Delta = (q_0, p_0, p_1) \times (y, n) = [q_0, y], [q_0, n], [p_0, y], [p_0, n],$
$\quad [p_1, y], [p_1, n]$
$\Sigma' = \Sigma$

$\Delta' = \Delta$

$q_0' = [q_0, b_0]$ where b_0 is an arbitrarily selected member of Δ.

$\quad = [q_0, n]$ where $b_0 = n$

Now determine δ' and λ' for each state of Moore machine and for each input symbol.

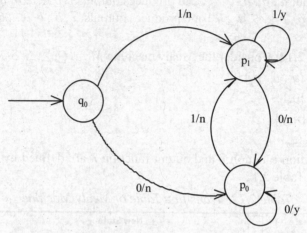

Fig. 2.18: Transition Diagram of the Mealy machine

For state $[q_0, y]$ and inputs 0, 1:

$\quad \delta'([q_0, y], 0) = [\delta(q_0, 0), \lambda'(q_0, 0)]$ [Theorem 2.4]

$\quad\quad\quad\quad\quad = [p_0, n]$ $[\delta(q_0, 0) = p_0, \lambda(q_0, 0) = n]$

$\quad \delta'([q_0, y], 1) = [\delta(q_0, 1), \lambda(q_0, 1)]$

$\quad\quad\quad\quad\quad = [p_1, n]$ $[\delta(q_0, 1) = p_1, \lambda(q_0, 1) = n]$

$\quad\quad \lambda'[q_0, y] = y$

For state $[q_0, n]$ and inputs 0, 1:

$\quad \delta'([q_0, n], 0) = [\delta(q_0, 0), \lambda(q_0, 0)]$ [Theorem 2.4]

$\quad\quad\quad\quad\quad = [p_0, n]$ $[\delta(q_0, 0) = p_0, \lambda(q_0, 0) = n]$

$\quad \delta'([q_0, n], 1) = [\delta(q_0, 1), \lambda(q_0, 1)]$

$\quad\quad\quad\quad\quad = [p_1, n]$ $[\delta(q_0, 1) = p_1, \lambda(q_0, 1) = n]$

$\quad\quad \lambda'[q_0, n] = n$

For state $[p_0, y]$ and inputs 0, 1:

$\quad \delta'([p_0, y], 0) = [\delta(p_0, 0), \lambda(p_0, 0)]$ [Theorem 2.4]

$\quad\quad\quad\quad\quad = [p_0, y]$

$\quad \delta'([p_0, y], 1) = [\delta(p_0, 1), \lambda(p_0, 1)]$

$\quad\quad\quad\quad\quad = [p_1, n]$ $[\delta(p_0, 1) = p_1, \lambda(p_0, 1) = n]$

$\quad\quad \lambda'[p_0, y] = y$

For state $[p_0, n]$ and inputs 0, 1:

$$\delta'\,([p_0, n], 0) = [\delta\,(p_0, 0), \lambda\,(p_0, 0)] \quad \text{[Theorem 2.4]}$$
$$= [p_0, y] \qquad\qquad [\delta\,(p_0, 0) = p_0, \lambda\,(p_0, 0) = y]$$
$$\delta'\,([p_0, n], 1) = [\delta\,(p_0, 1), \lambda\,(p_0, 1)]$$
$$= [p_1, n] \qquad\qquad [\delta\,(p_0, 1) = p_1, \lambda\,(p_0, 1) = n]$$
$$\lambda'[p_0, n] = n$$

For state $[p_1, y]$ and inputs 0,1:

$$\delta'\,([p_1, y], 0) = [\delta\,(p_1, 0),\ \lambda\,(p_1, 0)] \quad \text{[Theorem 2.4]}$$
$$= [p_0, n] \qquad\qquad [\delta\,(p_1, 0) = p_0, \lambda\,(p_1, 0) = n]$$
$$\delta'\,([p_1, y], 1) = [\delta\,(p_1, 1), \lambda'(p_1, 1)]$$
$$= [p_1, y] \qquad\qquad [\delta\,(p_1, 1) = p_1, \lambda'(p_1, 1) = y]$$
$$\lambda'[p_1, y] = y$$

For state $[p_1, n]$ and input 0,1: $\qquad\qquad$ [Theorem 2.4]

$$\delta'\,([p_1, n], 0) = [\delta\,(p_1, 0), \lambda'(p_1, 0)]$$
$$= [p_0, n] \qquad\qquad [\delta\,(p_1, 0) = p_0, \lambda'(p_1, 0) = n]$$
$$\delta'\,([p_1, n], 1) = [\delta\,(p_1, 1), \lambda'(p_1, 1)]$$
$$= [p_1, y] \qquad\qquad [\delta\,(p_1, 1) = p_1, \lambda\,(p_1, 1) = y]$$
$$\lambda'[p_1, n] = n$$

From the above computed six tuples, we get the transition table of Moore machine as shown in Table 2.13.

Table 2.13: Transition Table of Moore Machine

Old State	New State		Output(λ)
	Input 0	Input 1	
$-[q_0, n]$	$[p_0, n]$	$[p_1, n]$	n
$[q_0, y]$	$[p_0, n]$	$[p_1, n]$	y
$[p_0, y]$	$[p_0, y]$	$[p_1, n]$	y
$[p_0, n]$	$[p_0, y]$	$[p_1, n]$	n
$[p_1, y]$	$[p_0, n]$	$[p_1, y]$	y
$[p_1, n]$	$[p_0, n]$	$[p_1, y]$	n

In the above Table, we observe that the machine can never enter the state $[q_0, y]$. Thus, it may be removed.

(iii) The Transition diagram of Moore machine is shown in Figure 2.19.

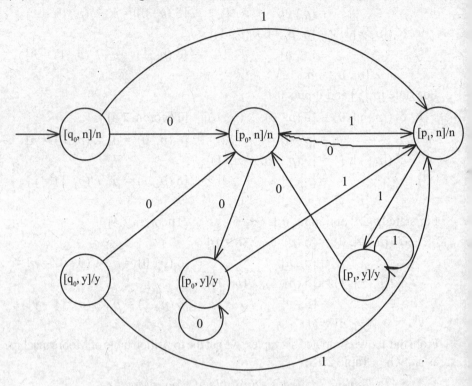

Fig. 2.19: Transition Diagram of Moore Machine

2.10 Minimization of Finite Automata

We know that any Deterministic Finite Automaton $M = (Q, \Sigma, \delta, q_0, F)$ defines a unique language (unique regular language). But the converse is not true. There are many different DFAs that can be used to define (accept) a given language. There may be considerable differences in the number of states of such equivalent automata. Representation of an automaton, for the purpose of computation, requires space proportional to the number of states it has. However, if the results are to be applied in a practical setting, the automaton, with the minimum number of states, is preferred over other equivalent machines due to storage efficiency.

Sometimes a DFA will have more states than necessary. For every DFA, there is an essentially unique minimum state equivalent DFA. Some DFAs contain unreachable states as shown in Example 2.13. Some DFAs may contain the states that are not accepting states and have no out-going transitions except to themselves. Such states are called dead states (trap states). Obviously in an automaton unreachable and dead states are unnecessary and can be eliminated. Moreover, a DFA may have equivalent states. The two states p and q are *equivalent*, written $p \equiv q$, if both $\delta(p, x)$ and $\delta(q, x)$ are accepting states, or both of them are non-accepting states for all $x \in \Sigma^*$, i.e., both behave exactly the same way.

Equivalent states are sometimes called *indistinguishable states*. Therefore states p and q of a DFA are *indistinguishable* if

$$\delta(p, x) \in F \text{ implies } \delta(q, x) \in F,$$

and

$$\delta(p, x) \notin F \text{ implies } \delta(q, x) \notin F,$$

for all $x \in \Sigma^*$.

The states p and q of a DFA are *distinguishable* if there exists some string $x \in \Sigma^*$ such that

$$\delta(p, x) \in F \text{ and } \delta(q, x) \notin F$$

or

$$\delta(p, x) \notin F \text{ and } \delta(q, x) \in F$$

Indistinguishable has the properties of equivalence relations and therefore partitions the set Q into disjoint equivalence classes.

If two states are *equivalent* (or *indistinguishable*) then transitions to one can be replaced by the transitions to the other state. Two equivalent states can therefore be merged together into one common state. Now, in order to reduce the number of states of a DFA, how do we decide what states are to be merged together? The complexity of finding equivalent classes can be reduced by applying the concept of k-equivalence relation and its properties

k-equivalence relation: The two states q_1 and q_2 are k-equivalent ($k \geq 0$) if both $\delta(q_1, x)$ and $\delta(q_2, x)$ are accepting or both are non-accepting states for all strings x of length k or less. In particular, any two accepting states are 0-equivalent and any two non-accepting states are also 0-equivalent.

We observe:

1. k-equivalence relation is an equivalence relation defined on Q. Recall that an equivalence relation is reflexive, symmetric and transitive.

2. Recall that an equivalence relation defined in the set S, partitions S into mutually disjoint equivalence classes. k- equivalence relation, therefore partitions the set Q into disjoint equivalent classes. We denote the set of k-equivalence classes by π_k.

3. If states q_1 and q_2 are k-equivalent for all $k \geq 0$, then they are equivalent.

4. If states q_1 and q_2 are $(k+1)$ equivalent, then they are k-equivalent.

5. $\pi_n = \pi_{n+1}$ for some n, where π_n denotes the set of equivalence classes under n-equivalence.

Theorem 2.6: Two states q_1 and q_2 are $(k+1)$ equivalent if

(*i*) They are k-equivalent, (ii) $\delta(q_1, a)$ and $\delta(q_2, a)$ are also k-equivalent for every $a \in \Sigma$.

Proof: Assume q_1 and q_2 are not $(k+1)$-equivalent. Then there exists a string $w = aw_1$ of length $k+1$ such that $\delta(q_1, aw_1)$ is a final state and $\delta(q_2, aw_1)$ is not a final state (or vice-versa). So, $\delta(\delta(q_1, a), w_1)$ is a final state and $\delta(\delta(q_2, a), w_1)$ is not a final state (or vice-versa). As w_1 is a string of length k, $\delta(q_1, a)$ and $\delta(q_2, a)$ are not k-equivalent. This is a contradiction and hence result is proved.

Based on the above discussion, two algorithms to construct a minimum state finite automaton are given in Algorithm 2.8 and Algorithm 2.9.

Algorithm 2.8: Algorithm 1 for construction of Minimum State Finite Automaton

---

Algorithm 1 (Construction of Minimum State Finite Automaton): The following steps are used as follows.

Step 1: Construct the transition table of DFA if it is not given.

Step 2: Construct π_0 as follows: By the definition of 0-equivalence, $\pi_0 = \{Q_1^0, Q_2^0\}$ where Q_1^0 is the set of all final states and $Q_2^0 = Q - Q_1^0$.

Step 3: Construct π_{k+1} from π_k as follows. Let Q_i^k be an element in π_k. If q_1 and q_2 are in Q_i^k, they are $(k+1)$ equivalent provided $\delta(q_1, a)$ and $\delta(q_2, a)$ are k-equivalent. Further, find out whether $\delta(q_1, a)$ and $\delta(q_2, a)$ are in the same equivalence class in π_k for every $a \in \Sigma$. If so, q_1 and q_2 are $(k+1)$-equivalent. In this way, check each $Q_i^k \in \pi_k$ to get all the elements of π_{k+1}.

Step 4: Construct π_k for $n = 1, 2, 3 \ldots$ until $\pi_n = \pi_{n+1}$.

Step 5: For the desired minimum state automaton, the states are the equivalence classes obtained in Step 4, i.e. the elements of π_n. The state table is obtained by replacing a state q by the corresponding equivalence class $[q]$.

Example 2.13: Construct a minimum state deterministic finite automaton equivalent to deterministic finite automaton given in Figure 2.20.

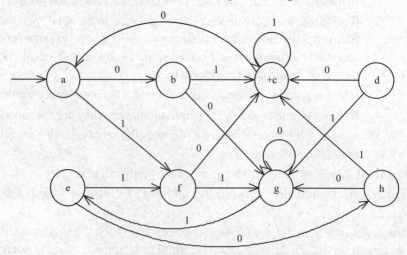

Fig. 2.20: Transition Diagram of DFA

Solution:

According to Step 1, we first construct a transition table of the given automaton as shown in Table 2.14.

As in Step 2, we now construct π_0.

We know $\pi_0 = \{ Q_1^0, Q_2^0 \}$

$Q_1^0 = $ set of all final states $= \{c\}$

$Q_2^0 = Q - Q_1^0$

$\quad = \{a, b, c, d, e, f, g, h\} - \{c\}$

$\quad = \{a, b, d, e, f, g, h\}$

So, $\pi_0 = \{ \{c\}, \{a, b, d, e, f, g, h\}\}$

Table 2.14: Transition Table of DFA

Input States	0	1
−a	b	f
b	g	c
+c	a	c
d	c	g
e	h	f
f	c	g
g	g	e
h	g	c

Following Step 3, consider $Q_1^0 \in \pi_0$. $Q_1^0 = \{c\}$ cannot be further partitioned. So, $Q_1' = \{c\}$.

Now consider the second element from π_0, i.e., $Q_2^0 = \{a, b, d, e, f, g, h\}$. Corresponding to $a, b \in Q_2^0$, the entries under the 0-column, b and g respectively, lie in Q_2^0 but the entries under 1-column are f and c, respectively where $f \in Q_2^0$ and $c \in Q_1^0$. Therefore, a and b are not 1-equivalent.

Corresponding to $a, d \in Q_2^0$, the entries in the 0-column are b and c, respectively. But $b \in Q_2^0$ and $c \in Q_1^0$. Therefore, a and d are not 1-equivalent.

Corresponding to $a, e \in Q_2^0$, the entries under the 0-column are b and h respectively and both belong to Q_2^0. The entries under 1-column are f and f, respectively and $f \in Q_2^0$. Therefore, a and e are 1-equivalent.

Similarly a and f are not 1-equivalent , a and g are 1-equivalent and a and h are not 1-equivalent.

Hence $\{a, e, g\} \in \pi_1$. So, $Q_2' = \{a, e, g\}$.

Now, consider the $\{b, d, f, h\} \subset Q_2^0$.

As above, we can prove that neither b, d nor, b, f are 1-equivalent but b, h are 1-equivalent. Hence $\{b, h\} \in \pi_1$. So, $Q_3' = \{b, h\}$.

Next, consider $\{d, f\} \subset Q_2^0$.

Since d and f are 1-equivalent, $\{d, f\} \in \pi_1$.

Hence, $\pi_1 = \{ \{c\}, \{a, e, g\}, \{b, h\}, \{d, f\} \}$.

Now we consider the elements of π_1 for 2-equivalence.

We see $\{c\} \in \pi_2$ as the set cannot be partitioned further.

Next consider $\{a, e, g\} \in \pi_1$. Corresponding to a and e the entries under the 0-column are b and h, respectively and both belong to the same equivalence class in π_1. The entries under 1-column, f and f are obviously in the same equivalence class of π_1. Therefore, a and e are 2-equivalent.

Corresponding to a and g the entries under the 0-column, g and h, respectively, are in different equivalence classes of π_1. Therefore, a and g are not 2-equivalent.

Hence $\{a, e, g\}$ is partitioned into sets $\{a, e\}$ and $\{g\}$.

Consider $\{b, h\} \in \pi_1$. Clearly, corresponding to b and h, the entries under the 0-column, g and g, are in the same equivalence class in π_1 and similarly the entries under 1-column, c and c, are in the same equivalence class in π_1. Therefore, b and h are 2-equivalent.

Consider $\{d, f\} \in \pi_1$. The entries under the 0-column corresponding to d and f are c and c; hence in the same equivalence class π_1, and the entries under 1-column, g and g, which are again in the same equivalence class in π_1. Therefore, d and f are 2-equivalent.

Hence, $\pi_2 = \{\{c\}, \{a, e\}, \{g\}, \{b, h\}, \{d, f\}\}$.

Proceeding in the same way we see $\pi_3 = \{ \{c\}, \{a, e\}, \{g\}, \{b, h\}, \{d, f\} \}$.

As $\pi_2 = \pi_3$, the process stops. Therefore, the minimum state automaton is $M' = (Q', \{0, 1\}, \delta', q_0', F')$ where

$$Q' = \{[c], [a, e], [g], [b, h], [d, f]\}$$

$$\Sigma = \{0, 1\}$$

$$q_0' = [a, e]$$

$F' = [c]$ and δ' is defined by the transition table given in Table 2.15.

Table 2.15: Transition Table of Minimum State DFA

Input States	0	1
$-[a, e]$	$[b, h]$	$[d, f]$
$[b, h]$	$[g]$	$[c]$
$[g]$	$[g]$	$[a, e]$
$[d, f]$	$[c]$	$[g]$
$+[c]$	$[a, e]$	$[c]$

Here the equivalent states *a* and *e* are merged together into one common state. Similarly states *b* and *h* are considered as one state and so are states *d* and *f* as shown in Figure 2.21.

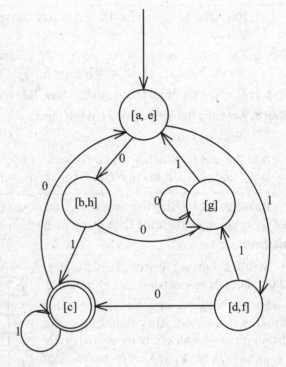

Fig. 2.21: Transition Diagram of Minimum State DFA

Algorithm 2.9: Algorithm for construction of Minimum State Finite Automaton

Algorithm 2 (Construction of Minimum State Finite Automaton): Let us assume $M = (Q, \Sigma, \delta, q_0, F)$ be a DFA. The following steps are used to construct a reduced DFA $M' = (Q', \Sigma, \delta', q_0', F')$.

Step 1: Construct the transition diagram of M if it is not given. Remove all inaccessible states. This can be done by enumerating all simple paths of the graph of DFA starting at the initial state. Any state, not part of some path, is inaccessible.

Step 2: We construct a table that has an entry D in the cell (p, q), for each pair of states (p, q) of M, if p and q are distinguishable (not equivalent). In case p and q are indistinguishable (equivalent), the cell (p, q) has entry ID.

Step 3: Repeat the following step until no previously unmarked pairs are marked. For all pairs of states (p, q) and all $a \in \Sigma$, compute $\delta(p, a) = p_a$ and $\delta(q, a) = q_a$. If the pair (p_a, q_a) is marked distinguishable, mark (p, q) distinguishable as well.

Step 4: Find the sets of indistinguishable states. Partition the states into sets of equivalent states and sets each containing one distinguishable state.

Step 5: States of DFA are renamed to $q_0, q_1, \dots q_{n-1}$ where n is the number of states. For each set $\{q_i, q_j, \dots q_k\}$ of such indistinguishable states, create a state labeled $ij, \ldots k$ for M. And also create label l for each distinguishable state q_l.

Step 6: The initial state q_0' is that state of M' whose label includes 0 or in other words that state of M' which contains q_0.

Step 7: F' is the set of all those states whose labels contain i such that $q_i \in F$.

Step 8: For each transitition of M of the form

$$\delta(q_r, a) = q_p$$

find the sets to which q_r and q_p belong. if $q_r \in '\{q_i, q_j, \ldots q_k\}$, and $q_p \in \{q_l, q_m, \ldots q_n\}$ add to δ' a transition rule $\delta'(ij\ldots k, a) = lm\ldots n$.

Example 2.14: Using the algorithm given in Algorithm 2.9, construct a minimum state finite automaton for the DFA given in the Figure 2.20.

Solution:

Step 1: From the given diagram, it is clear that the state d is inaccessible. So, eliminate d.

Step 2: Now we construct the table that indicates the distinguishable and indistinguishable states. Obviously (a, c), (b, c), (c, e), (c, f), (c, g) and (c, h) are pairs of distinguishable states, so the entry in the cell corresponding to each of these pairs is D. Table 2.16 shows the pair of distinguishable states.

Table 2.16

	a	b	c	e	f	g
b						
c	D	D				
e			D			
f			D			
g			D			
h			D			

Step 3: To find further distinguishable pairs, we consider pairs of states corresponding to empty cells one-by-one. So first consider the pair (a, b). Now

$\delta(a, 0) = b$ and $\delta(b, 0) = g$. Here (b, g) is not distinguishable yet.

$\delta(a, 1) = f$ and $\delta(b, 1) = c$. Here (c, f) is distinguishable. Thus (a, b) is also distinguishable. So cell (a, b) has entry D.

The modified table is shown in Table 2.17:

Table 2.17

	a	b	c	e	f	g
b	D					
c	D	D				
e			D			
f			D			
g			D			
h			D			

For the pair (a, e):

$\delta(a, 0) = b$ and $\delta(e, 0) = h$. Here (b, h) is not distinguishable yet.

$\delta(a, 1) = f$ and $\delta(e, 1) = f$. So (a, e) is not yet distinguishable.

For the pair (a, f):

$\delta(a, 0) = b$ and $\delta(f, 0) = c$. Here (b, c) is distinguishable.

Thus (a, f) is also distinguishable. So put D in the cell (a, f).

For the pair (a, g):

$\delta(a, 0) = b$ and $\delta(g, 0) = g$.

$\delta(a, 1) = f$ and $\delta(g, 1) = e$. Here, we can see that both (b, g) and (f, e) are not yet distinguishable. So, (a, g) is also not distinguishable yet.

For the pair (a, h):

$\delta(a, 0) = b$ and $\delta(h, 0) = g$.

$\delta(a, 1) = f$ and $\delta(h, 1) = c$. Here (f, c) is distinguishable.

Thus (a, h) is also distinguishable. So put D in the cell (a, h).

For the pair (b, e):

$\delta(b, 0) = g$ and $\delta(e, 0) = h$.

$\delta(b, 1) = c$ and $\delta(e, 1) = f$. Here, we can see that (c, f) is distinguishable. Thus, (b, e) is also distinguishable. So, we put D in the cell (b, e).

For the pair (b, f):

$\delta(b, 0) = g$ and $\delta(f, 0) = c$. Here, we can see that (c, g) is distinguishable. Thus, (b, f) is also distinguishable. So, we put D in the cell (b, f).

For the pair (b, g):

$\delta(b, 0) = g$ and $\delta(g, 0) = g$.

$\delta(b, 1) = c$ and $\delta(g, 1) = e$. Here, we can see that (c, e) is distinguishable. So, (b, g) is also distinguishable. Therefore (a, g) and (a, h) are also distinguishable. So, we put D in the cells corresponding to each of (b, g), (a, g) and (a, h).

For the pair (b, h):

$\delta(b, 0) = g$ and $\delta(h, 0) = g$.

$\delta(b, 1) = c$ and $\delta(h, 1) = c$. Here, we see on input 1, the machine moves to the final state either from state b or h. So, (b, h) is indistinguishable. Therefore (a, e) is also indistinguishable. Put ID in the cells (b, h) and (a, e).

For the pair (e, f):

$\delta(e, 0) = h$ and $\delta(f, 0) = c$. Here, we can see that (c, h) is distinguishable. So, (e, f) is also distinguishable. Therefore, we put D in the cell (e, f).

For the pair (e, g):

$\delta(e, 0) = h$ and $\delta(g, 0) = g$.

$\delta(e, 1) = f$ and $\delta(g, 1) = e$. Here (e, f) is distinguishable. So, (e, g) is also distinguishable. Therefore, we put D in the cell (e, g).

For the pair (e, h):

$\delta(e, 0) = h$ and $\delta(h, 0) = g$.

$\delta(e, 1) = f$ and $\delta(h, 1) = c$. Here, (c, f) is distinguishable. So, (e, h) is also distinguishable. Therefore, we put D in the cell (e, h).

For the pair (f, g):

$\delta(f, 0) = c$ and $\delta(g, 0) = g$. Here (c, g) is distinguishable. So, (f, g) is also distinguishable. Therefore, we put D in the cell (f, g).

For the pair (f, h):

$\delta(f, 0) = c$ and $\delta(h, 0) = g$. Here (c, g) is distinguishable. So, (f, h) is also distinguishable.

For the pair (h, g):

$\delta(h, 0) = g$ and $\delta(g, 0) = g$.

$\delta(h, 1) = c$ and $\delta(g,1) = e$. Here (c, e) is distinguishable. So, (h, g) is also distinguishable.

Finally, we get the table as shown in Table 2.18.

From the Table 2.18, we can see that (a, e) and (b, h) are non–distinguishable state. Therefore $a \equiv e$ and $b \equiv h$.

Step 4: $Q' = \{[c], [a, e], [b, h], [f], [g]\}$. States a, b, c, e, f, g are renamed to q_0, q_1, q_2, q_3, q_4, q_5 and q_6. Therefore, all of the states have been portioned into states $\{\{q_2\}, \{q_0, q_3\}, \{q_1, q_6\}, \{q_4\}, \{q_5\}\}$. $Q' = \{2, 03, 16, 4, 5\}$.

$\Sigma = \{0,1\}$

Step 5: $q_0' = \{03\}$

Table 2.18

b	D				
c	D	D			
e	ID	D	D		
f	D	D	D		
g	D	D	D	D	D
h	D	ID	D	D	D
a	b	c	e	f	g

Table 2.19: Transition Table

Input / States	0	1
−03	16	4
16	5	2
5	5	03
4	2	5
+2	03	2

Step 6: $F' = \{2\}$ and δ' is defined by the transition table given in Table 2.19.

2.11 The Myhill-Nerode Theorem

The Myhill-Nerode theorem was proposed by John Myhill and Anil Nerode. Minimization of DFA is based on this theorem. We can also associate natural equivalence relation R_M on strings associated with a finite automaton. Let $M = (Q, \Sigma, \delta, q_0, F)$ be a DFA. For x and y in Σ^*, we define xR_My if and only if $\delta(q_0, x) = \delta(q_0, y)$. R_M divides the set Σ^* into equivalence classes, one class corresponding to each state that is reachable from q_0. Further,

if xR_My, then xzR_Myz for all z in Σ^* since

$$\delta(q_0, xz) = \delta(\delta(q_0, x), z) = \delta(\delta(q_0, y), z) = \delta(q_0, yz)$$

As equivalence relation R such that xRy implies $xzRyz$ is said to be right invariant with respect to concatenation.

For any language L, a natural equivalence relation R_L can be defined such that xR_Ly, x and y in Σ^* exists if and only if for each $z \in \Sigma^*$ either both or neither of xz and yz is in L. If L is a regular set (language defined by a DFA) then clearly the number of equivalence classes (index) is always finite.

Theorem 2.5 (The Mehill-Nerode Theorem): The following three statements are equivalent:

1.   The set $L \subseteq \Sigma^*$ is accepted by some finite automaton.

2. L is the union of some of the equivalence classes of a right invariant equivalence relation of finite index.

3. Let equivalence relation R_L be defined by: xR_Ly if and only if for all z in Σ^*, xz is in L exactly when yz is in L. Then R_L is of finite index.

Proof:

For statements (1) and (2), we assume that L is accepted by some DFA $M = (Q, \Sigma, \delta, q_0, F)$. Let R_M is the equivalence relation such that xR_My if and only if $\delta(q_0, x) = \delta(q_0, y)$. As discussed above, R_M is right invariant and the number of equivalence classes (index) is finite, since index is at the most equal to the number of states in Q. The set L is the union of those equivalence classes that include a string x such that $\delta(q_0, x)$ is in F, that is, the equivalence classes corresponding to final states.

Further, for statements (2) and (3), we show that any equivalence relation E satisfying (2) is a refinement of R_L. That is each equivalence class of E is entirely contained in some equivalence class of R_L. Thus index of R_L cannot be greater than the index of E. So, it is finite. Let us assume that xEy. Then since E is right invariant, for each z in Σ^*, $xzEyz$, and thus yz is in L if and only if xz is in L. Thus xR_Ly, and hence the equivalence class of x in E is contained in the equivalence class of x in R_L. Therefore, we can conclude that each equivalence class of E is contained within some equivalence class of R_L.

For statements (3) and (1) we must show that R_L is right invariant. Suppose xR_Ly, and let w is in Σ^*. We have to prove that xwR_Lyw. That is, for any z, xwz is in L exactly when ywz is in L. But, we know for xR_Ly that for any v, xv is in L exactly when yv is in L. Let $v = vz$ to prove that R_L is right invariant. Now let Q' be finite set of equivalence classes of R_L and $[x]$ the element of Q' containing x. Define $\delta'([x], a) = [xa]$. If we choose y instead of x, we obtain $\delta'([x], a) = [ya]$. But xR_Ly, so xz is in L exactly when yz is in L. If $z = az'$, xaz' is in L exactly when yaz' is in L, so xaR_Lya and $[xa] = [ya]$. Let $q_0' = [\varepsilon]$ and let $F' = \{[x] \mid x \text{ is in } L\}$. The finite automaton $M = (Q', \Sigma, \delta', q_0', F')$ accepts L, since $\delta'(q_0', x) = [x]$ and thus x is in $L(M')$ if and only if $[x]$ is in F'.

2.12 Summary

1. Finite Automata and Regular languages were developed by Kleene, Mealy, Moore, Robin and Scott in the 1950s.

2. Finite Automata are simple computational models for computers with extremely limited memory, the memory being limited by the number of states.

3. In computer science, finite automata theory is successfully applied in various design problems like design of switching circuits, design of lexical analyzers, design of editors and other text processing programs, etc.

4. Other important non-computer applications for finite automata can be found in various household appliances like dishwashers, washing machines, electronic

thermostats (refrigerators) as well as parts of digital watches and calculators.

5. Every finite automaton defines a unique regular language. But the converse is not true. For every DFA, there is an essentially unique minimum state equivalent DFA.

6. The finite automata have binary output, i.e., either they accept the string or do not accept the string. There are two distinct ways of adding output capability to FA. Moore machine associates output with each state and Mealy machine associates output with the transition function.

2.13 Exercises

Objective Questions

1. The word "Finite" in Finite Automaton refers to:
    (a) Finite number of states
    (b) Finite number of symbols in the alphabet
    (c) Both (a) and (b)
    (d) None of these

2. The word "Automaton" in Finite Automaton means that the:
    (a) Change of the state is totally governed by the input and state
    (b) Change of the state is totally governed by the input only
    (c) Change of the state is totally governed by the state only
    (d) None of these

3. The word deterministic in DFA means that the next state of a DFA can be identified by:
    (a) Knowing the current state
    (b) Knowing the input symbol
    (c) Knowing the current state and the input symbol
    (d) None of these

4. Which one is false for DFA $M = (Q, \Sigma, \delta, q_0, F)$?
    (a) $q_0 \in Q$ (b) δ from $Q \times \Sigma$ to Q
    (c) $F \in Q$ (d) None of these

5. A transition diagram is also known as:
    (a) State transition graph   (b) State diagram
    (c) Both (a) and (b)   (d) None of these

6. Which one is not a representation of a finite automaton?
    (a) State transition graph   (b) Transition table
    (c) $M = (Q, \Sigma, \delta, q_0, F)$ (d) $M = (Q, \Sigma, \delta, F)$

7. Transition table is also known as:
    (a) Transition system table   (b) State table

(c)   Transition function table   (d)   All of these

8.   Which one is not a way to indicate the final state of a finite automaton?

final

(a)

(b)

(c)

(d)

9.   Which one is not true for NFA?

(a) $q_0 \in Q$

(b) δ maps from $Q \times \Sigma$ to 2^Q

(c)   Next state of NFA is partially determined by knowing current state and input symbol

(d)   Next state of NFA is determined by the current input symbol only

10.   The major difference between a Moore and Mealy machine is that:

(a)   Output of Moore machine depends on the present state and present input

(b)   Output of Moore depends only on the present state

(c)   Output of Moore depends only on the present input

(d)   All of these

11.   The major difference between a Moore and Mealy machine is that:

(a)   Output of Mealy is associated with the transition function

(b)   Output of Mealy depends on the present state and present input symbol

(c)   Both (a) and (b)

(d)   None of these

12.   Which one is false?

(a)   Output is associated with state in Moore machine

(b)   Output is associated with transition function in Mealy machine

(c)   Moore and Mealy both act as a language recognizer

(d)   None of these

13.   Let L be a language recognizable by a finite automaton. The language REVERSE(L) = $\{x | x = \bigcup^R, \bigcup \in L\}$ is a:

(a)   Regular language   (b)   Context-free language

(c)   Non-regular language   (d)   None of these

14.   Let L be a language recognizable by a finite automaton. The language FRONT(L) = $\{x | x$ is prefix of y where $y \in L\}$ is a:

(a)   Regular language   (b)   Context-free language

(c)   Non-regular language   (d)   None of these

15. Can a DFA simulate an NFA?
    (a) No   (b) Sometimes
    (c) Generally   (d) Yes

16. The following Figure represents:

    1/0, 0/1

    (a) A Moore machine   (b) A Mealy machine
    (c) A DFA   (d) All of these

17. The following machine accepts:

    (a) All strings   (b) ε
    (c) No string   (d) None of these

18. In the following two Figures:

    and

    (a) Both are equivalent   (b) Second accepts ε-only
    (c) First accepts nothing   (d) None of these

19. The main difference between DFA and NFA is:
    (a) In DFA, ε-transition may present
    (b) In NFA, ε-transition may present
    (c) In DFA, for any given state, there can not be any alphabet leading to two different states
    (d) In NFA, for any given state, there can not be any alphabet leading to two different states

20. Running time of NFA to DFA conversion including the case where the NFA has ε-transition is:
    (a) $O(n^3)$ (b) $O(n^3 2^n)$
    (c) $O(n^3 3^2)$ (d) $O(n^2 2^n)$

21. If two finite automata are equivalent, they should have the same number of:
    (a) States   (b) Edges
    (c) States and edges   (d) None of these

22. Two finite automata are equivalent if:
    (a) They have same number of states and edges

(b) Both accept the same language

(c) Both should be either DFAs or NFAs

(d) None of these

23. Which one is false for NFA with ε-transition? Let us assume δ and $\hat{\delta}$ be transition and extended transition functions, respectively.

(a) δ maps from $Q \times (\Sigma\{\varepsilon\})$ to 2^Q

(b) $\hat{\delta}$ maps from $Q \times (\Sigma^* \cup \{\varepsilon\})$ to 2^Q

(c) $\hat{\delta}(q, a) = \varepsilon\text{-closure}(\delta(\hat{\delta}(q, \varepsilon), a))$

(d) None of these

24. Theory of Automata does not play an important role in the design of:

(a) Lexical analyzer

(b) Editor

(c) Control mechanism of washing machine

(d) None of these

25. The applications of finite automata include:

(a) Text processing program (b) Lexical analyzer

(c) Operating system (d) Only (a) and (b)

26. Which one is not the application of finite automata?

(a) Control mechanism of fridge (b) Design of editor

(c) Design of lexical analyzer (d) None of these

27. A finite automata can recognize:

(a) Only regular grammar

(b) Regular grammar and some of the non-regular grammar

(c) Context free grammar

(d) None of these

28. Which of the following statements is true?

(a) A Mealy and Moore machine generates no language as such

(b) A Moore machine has no final state

(c) A finite automata accept left and right linear grammar

(d) All of the above

29. Which one is false of FA?

(a) Finite Automata accept left-linear grammar

(b) The finite automaton in which output is associated with state only is called Moore machine

(c) The finite automaton in which the movement of read head is either direction (left or right) is called a two way finite automaton

(d) None of these

30. The trap state of finite automaton is a state from which:

(a) It can never escape   (b) It can always escape

(c) It can occasionally escape   (d) It can occasionally stay

31. Which one is false for trap state of finite automata?

(a) Trap state may be final state

(b) Trap state may be non-final state

(c) Trap state will always be a final state

(d) None of these

32. Which one is false?

(a) Every DFA defines a unique regular language

(b) For a given regular language, there are many DFAs that accept it.

(c) For a given regular language, there are many DFAs that do not accept it.

(d) None of these

33. Two states p and q of a DFA are called distinguishable by a string $x \in \Sigma^*$:

(a) $\delta(p, x) \in F$ implies $\delta(q, x) \in F$ (b) $\delta(p, x) \notin F$ implies $\delta(q, x) \notin F$

(c) $\delta(p, x) \in F$ implies $\delta(q, x) \notin F$ (d) None of these

34. Two states p and q of a DFA are called distinguishable by a string $x \in \Sigma^*$, if:

(a) $\delta(p, x) \notin F$ implies $\delta(q, x) \in F$ (b) $\delta(p, x) \in F$ implies $\delta(q, x) \in F$

(c) $\delta(q, x) \notin F$ implies $\delta(q, x) \notin F$ (d) None of these

35. Two states p and q of a DFA are called indistinguishable if:

(a) $\delta(p, x) \in F$ implies $\delta(q, x) \in F$, for some $x \in \Sigma^*$

(b) $\delta(p, x) \notin F$ implies $\delta(q, x) \notin F$

(c) $\delta(p, x) \in F$ implies $\delta(q, x) \notin F$

(d) None of these

36. Two states p and q of a DFA are called indistinguishable if:

(a) $\delta(p, x) \notin F$ implies $\delta(q, x) \notin F$, for some $x \in \Sigma^*$

(b) $\delta(p, x) \notin F$ implies $\delta(q, x) \notin F$, for all $x \in \Sigma^*$

(c) $\delta(p, x) \in F$ implies $\delta(q, x) \in F$, for some $x \in \Sigma^*$

(d) $\delta(p, x) \in F$ implies $\delta(q, x) \in F$, for all $x \in \Sigma^*$

37. Which one is false for indistinguishable states p and q of a DFA ?

(a) $\delta(p, x) \in F$ implies $\delta(q, x) \in F$, for all $x \in \Sigma^*$

(b) $\delta(p, x) \notin F$ implies $\delta(q, x) \notin F$, for all $x \in \Sigma^*$

(c) $\delta(p, x) \in F$ and $\delta(q, x) \notin F$, for all $x \in \Sigma^*$

(d) None of these

38. Which one is false for distinguishable states p and q of a DFA ?

(a) $\delta(p, x) \in F$ implies $\delta(q, x) \notin F$, for some $x \in \Sigma^*$

(b) $\delta(p, x) \notin F$ implies $\delta(q, x) \in F$, for some $x \in \Sigma^*$

(c) $\delta(p, x) \in F$ and $\delta(q, x) \in F$, for all $x \in \Sigma^*$

(d) None of these

39. Indistinguishability of states p and q of a DFA has the property of:

    (a) A reflexive relation only
    (b) A symmetric relation only
    (c) A transitive relation only
    (d) An equivalence relation

40. Consider the following NFA with ε-moves:

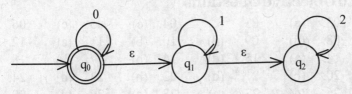

Find $\hat{\delta} (q_0, 1)$.

(a) $\{q_0, q_1, q_2\}$
(b) $\{q_1, q_2\}$
(c) $\{q_1\}$
(d) None of these

41. The following DFA accepts the set of all strings over $\{a, b\}$ that:

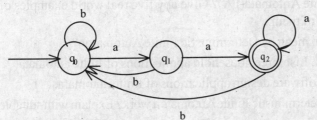

(a) Begin with either a or b
(b) End with a
(c) End with aa
(d) Contain substring aa

42. The machine shown in the figure:

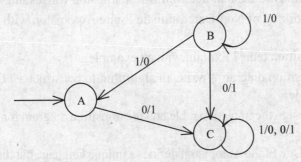

(a) Complements a given bit pattern
(b) Find 2's complement of a given bit pattern
(c) Increments a given pattern by 1
(d) Changes the sign bit

43. Myhill-Nerode theorem was proposed by:
  (a) John Myhill and Anil Nerode   (b) Anil Myhill and John Nerode
  (c) S. Myhill and A. Nerode   (d) None of these

44. Let $L_1 = \{\phi\}$ and $L_2 = \{a\}$. Which one is the value of $L_1 L_2 {}^* \cup L_1{}^*$?
  (a) $\{\varepsilon\}$ (b) a^*
  (c) $\{\varepsilon, a\}$ (d) ϕ

Answers to Objective Questions

01.	(c)	02.	(a)	03.	(c)	04.	(c)	05.	(c)	06.	(d)
07.	(d)	08.	(d)	09.	(d)	10.	(b)	11.	(c)	12.	(c)
13.	(a)	14.	(a)	15.	(d)	16.	(b)	17.	(b)	18.	(d)
19.	(c)	20.	(b)	21.	(d)	22.	(b)	23.	(d)	24.	(d)
25.	(d)	26.	(d)	27.	(a)	28.	(d)	29.	(d)	30.	(a)
31.	(d)	32.	(c)	33.	(c)	34.	(a)	35.	(b)	36.	(b)
37.	(c)	38.	(c)	39.	(d)	40.	(b)	41.	(c)	42.	(a)
43.	(a)	44.	(b)								

Review Questions

1. What is Finite Automata(FA)? Give any five real world examples of a FA and explain one of them .

2. What do you mean by Deterministic Finite Automaton?

3. Define DFA. List three household applications of finite automata.

4. Give three software design applications of finite automata.

5. How does Deterministic Finite Automaton work? Explain with suitable example.

6. Write the difference between DFA computing and NFA computing. Also justify the name DFA.

^7. Prove that all finite languages are regular.

8. Explain deterministic and non-deterministic automaton with examples.

9. Explain the working of Non-Deterministic Finite Automaton with a suitable example.

10. What is a transition table? Explain with an example.

11. What is a transition diagram? Write an algorithm to construct a TD. Explain with an example.

^12. Discuss and design the transition table and the transition diagram for automatic doors.

13. Any Deterministic Finite Automaton defines a unique language but the converse is not true. Justify it with the help of a suitable example.

14. Why do we minimize DFA?

^15. What is a trap state in FA? State and explain the properties of transition functions.

16. What do you mean by the extended transition function of DFA? Is it necessary

to use a different symbol for the extended transition function than that of the transition function? Give the reason for your answer.

ᴬ17. Suppose δ is the transition function of a DFA. Prove that for any input strings x and y, $\delta(q, xy) = \delta(\delta(q, x), y)$.

ᴬ18. Suppose δ is the transition function of a DFA. If $\delta(q, x) = \delta(q, y)$, prove that $\delta(q, xz) = \delta(q, yz)$ for all strings z in Σ^+.

ᴬ19. Design deterministic finite automaton accepting the following languages over the alphabet $\{0, 1\}$:

  (i)   The set of all words.

  (ii)   The set of all words ending in 00.

  (iii) The set of all words except ε.

  (iv) The set of all words that begin with 0.

  (v)   The set of all words with three consecutive 0s.

  (vi) The set of all words with exactly two 0s.

  (vii) The set of all words that have 0s in multiple of three.

  (viii)The set of all words that have exactly four 1s.

  (ix) The set of all words that end with 0.

  (x)   The set of all words that have exactly one 1.

  (xi) The set of all words that have 0 and 1 as second and fourth symbol.

  (xii) The set of all words that either begin with 01 or end with 01.

  (xiii)The set of all words that have different first and last symbols.

  (xiv)The set of all words that have at least two 1s.

  (xv) The set of all words that have even number of 0s.

  (xvi)The set of all words in which each 0 is followed by at least one 1.

  (xvii) The set of all words that ends up in either 00 or 11.

  (xviii) The set of all words with no more than three 1's.

20. Build an FA that accepts only the word baa over the alphabet $\{a, b\}$.

21. Construct an FA that accepts the two strings 100 and 01 over the alphabet $\{0, 1\}$.

22. The following (see Figure 2.22) are the state diagrams of two DFAs, M_1 and M_2. Answer the following questions about each of these machines:

  (i)   What is the start state?

  (ii)   What is the set of accept states?

  (iii) What sequence of states does each machine go through on input aabb?

  (iv) Do both the machines accept the string aabb?

  (v)   Do both the machines accept the string ε?

  (vi) Give the formal description of the machines M_1 and M_2.

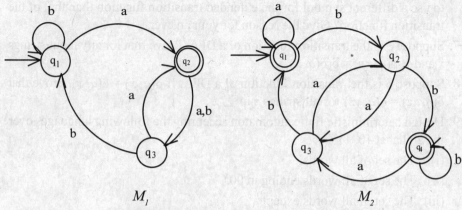

M_1 M_2

Figure 2.22: State diagrams of M_1 and M_2.

A23. Describe in English the language accepted by the following DFAs as shown in Figure 2.23:

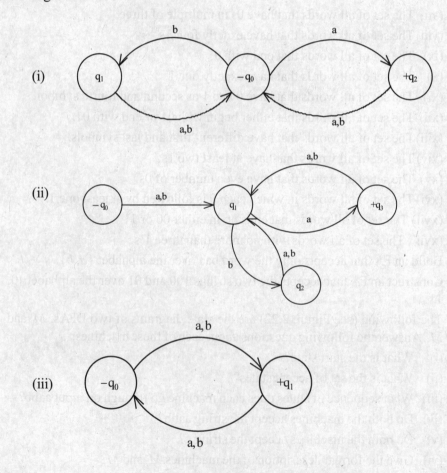

(i)

(ii)

(iii)

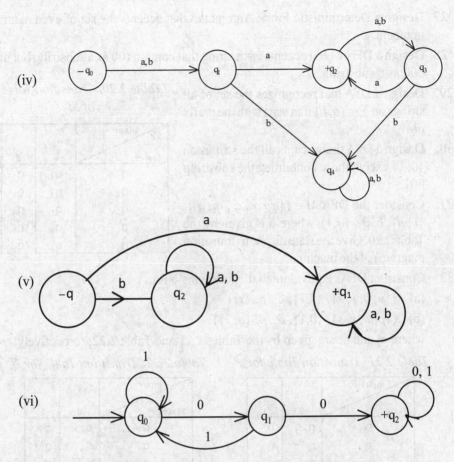

Figure 2.23: State diagram of DFAs

24. Design Deterministic Finite Automata for the following languages:
    (i) $L = \{w: n_a(w) = 1, w \in (a, b)^*\}$
    (ii) $L = \{w: n_a(w) \geq 1, w \in (a, b)^*\}$
    (iii) $L = \{w: n_a(w) \geq 1 \text{ and } n_b(w) = 2, w \in (a, b)^*\}$
    (iv) $L = \{w_1 ab w_2 : w_1, w_2 \in (a, b)^*\}$
    (v) $L = \{a^m b^n : m, n > 0\}$
    (vi) $L = \{(ab)^n : n \geq 0\}$
    ^(vii) $L = \{a^n b : n \geq 0\}$
    ^(viii) $L = \{b^m a b^n : m, n > 0\}$
    ^(ix) $L = \{ab^5 wbb : w \in (a, b)^*\}$
    ^(x) $L = \{w : |w| \bmod 3 = 0\}$
    (xi) $L = \{w : n_a(w) \bmod 3 > n_b(w) \bmod 3 \}$

^25. Design a Deterministic Finite Automaton that accepts the set of all integers.

^26. Design a Deterministic Finite Automaton that accepts the set of signed integers.

[A]27. Design a Deterministic Finite Automaton that accepts the set of even natural numbers.

[A]28. Design a DFA which accepts each string that contains 00 as a substring but not 000 as a substring.

29. Design a DFA that recognizes the set of all strings on $\Sigma = \{a, b\}$ that start with the prefix ab.

Table 2.20: Transition Table of M

Input States	u	d
q_1	q_1	q_2
q_2	q_1	q_3
q_3	q_2	q_4
q_4	q_3	q_5
q_5	q_4	q_5

30. Design a DFA that accepts all the strings on $\{0, 1\}$ except those containing the substring 001.

31. Consider the DFA $M = (\{q_1, q_2, q_3, q_4, q_5\}, \{u, d\}, \delta, q_1, \{q_3\})$, where δ is given by the Table 2.20. Give the state diagram (transition diagram) of the machine.

32. Construct DFAs equivalent to the following NFAs :

(a) $(\{p, q, r, s\}, \{0,1\}, \delta_1, p, \{s\})$

(b) $(\{p, q, r, s\}, \{0,1\}, \delta_2, p, \{q, s\})$

where δ_1 and δ_2 are given by the Tables 2.21 and Table 2.22, respectively:

Table 2.21: Transition Table for δ_1

Input States	0	1
p	p, q	p
q	r	r
r	s	-
s	s	s

Table 2.22: Transition Table for δ_2

Input States	0	1
p	q, s	q
q	r	q, r
r	s	p
s	-	p

[A]33. Prove that for every NFA with an arbitrary number of final states there is an equivalent NFA with only one final state. Can we make similar claim for DFAs?

34. Construct a non-deterministic finite automaton with three states accepting all words that end with 00. Use it to construct a DFA accepting the same set of strings.

35. Construct a non-deterministic finite automation accepting $\{ab, ba\}$. Use it to construct an equivalent DFA.

36. Construct a non-deterministic finite automaton accepting the set of all strings over $\{a, b\}$ ending in aba. Use it to construct an equivalent DFA.

[A]37. Construct a non-deterministic automaton which accepts all words over $\Sigma = \{0, 1\}$ which end in 1 but do not contain the substring 00.

[A]38. (i) Construct a non-deterministic automaton for $L = \{a^n : n \geq 0\} \cup \{b^n a : n \geq 1\}$

(ii) Find an NFA without ε-transitions and with a single final state that accepts the set $\{a\} \cup \{b^n : n \geq 1\}$.

^39. Design an NFA with no more than 5 states for the set $L = \{abab^n : n \geq 0\}$
$\cup \{aba^n : n \geq 0\}$

40. Design an NFA with 3 states that accepts the language $\{ab, abc\}^*$.

^41. Design an NFA that accepts the language $L = \{bb^*(a + b)\}$.

^42. Design an NFA that accepts the language $L = \{ab \cup aba)\}^*$.

43. Design an NFA that accepts the language $L = \{ab)^* (ba)^* \cup aa\}^*$.

44. Design an NFA that accepts the language $\{ab, ba\}$.

45. Construct NFAs equivalent to each of the following NFAs with ε-moves as described in the following Figures 2.24 (i-iv):

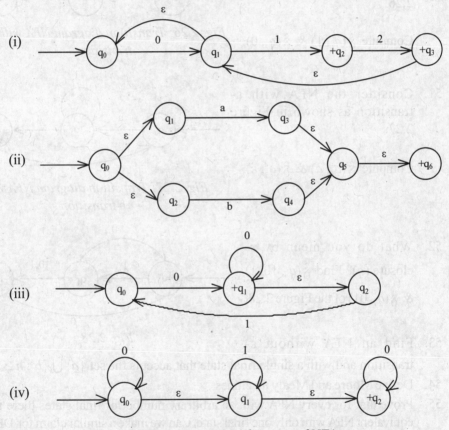

Fig. 2.24 (i-iv): Transition diagram of NFAs

46. What do you mean by the extended transition function of an NFA? Is it necessary to use different symbols for extended transition function and the transition function? Give the reason for your answer.

47. What do you mean by the extended transition function of an NFA with ε-transition? Is it necessary to use different symbols for extended transition function and the transition function? Give the reason for your answer.

48. Consider the NFA (see Figure 2.25) with ε-transition:

    Compute $\hat{\delta}(q_0, 1)$ & $\hat{\delta}(q_2, 0)$.

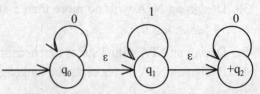

Fig. 2.25: Transition diagram NFA with ε-transition

49. What is the difference between NFA and NFA with ε-move?

50. Consider the NFA with ε-transition as shown in Figure 2.26.

    Compute $\hat{\delta}(q_0, 1)$ & $\hat{\delta}(q_2, 0)$.

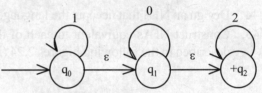

Fig. 2.26: Transition diagram NFA with ε-transition

51. Consider the NFA with ε-transition as shown in Figure 2.27.

    Compute $\hat{\delta}(q_0, a)$ & $\hat{\delta}(q_1, \varepsilon)$.

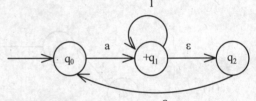

Fig. 2.27: Transition diagram NFA with ε-transition

52. What do you mean by ε-closure (q)? Find $\hat{\delta}(q_0, 1011)$ & $\hat{\delta}(q_1, 01)$ of the Figure 2.28.

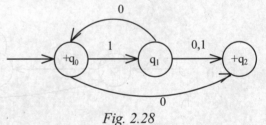

Fig. 2.28

53. Find an NFA without ε-transition and with a single final state that accepts the set $\{a\} \bigcup \{b^n : n \geq 1\}$.

54. Define Moore and Mealy machines.

55. Prove that for every NFA with an arbitrary number of final states there is an equivalent NFA with only one final state. Can we make a similar claim for DFAs?

56. What is the limitation of FA? Differentiate between the Moore and Mealy machines with examples.

57. What do you mean by Automata with output capability?

58. What is a Moore machine?

^59. Construct a Moore machine that determines whether an input string contains an even or odd number of 1s. The machine should give 'E' as output if an even number of 1s are in the string and 'O' otherwise.

^A60. Design a Moore machine which adds binary numbers.

^A61. Design a Moore machine to find 2's complement of a given binary number.

62. Design a Moore machine for incrementing a given binary number by 1.

63. Design a Moore machine for a binary input sequence such that if it has a substring 101 the machine outputs A, if input has substring 110 it outputs B, otherwise it outputs C.

^A64. Design a Moore machine to generate 1's complement of a given binary number.

65. Design a Moore machine to find out residue mod 3 of a given binary number.

^A66. Design a Moore machine to find out residue modulo 5 of input treated as a ternary number.

67. What do you mean by a Mealy machine? Write the procedure of drawing Transition Diagram of the Mealy machine. Explain with suitable example.

68. Construct a Moore Machine equivalent to the Mealy Machine given in the Table 2.23:

Table 2.23: Transition Table of Mealy Machine

Old State	New State			
	Input a		Input b	
	state	output	state	output
$-q_0$	q_1	0	q_3	0
q_1	q_0	0	q_1	1
q_2	q_1	1	q_2	0
q_3	q_2	0	q_0	1

69. Construct a Mealy Machine equivalent to the Moore Machine given in the Table 2.24:

Table 2.24: Transition Table of Moore Machine

Old State	New State		Output
	Input a	Input b	
$-q_0$	q_1	q_2	0
q_1	q_2	q_3	0
q_2	q_3	q_4	1
q_3	q_4	q_4	0
q_4	q_0	q_0	0

70. Draw a Mealy machine equivalent to the following circuit as depicted in Figure 2.29.

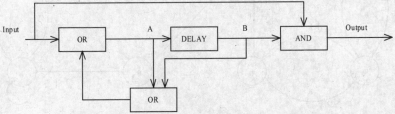

Fig. 2.29: Sequential Feedback Circuit

[A]71. Draw a Mealy machine equivalent to the following circuit as given in Figure 2.30:

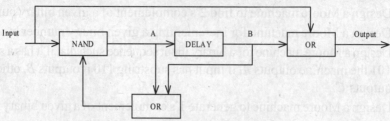

Fig. 2.30: Sequential Feedback Circuit

[A]72. Construct a Mealy machine which can output EVEN, ODD according as the total member of 1s encountered in the input string is even or odd. The input symbols are 0 and 1.

[A]73. Construct a Mealy machine which determines residue mod 4 for each binary string treated as binary integer.

74. Construct a Mealy machine which has input as binary number and output is the sum of three consecutive symbols. (Output is in decimal).

75. Design a Mealy machine which will generate 1s complement of given number.

[A]76. Design a Mealy machine which will increment the given number by 1.

77. Construct a Mealy machine that scans sequences of 0s and 1s and generates output '*A*' if the input string terminates in 00, output '*B*' if the string terminates in 11 and output '*C*' otherwise.

[A]78. Construct a minimum state automaton equivalent to a given DFA M whose transition table is as shown in Table 2.25.

Table 2.25: Transition Table

Input States	a	b
$-q_0$	q_1	q_4
q_1	q_2	q_3
$+q_2$	q_7	q_8
$+q_3$	q_8	q_7
q_4	q_5	q_6
$+q_5$	q_7	q_8
$+q_6$	q_7	q_8
q_7	q_7	q_7
q_8	q_8	q_8

79. Construct the minimum state automaton for the DFA as given in Figure 2.31.

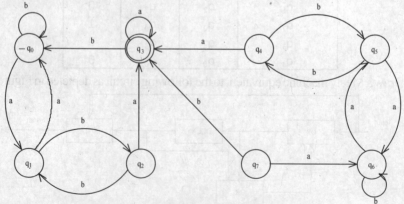

Fig. 2.31: Transition diagram of DFA

80. Construct the minimum state automaton equivalent to the DFA as given in Figure 2.32.

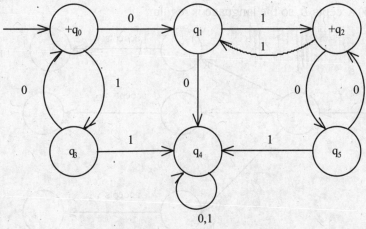

Fig. 2.32: Transition diagram of DFA

81. Construct a minimum state automaton equivalent to a DFA M whose transition table is given in Table 2.26:

Table 2.26: Transition Table of M

States	Input	
	0	1
$-q_0$	q_1	q_2
q_1	q_3	q_4
q_2	q_5	q_6
q_3	q_3	q_4
q_4	q_5	q_6
$+q_5$	q_3	q_4
q_6	q_5	q_6

82. Minimize the states in the DFA depicted in the Figure 2.33:

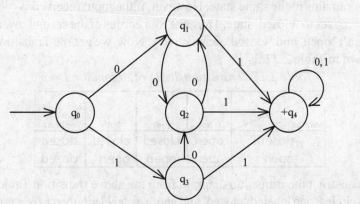

Fig. 2.33: Transition diagram of DFA

Answers/Hints for Selected Review Questions

7. Suppose that $L = \{w_1, w_2, \ldots w_n\}$. Then the NFA with ε-transition (see Figure 2.34) accepts L, so the language is regular.

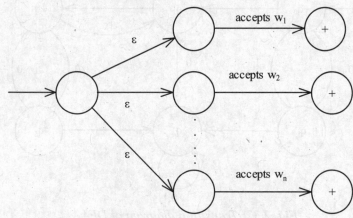

Fig. 2.34: NFA with ε-transition

12. In this problem, we can see that the machine has two states - closed and open. The transition table, therefore, has two rows labeled closed and open respectively. Assume closed state is the start of the machine. The input symbols are the four input signals 'front', 'rear', 'both' and 'neither'. So, the table has four columns labeled front, rear, both and neither, respectively. The controller of the automatic door moves from state to state, depending on the input it receives. While in 'closed' state, if the input received is 'front', the door moves to 'open' state, and if the input received is 'neither',' rear' or 'both', the door remains in 'closed' state (with input 'both', the door stays in the same state because opening the door may be risky as someone is on the rear pad). Accordingly, the four entries in the first row of the table are 'open', 'closed', 'closed' and 'closed' respectively.

Now, while in 'open' state, the input received is 'rear', 'both' or 'front', the door remains in the same state. However, if the input received is 'neither', the door moves to 'closed' state. Thus, the four entries of the second row are 'open' 'open', 'open' and 'closed', respectively. Now, we get the Transition Table as shown in Table 2.27.

Table 2.27: Transition Table of Automatic Door

Input / States	front	rear	both	neither
-closed	open	closed	closed	closed
open	open	open	open	closed

To construct the transition diagram from the above transition Table, we draw two circles, one labeled 'closed' and another 'labeled' open to represent the two states of the machine. Since the entry in the cell (closed, front) is 'open' we draw an arch labeled 'front' from the state closed to state open. Repeating the process for each cell entry, we get the transition diagram as depicted in Figure 2.35:

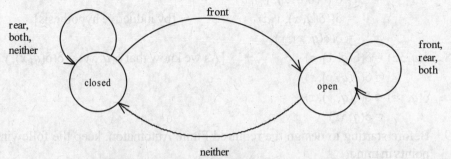

rear, both, neither

front

front, rear, both

closed

open

neither

Fig. 2.35: Transition Diagram of Automatic Door

15. The trap state of FA is a state from which it can never escape. For example, the state q_1 is a trap state of the DFA as shown in Figure 2.36. There are two properties of transition functions:

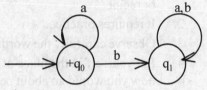

Fig. 2.36: FA with a trap state q_1.

(i) $\delta(q, \varepsilon) = q$ exists in a Finite Automaton. This means that Finite Automaton does not change its state without an input symbol. In other words, the state of system can be changed only by an input symbol.

(ii) For all strings 'x' and input symbol 'a',
$$\delta(q, ax) = \delta(\delta(q, a), x)$$
$$\delta(q, xa) = \delta(\delta(q, x), a)$$

The above property states that the state after the automaton consumes or reads the first symbol of a string 'ax' and the state after the automaton consumes a prefix 'x' of string 'xa'.

17. We prove $\delta(q, xy) = \delta(\delta(q, x), y)$ by the method of induction on $|y|$, i.e., length of string y.

Basis: Let us assume $|y| = 1$, and $y = a \in \Sigma$

Then $\delta(q, xy) = \delta(q, xa)$

$\qquad\qquad = \delta(\delta(q, x), a)$ [As we know $\delta(q, wa) = \delta(\delta(q, w), a)$

$\qquad\qquad = $ RHS

Induction: Assume

$\qquad \delta(q, xy) = \delta(\delta(q, x), y)$

for all strings x and y with $|y| = n$.

Let $y = y_1 a$ where $|y_1| = n$

$\qquad \delta(q, xy) = \delta(q, xy_1 a)$

$\qquad\qquad\quad = \delta(q, x_1 a)$ [assume $xy_1 = x_1$]

$$= \delta(\delta(q, x_1), a) \qquad [\delta(q, wa) = \delta(\delta(q, w), a)]$$
$$= \delta(\delta(q, xy_1), a)$$
$$= \delta\,(\delta(\delta(q, x), y_1), a)$$
$$= \delta((\delta(q, x), y_1 a) \qquad [\text{by inductive hypothesis}]$$
$$= \delta(\delta(q, x), y)$$

18. $\delta(q, xz) = \delta(\delta(q, x), z) \qquad [\text{As we know that } \delta(q, xy) = \delta(\delta(q, x), y)]$
$$\qquad\quad = \delta(\delta(q, y), z)$$
$$\delta(q, yz) = \delta(\delta(q, y), z)$$
$$\qquad\quad = \delta(q, xz)$$

19. Before starting to design the required Finite Automaton, keep the following points in mind.

1. Design is a creative process. There is no panacea in the form of methods or recipe.

2. It requires practice.

3. Observe carefully the words recognized (accepted) by the FA.

4. Put yourself in the place of the machine you are trying to design and see how you would go about performing the machine's task.

5. Pretending to be the automaton, determine whether the input received is a member of the language the automaton is supposed to recognize.

(i) According to the problem, we have to design a FA which accepts all words over the alphabet $\{0,1\}$, i.e., $\{\varepsilon, 0, 1, 00, 01, 10, 11, \dots\}$. We can design the desired Automaton as follows (see Figure 2.37):

Here $Q = \{q_0\}$, q_0 is the initial state as well as the final state and $\Sigma = \{0, 1\}$.

Fig. 2.37

(ii) According to the problem, the required FA accepts all words ending in 00 over the alphabet $\{0, 1\}$, i.e., the language $\{00, 100, 000, 0000, 0100, 1000, 1100, \dots\}$. We can design the desired machine as an Automaton with three states as depicted in Figure 2.38:

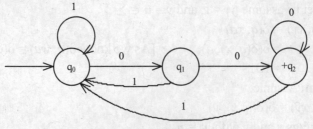

Fig. 2.38

Here q_0 is the start state and q_2 is the final state. While in state q_0, the FA does not change state with input 1 but with input 0 it moves to state q_1. While in state q_1, on input 1, it goes to the state q_0 and on input 0 it goes to state q_2. While in q_2, the machine remains in the same state if the input is 0 but if the input is 1, it goes back to state q_0. We observe that reading two or more consecutive zeroes, the machine always goes to the final state.

Here $Q = \{q_0, q_1, q_2\}$, q_0 is the initial state, q_2 is the final state and $\Sigma = \{0, 1\}$.

(iii) According to the problem, we have to design a FA which accepts all words except ε over the alphabet $\{0, 1\}$, i.e., the set $\{0, 1, 00, 01, 10, 11, 000, 001, 010, 011, 100, \ldots\}$. The desired Automaton is a two state machine as shown in Figure 2.39.

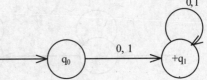

Fig. 2.39: Transition diagram

Here $Q = \{q_0, q_1\}$, q_0 is the initial state, q_1 is the final state, and $\Sigma = \{0, 1\}$.

(iv) According to the problem, we have to design a FA which accepts all words that begin with 0 over the alphabet $\{0, 1\}$, i.e., the set $\{0, 00, 01, 000, 001, 010, 011, \ldots\}$. The desired Automaton is a three state machine as given in Figure 2.40.

$Q = \{q_0, q_1, q_2\}$, q_0 is the initial state, q_1 is the final state and $\Sigma = \{0,1\}$.

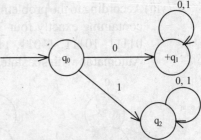

Fig. 2.40: Transition diagram

(v) In this case, we have to construct a FA that accepts all words having at least three consecutive zeroes over the alphabet $\{0, 1\}$, i.e., $\{000, 0000, 1000, 0001, 00000, 00001, \ldots\}$. The required Automaton is as shown in Figure 2.41.

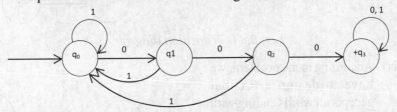

Fig. 2.41: Transition diagram

(vi) In this case, we have to construct a FA that accepts all words with exactly two 0s over the alphabet $\{0, 1\}$, i.e., $\{00, 100, 001, 1100, 0011 \ldots\}$. The required Automaton is as depicted in Figure 2.42.

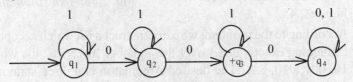

Fig. 2.42: Transition diagram

(vii) We need to design a FA that accepts all words that have 0's in multiple of three over the alphabet {0, 1}, i.e., the words having 3, 6, 9 …. zeroes. The position of 1's and 0's do not matter. The desired automaton is a four state machine as shown in Figure 2.43:

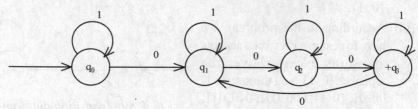

Fig. 2.43: Transiton diagram

[Every multiple of a number is greater than or equal to that number. Thus multiple of three means 3, 6, 9... zeroes]

(viii) According to the problem, we have to design a FA which accepts all words containing exactly four 1's over the alphabet {0,1}, i.e., the set {1111, 01111, 10111, 11011, 11101, 11110, …}. We can design the desired Automaton with six states as given in Figure 2.44.

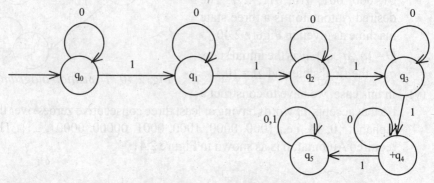

Fig. 2.44: Transition diagram

(ix) According to the problem, we have to design a FA that accepts all words ending with 0 over the alphabet {0, 1}, i.e., the words {0, 00, 10, 110, 010, 000, …}. We can design the desired Automaton with two states as depicted in Figure 2.45.

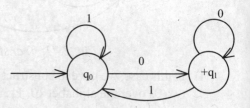

Fig. 2.45: Transition diagram

(x) According to the problem, we can construct a FA which accepts all words containing exactly one 1 over the alphabet {0,1}, i.e., the words {1, 01, 10, 001, 010, …}. The desired Automaton is a three state machine as given in Figure 2.46.

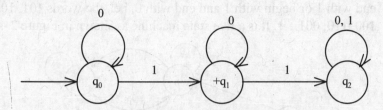

Fig. 2.46: Transition diagram

(xi) According to the problem, we can construct a FA which accepts all words that have 0 and 1 as second and fourth symbol. The desired Automaton is a three state machine as depicted in Figure 2.47.

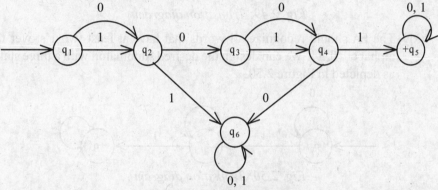

Fig. 2.47: Transition diagram

(xii) In this problem, we have to design a FA which accepts all words that either begin with 01 or end with 01 over the alphabet $\{0, 1\}$, i.e., the words $\{01, 010, 011, 001, 101 \ldots\}$. The desired machine is a six state FA as given in Figure 2.48.

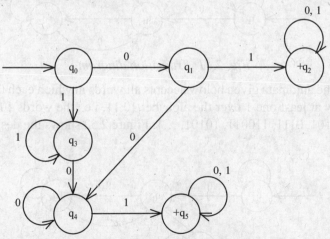

Fig. 2.48: Transition diagram

(xiii) The desired automata should accept all words that either begin with 0 and end with 1 or begin with 1 and end with 0, i.e., the words {01, 10, 011, 100, 110, 001...}. It is a five state machine as shown in Figure 2.49.

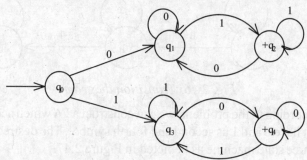

Fig. 2.49: Transition diagram

(xiv) The FA should recognize all words that have at least two 1's over the alphabet {0, 1}. We can design the desired Automaton with a three states as depicted in Figure 2.50.

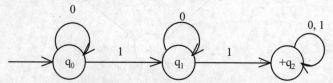

Fig. 2.50: Transition diagram

(xv) The FA to be designed should recognize all words that have even number of 0's over the alphabet {0,1}, i.e., the words {001, 010, 100, 0011, 1001, ...}. We can design the Automaton as shown in Figure 2.51.

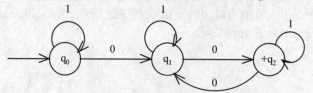

Fig. 2.51: Transition diagram

(xvi) The automata given below accepts all words in which each 0 is followed by at least one 1 over the alphabet {0,1}, i.e., the words {01, 011, 101, 0101, 0111, 110011, 10101, ...}. Figure 2.52 shows the desired DFA.

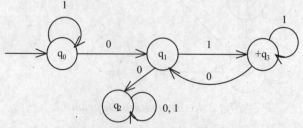

Fig. 2.52: Transition diagram

(xvii) Here we have to design a FA which accepts all words that ends with either 00 or 11 over the alphabet {0,1}, i.e., the words {00, 11, 000, 011, 100, 111 …}. The desired Automaton is a five states machine as given in Figure 2.53.

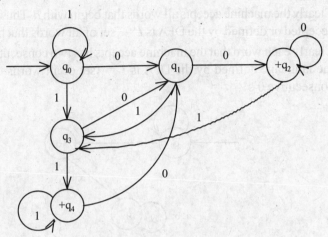

Fig. 2.53: Transition diagram

(xviii) We split the problem into three cases each with an accepting state as follows:

1. Words with single 1.
2. Words with only two 1s.
3. Words with only three 1s.

Four and more 1's must send the machine into a non-accepting state.

We design the desired automaton with five states as depicted in Figure 2.54.

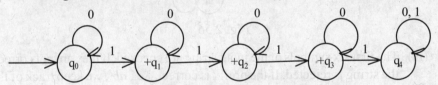

Fig. 2.54: Transition diagram

23. (i) The set of words accepted by the machine is {a, aba, baa, aaa, bba, …}. We observe that every word the machine accepts has odd length and ends with letter a. Thus, the language accepted/defined by the DFA is $L = \{w|\ w$ is of odd length and ends with $a\}$.

(ii) The set of words accepted by the machine is {aa, ba, $aaaa$, $aaba$, $abaa$, $abba$, …}. We observe that every word the machine accepts, is of even length and ends with letter a. Thus, the language accepted/defined by the DFA is $L = \{w|\ w$ is of even length and ends with $a\}$.

(iii) The set of words accepted by the machine is {a, b, aaa, baa, bab, bbb, abb, aba, …}, each of which is of odd length. Thus, the language accepted or defined by the DFA is $L = \{w|\ w$ has odd length}.

(iv) We observe that every word the machine accepts is of even length, ends with *a* and begin with *aa* or *ba*. Thus, the language accepted or defined by the DFA is $L = \{$set of words that begin with *aa* or *ba*, have even length and end with *a*$\}$.

(v) Clearly the machine accepts all words that begin with *a*. Thus, the language accepted or defined by the DFA is $L = \{$set of all words that begin with *a*$\}$.

(vi) Clearly each word that the machine accepts has two consecutive 0's. Thus, the language defined by the DFA is $L = \{$set of all words that have two consecutive 0's$\}$.

24. (vii)

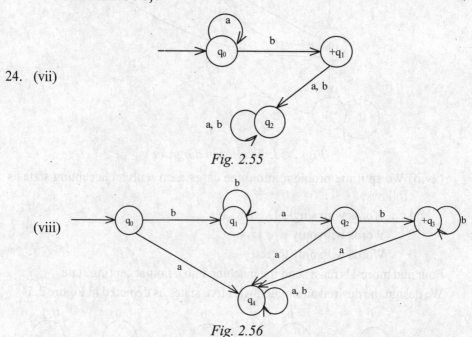

Fig. 2.55

(viii)

Fig. 2.56

(ix) The first six symbols of the input string are checked. If they are not correct, the string is rejected. If the prefix is correct, i.e., ab^5, we keep track of the last two symbols read, and in case these are *bb*, the DFA moves to an accepting state. Figure 2.57 shows the transition diagram of DFA.

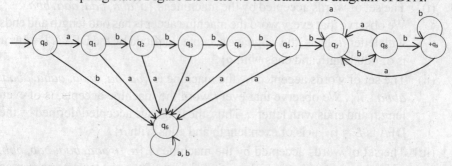

Fig. 2.57

(x) $|w|$ mod 3 = 0 if $|w|$ is a multiple of 3 that is 0, 3, 6, 9........etc. The machine recognizes all words of length 0, 3, 6, and so on. Figure 2.58 depicts the transition diagram of the DFA.

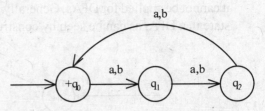

Fig. 2.58: Transition diagram

25.

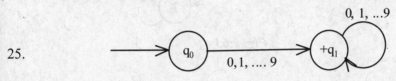

Fig. 2.59

26.

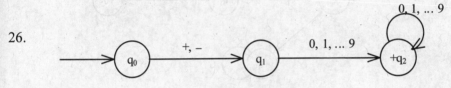

Fig. 2.60

27.

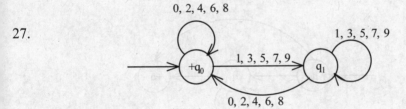

Fig. 2.61

28.

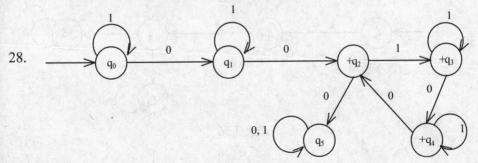

Fig. 2.62

33. We introduce a new final state p_f and for every $q \in F$ add the transitions $\delta(q, \varepsilon)$ = $\{p_f\}$. Then make p_f the only final state. We can easily argue that if originally $\hat{\delta}(q_0, w) \in F$, then $\hat{\delta}(q_0, w) = \{p_f\}$ after the modification, so both the original and modified NFAs are equivalent. Since this construction requires ε-transitions,

it cannot be applied for DFAs. Generally, it is impossible to have only one final
state in a DFA, as can be seen by constructing DFAs that accepts $\{\varepsilon, a\}$.

37.

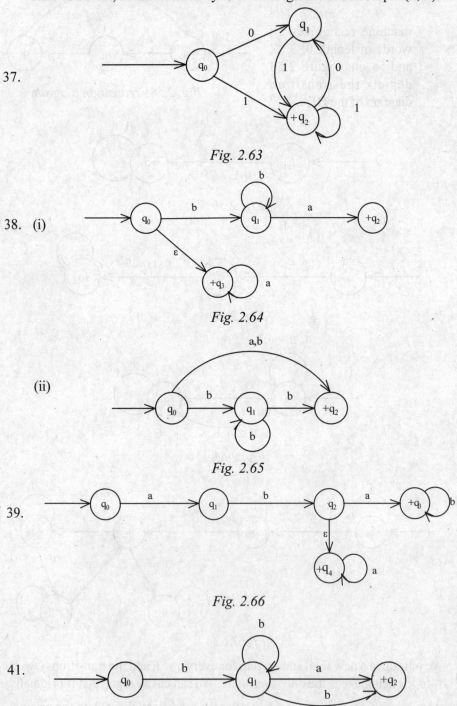

Fig. 2.63

38. (i)

Fig. 2.64

(ii)

Fig. 2.65

39.

Fig. 2.66

41.

Fig. 2.67

42.

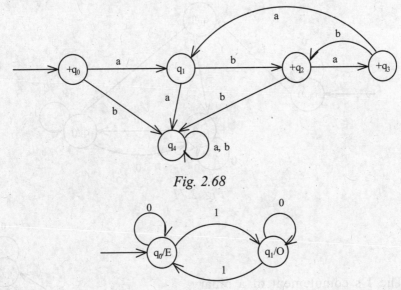

Fig. 2.68

59.

Fig. 2.69

60. When we add two binary numbers, we start from the least significant bit, i.e. from right most bit of both numbers and add them. We then add the next significant bits from both the numbers. In case a carry was generated while adding previous bits, it is propagated forward and added along with the next significant bits. We have four possible cases.

$0 + 0 = 0$, output is 0 and carry $= 0$
$0 + 1 = 1$, output is 1 and carry $= 0$
$1 + 1 = 0$, output is 0 and carry $= 1$
$1 + 1 + 1 = 1$, output is 1 and carry $= 1$.

We can represent these cases by four states q_0, q_1, q_2, and q_3, respectively. We take the input as (i, j) when i^{th} and j^{th} bits are to be added. Figure 2.70 shows the required Moore machine.

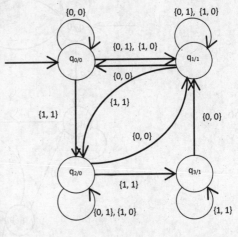

Fig. 2.70

61. To obtain the 2's complement of a binary number, we scan the number starting from the least significant bit and move forward till a 1 in encountered. We then modify the rest of the string(not yet scanned) by changing 0's into 1's and 1's into 0's. Figure 2.71 represents the Moore machine.

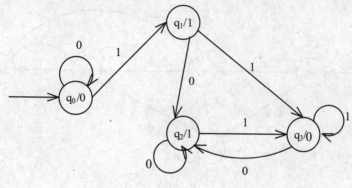

Fig. 2.71

64. The 1's complement of a binary number is obtained by replacing 0s by 1s and 1s by 0s. Figure 2.72 depicts the Moore machine.

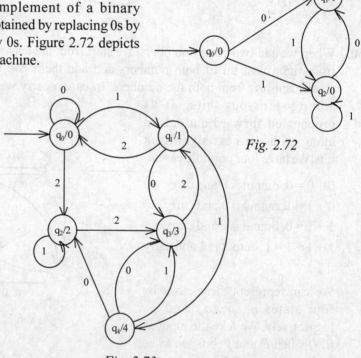

Fig. 2.72

66.

Fig. 2.73

71. We can identify four states based on whether or not there is current at points A and B in the circuit. The meaning of NAND and OR are as usual. The DELAY delays transmission of the signal along the wire by one clock pulse. The Delay is sometimes called a D flip-flop. The current in a wire is denoted by the value 1, no current by 0.

Thus,

q_0 means $A = 0$ and $B = 0$

q_1 means $A = 0$ and $B = 1$

q_2 means $A = 1$ and $B = 0$

q_3 means $A = 1$ and $B = 1$

The operation of the given circuit is such that after an input 0 or 1 the state changes according to the following rules:

new B = old A

new A = (input) NAND (old A OR old B)

output = (input) OR (old B)

At various discrete pulses of a time clock input is received, the state changes, and output is generated.

Suppose, we are in state q_0 and we receive the input 0.

new B = old A = 0

new A = (input) NAND (old A OR old B)

= (0) NAND (0 OR 0)

= 0 NAND 0

= 1

output = (input) OR (old B)

= 0 OR 0 = 0

The new state is q_2 (since new A = 1, new B = 0).

If we are in state q_0 and receive the input 1.

new B = old A = 0

new A = (input) NAND (old A OR old B)

= (1) NAND (0 OR 0)

= 1 NAND 0

= 1

output = (input) OR (old B)

= 1 OR 0 = 1

The new state is q_2 (since new A = 1, new B = 0).

If we are in state q_1 and receive the input 0.

new B = old A = 0

new A = (input) NAND (old A OR old B)

= (0) NAND (0 OR 1)

= 0 NAND 1

= 1

output = (input) OR (old B)

= 0 OR 1 = 1

The new state is q_2 (since new $A = 1$, new $B = 0$).

If we are in state q_1 and receive the input 1.

$\quad$ new B = old $A = 0$

$\quad$ new A = (input) NAND (old A OR old B)

$\qquad$ = (1) NAND (0 OR 1)

$\qquad$ = 1 NAND 1

$\qquad$ = 0

$\quad$ output = (input) OR (old B)

$\qquad$ = 1 OR 1 = 1

The new state is q_0 (since new $A = 0$, new $B = 0$).

If we are in state q_2 and receive the input 0.

$\quad$ new B = old $A = 1$

$\quad$ new A = (input) NAND (old A OR old B)

$\qquad$ = (0) NAND (1 OR 0)

$\qquad$ = 0 NAND 1

$\qquad$ = 1

$\quad$ output = (input) OR (old B)

$\qquad$ = 0 OR 0 = 0

The new state is q_3 (since new $A = 1$, new $B = 1$).

If we are in state q_2 and receive the input 1.

$\quad$ new B = old $A = 1$

$\quad$ new A = (input) NAND (old A OR old B)

$\qquad$ = (1) NAND (1 OR 0)

$\qquad$ = 1 NAND 1

$\qquad$ = 0

$\quad$ output = (input) OR (old B)

$\qquad$ = 1 OR 0 = 1

The new state is q_1 (since new $A = 0$, new $B = 1$).

If we are in state q_3 and receive the input 0.

$\quad$ new B = old $A = 1$

$\quad$ new A = (input) NAND (old A OR old B)

$\qquad$ = (0) NAND (1 OR 1)

$\qquad$ = 0 NAND 1

$\qquad$ = 1

$\quad$ output = (input) OR (old B)

$\qquad$ = 0 OR 1 = 1

The new state is q_3 (since new $A = 1$, new $B = 1$)

If we are in state q_3 and receive the input 1.

new B = old $A = 1$

new A = (input) NAND (old A OR old B)

= (1) NAND (1 OR 1)

= 1 NAND 1

= 0

output = (input) OR (old B)

= 1 OR 1 = 1

The new state is q_1 (since new $A = 0$, new $B = 1$)

The action of the above sequential feedback circuit is equivalent to the Mealy machine represented by the following transition Table (see Table 2.28).

Table 2.28

Old State	New State				
	Input 0			Input 1	
	state	output(λ)		state	output(λ)
$-q_0$	q_2	0		q_2	1
q_1	q_2	1		q_0	1
q_2	q_3	0		q_1	1
q_3	q_3	1		q_1	1

The transition diagram of the above Mealy machine is given in Figure 2.74:

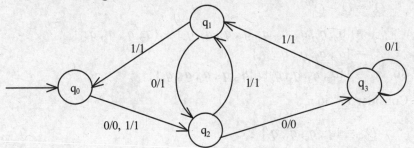

Fig. 2.74: Mealy machine

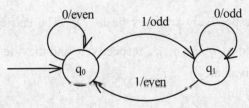

Fig. 2.75

73. When a number is divided by 4, the remainder is 0, 1, 2 or 3. So, the Mealy machine will have four states with outputs 0, 1, 2, and 3, respectively. Figure 2.76 depicts the Mealy machine.

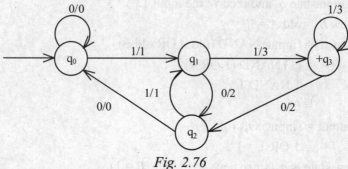

Fig. 2.76

76. To increment a binary number by 1, we scan the binary number from right han $\cdot$
(LSB) 1-bit at a time and replace each 1 by 0 till we encounter a 0. The first $\cdot$
encountered is replaced by 1 and the rest of the string (the part of the string no $\cdot$
yet scanned) is kept unaltered.
Figure 2.77 represents the
desired machine.

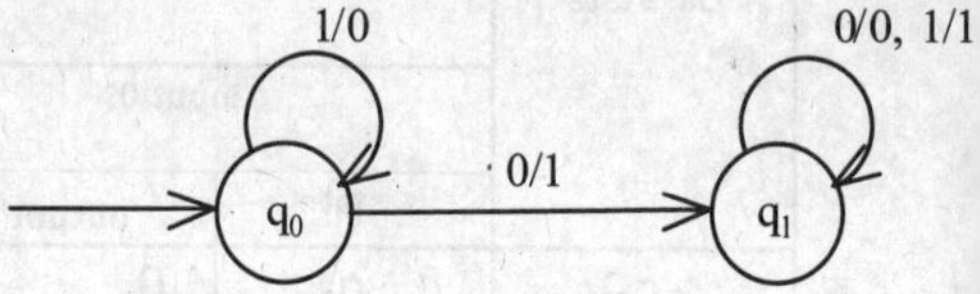

78. First construct π_0 as

$$\pi_0 = \{Q_1^0, Q_2^0\}$$

Fig. 2.77

Q_1^0 = set of all final states

$= \{q_2, q_3, q_5, q_6\}$

$Q_2^0 = Q - Q_1^0$

$= \{q_0, q_1, q_2, q_3, q_4, q_5, q_6, q_7, q_8\} - \{q_2, q_3, q_5, q_6\}$

$= \{q_0, q_1, q_4, q_7, q_8\}$

So, $\pi_0 = \{\{q_2, q_3, q_5, q_6\}, \{q_0, q_1, q_4, q_7, q_8\}\}$

Consider Q_1^0 in π_0.

$$Q_1^0 = \{q_2, q_3, q_5, q_6\}$$

Let us consider $q_2, q_3 \in Q_1^0$. The entries under 0-column corresponding to q $\cdot$
q_3 are q_7, q_8, respectively and they lie in Q_2^0. The entries under 1-colum $\cdot$
corresponding to q_2, q_3 are q_8, q_7, respectively and they lie in Q_2^0. Therefore
q_2, q_3 are 1-equivalent.

Next consider q_2, q_5.

The entries under 0-column corresponding to q_2, q_5 are q_7, q_7; they lie in Q_2^0

The entries under 1-column corresponding to q_2, q_5 are q_8, q_8; they lie in Q_2^0
Therefore, q_2, q_5 are 1-equivalent.

Next consider to q_2, q_6.

The entries under 0-column corresponding to q_2, q_6 are q_7, q_7; they lie in Q_2^0.

The entries under 1-column corresponding to q_2, q_6 are q_8, q_8; they lie in Q_2^0.
Therefore, q_2, q_6 are 1-equivalent.

Hence $\{q_2, q_3, q_5, q_6\}$ is a subset of π_1. So, $Q_1' = \{q_2, q_3, q_5, q_6\}$.

Now consider another set of π_0, i.e., So, $Q_2^0 = \{q_0, q_1, q_4, q_7, q_8\}$.

Let us take $q_0, q_1 \in Q_2^0$.

The entries under 0-column corresponding to q_0, q_1 are $q_1, q_2; q_1 \in Q_2^0, q_2 \in Q_1'$.

The entries under 1-column corresponding to q_0, q_1 are $q_4, q_3; q_4 \in Q_2^0, q_3 \in$

Q_1^0. Therefore, q_0, q_1 are not 1-equivalent.

Next consider $q_0, q_4 \in Q_2^0$.

The entries under 0-column corresponding to q_0, q_4 are $q_1, q_5; q_1 \in Q_2^0, q_5 \in Q_1$.

The entries under 1-column corresponding to q_0, q_4 are $q_4, q_6; q_4 \in Q_2^0, q_6 \in Q_1$.
Therefore, q_0, q_4 are not 1-equivalent.

Next consider $q_0, q_7 \in Q_2^0$.

The entries under 0-column corresponding to q_0, q_7 are q_1, q_7; they lie in Q_2^0.

The entries under 1-column corresponding to q_0, q_7 are q_4, q_7; they lie in Q_2^0.
Therefore, q_0, q_7 are 1-equivalent.

Next consider $q_0, q_8 \in Q_2^0$.

The entries under 0-column corresponding to q_0, q_8 are q_1, q_8; they lie in Q_2^0.

The entries under 1-column corresponding to q_0, q_8 are q_4, q_8; they lie in Q_2^0.
Therefore, q_0, q_8 are 1-equivalent.

Hence $\{q_0, q_7, q_8\}$ is a subset of π_1. So, $Q_1' = \{q_0, q_7, q_8\}$.
Now we consider a subset $\{q_1, q_4\}$.
Next consider q_1, q_4.
The entries under 0-column corresponding to q_1, q_4 are q_2, q_5; they lie in Q_1'.
The entries under 1-column corresponding to q_1, q_4 are q_3, q_6; they lie in Q_1'.
Therefore, q_1, q_4 are 1-equivalent.
Hence $\{q_1, q_4\}$ is a subset of π_1. So, $Q_3' = \{q_1, q_4\}$.

Therefore $\pi_1 = \{\{q_2, q_3, q_5, q_6\}, \{q_0, q_7, q_8\}, \{q_1, q_4\}\}$.

The $\{q_2, q_3, q_5, q_6\}$ is also in π_2 as it cannot be further partitioned.

Now consider $\{q_0, q_7, q_8\}$ subset of π_1.

Now, consider q_0, q_7.

The entries under 0-column corresponding to q_0, q_7 are q_1, q_7; they lie in different equivalence class of π_1. The entries under 1-column corresponding to q_0, q_7 are q_4, q_7; they lie in different equivalence class of π_1. Therefore, q_0, q_7 are not 2-equivalent.

Next, consider q_0, q_8.

The entries under 0-column corresponding to q_0, q_8 are q_1, q_8; they lie in different equivalence class of π_1. The entries under 1-column corresponding to q_0, q_8 are q_4, q_8; they lie in different equivalence class of π_1. Therefore, q_0, q_8 are not 2-equivalent.

Hence $\{q_0, q_7, q_8\}$ is partitioned into two subsets $\{q_0\}$ and $\{q_7, q_8\}$.

Therefore $\{q_0\}$ in π_2 as it cannot be further partitioned.

Next consider $\{q_7, q_8\}$.

The entries under 0-column corresponding to q_7, q_8 are q_7, q_8; they lie in same equivalence class of π_1. The entries under 1-column corresponding to q_7, q_8 are q_7, q_8; they lie in same equivalence class of π_1. Hence q_7, q_8 are 2-equivalent.

Next consider $\{q_1, q_4\}$.

The entries under 0-column corresponding to q_1, q_4 are q_2, q_5; they lie in same equivalence class of π_1. The entries under 1-column corresponding to q_1, q_4 are q_3, q_6; they lie in same equivalence class of π_1. Hence $\{q_1, q_4\}$ is 2-equivalent.

Thus $\pi_2 = \{\{q_2, q_3, q_5, q_6\}, \{q_0\}, \{q_7, q_8\}, \{q_1, q_4\}\}$.

q_2 is 3 equivalent to q_3, q_5 and q_6. So, $\{q_2, q_3, q_5, q_6\} \in \pi_3$.

q_0 is 3 equivalent as it cannot be further partitioned.

q_7 is 3 equivalent to q_8 so $q_7, q_8 \in \pi_3$.

q_1 is 3 equivalent to q_4 so $q_1, q_4 \in \pi_3$.

Thus $\pi_3 = \{\{q_2, q_3, q_5, q_6\}, \{q_0\}, \{q_7, q_8\}, \{q_1, q_4\}\}$.

Therefore $\pi_3 = \pi_2$, so minimum state automaton is $M' = (Q', \{0, 1\}, \delta', q_0', F')$ where

$$Q' = \{[q_0], [q_7, q_8], [q_1, q_4], [q_2, q_3, q_5, q_6]\}$$
$$q_0 = [q_0]$$
$$F' = [q_2, q_3, q_5, q_6]$$

δ' is defined in Table 2.29.

Table 2.29: Transition Table of minimum state DFA

Input States	0	1
$-[q_0]$	$[q_1, q_4]$	$[q_1, q_4]$
$[q_7, q_8]$	$[q_7, q_8]$	$[q_7, q_8]$
$[q_1, q_4]$	$[q_2, q_3, q_5, q_6]$	$[q_2, q_3, q_5, q_6]$
$+[q_2, q_3, q_5, q_6]$	$[q_7, q_8]$	$[q_7, q_8]$

Figure 2.78 depicts the transition graph.

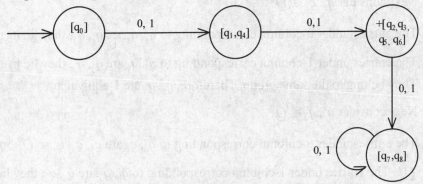

Fig. 2.78: Transition diagram of minimum state DFA

81. First, we will construct π_0, as we know

$$\pi_0 = \{Q_1^0,\ Q_2^0\}$$

$$Q_1^0 = \text{set of all final states}$$

$$= \{q_5\}$$

$$Q_2^0 = Q - Q_1^0$$

$$= \{q_0, q_1, q_2, q_3, q_4, q_5, q_6\} - \{q_5\}$$

$$= \{q_0, q_1, q_2, q_4, q_3, q_4, q_6\}$$

So, $\pi_0 = \{\{q_5\}, \{q_0, q_1, q_2, q_3, q_4, q_6\}\}$

Consider Q_1^0 in π_0.

$Q_1^0 = \{q_5\}$ cannot be further portioned. So, $Q_1' = \{q_5\}$.

Now consider another set of π_0, i.e., so, $Q_2^0 = \{q_0, q_1, q_2, q_3, q_4, q_6\}$.

Let us take $q_0, q_1 \in Q_2^0$.

The entries under 0-column corresponding to q_0, q_1 are q_1, q_3; they lie in Q_2^0.

The entries under 1-column corresponding to q_0, q_1 are q_2, q_4; they lie in Q_2^0.

They belong to the same group. Therefore, q_0, q_1 are 1-equivalent.

Next consider $q_0, q_2 \in Q_2^0$.

The entries under 0-column corresponding to q_0, q_2 are $q_1, q_5; q_1 \in Q_2^0, q_5 \in Q_1^0$. The entries under 1-column corresponding to q_0, q_2 are q_2, q_6; they lie in Q_2^0. Therefore, q_0, q_2 are not 1-equivalent.

Next consider $q_0, q_3 \in Q_2^0$.

The entries under 0-column corresponding to q_0, q_3 are q_1, q_3; they lie in Q_2^0.

The entries under 1-column corresponding to q_0, q_3 are q_2, q_4; they lie in Q_2^0. They belong to the same group. Therefore, q_0, q_3 are 1-equivalent.

Next consider $q_0, q_4 \in Q_2^0$.

The entries under 0-column corresponding to q_0, q_4 are $q_1, q_5; q_1 \in Q_2^0, q_5 \in Q_1^0$. The entries under 1-column corresponding to q_0, q_4 are q_2, q_6; they lie in Q_2^0. Therefore, q_0, q_4 are not 1-equivalent.

Next consider $q_0, q_6 \in Q_2^0$.

The entries under 0-column corresponding to q_0, q_6 are $q_1, q_5; q_1 \in Q_2^0, q_5 \in Q_1^0$. The entries under 1-column corresponding to q_0, q_6 are q_2, q_6; they lie in Q_2^0. Therefore, q_0, q_6 are not 1-equivalent.

Hence $\{q_0, q_1, q_3\}$ is a subset of π_1. So, $Q_2' = \{q_0, q_1, q_3\}$.

Now we consider a subset $\{q_2, q_4, q_6\}$.

Next consider q_2, q_4.

The entries under 0-column corresponding to q_2, q_4 are q_5, q_5; they lie in the same group. The entries under 1-column corresponding to q_2, q_4 are q_6, q_6; they lie in the same group. Therefore, q_2, q_4 are 1-equivalent.

Next consider q_2, q_6.

The entries under 0-column corresponding to q_5, q_5 are q_5, q_5; they lie in the same group. The entries under 1-column corresponding to q_2, q_6 are q_6, q_6; they lie in the same group. Therefore, q_2, q_6 are 1-equivalent.

Hence $\{q_2, q_4, q_6\}$ is a subset of π_1. So, $Q_3' = \{q_2, q_4, q_6\}$.

Therefore $\pi_1 = \{\{q_5\}, \{q_0, q_1, q_3\}, \{q_2, q_4, q_6\}\}$.

The $\{q_5\}$ is also in π_2 as it can not be further partitioned.

Now consider $\{q_0, q_1, q_3\}$ subset of π_1.

Now, consider q_0, q_1.

The entries under 0-column corresponding to q_0, q_1 are q_1, q_3; they lie in same equivalence class of π_1. The entries under 1-column corresponding to q_0, q_1 are q_2, q_4; they lie in same equivalence class of π_1. Therefore, q_0, q_1 are 2-equivalent.

Next, consider q_0, q_3.

The entries under 0-column corresponding to q_0, q_3 are q_1, q_3; they lie in same equivalence class of π_1. The entries under 1-column corresponding to q_0, q_3 are q_2, q_4; they lie in same equivalence class of π_1. Therefore, q_0, q_3 are 2-equivalent.

Therefore $\{q_0, q_1, q_3\}$ are 2-equivalent.

Next consider $\{q_2, q_4, q_6\}$.

Let us take q_2 and q_4.

The entries under 0-column corresponding to q_2, q_4 are q_5, q_5; they lie in same equivalence class of π_1. The entries under 1-column corresponding to q_2, q_4 are q_6, q_6; they lie in same equivalence class of π_1. Hence q_2, q_4 are 2-equivalent.

Next consider $\{q_2, q_6\}$.

The entries under 0-column corresponding to q_2, q_6 are q_2, q_5; they lie in same equivalence class of π_1. The entries under 1-column corresponding to q_2, q_4 are q_6, q_6; they lie in same equivalence class of π_1. Hence $\{q_1, q_4\}$ is 2-equivalent.

Therefore $\{q_2, q_4, q_6\}$ are 2-equivalent.

Thus $\pi_2 = \{\{q_5\}, \{q_0, q_1, q_3\}, \{q_2, q_4, q_6\}\}$.

Therefore $\pi_3 = \pi_2$, so minimum state automaton is $M' = (Q', \{0, 1\}, \delta', q_0', F')$ where

$$Q' = \{[q_5], [q_0, q_1, q_3], [q_2, q_4, q_6]\}$$
$$q_0' = [q_0, q_1, q_3]$$
$$F' = [q_5]$$

δ' is defined in the Table 2.30.

Table 2.30: Transition Table of minimum state DFA

Input \ States	0	1
$-[q_0, q_1, q_3]$	$[q_0, q_1, q_3]$	$[q_2, q_4, q_6]$
$[q_2, q_4, q_6]$	$[q_5]$	$[q_2, q_4, q_6]$
$[q_5]$	$[q_0, q_1, q_3]$	$[q_2, q_4, q_6]$

Figure 2.79 shows the required minimum state DFA M'.

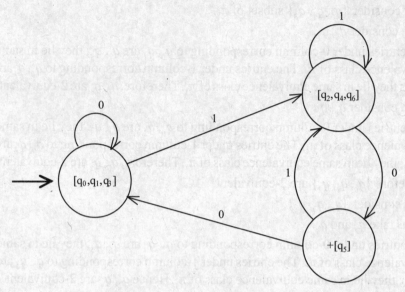

Fig. 2.79: Transition diagram of minimum state DFA M'

Programming Problems

1. Consider the Deterministic Finite Automaton $M = (\{q_1, q_2, q_3, q_4, q_5, q_6\}, \{a, b\}, \delta, q_1, \{q_5, q_6\})$ where δ is given by the Table 2.31.

Table 2.31: Transition Table

Input States	a	b
$-q_1$	q_3	q_5
q_2	q_4	q_2
q_3	q_1	q_6
q_4	q_4	q_3
$+q_5$	q_2	q_4
$+q_6$	q_3	q_4

   Write a C++ program to simulate this finite automaton.
2. Write an interactive C++ /Java program to simulate the NFA.
3. Write an interactive C++ /Java program to simulate the NFA with ε-transition.
4. Write an interactive C++ /Java program to simulate the Moore machine.
5. Write an interactive C++ /Java program to simulate the Mealy machine.
6. Write an interactive C++ /Java program that produces a minimal DFA for an given DFA.

Chapter 3
Regular Expressions

In this Chapter we will study about regular expressions which are one of the ways to represent the regular languages. This representation has important practical applications. We will discuss the identities for Regular expressions, Transition graph and Kleene's theorem. The correspondence between regular expression and finite automaton will be explored. Finally, we will present Arden's theorem and demonstrate its use to convert finite automata into regular expressions. The Chapter also gives adequate emphasis on illustrative examples to facilitate thorough understanding of the concepts presented here.

Objectives: The objective of this Chapter is to introduce regular expression. After learning the contents of this Chapter, you will be able to:

1. Define and characterize the language associated with Regular expressions,
2. Explain Transition graph and its conversion into a Regular expression,
3. Illustrate the steps in the conversion of given DFA and NFA into Regular expressions and
4. State and explain Kleene's and Arden's theorem.

3.1 Regular Expressions, Operators and their precedence

Regular expressions are notations used to represent languages. The representation involves a combination of strings of symbols from some alphabet Σ, parentheses, and the operators union (denoted by $\cup$ or $+$), concatenation (denoted by .) and Kleene closure (denoted by $*$). The precedence of the operators, from highest to lowest, is $*$, ., $+$.

3.1.1 Definition

Formally a *regular expression* over the alphabet Σ is defined by the following rules:

1. ϕ, ε, and $a \in \Sigma$ are all regular expressions. These are called *primitive regular expressions*.

2.   If r_1 and r_2 are regular expressions, then $r_1 + r_2$ and $r_1 r_2$ are also regular expressions.

3.   If r is a regular expression then $r*$ is also a regular expression.

4.   If r is a regular expression then r^+ (*positive closure*) is also a regular expression.

5.   If r is a regular expression then (r) is also a regular expression.

6.   A string is a regular expression if and only if it can be derived from the primitive regular expressions by a finite number of applications of the rules 2, 3 and 4.

7.   Nothing else is a regular expression.

3.1.2 Language Associated with Regular Expressions

A regular expression can be considered an algebraic formula to generate a pattern of a set of strings, called the language of the expression. The language represented by the regular expression r is formally denoted by $L(r)$ and is defined by the following rules:

1.   The language associated with the regular expression a (for each a in Σ) is $\{a\}$, ϕ is $\{\phi\}$ and with ε is $\{\varepsilon\}$.

2.   If r_1 and r_2 are regular expressions corresponding to languages L_1 and L_2 respectively, then

   (i)   The regular expression $r_1 + r_2$ is associated with the language $L_1 \cup L_2$, i.e., $L(r_1 + r_2) = L_1 + L_2$.

   (ii) The regular expression $r_1 r_2$ is associated with the language $L_1 L_2$, i.e., $L(r_1 r_2) = L_1 L_2$.

   (iii) The regular expression $r*$ is associated with the language $L*$, i.e., language $L(r*) = L*$.

Two regular expressions r_1 and r_2 are said to be equivalent if both represent the same set of strings, and we will write $r_1 = r_2$.

Example 3.1: Write the regular expressions of the following sets:

(i) $\{\varepsilon, x, xx, xxx\}$

(ii) $\{\varepsilon, xx, xxxx, ...\}$

(iii) $\{01, 10\}$

Solution:

(i)   The set $\{\varepsilon, x, xx, xxx\}$ is represented by $\varepsilon + x + xx + xxx$.

(ii) The set $\{\varepsilon, xx, xxxx ...\}$ is represented by $\{\varepsilon + xx + xxxx, ...\}$. Here, we can also see that the set contains either ε or word of even number of x's, i.e., a string of the form $(xx)^n$, $n \geq 0$. So, the regular expression can be represented by $(xx)^*$.

(iii) The set $\{01, 10\}$ is represented by $01 + 10$.

3.1.3   Algebraic Laws for Regular Expressions

Let p, q and r are regular expressions. Then:

$I_1 : \phi + p = p$ [ϕ is the identity for union]

$I_2 : \phi p = p\phi = \phi$ [ϕ is the zero for concatenation. That is concatenating empty set to any set yields the empty set]

$I_3 : \varepsilon p = p\varepsilon = p$ [ε is the identity for concatenation]

$I_4 : \varepsilon^* = \varepsilon$ and $\phi^* = \varepsilon$

$I_5 : p + p = p$

$I_6 : p^*p^* = p^*$

$I_7 : pp^* = p^*p$

$I_8 : (p^*)^* = p^*$

$I_9 : \varepsilon + pp^* = p^* = p^*p + \varepsilon$

$I_{10} : (pq)^*p = p(qp)^*$

$I_{11} : (p + q)^* = (p^*q^*)^* = (p^* + q^*)^*$

$I_{12} : (p + q)r = pr + qr$ and $r(p + q) = rp + rq$

Example 3.2: Prove that

(i) $\varepsilon + 1^*(011)^*(1^*(011)^*)^* = (1 + 011)^*$

(ii) $(1 + 00^*1) + (1 + 00^*1)(0 + 10^*1)^*(0 + 10^*1) = 0^*1(0 + 10^*1)^*$

Solution:

(i)   Let $p_1 = 1^*(011)^*$

$\varepsilon + 1^*(011)^*(1^*(011)^*)^* = \varepsilon + p_1(p_1)^*$

$\quad\quad = p_1^*$ [from identity I_9]

$\quad\quad = (1^*(011)^*)^*$

$\quad\quad = (p_2^*p_3^*)^*$ where $p_2 = 1$ and $p_3 = 011$

$\quad\quad = (p_2 + p_3)^*$ [identity I_{11}]

$\quad\quad = (1 + 011)^*$

(ii) $(1 + 00^*1) + (1 + 00^*1)(0 + 10^*1)^*(0 + 10^*1)$

$$= (1 + 00*1)(\varepsilon + (0 + 10*1)*(0 + 10*1)) \qquad \text{[identity } I_{12}]$$
$$= (1 + 00*1)(\varepsilon + p_1*p_1) \qquad \text{where } p_1 = (0 + 10*1)$$
$$= (1 + 00*1)p_1* \qquad \text{[identity } I_9]$$
$$= (1 + 00*1)(0 + 10*1)*$$
$$= (\varepsilon + 00*)1(0 + 10*1)* \qquad \text{[identity } I_{12}]$$
$$= 0*1(0 + 10*1)* \qquad \text{[identity } I_9]$$

3.2   Transition Graph (TG)

Transition graph was invented by John Myhill in 1957 to simplify the proof of Kleene's Theorem. It is a mathematical model of a system which can read more than one input letter at a time. Formally, we can define it as follows:

A *Transition graph* is a five tuple $(Q, \Sigma, \delta, Q', F)$ where

        Q-finite set of states,

        Σ-input alphabet,

        $Q' \subseteq Q$ is a set of start states,

        $F \subseteq Q$ is a set of final states,

$\delta(Q, w)$ is a transition function that shows how to go from one state to another based on reading specified substrings of input letter (possibly even the null string ε). It is non-deterministic. The algorithm for the construction of transition table is given in the Algorithm 3.1.

Algorithm 3.1: Algorithm for construction of transition table of TG.

Algorithm (Construction of Transition Table): Let $M = (Q, \Sigma, \delta, Q', F)$ be a transition graph. Following steps are used to construct the transition table.

Step 1: Draw a table where number of rows indicates number of states and number of columns indicates number of substrings of alphabet characters that are ever used as label for any edge in the Transition graph.

Step 2: Label the rows with states of Transition graph and columns with labels of edges.

Step 3: For each transition function $\delta(q, w) = p$, enter p into cell (q, w).

Step 4: Start state is preceded by '−' and final state by ' + '.

Example 3.3: Consider the Transition graph in Figure 3.1:

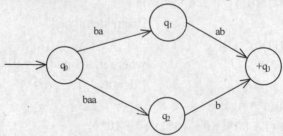

Fig. 3.1: Transition Graph

We see that q_0, q_1, q_2, and q_3 are states of the machine. So, the rows of the table will have the labels q_0, q_1, q_2, and q_3. The labels of edges are b, ab, ba and baa. Therefore, columns will be labeled with b, ab, ba and baa. We observe that q_0 is the initial state and q_3 is a final state. Therefore, row label q_0 is preceded by $-$ sign and q_3 by $+$ sign in the table. There is an edge labeled ba from state q_0 to state q_1, i.e., $\delta(q_0, ba) = q_1$. So, the entry in the cell (q0, ba) is q_1. We repeat this process for each transition function value. The transition table is depicted in the Table 3.1.

Table 3.1: Transition Table of TG

States \ Input	b	ab	ba	baa
$-q_0$	ϕ	ϕ	q_1	q_2
q_1	ϕ	q_3	ϕ	ϕ
q_2	q_3	ϕ	ϕ	ϕ
$+q_3$	ϕ	ϕ	ϕ	ϕ

3.3 Kleene's Theorem

Any language that can be defined by

1. Regular expression or
2. Finite automaton or
3. Transition graph

Can be defined by all the above three methods. In the next sections, we will prove this theorem.

3.4 Finite Automata and Regular Expression

In this section, we will prove that regular expressions and finite automata have equivalent expressive power: languages defined or accepted by finite automata are precisely the languages represented by regular expressions. That is why finite Automata definable languages are called regular languages.

3.4.1 Regular Expression to FA

Theorem 3.1: For every regular expression r, there is a corresponding NFA with ε-transitions that accepts the language $L(r)$ represented by r.

Proof: The proof is by the principal of induction on the total number of operators in the regular expression r. Assume that there is an NFA M with ε-transitions having one final state and no moves out of this final state, such that $L(M) = L(r)$.

Basis: Let the number of operators in the regular expression be zero. The regular expression r must be ε, ϕ or a from some a in Σ. The transition diagrams of NFA given in the figure 3.2 will clearly represent three regular expressions.

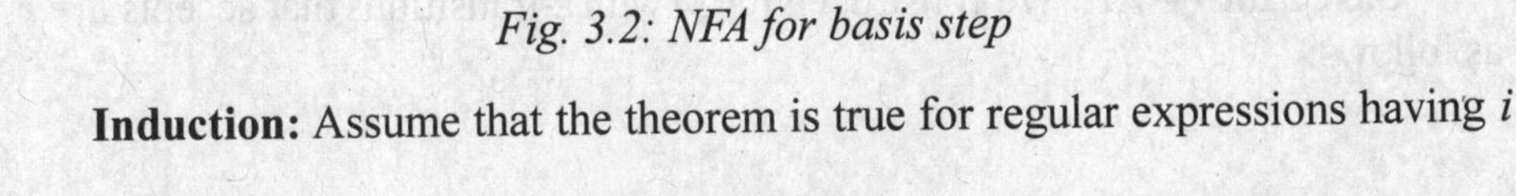

$r = \varepsilon$ $r = \phi$ $r = a$

Fig. 3.2: NFA for basis step

Induction: Assume that the theorem is true for regular expressions having i

operators, $i \geq 1$. Let r have $i + 1$ operators. There are three cases depending on the outermost operator in r which can be either $+$,. or $*$, that is

$$r = r_1 + r_2 \text{ or } r = r_1 . r_2 \text{ or } r = r_1*$$

where r_1 and r_2 are regular expressions having i or less operators. By induction hypothesis, language defined by r_1, i.e., $L(r_1)$ and language defined by r_2, i.e., $L(r_2)$ are recognized by NFAs with ε transitions say

$$M_1 = (Q_1, \Sigma_1, \delta_1, q_1, \{f_1\}) \text{ and } M_2 = (Q_2, \Sigma_2, \delta_2, q_2, \{f_2\}), \text{ respectively.}$$

Let us assume that Q_1 and Q_2 are distinct.

Case 1 for $r_1 + r_2$: Now we construct an NFA M with ε-transitions that accept $L(r_1 + r_2)$ with q_0 as a new initial state and f_0 as a new final state as follows :

$$M = (Q_1 \cup Q_2 \cup \{q_0, f_0\}, \Sigma_1 \cup \Sigma_2, \delta, q_0, \{f_0\}),$$

where δ is defined by

(i) $\delta(q_0, \varepsilon) = \{q_1, q_2\}$,

(ii) $\delta(q, a) = \delta_1(q, a)$ for q in $Q_1 - \{f_1\}$ and a in $\Sigma_1 \cup \{\varepsilon\}$,

(iii) $\delta(q, a) = \delta_2(q, a)$ for q in $Q_2 - \{f_2\}$ and a in $\Sigma_2 \cup \{\varepsilon\}$,

(iv) $\delta(f_1, \varepsilon) = \delta(f_2, \varepsilon) = \{f_0\}$.

Now from the above definition of δ, we can say that all moves of M_1 and M_2 are present in M since we know that there are no transitions out of f_1 in M_1 or f_2 in M_2. Figure 3.3 depicts the transition diagram of M.

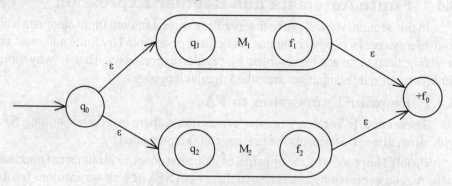

Fig. 3.3: NFA for M

Obviously for any path from q_0 to f_0, M either moves to q_1 or q_2 on ε transition and then make exactly the same moves as either M_1 or M_2 would to reach f_1, or f_2 and then go to f_0 on ε. Hence there is a path labeled x in M from q_0 to f_0 if and only if there is a path labeled x in M_1 from q_1 to f_1 or a path from q_2 to f_2. Thus $L(M) = L(M_1) \cup L(M_2) = L(M_1) + L(M_2)$.

Case 2 for $r = r_1 r_2$: We construct NFA M with ε-transitions that accepts $L(r_1 r_2)$ as follows:

$M = (Q_1 \cup Q_2, \Sigma_1 \cup \Sigma_2, \delta, \{q_1\}, \{f_2\})$ where q_1 is the initial state, f_2 is the final state and

δ defined by

(i) $\delta(q, a) = \delta_1(q, a)$ for q in $Q_1 - \{f_1\}$ and a in $\Sigma_1 \cup \{\varepsilon\}$,

(ii) $\delta(f_1, \varepsilon) = \{q_2\}$,

(iii) $\delta(q, a) = \delta_2(q, a)$ for q in Q_2 and a in $\Sigma_2 \cup \{\varepsilon\}$.

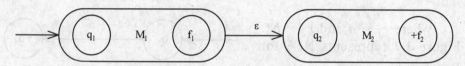

Fig. 3.4: NFA for M

The Figure 3.4 depicts the transition diagram of M. In this Figure, we can see that every path in M from q_1 to f_2 is a path labeled by some string x from q_1 to f_1, followed by an edge from f_1 to q_2 labelled ε, followed by a path labeled by some string y from q_2 to f_2. Therefore, $L(M) = \{xy \mid x$ is in $L(M_1)$ and y is in $L(M_2)\}$. Thus $L(M) = L(M_1)L(M_2)$.

Case 3 for $r = r_1{}^*$: We construct NFA M as follows:

$$M = (Q_1 \cup \{q_0, f_0\}, \Sigma_1, \delta, q_0, \{f_0\})$$

where δ is defined by

(i) $\delta(q_0, \varepsilon) = \delta(f_1, \varepsilon) = \{q_1, f_0\}$

(ii) $\delta(q, a) = \delta_1(q, a)$ for q in $Q_1 - \{f_1\}$ and a in $\Sigma_1 \cup \{\varepsilon\}$

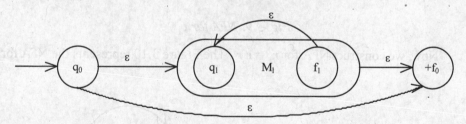

Fig. 3.5: NFA for M

The Figure 3.5 depicts the transition diagram of M. Any path from q_0 to f_0 consists either of a move from q_0 to f_0 on ε or a move from q_0 to q_1 on ε, followed by some number (possibly zero) of paths from q_1 to f_1 then back to q_1 on ε, each labeled by a string in $L(M_1)$, followed by a path from q_1 to f_1 on a string in $L(M_1)$ and then to f_0 on ε. Therefore, $L(M) = L(M_1)^*$.

Example 3.4: Construct an NFA for the regular expression $ab^* + b$.

Solution: We start construction from smallest sub expression to larger sub expressions until we have an NFA for the original expression.

Let $r = ab^* + b$.

It can be written as

$$r = r_1 + r_2$$

where $r_1 = ab^*$ and $r_2 = b$.

We draw the NFA for r_2 as shown in Figure 3.6:

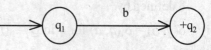

Fig. 3.6: NFA for r$_2$

Now we may rewrite r_1 as

$$r_1 = r_3 r_4$$

where $r_3 = a$ and $r_4 = b^*$. Figure 3.7 represents NFA for r_3.

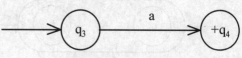

Fig. 3.7: NFA for r$_3$

Now we rewrite r_4 as

$$r_4 = r_5^* \text{ where } r_5 = b.$$

Figure 3.8 represents the NFA for r_5:

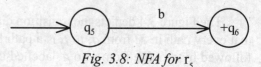

Fig. 3.8: NFA for r$_5$

Next, we construct r_4. Figure 3.9 represents the NFA for r_4.

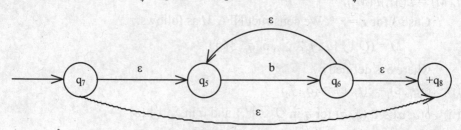

Fig. 3.9: NFA for r$_4$

Now, we construct NFA for $r_1 = r_3 r_4$. The Figure 3.10 represents the NFA for r_1.

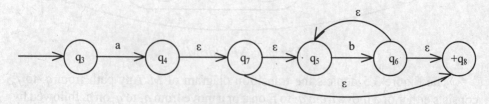

Fig. 3.10: NFA for r$_1$

Finally, we construct NFA for $r = r_1 + r_2$. The following Figure 3.11 represents the NFA for r.

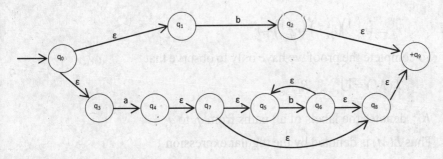

Fig. 3.11: NFA for r

3.4.2 DFA to Regular Expression

Theorem 3.2: For every DFA M, there is a corresponding regular expression r that represents the same language as accepted by M.

Proof: Let L be the set of strings accepted by the DFA

$$M = (\{q_1, \ldots q_n\}, \Sigma, \delta, q_1, F)$$

Let R_{ij}^k denotes the set of all strings x such that $\delta(q_i, x) = q_j$ and the finite automaton moves from state q_i to state q_j without going through any state numbered higher than k. Going through a state, we mean both entering and then leaving. The value of i or j may be greater than k.

Now, we can define R_{ij}^k recursively.

$$R_{ij}^k = R_{ik}^{k-1}\left(R_{kk}^{k-1}\right)^k R_{kj}^{k-1} \bigcup R_{ij}^{k-1},$$

$$R_{ij}^0 = \begin{cases} \{a \mid \delta(q_i, a) = q_j \ \ if \ \ i \neq j, \\ \{a \mid \delta(q_i, a) = q_j \bigcup \{\in\} \ \ if \ \ i = j. \end{cases}$$

We have to show that for each i, j and k there exists a regular expression r_{ij}^k which represents the language R_{ij}^k.

Basis: Let k be zero. R_{ij}^0 is then a finite set of strings each of which is either ε or a single symbol. Thus R_{ij}^k can be written as $a_1 + a_2 \ldots + a_p$ (or as $a_1 + a_2 \ldots + a_p + \varepsilon$ if $i = j$), where $\{a_1, a_2, \ldots a_p\}$ is the set of all symbols a such that $\delta(q_i, x) = q_j$. If there are no such a's, then ϕ (or ε in the case $i = j$) serves as R_{ij}^0.

Induction: We can see that the recursive formula for obtaining the language R_{ij}^k involves regular expression operators only, that is union, concatenation, and closure. By the induction hypothesis, for each l and m there exists a regular expression r_{1m}^{k-1} such that $L\left(r_{1m}^{k-1}\right) = R_{1m}^{k-1}$. Thus for r_{ij}^k we can write the regular expression

$$r_{ij}^k = \left(r_{ik}^{k-1}\right)\left(r_{kk}^{k-1}\right)^*\left(r_{kj}^{k-1}\right) + r_{ij}^{k-1}$$

To complete the proof we have only to observe that

$$L(M) = \bigcup_{q_j . in\, F} R_{1j}^n$$

R_{1j}^n denotes the labels of all paths from q_1 to q_j.

Thus $L(M)$ is denoted by the regular expression

$$r_{1j_1}^n + r_{1j_2}^n + ...r_{1j_p}^n$$

where $F = \{q_{j_1}, q_{j_2},...q_{j_p}\}$.

Example 3.5: Construct regular expression of the FA given in Figure 3.12.

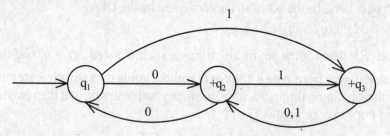

Fig. 3.12: Transition diagram

Solution:

The regular expression for the given FA will be

$$r_{12}^3 + r_{13}^3$$

To compute the values of r_{ij}^k for all i, j, we construct the Table 3.2 for $r_{12}^3 + r_{13}^3$.

Table 3.2: Format of table for r_{ij}^k for all i and j and $k = 0, 1, 2$

	$k = 0$	$k = 1$	$k = 2$
r_{11}^k			
r_{12}^k			
r_{13}^k			
r_{21}^k			
r_{22}^k			
r_{23}^k			
r_{31}^k			
r_{32}^k			
r_{33}^k			

Starting with $k = 0$ we have:

$r_{11}^0 = \varepsilon$ (There is no path from q_i to q_j but $i = j$)

$r_{12}^0 = 0$ (There is path q_1 to q_2 labeled 0)

$r_{13}^0 = 1$ (There is path q_1 to q_3 labeled 1)

$r_{21}^0 = 0$ (There is path from q_2 to q_1 labeled 0)

$r_{22}^0 = \varepsilon$ (There is no path from q_i to q_j but $i = j$)

$r_{23}^0 = 1$ (There is path q_2 to q_3 labeled 1)

$r_{31}^0 = \phi$ (There is a path from q_3 to q_1 but $1 \Leftrightarrow 3$)

$r_{32}^0 = 0 + 1$ (There are two paths labeled 0 and 1)

$r_{33}^0 = \varepsilon$ (There is no bath p from q_i to q_j but $i = j$)

After entering the values, we get the Table 3.3.

Table 3.3: Tabulation of r_{ij}^k for $k = 0$

	$k = 0$	$k = 1$	$k = 2$
r_{11}^k	ε		
r_{12}^k	0		
r_{13}^k	1		
r_{21}^k	0		
r_{22}^k	ε		
r_{23}^k	1		
r_{31}^k	ϕ		
r_{32}^k	$0 + 1$		
r_{33}^k	ε		

Next, we compute r_{ij}^1 for all i & j as follows:

$$r_{11}^1 = r_{11}^0 (r_{11}^0)^* r_{11}^0 \cup r_{11}^0$$
$$= \varepsilon\,(\varepsilon)^*\varepsilon + \varepsilon$$
$$= \varepsilon + \varepsilon$$
$$= \varepsilon$$

$$r_{12}^1 = r_{11}^0 (r_{11}^0)^* r_{12}^0 \cup r_{12}^0$$
$$= \varepsilon\,(\varepsilon)^*0 + 0$$

$$= \varepsilon 0 + 0$$
$$= 0 + 0$$
$$= 0$$

$$r_{13}^1 = r_{11}^0 (r_{11}^0)^* r_{13}^0 \cup r_{13}^0$$
$$= \varepsilon(\varepsilon)^* 1 + 1$$
$$= 1 + 1$$
$$= 1$$

$$r_{21}^1 = r_{21}^0 (r_{11}^0)^* r_{11}^0 \cup r_{21}^0$$
$$= 0(\varepsilon)^* \varepsilon + 0$$
$$= 0 \varepsilon \varepsilon + 0 \qquad\qquad [\varepsilon^* = \varepsilon]$$
$$= 0 + 0$$
$$= 0$$

$$r_{22}^1 = r_{21}^0 (r_{11}^0)^* r_{12}^0 \cup r_{22}^0$$
$$= 0(\varepsilon)^* 0 + \varepsilon$$
$$= 0 \varepsilon 0 + \varepsilon \qquad\qquad [\varepsilon^* = \varepsilon]$$
$$= 00 + \varepsilon$$
$$= \varepsilon + 00$$

$$r_{23}^1 = r_{21}^0 (r_{11}^0)^* r_{13}^0 \cup r_{23}^0$$
$$= 0(\varepsilon)^* 1 + 1$$
$$= 0 \varepsilon 1 + 1 \qquad\qquad [\varepsilon^* = \varepsilon]$$
$$= 01 + 1$$
$$= 1 + 01$$

$$r_{31}^1 = r_{31}^0 (r_{11}^0)^* r_{11}^0 \cup r_{31}^0$$
$$= \phi \varepsilon \varepsilon + \phi$$
$$= \phi \varepsilon + \phi$$
$$= \phi$$

$$r_{32}^1 = r_{31}^0 (r_{11}^0)^* r_{12}^0 \cup r_{32}^0$$
$$= \phi(\varepsilon)^* 0 + (0 + 1)$$
$$= \phi + (0 + 1) \qquad\qquad [\phi + p = p]$$
$$= 0 + 1$$

$$r_{33}^1 = r_{31}^0 (r_{11}^0)^* r_{13}^0 \cup r_{33}^0$$
$$= \phi(\varepsilon)1 + \varepsilon$$
$$= \phi + \varepsilon \qquad\qquad [\phi p + p\phi = \phi]$$
$$= \varepsilon$$

The Table 3.4 now has the following entries:

Next, we compute r_{ij}^2 for all i and j.

$$r_{11}^2 = r_{12}^1 (r_{22}^1)^* r_{21}^1 \cup r_{11}^1$$
$$= 0(\varepsilon + 00)^* 0 + \varepsilon$$
$$= 0(00)^* 0 + \varepsilon$$
$$= \varepsilon + 0(00)^* 0$$
$$= (00)^*$$

$$r_{12}^2 = r_{12}^1 (r_{22}^1)^* r_{22}^1 \cup r_{12}^1$$
$$= 0(\varepsilon + 00)^* (\varepsilon + 00) + 0$$
$$= 0((\varepsilon + 00)^* (\varepsilon + 00) + \varepsilon)$$
$$= 0(\varepsilon + (\varepsilon + 00)(\varepsilon + 00)^*)$$
$$= 0(\varepsilon + 00)^* \qquad [\varepsilon + pp^* = p^*]$$
$$= 0(00)^* \qquad [(\varepsilon + 00)^* = (00)^*]$$

$$r_{13}^2 = r_{12}^1 (r_{22}^1)^* r_{23}^1 \cup r_{13}^1$$
$$= 0(\varepsilon + 00)^* (1 + 01) + 1$$
$$= 0(00)^* (\varepsilon + 0)1 + 1$$
$$= 00^* 1 + 1 \qquad [(00)^* (\varepsilon + 0) = 0^*]$$
$$= (00^* \varepsilon + \varepsilon)1$$
$$= (00^* + \varepsilon)1$$
$$= 0^* 1 \qquad [\varepsilon + pp^* = P^*]$$

$$r_{21}^2 = r_{22}^1 (r_{22}^1)^* r_{21}^1 \cup r_{21}^1$$
$$= (\varepsilon + 00)(\varepsilon + 00)^* 0 + 0$$
$$= 0 + (\varepsilon + 00)(\varepsilon + 00)^* 0$$
$$= 0(\varepsilon + (\varepsilon + 00)(\varepsilon + 00)^*)$$
$$= 0(\varepsilon + 00)^* \qquad [\varepsilon + pp^* = p^*]$$
$$= 0(00)^*$$

$$r_{22}^2 = r_{22}^1 (r_{22}^1)^* r_{22}^1 \cup r_{22}^1$$
$$= (\varepsilon + 00)(\varepsilon + 00)^* (\varepsilon + 00) + (\varepsilon + 00)$$
$$= (\varepsilon + 00)(\varepsilon + (\varepsilon + 00)(\varepsilon + 00)^*)$$
$$= (\varepsilon + 00)(\varepsilon + 00)^* \qquad [\varepsilon + pp^* = p^*]$$
$$= (\varepsilon + 00)(00)^*$$
$$= (00)^*$$

Table 3.4: *Tabulation of r_{ij}^k for $k = 0$ & $k = 1$*

	$k = 0$	$k = 1$	$k = 2$
r_{11}^k	ε	ε	
r_{12}^k	0	0	
r_{13}^k	1	1	
r_{21}^k	0	0	
r_{22}^k	ε	$\varepsilon + 00$	
r_{23}^k	1	$1 + 01$	
r_{31}^k	ϕ	ϕ	
r_{32}^k	$0 + 1$	$0 + 1$	
r_{33}^k	ε	ε	

$$r_{23}^2 = r_{22}^1 (r_{22}^1)^* r_{23}^1 \cup r_{23}^1$$

$$= (\varepsilon + 00)(\varepsilon + 00)^*(1 + 01) + (1 + 01)$$

$$= (\varepsilon + 00)(\varepsilon + 00)^* + \varepsilon(1 + 01)$$

$$= (\varepsilon + 00)^*(\varepsilon + 0)1 \qquad [\varepsilon + pp^* = p^* \text{ and } (p + q)r^* = pr + qr]$$

$$= (00)^*(\varepsilon + 0)1$$

$$= 0^*1 \qquad\qquad\qquad [(00)^* (\varepsilon + 0) = 0^*]$$

$$r_{31}^2 = r_{32}^1 (r_{22}^1)^* r_{21}^1 \cup r_{31}^1$$

$$= (0 + 1)(\varepsilon + 00)^*0 + \phi$$

$$= (0 + 1)(\varepsilon + 00)^*0$$

$$= (0 + 1)(00)^*0$$

$$r_{32}^2 = r_{32}^1 (r_{22}^1)^* r_{22}^1 \cup r_{32}^1$$

$$= (0 + 1)(\varepsilon + 00)(\varepsilon + 00) + (0 + 1)$$

$$= (0 + 1)((\varepsilon + 00)^*(\varepsilon + 00) + \varepsilon)$$

$$= (0 + 1)(\varepsilon + 00)^* \qquad [\varepsilon + pp^* = p^*]$$

$$= (0 + 1)(00)^*$$

$$r_{33}^2 = r_{32}^1 (r_{22}^1)^* r_{23}^1 \cup r_{33}^1$$

$$= (0 + 1)(\varepsilon + 00)^*(1 + 01) + \varepsilon$$

$$= (0 + 1)(00)^*(1 + 01) + \varepsilon$$

$$= (0 + 1)(00)^*(\varepsilon + 0)1 + \varepsilon$$

$$= (0 + 1)0^*1 + \varepsilon$$

$$= \varepsilon + (0 + 1)0^*1$$

With above entries we get the Table 3.5.

Next, we compute

$$r_{12}^3 = r_{13}^2 (r_{33}^2)^* r_{32}^2 \cup r_{12}^2$$

$$= 0^*1(\varepsilon + (0 + 1)0^*1)^*(0 + 1)(00)^* + 0(00)^*$$

$$= 0^*1((0 + 1)0^*1)^*(0 + 1)(00)^* + 0(00)^*$$

$$r_{13}^3 = r_{13}^2 (r_{33}^2)^* r_{33}^2 \cup r_{13}^2$$

$$= 0^*1(\varepsilon + (0 + 1)0^*1)^*(\varepsilon + (0 + 1)0^*1) + 0^*1$$

$$= 0^*1((0 + 1)0^*1)^*$$

Table 3.5: Tabulation of r_{ij}^k for $k = 0$, $k = 1$ and $k = 2$

	$k = 0$	$k = 1$	$k = 2$
r_{11}^k	ε	ε	$(00)^*$
r_{12}^k	0	0	$0(00)^*$
r_{13}^k	1	1	0^*1
r_{21}^k	0	0	$0(00)^*$
r_{22}^k	ε	$\varepsilon + 00$	$(00)^*$
r_{23}^k	1	$1 + 01$	0^*1
r_{31}^k	ϕ	ϕ	$(0 + 1)(00)^*0$
r_{32}^k	$0 + 1$	$0 + 1$	$(0 + 1)(00)^*$
r_{33}^k	ε	ε	$\varepsilon + (0 + 1)0^*1$

Hence $r_{12}^3 + r_{13}^3 = 0*1((0+1)0*1)*(0+1)(00)* + 0(00)* + 0*1((0+1)0*1)*$

$$= 0*1((0+1)0*1)*(\varepsilon + (0+1)(00)*) + 0(00)*$$

3.4.3 TG to Regular Expression

Theorem 3.3: Every language that can be defined by a transition graph can also be defined by a regular expression.

Proof:

We present an algorithm that starts with a transition graph and ends up with a regular expression that defines the same language as the transition graph. The algorithm is given in Algorithm 3.2.

Algorithm 3.2: Algorithm for conversion of transition graph into regular expression

---

Algorithm(Convert a transition graph into corresponding regular expression):

Step 1: If the transition graph has many start states then we convert it so that it has only one start state as follows:

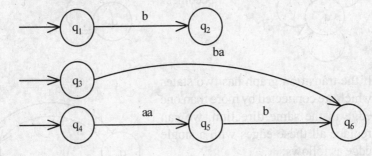

becomes

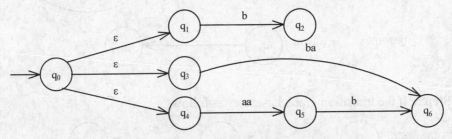

Step 2: If the transition graph has many final states, then it can be modified to have a unique final states as follows:

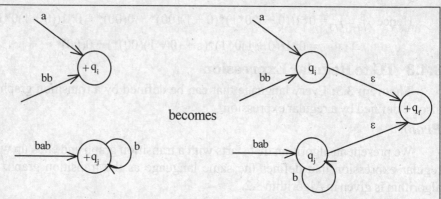

becomes

Step 3: If the transition graph has some state q_n (which is neither a start state nor a final state) that has more than one loop then we can replace all the loops by a single loop as follows:

becomes

Step 4: If the transition graph has two states which are connected by more than one edge in the same direction, we can replace all these edges with a single edge as follows:

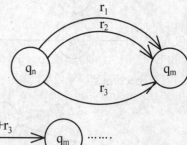

becomes ....

Step 5: If the transition graph has states as follows:

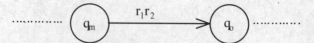

then we replace above as follows:

.... q_m —— $r_1 r_2$ —→ q_o ....

Step 6: If the transition graph has states as follows:

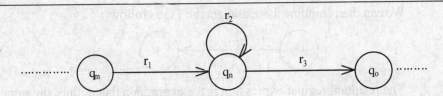

then we replace above as follows:

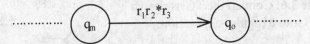

Step 7: If the state q_m in the transition graph is connected to state q_n and state q_n is connected to more than one state (say to q_{n_1}, q_{n_2} and q_{n_3}), and state q_n also has self loop as follows:

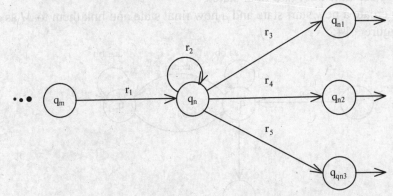

then we eliminate the edge from state q_m to state q_n, add edges to q_{n_1}, q_{n_2}, q_{n_3} from state q_m and delete the state q_n as follows:

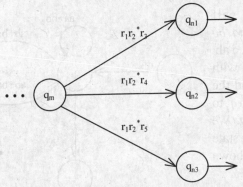

Step 8: We can repeat the above steps until we have eliminated all the states from the transition graph except the unique start state and the unique final state. Finally, we get the TG as follows:

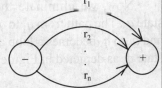

We can then combine these and get the TG as follows:

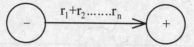

The resultant regular expression is the expression that defines the same language as defined by the Transition graph originally.

Example 3.6: Convert the TG as shown in Figure 3.13 into a regular expression.

Solution:

Let the Transition graph be denoted by *M*.

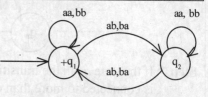

Fig. 3.13: Transition Graph M

First we separate start and final states. For this we create a new start state and a new final state and link them to *M* as as shown in Figure 3.14:

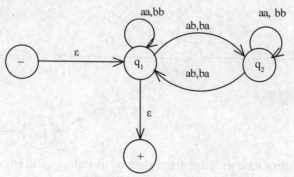

Fig. 3.14: Transition Graph M

State q_1 has self transitions labeled with *aa, bb* and transition to q_2 labeled ab, ba. We replace the first with loop labeled *aa + bb* and the second by transition from q_1 to q_2 labeled with *ab + ba*. We repeat this process for the state q_2 also and get the TG as shown in Figure 3.15

Now, we eliminate the state q_2. The path from q_1 to q_2 and q_2 to q_1 becomes a loop at state q_1 as depicted in Figure 3.16.

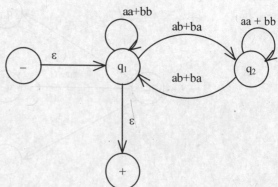

Fig. 3.15: Transition Graph M

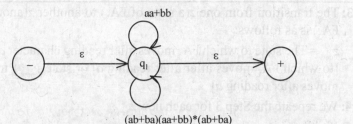

(ab+ba)(aa+bb)*(ab+ba)

Fig. 3.16: Transition Graph M

The state q_1 has two loops labeled $(aa + bb)$ and $(ab + ba)(aa + bb)*(ab + ba)$. We can replace these by a single loop labeled $(aa + bb) + (ab + ba)(aa + bb)*(ab + ba)$. We get the following TG as given in Figure 3.17.

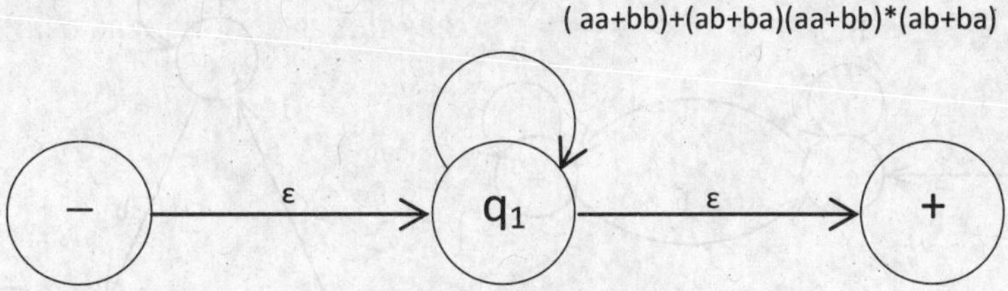

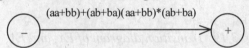

Fig. 3.17: Transition Graph M

Finally, we get the TG as shown in Figure 3.18.

$$(aa+bb)+(ab+ba)(aa+bb)*(ab+ba)$$

Fig. 3.18: Final Transition Graph M

The following regular expression corresponds to the above TG:
$$(aa + bb) + (ab + ba)(aa + bb)*(ab + ba)$$

Example 3.7: FA_1 and FA_2 are two Finite Automata which define the languages L_1 and L_2, respectively. Write an algorithm to construct a Finite Automaton FA_3 which accepts the language $L_1 \bigcup L_2$.

Solution:

The algorithm for the construction of finite automaton that accepts the language $L_1 \bigcup L_2$ is given in Algorithm 3.3.

Algorithm 3.3: Algorithm for construction of FA for $L_1 \bigcup L_2$

Algorithm: Finite automata FA_1 and FA_2 define the languages L_1 and L_2, respectively. The following steps are used to construct FA_3 that will define the language $L_1 \bigcup L_2$:

Step 1: Let the states of FA_1 be $x_1, x_2, \ldots$ where x_1 is a starting state and the states of FA_2 be $y_1, y_2, \ldots$ where y_1 is the start state. Let the states of FA_3 be z_1, z_2, z_3 where each z is of the form "$x_{Something} \cdot y_{Something}$".

Step 2: Starting state of FA_3 be z_1 and $z_1 = x_1$ or y_1

Step 3: The transition from one z(a state of FA_3) to another z(another state of FA_3) is as follows:

z_{new} = The state to which FA_3 moves after reading character a = State x_{new} [to which FA_1 moves after after reading a] or state y_{new} [to which FA_2 moves after reading a]

Step 4: We repeat the Step 3 for each new z_{new}.

Step 5: If either x or y is a final state, then the corresponding z is a final state.

Example 3.8: (Application of algorithm given in Algorithm 3.3):

Consider the deterministic finite automata FA_1 and FA_2 as shown in Figure 3.19 recognizing the languages L_1 and L_2, respectively.

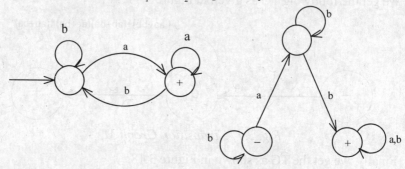

FA₁   FA₂

Fig. 3.19: Transition diagram of FA_1 and FA_2

Construct FA_3 that recognizes the language $L_1 \cup L_2$.

Solution:

Step 1: Let the states of FA_1 be x_1 and x_2 and FA_2 be y_1, y_2, and y_3. Thus we have FA_1 and FA_2 as given in Figure 3.20.

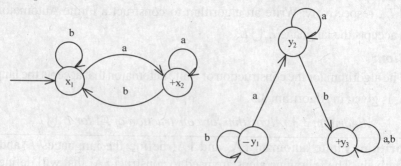

Fig. 3.20: Transition diagram of FA_1 and FA_2

Step 2: Start state of FA_3 is $z_1 = x_1$ or y_1

Step 3: While in state z_1 if FA_3 reads a, it goes to z_2 where $z_2 = x_2$(if $z_1 = x_1$) or $z_2 = y_2$(if $z_1 = y_2$.), and if FA_3 reads b it goes to z_1 (x_1 or y_1).

Step 4: Next, while in state z_2, if FA_3 reads a, it moves to z_2 (either to x_2 or y_2).

However, If it reads b, it goes to $z_3 = (x_1 \text{or } y_3)$.

Again on input a, FA_3 moves from state z_3 to z_4 (x_2 or y_3) and on input b it moves to z_3 (x_1 or y_3).

From state z_4, on input a, it goes to z_4 (x_2 or y_3), and on input b it goes to z_3 (x_1 or y_3).

This Step is now complete as no further new state is generated by the machine.

Step 5: The final states of FA_3 are states z_2, z_3 and z_4 that since each of these contain either final state of FA_1 or of FA_2.

Table 3.6

Input States	a	b
$-z_1$	z_2	z_1
$+z_2$	z_2	z_3
$+z_3$	z_4	z_3
$+z_4$	z_4	z_3

Finally, we get the transition table and the transition diagram of FA_3 which recognize the language defined by $L_1 \cup L_2$ as given in Table 3.6 and Figure 3.21.

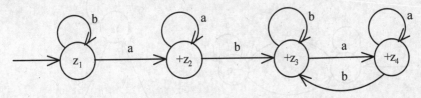

Fig. 3.21: Transition diagram of FA_3

Example 3.9: FA_1 and FA_2 are two Finite Automata which define the language L_1 and L_2, respectively. Write the algorithm to construct a Finite Automaton FA_3 that accepts the language $L_1 L_2$.

Solution:

The algorithm for the construction of FA_3 which accepts the language $L_1 L_2$ is given in Algorithm 3.4:

Algorithm 3.4: Algorithm for construction of FA_3 for language $L_1 L_2$

Algorithm: Finite automata FA_1 and FA_2 define the languages L_1 and L_2 respectively. The following steps are used to construct a Finite Automaton FA_3 that will accept the language $L_1 L_2$:

Step 1: Assume the states of FA_1 be $x_1, x_2 \ldots$ where x_1 is a start state and the states of FA_2 be $y_1, y_2 \ldots$ where y_1 is the start state.

Step 2: The start state of FA_3 will be $z_1 (= x_1)$.

Step 3: (a) FA_3 will have one z state corresponding to every non-final state x_i in FA_1 and on any input alphabet the behavior of state z will be similar to that of the state x_i.

(b) Corresponding to each final state x_j in FA_1, FA_3 will have one z state that represents the options that $z = x_j$ and the machine continues to be in FA_1 or $z = y_1$ and the machine is ready to start in FA_2 or $z =$ the state in FA_2 to which it moves from y_1. The transitions from one z

---

state to another z state for each input is determined uniquely by the transition rules in FA_1 and FA_2.

Step 4: We repeat the Step 3 for each new state formed during Step 3.

Step 5: The final states of FA_3 are those states that include the final state of FA_3.

Example 3.10: (Application of Algorithm given in Algorithm 3.4).

Consider the Deterministic Finite Automaton FA_1 and FA_2 recognizing the language L_1 and L_2, respectively given in Example 3.8. Construct FA_3 that recognize the language L_1L_2.

Solution:

Step 1: Let the states of FA_1 be x_1 and x_2 and FA_2 be y_1, y_2, and y_3. FA_1 and FA_2, then, are given in Figure 3.22.

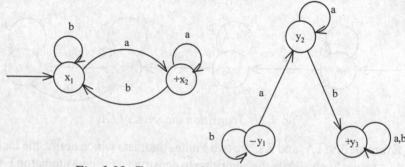

Fig. 3.22: Transition diagram of FA$_1$ and FA$_2$

Step 2: The start state of FA_3 will be x_1, the start state of FA_1.

Step 3: FA_3 will have a state corresponding to non-final state x_1 in FA_1 and on any input it will behave like the state x_1. Assume the state is z_1.

Step 4: Corresponding to the final state x_2 of FA_1, FA_3 will have a state; say has z_2. Then, either, $z_2 = x_2$ and machine is still running in FA_1 or $z_2 = y_1$ and machine is to begin to run in FA_2 or machine is in FA_2. Let while in state z_2, the machine on input a moves to state z_3 then either $z_3 = z_2 = x_2$ (machine being in FA_1, on input a state x_2 loops back to itself) or $z_3 = y_1$ (machine enters FA_2) or $z_3 = y_2$ (the machine in FA_2, on input a state y_1 moves to y_2, i.e., $z_3 = (x_2$ or y_1 or $y_2)$. Let the machine z_4 from state z_2 on input b then clearly $z_4 = x_1$ or $z_4 = y_1$ or z_2 goes back to y_1, i.e., $z_4 = x_1$ or y_1.

If machine is in state z_3 then on input a it moves to x_2 or y_1 or y_2, i.e., to z_3 only and on input b it goes to $(x_1$ or y_1 or $y_3)$. Let $z_5 = (x_1$ or y_1 or $y_3)$. z_5 is a final state of FA_3 as it includes y_3, the final state of FA_2.

If machine is in state z_4 then on input a it goes to $z_6 = (x_2$ or $y_2)$ and on input b it goes to$(x_1$ or $y_1)$, i.e., to z_4.

If machine is in state z_5 and reads an a, it goes to state $z_7 = (x_2$ or y_2 or $y_3)$ and if it reads b, it goes to $(x_1$ or y_1 or $y_3) = z_5$.

If machine is in state z_6 and read an a, it goes to $(x_2$ or y_1 or $y_2) = z_3$ and if it reads b it goes to $(x_1$ or y_1 or $y_3) = z_5$.

If machine is in state z_7 and reads an a, it goes to $(x_2$ or y_2 or $y_3) = z_7$ and if it reads b, it goes to state $(x_1$ or y_1 or $y_3) = z_5$.

Step 5: As we know that the final states of FA_2 are those states that include final states of FA_2. Therefore, final states of FA_3 will be z_5 and z_7.

We get the following transition diagram for FA_3 which recognizes the language L_1L_2 as shown in Figure 3.23.

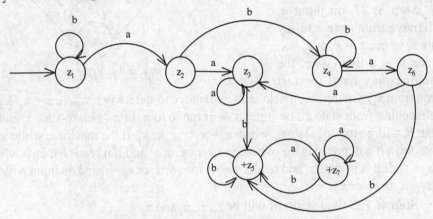

Fig. 3.23: Transition diagram of FA₃

Example 3.11: Given a Deterministic Finite Automaton FA which defines the language L. Draw a Finite Automaton which accepts the language L^*.

Solution:

The algorithm for construction of FA which defines the language L^* is given in Algorithm 3.5.

Algorithm 3.5: Algorithm for construction of FA for L^*

Algorithm: Let the finite automaton FA_1 defines the language L^*.

Step 1: Let the states of FA be x_1, x_2 ...where x_1 is a start state. Each state in FA_1 corresponds to some collection of x states of FA. Each time when we reach a final state, then it is possible that we have to start all over again at x_1, i.e., the start state of FA.

Step 2: The start state of FA_1 will be start state of FA.

Step 3: The transition from one collection of x states to another on any input alphabet is obtained completely by the transition rules of FA.

Step 4: Final states of FA_1 will be the states which contain the final states of FA.

Example 3.12: (Application of an algorithm given in Algorithm 3.5).

Consider the DFA M as given in Figure 3.24, which recognizes the language defined by the regular expression r.

Construct the DFA that recognizes the language $L(r^*)$.

Solution:

Step 1: States of the given DFA M are $x_1, x_2 \ldots$

Step 2: Assume the start state of the required DFA M_1 be z_1 where $z_1 = x_1$.

Step 3: M_1 on input a, will move from state z_1 to say state z_2, where $z_2 = x_2$ or $z_2 = x_1$ (since x_2 is a final state, the machine may have to start

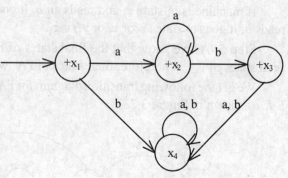

Fig. 3.24: DFA M

again from x_1). On input b, machine M_1 will move to state, say z_3 where $z_3 = x_4$. Again the machine from state z_2, on input a, will move to x_2 or x_1, i.e., to state z_2 and on input b, will go to, say, state z_4, where $z_4 = x_3$ or x_4 or x_1. If the machine, while in z_4, reads an a, it will go to state z_5 where $z_5 = x_4$ or x_2 or x_1 and if it reads b then it will go to $x_4 = z_3$. If it is in state z_5 and read a it goes to x_4 or x_2 or $x_1 = z_5$ and on input b it goes to $z_4 = x_4$ or x_3 or x_1.

Step 4: The final states of will be z_1, z_2, z_4 and z_5.

We get the transition diagram of the DFA M_1 as given in Figure 3.25:

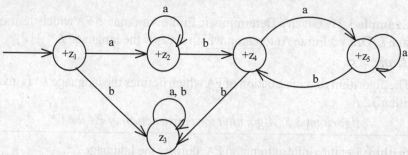

Fig. 3.25: Transition diagram of DFA M_1

In the next section, we consider Arden's theorem and how it is used to find a regular expression corresponding to given DFA.

3.4.4. Arden's Theorem

Let p and q are two regular expressions over alphabet Σ. If p does not contain ε, then the following equation in r, namely

$$r = q + rp \qquad \ldots (1)$$

has a unique solution (i.e., one and only one solution) given by

$$r = qp^*.$$

Proof: To show that $r = qp^*$ is a solution of $r = q + rp$, we substitute the $r = qp^*$ in (1)

We get

$$\text{RHS} = q + (qp^*)p$$

$$= q(\varepsilon + p^*p)$$

$$= qp^* \qquad \qquad [\varepsilon + p^*p = p^* = \varepsilon + pp^*]$$

$$\text{LHS} = qp^*$$

Therefore, $r = qp^*$ is a solution. Now, we will prove $r = qp^*$ is one and the only ne solution of (1).

Now $r = q + rp$

$$= q + (q + rp)p \qquad [\text{ replacing } r \text{ by } q + rp \text{ in the RHS}]$$

$$= q + qp + rpp$$

$$= q + qp + rp^2$$

$$= q + qp + (q + rp)p^2$$

$$= \dots\dots\dots\dots\dots\dots\dots$$

$$= q + qp + qp^2 + \dots qp^i + rp^{i+1}$$

$$= q(\varepsilon + p + p^2 + \dots + p^i) + rp^{i+1} \quad \text{ for } i \geq 0 \qquad \qquad \dots(2)$$

Suppose R be a solution of (1). We will prove that $R = qp^*$. R satisfies both (1) nd (2). Let x be a string of length i in the set recognized by R. Then x belongs to the et $q(\varepsilon + p + p^2 + \dots + p^i) + Rp^{i+1}$. As p does not contain ε, Rp^{i+1} has no string of ength less than $i + 1$ and so x is not in the set Rp^{i+1}. This means that x belongs to the et $q(\varepsilon + p + p^2 + \dots + p^i)$, and hence the set represented by qp^*. Hence the set ecognized by R is a subset of the set recognized by qp^*. Now let us consider a string in the set qp^*. Then x is in the set qp^k for some k $\geq$ 0, and hence in q($\varepsilon + p + p^2 +$ .. $+ p^k$). So x is in the RHS of 2. Thus, the set recognized by qp^* is subset of the set ecognized by R. Hence R and qp^* represent the same set. This proves the uniqueness f the solution of (1).

.4.5 Algebraic Method using Arden's Theorem

The Algorithm for construction of regular expression from finite automation is iven in Algorithm 3.5.

Algorithm 3.5: Algorithm for conversion of finite automaton into regular
expression

Algorithm (Conversion of Finite Automaton into Regular expression): Let M = $(Q, \Sigma, \delta, q_0, F)$ be a finite automaton. Suppose the states of an automaton are $q_1, q_2, \dots q_n$. Let q_i represents the set of strings accepted by the system even though q_i is a final state. Let α_{ij} denotes the set of labels of the edges from q_i to q_j. When there is no such edge, $\alpha_{ij} - \phi$ The following steps are used to convert the given finite automaton into a regular expression:

Step 1: Draw the transition diagram of finite automaton if it is not given.

Step 2: We have to determine the following set of equations in $q_1, q_2, \dots q_n$:

$$q_1 = q_1 \, \alpha_{11} + q_2 \, \alpha_{21} + q_3 \, \alpha_{31} + \dots\dots q_n \, \alpha_{n_1} + \varepsilon$$

$$q_2 = q_1 \, \alpha_{12} + q_2 \, \alpha_{22} + q_3 \, \alpha_{32} + \dots\dots q_n \, \alpha_{n_2}$$

$$q_n = q_1 \alpha_{1n} + q_2 \alpha_{2n} + q_3 \alpha_{3n} + \ldots\ldots q_n \alpha_{nn}$$

By repeatedly applying substitutions and Arden's theorem, we are able to express q_i in terms of α_{ij}'s.

Step 3: We take the 'union' ('+') of all q_i corresponding to the final states.

Example 3.13: Find regular expression for the language accepted by the DFA given in Figure 3.26.

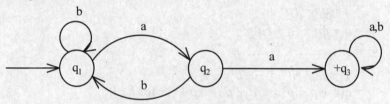

Fig. 3.26: Transition diagram of DFA

Solution:

The Equations for the states q_1, q_2 and q_3 can be written as

$$q_1 = q_1 b + q_2 b + \varepsilon \qquad \ldots (1$$
$$q_2 = q_1 a \qquad \ldots (2$$
$$q_3 = q_2 a + q_3 a + q_3 b \qquad \ldots (3$$

Substituting the value of q_2 in Equation (1), we get

$$q_1 = q_1 b + q_1 a b + \varepsilon$$
$$= \varepsilon + q_1 (b + ab)$$
$$= \varepsilon (b + ab)^* \qquad \text{[since by Arden's theorem } r = qp^* \text{ is a solution of}$$
$$= q + rp]$$
$$= (b + ab)^*$$

Now, we substitute the value of q_2 in q_3, we get

$$q_3 = q_1 aa + q_3 a + q_3 b$$
$$= q_1 aa + q_3 (a + b)$$
$$= q_1 aa (a + b)^*$$
$$q_3 = (b + ab)^* aa (a + b)^*$$

As q_3 is the final state, therefore regular expression corresponding to the given DFA is $= (b + ab)^* aa (a + b)^*$.

Example 3.14: Construct regular expression corresponding to the transition diagram of DFA given in Figure 3.27.

Solution:

Following Equations represent the above diagram are given as follows:

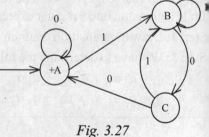

Fig. 3.27

$$A = A0 + C0 + \varepsilon \qquad\qquad \text{...(1)}$$
$$B = A1 + B1 + C1 \qquad\qquad \text{...(2)}$$
$$C = B0 \qquad\qquad \text{...(3)}$$

Now, substitute the value of $C = B0$ in Equation (2), we get:

$$B = A1 + B1 + B01$$
$$= A1 + B(1 + 01)$$
$$= A1(1 + 01)^* \qquad\qquad \text{[by Arden's theorem]}$$

Now, substitute the value of B in Equation (3), we get:

$$C = A1(1 + 01)^*0$$

Next, we substitute the value of C in Equation (1), we get:

$$A = A0 + A1(1 + 01)^*00 + \varepsilon$$
$$= \varepsilon(0 + 1(1 + 01)^*00)^* \qquad\qquad \text{[by Arden's theorem]}$$

A is a final state, therefore regular expression corresponding to the given transition diagram is $(0 + 1(1 + 01)^*00)^*$.

3.5 Distinguishing One String from Other

Every finite automaton defines a language over some alphabet. To recognize a language L, FA needs to adequately distinguish strings from each other. The number of states the FA should have, in order to recognize L, depends on the number of strings that must be distinguished from each other. However, the fact is, there are groups of strings so that, to recognize L, it is not necessary for the machine to distinguish strings within the same group. A consequence to this is to distinguish strings from one another, the machine need not to remember which string within the group it has read so far. It is enough for the machine to remember which particular group the string belongs to.

3.5.1 Definition

If L is a language over the alphabet Σ and x, y, z are strings in Σ^*, then x and y are said to be *distinguishable* by z with respect to L if either $xz \in L$ and $yz \notin L$ or $xz \notin L$ and $yz \in L$.

Similarly, x and y are said to be *distinguishable* with respect to L or *L-distinguishable* if there is some $z \in \Sigma^*$ that distinguishes them.

Equivalently, x and y are *L-distinguishable* if $L/x \neq L/y$, where $L/x = \{z \in \Sigma^* | xz \in L\}$ and $L/y = \{z \in \Sigma^* | yz \in L\}$.

To show that two strings x and y are distinguishable with respect to a language L, it is sufficient to find one string z such that one of the two string xz, yz is in L and other is not.

Example 3.15: Consider the language

$L = (0 + 1)^*10$, the set of all strings in $\{0, 1\}^*$ that end in 10.

The strings 00 and 01 are distinguishable with respect to L, because choosing z to be the string 0; we find $000 \notin L$ and $010 \in L$. The two strings 0 and 00 are indistinguishable with respect to L, because the two sets $L/0$ and $L/00$ are equal; each is just the set L itself.

3.5.2 Distinguishability Lemma

For any DFA $M = (Q, \Sigma, \delta, q_0, F)$, if x and y are two strings in Σ^* that are distinguishable with respect to $L(M)$, then

$$\delta^*(q_0, x) \neq \delta^*(q_0, y)$$

Proof:

Since strings x and y are distinguishable with respect to L, there is a string z in Σ^* such that exactly one of the two strings xz and yz is in L. Again, from the assumption that M accepts L it follows that exactly one of the states $\delta^*(q_0, xz)$ and $\delta^*(q_0, yz)$ is an accepting state, that is

$$\delta^*(q_0, xz) = \delta^*(q_0, yz) \qquad \qquad ...(1)$$

Now for any x and y in Σ^*, and any $q \in Q$,

$$\delta(q, xy) = \delta(\delta(q, x), y)$$

Hence $\delta^*(q_0, xz) = \delta^*(\delta^*(q_0, x), z)$ and $\delta^*(q_0, yz) = \delta^*(\delta^*(q_0, y), z)$ ...(2)

From (1) and (2), it follows that

$$\delta^*(q_0, x) \neq \delta^*(q_0, y).$$

3.5.3 Distinguishability Theorem

For any language $L \subseteq \Sigma^*$, there are n strings in Σ^*, such that each is distinguishable from all the others with respect to L. Then every FA recognizing L must have at least n states.

Proof:

Assume $x_1, x_2, x_3, \ldots x_n$ are n strings, each distinguishable from all the others with respect to L. Assume that DFA $M = (Q, \Sigma, \delta, q_0, F)$ recognizes L. Since any two strings from $x_1, x_2, x_3, \ldots x_n$ are distinguishable with respect to L, it follows from the Distinguishability Lemma that each of the states $\delta^*(q_0, x_1), \delta^*(q_0, x_2) \ldots \delta^*(q_0, x_n)$ is distinct. Hence, M has at least n states.

Example 3.16:. Design an FA to accept
$L = (bb + bba)^*a$.

Solution:

It is clear that a is in L, ε and b are not in L and ε and b are L-distinguishable since $\varepsilon a \in L$, $ba \notin L$). The machine, from the start state q_0, on input a will move to the final state q_1 and on input b to state q_2. The Figure 3.28 represents the partial FA.

L contains a but no string that begins with a. Introduce state q_3 to take care of invalid prefixes. We get the FA as shown in Figure 3.29.

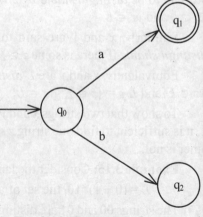

Fig. 3.28: Transition diagram of partial FA.

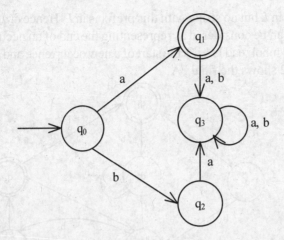

Fig. 3.29: Transition diagram of partial FA

The machine, with an input that starts with *bb* needs to move out of state q_2 since *b* and *bb* are *L*-distinguishable. Introduce state q_4 for this. Now, we get FA as shown in Figure 3.30.

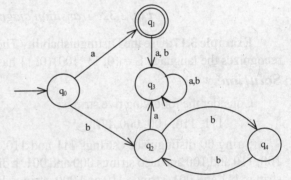

Fig. 3.30: Transition diagarm of partial FA

However, $bba \in L$. Hence create accepting state q_5 for $\delta(q_4, a)$. Now we get FA as given in Figuer 3.31.

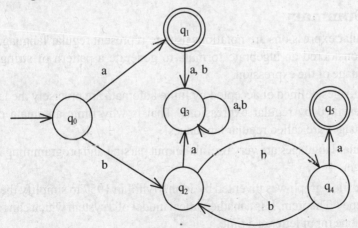

Fig. 3.31: Transition diagram of partial FA

Now *bba* is in *L* but no string with this prefix is in *L*. Hence $\delta(q_5, a)$ must be q_1. States q_4 and q_5 can be considered as representing the end of an occurrence of *bb* or *bba*; if the next symbol read is *b* it's the start of a new occurrence and FA moves back to q_2. Figure 3.32 shows the final FA.

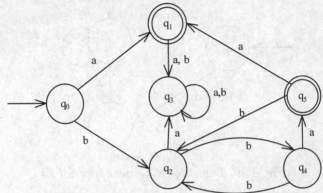

Fig. 3.32: Transition diagram of FA

Example 3.17: Use the Distinguishability Theorem to prove that any DFA that recognizes the language L = {0, 1}*{00}(0, 1} has at least 5 states.

Solution:

Consider the following five strings:

111, 110, 100, 000, 001.

String 00 distinguishes strings 111 and 110, 0 distinguishes strings 111 and 100, 110 and 100 and also strings 000 and 001. ε distinguishes strings 111 and 000, strings 111 and 001, strings 110 and 000, strings 110 and 001, strings 100 and 000 as well as strings 100 and 001 with respect to *L*. The above 5 strings are, therefore, pair wise distinguishable with respect to *L*. It then follows from the Distinguishability theorem that any DFA that recognizes *L* has at least 5 states.

3.6   Summary

1. Regular expressions are notations used to represent regular languages. It can be considered an algebraic formula to generate a pattern of strings, called language of the expression.

2. Languages defined or accepted by finite automata are precisely the languages represented by regular expressions. That is why finite automata definable languages are called regular languages.

3. Regular languages are very useful in input parsing and programming language design.

4. Transition graph was invented by John Myhill in 1957 to simplify the proof of Kleene's Theorem. It is a mathematical model of a system which can read more than one input letter at a time.

5. A regular language can be defined as a language recognized by a finite automaton.

The equivalence of regular expressions, transition graphs and finite automata is known as Kleene's theorem.

5. Arden's rule, also known as Arden's lemma, is a mathematical statement about a certain form of language equations.

7. There are wide varieties of applications of regular expressions including the description of lexical analyzers, defining XML (eXtensible Markup Language) document types and description of protein motifs (meaningful "words" in protein sequences are called motifs).

8. Many programming languages like Java, Python and Perl as well as System utilities like grep program in UNIX system support regular expression.

9. Grep (Global regular expression print) is a command-line utility which is used for searching plain-text data sets for lines matching a regular expression.

3.7 Exercises

Objective Questions

1. Any given transition graph has an equivalent:
   (a) Regular expression
   (b) DFA
   (c) NFA
   (d) All of these

2. Which of the following regular expressions is true?
   (a) $(r^*)^* = r^*$
   (b) $(r + s)^* = r^* + s^*$
   (c) $r^*s^* = r^* + s^*$
   (d) All of these

3. The language accepted by the following FA is:
   (a) $(a + b)^*b$
   (b) $(a + b)^*a$
   (c) a^*
   (d) a^*b^*a

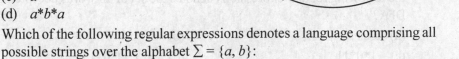

4. Which of the following regular expressions denotes a language comprising all possible strings over the alphabet $\Sigma = \{a, b\}$:
   (a) a^*b^*
   (b) $(a + b)^*$
   (c) $(ab)^*$
   (d) $(a + b^*)$

5. Which of the following regular expressions over the alphabet $\Sigma = \{a, b\}$ represents the set of words that contain an even number of a's?
   (a) $(b^*aab^*)^* + b^*$
   (b) $(b^*aab^*)^*$
   (c) $(b^*ab^*ab^*)^* + b^*$
   (d) $(b^*ab^*ab^*)^* + b^*$

6. Which of the following regular expressions over the alphabet $\Sigma = \{a, b\}$ denotes the language defined by the set $L = \{w \mid w \bmod 3 = 0\}$?
   (a) $((a + b)(a + b)(a + b))^*$
   (b) $(aaa)^* + (bbb)^*$
   (c) $((a + b)a(a + b))^*$
   (d) $((a + b)b(a + b))^*$

7. Which of the following regular expressions denotes the language defined by th
    set $L = \{a^n b^m, n \geq 4, m \leq 3\}$?
    (a) $a^4 a^*(b + bb + bbb)$ (b) $aaaaa^*(b + bb + bbb)$
    (c) $aaaaa^*(\varepsilon + b + bb + bbb)$ (d) None of these

8. A language is denoted by a regular expression $L = x^*(x + yx)$. Which of th
    following is not a legal string in L?
    (a) yx (b) x
    (c) xyx (d) $xyxyx$

9. Regular expression $(a + b)$ denotes the set:
    (a) $\{a, b\}$ (b) $\{a\}$
    (c) $\{\varepsilon, a, b\}$ (d) $\{ab\}$

10. Regular expression $(a + b)(a + b)$ denotes the set:
    (a) $\{a, b, ab, aa\}$ (b) $\{a, b, ba, bb\}$
    (c) $\{aa, ab, ba, bb\}$ (d) $\{a, b\}$

11. Which of the following regular expressions denotes zero or more instances o
    an a or b ?
    (a) $a + b$ (b) $(ab)^*$
    (c) $(a + b)^*$ (d) $a^*|b$

12. Consider the following regular expression :
    $R = (ab + abb)^* bbab$. Which of the following strings is NOT in the set denote
    by R?
    (a) $abbab$ (b) $ababbabbbab$
    (c) $ababab$ (d) $abbabbbab$

13. In following Figure, a DFA has start state q_0 and accepting state q_3. Which o
    the following regular expressions denotes the set of all words accepted by th
    DFA?
    (a) 001   (b) 10^*1^*0
    (c) 1^*0^*11 (d) $(0 + 1)^*011$

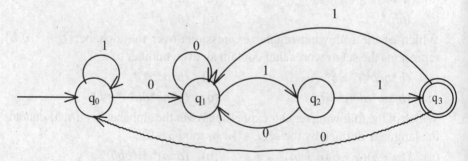

14. Let a and b be regular expressions, then, $(a^* + b^*)^*$ is equivalent to:

(a) $a \cap b$ (b) $(a \cup b)*$

(c) $(a \cap b)*$ (d) $a \cup b$

15. If L_1 and L_2 be languages over alphabet $\Sigma = \{a, b\}$ represented by regular expression $(a + b*)*$ and $(a + b)*$, respectively, then:

(a) $L_1 \subseteq L_2$ (b) $L_2 \subseteq L_1$

(c) $L_1 \cap L_2 = \phi$ (d) $L_1 = L_2$

16. Consider regular expression $(0 + 1)(0 + 1) \dots n$ times. Minimum state FA that recognizes the language represented by this regular expression contains:

(a) $n + 1$ states   (b) n states

(c) $n + 2$ states   (d) None of these

17. If L_1 and L_2 are languages over $\Sigma = \{a, b\}$ represented by regular expression $(ab + b)*$ and $((ab)*b*)*$, respectively, then:

(a) $L_1 \subseteq L_2$ (b) $L_2 \subseteq L_1$

(c) L_1 and L_2 are incomparable   (d) $L_1 = L_2$

18. The string 1101 does not belong to the set represented by:

(a) $110*(0 + 1)$ (b) $1(0 + 1)*101$

(c) $(10)*(01)*(00 + 11)*$ (d) $((11)* + 01)*$

19. Which of the following regular expressions over $\{0, 1\}$ denotes the set of all strings not containing 100 as a substring?

(a) $0*(1 + 0)*$ (b) $0*1010*$

(c) $0*1*01$ (d) $0*(10 + 1)*$

20. Which of the following pairs of regular expressions is equivalent?

(a) $b(ab)*$ and $(ba)*b$ (b) $x(xx)*$ and $(xx)*x$

(c) $a +$ and $a*a^+$ (d) All of these

21. Which one is used in regular expressions?

(a) Parenthesis   (b) Operator '+'

(c) Operator '.'   (d) All of these

22. Which one is not a notation of regular expressions?

(a) Operator '.'

(b) Strings of symbols from alphabet Σ

(c) Operator '*'

(d) None of these

23. Which one is not a notation of regular expressions?

(a) Union operator '$\cup$'   (b) Intersection operator '$\cap$'

(c) Star-closure '*'   (d) Operator '.'

24. Which one is not a primitive regular expression?

(a) ϕ (b) ε

(c) $a \in \Sigma$ (d) None of these

25. Which of the following regular expressions denotes the set of all strings with an even number of a's followed by an odd number of b's:

(a) $(aa)+(bb)*b$ (b) $2n(0)(2m+1)b \ n, m \geq 0$

(c) $(aa)*(bb)*b$ (d) None of these

26. Which one is not true for the transition graph?

(a) It is mathematically represented by the 5-tuple

(b) It has finite set of states

(c) It may have more than one start state

(d) Transition function shows how to go from one state to another on reading input symbol

27. Which of the following regular expressions denotes the set of all strings that has no pair of consecutive zeroes?

(a) $(1*011*)*$ (b) $(1*011*)*0$

(c) $(1*011*)*(0+\varepsilon)$ (d) None of these

28. Which one is not true for transition graph?

(a) It has only one start state which is an element of set of states

(b) It has a set of final states which is a subset of set of states

(c) Transition function show how to go from one state to another on reading substrings of some one alphabet Σ

(d) None of these

29. The basic purpose of invention of Transition graph is:

(a) To simplify the proof of Kleene's theorem

(b) To simplify the regular expression

(c) To convert regular expression to DFA

(d) All of these

30. Any language that can be defined by (i) Regular expression or (ii) Finite automaton or (iii) Transition graph

(a) Can be defined by only (i) and (ii)

(b) Can be defined by only (i) and (iii)

(c) Can be defined by only (ii) and (iii)

(d) Can be defined by (i), (ii) and (iii)

31. Any language that can be defined by regular expression or finite automaton or transition graph can be defined by all the three methods. This statement is known as:

(a) Arden's thorem   (b) Church's theorem

(c) Kleene's theorem   (d) Turing's thesis

32. The regular expression $a^*(a + b)^*$ is equivalent to:
    (a) $a^* + b^*$ (b) $(ab)^*$
    (c) a^*b^* (d) None of these

33. $(a + a^*)^*$ is equivalent to
    (a) $a(a^*)^*$ (b) a^*
    (c) aa^* (d) None of these

34. $(a^*b^*)^*$ is same as:
    (a) $(a + b)^*$ (b) $(ab)^*$
    (c) $(ba)^*$ (d) None of these

35. $\{a^{2n} \mid n \geq 1\}$ is represented by the regular expression:
    (a) $(aa)^*$ (b) a^*a^*
    (c) a^* (d) $(aa)+$

Answers to Objective Questions

01.	(d)	02.	(a)	03.	(b)	04.	(b)	05.	(d)	06.	(a)
07.	(c)	08.	(d)	09.	(a)	10.	(c)	11.	(c)	12.	(c)
13.	(d)	14.	(a)	15.	(d)	16.	(a)	17.	(d)	18.	(c)
19.	(c),(d)	20.	(c)	21.	(d)	22.	(d)	23.	(b)	24.	(d)
25.	(c)	26.	(d)	27.	(c)	28.	(a)	29.	(a)	30.	(d)
31.	(c)	32.	(c)	33.	(b)	34.	(a)	35.	(d)		

Review Questions

1. What is the reason of calling the language defined by Finite Automata a regular language?

2. What is the regular expression? Give recursive definition of the regular expression.

3. Discuss the language associated with regular expressions.

4. Define and discuss Transition graph with suitable example.

5. Prove that if r is a regular expression then there exist an NFA with ε-transition that accepts $L(r)$.

6. Prove that if L is accepted by a DFA, then L is represented by a regular expression.

7. What is Arden's theorem? Give an algorithm to convert the DFA into a regular expression.

8. A student walks into a class room and sees on the black-board a diagram of a transition graph with two states that accepts only the word ε. The student reverses the direction of exactly one edge learning all other edges and all labels and all + 's and −'s the same. But now the new transition graph accepts the language a^*. What was the original machine?

A9. Consider the following statements and state whether they are True or False.

Justify your answer.

    (a) $a* + b* \neq (a + b)*$ (b) $(ab)* = a*b*$

10. Is $(ab)*a = a(ba)*$? Prove or disprove.

11. Finite automaton M_1 and M_2 accept the languages generated by regular expressions r_1 and r_2, respectively. Construct automata for

    (i) $r_1 + r_2$ (ii) $r_1 r_2$ and   (iii) r_1*

^12. Construct a regular expression defining each of the following languages over the alphabet $\Sigma = \{a, b\}$:

    (i)   All words with double a within.

    (ii)   All words that have different first and last letters.

    (iii)   All words that have an odd number of a's.

    (iv)   All words that end with letter a.

    (v)   All words that do not have the substring ab.

    (vi)   All words with at least one a and at least one b.

    (vii) All words with at least two a's.

    (viii)All words with exactly two a's.

    (ix)   All words ending in aa.

    (x)   All words that begin with a and end with b.

    (xi)   All words that have the letter b in them.

    (xii) All words that have at least two letters that begin and end with a's that have nothing but b's inside.

    (xiii)All words in which all a's (if any) come before all the b's (if any).

    (xiv)All words that have a double letter in them.

    (xv) $L = \{w:|w| \text{ is even}\}$.

13. Describe in English, as briefly as possible, the language defined by each of these regular expressions:

    (a) $(b + ba)(b + a)*(ab + b)$

    (b) $(((a*b*)*ab) + ((a*b*)*ba))(b + a)*$

    ^(c) $(a + b)*b$

    ^(d) $((a + b)(a + b)a(a + b)*)$

    ^(e) $((a + b)(a + b))*$

    ^(f) $(aa + ab + ba + bb)*$

    (g) $(aa)*(bb)*b$

14. Simplify each of the following regular expressions:

    (a) $(a + b)*(a + \varepsilon)b*$

    (b) $(\phi* + b)b*$

    (c) $(ab)*a* \cup b$

    (d) $((ab)*)*$

(e) $((ab)^+)^*$

(f) $((a+b)(b+a))^*a((a+b)a)^* + a((b+a)b)^*$

15. Consider the Deterministic Finite Automata M_1 and M_2 as pictured in the Figure 3.33, which recognize the languages L_1 and L_2, respectively.

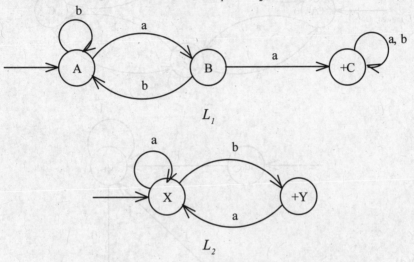

$$L_1$$

$$L_2$$

Fig. 3.33: Finite Automata M_1 and M_2

Draw Deterministic Finite Automaton recognizing the following languages:

a. $L_1 \cup L_2$ b. $L_1 L_2$

c. L_1^* d. $L_1 - L_2$

e. $L_1 \cup L_2$

16. Find regular expressions for the languages accepted by the following automata as given in Figure 3.34 (a-g).

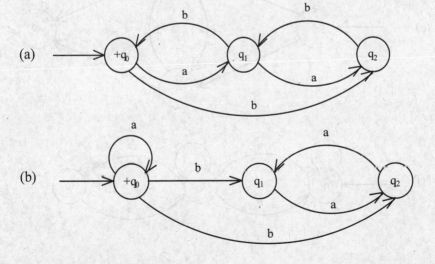

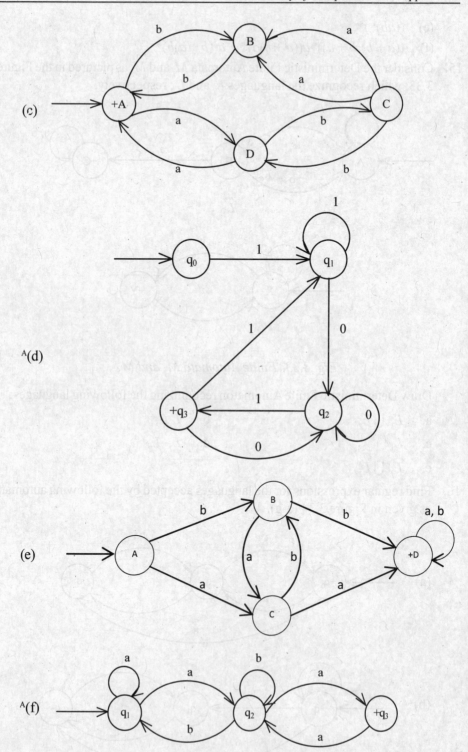

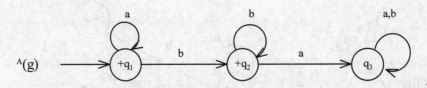

Fig. 3.34: Finite Automata

17. Give an NFA that accepts the language $L((a + b)*b(a + bb)*)$.
18. Convert the following regular expressions to NFA:
    (a) $a(abb)* + b$
    (b) $a^+ + (ab)^+$
    (c) $(a + b^+)a^+ b^+$
    (d) $(ab + a)*$
    (e) $(a + b)*aba$

^{A}19. Express the following sets by regular expressions:
    (a) $\{a, b, c\}$
    (b) $\{a^{2n + 1}|n>0\}$
    (c) $\{w \in \{a, b\}* \,|w$ has only one $a\}$
    (d) The set of all strings over $\{0, 1\}$ which has at most two zeros.
    (e) $\{a^2, a^5, a^8, \ldots\}$
    (f) $\{a^n| n$ is divisible by 2 or 3 or $n = 5\}$
    (g) The set of all strings over $\{a, b\}$ beginning and ending with a.
    (h) $\{w|w$ has no more than one b and $w \in \{a, b\}*\}$
    (i) $\{w \,|$ no two consecutive letters are same in w and $w \in \{a, b\}*\}$
20. Find the regular expressions corresponding to the following transition graphs as shown in Figure 3.35 (i-iv).

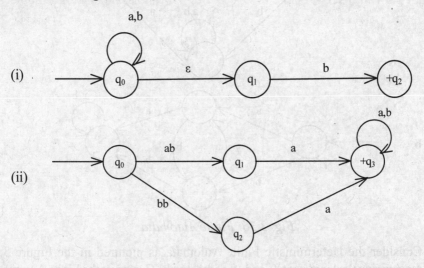

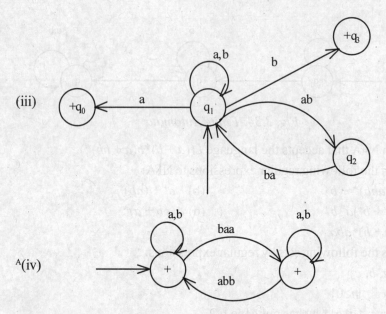

Fig. 3.35: Transition Graphs

21. Consider the Deterministic Finite Automata shown in the Figure 3.36 recognizing the language $L(r)$. Construct the Finite Automaton for accepting the language defined by the regular expression $r*$.

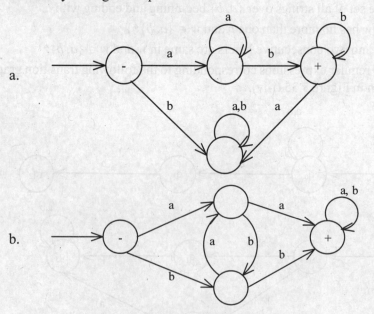

Fig. 3.36: Finite Automata

22. Consider the Deterministic Finite Automata as pictured in the Figure 3.37 recognizing the languages L_1 and L_2, respectively. Construct the Finite Automaton for accepting the language defined by $L_1 L_2$.

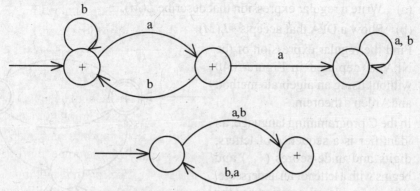

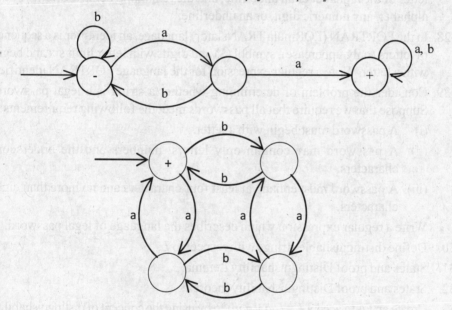

Fig. 3.37: Finite Automata

23. Consider the Deterministic Finite Automata as pictured in the Figure 3.38 recognizing the languages L_1 and L_2, respectively. Construct the Finite Automaton for accepting the language defined by L_1L_2 and $L_1 + L_2$.

Fig. 3.38: Deterministic Finite Automata

24. Consider the following DFA M as given in Figure 3.39.

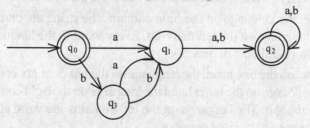

Fig. 3.39: DFA M

(a)   Write a regular expression that describe $L(M)$.

(b)   Show a DFA that accepts $\sim L(M)$.

^25. Find the regular expression of the NFA as depicted in Figure 3.40 without using an algebraic method and Arden's theorem.

^26. In the C programming language, an identifier is a sequence of letters, digits and underscores (_) and begins with a letter or an underscore. Write a regular expression for the C language identifier.

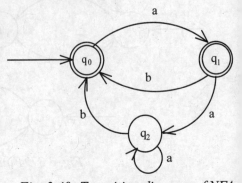

Fig. 3.40: Transition diagram of NFA

27.   In the C++ programming language, an identifier is a combination of alphanumeric characters, the first being a letter of the alphabet or an underline, and the remaining being any letter of the alphabet, any numeric digit, or an underline.

^28. In the FORTRAN (FORmula TRANslator) language, an identifier is a sequence of letters (only uppercase), symbol ($) and digits with letter limit six and begin with a letter. Write a regular expression for the language FORTRAN identifier.

^29. Consider the problem of determining whether a string is a legal password. Suppose that we require that all passwords meet the following requirements:

(i)   A password must begin with a letter.

(ii) A password may contain only letters, numbers and the underscore characters.

(iii) A password must contain at least four characters and no more than eight characters.

Write a regular expression which describes the language of legal password.

30.   Define distinguishable strings with respect to L.

31.   States and proof Distinguishability Lemma.

32.   States and proof Distinguishability theorem.

33.   Create an FA to accept $L = (aa + aab)^*b$ by using the concept of distinguishability of strings.

Answers/Hints for Selected Review Questions

9.   (a)   True, the language on the right contains the string ab, on the other hand the language on the left does not. Every word in the language on the left contains only a's or only b's.

      (b)   False, on the one hand, the language on the left does not contain the word *aaabbbbbb*, on the other hand the language on the right contains the word *aaabbbbbb*. The language on the left contains the word abab, while the language on the right does not.

12. (i) $(a+b)^* aa (a+b)^*$

   (ii) $a(a+b)^*b + b(a+b)^*a$

   (iii) $b^*a(b^*ab^*ab^*)^*$ or $b^*(ab^*ab^*)ab^*$ or $b^*ab^*(ab^*ab^*)^*$

   (iv) $(a+b)^*a$

   (v) $b^*(ba)^*a^*$

   (vi) $(a+b)^*a(a+b)^*b(a+b)^* + (a+b)^*b(a+b)^*a(a+b)^*$

   (vii) $(a+b)^*a(a+b)^*a(a+b)^*$

  (viii) $b^*ab^*ab^*$

   (ix) $(a+b)^*aa$

   (x) $a(a+b)^*b$

   (xi) $(a+b)^*b(a+b)^*$

  (xii) ab^*a

  (xiii) a^*b^*

  (xiv) $(a+b)^* (aa+bb)(a+b)^*$

  (xv) $((a+b)(a+b))^*$ or $(aa+ab+ba+bb)^*$

3. (c) Set of all strings over the alphabet $\Sigma = \{a, b\}$ that end in b.

  (d) Set of all strings of a's and b's such that there exists a third character, and it is an a.

  (e) Set of all strings of a's and b's having even length.

  (f) Set of all strings of a's and b's having even length.

6. (d) We get the following Equations:

$$q_0 = \varepsilon \qquad \qquad \dots(1)$$
$$q_1 = q_0 1 + q_1 1 + q_3 1 \qquad \dots(2)$$
$$q_2 = q_1 0 + q_2 0 + q_3 0 \qquad \dots(3)$$
$$q_3 = q_2 1 \qquad \qquad \dots(4)$$

Substituting the value of q_3 from (4) in Equation (3), we get

$$q_2 = q_1 0 + q_2 0 + q_2 10$$
$$= q_1 0 + q_2 (0 + 10)$$
$$= q_1 0(0 + 10)^* \qquad \dots\dots(5) \quad \text{[by Arden's theorem]}$$

Now substituting the above value of q_2 in Equation (4), we get

$$q_3 = q_1 0(0 + 10)^* 1 \qquad \dots(6)$$

After substituting the values of q_0 and q_3 from (1) and (6) in Equation (2) we get

$$q_1 = 1 + q_1 1 + q_1 0(0 + 10)^* 11$$
$$= 1 + q_1 (1 + 0(0 + 10)^* 11)$$
$$= 1(1 + 0(0 + 10)^* 11)^* \qquad \text{[by Arden's theorem]}$$

After substituting the value of q_1 in (5), we get

$$q_2 = 1(1 + 0(0 + 10)^* 11)^* 0(0 + 10)^*$$

Now we substitute the value of q_2 in (4), we get

$$q_3 = 1(1 + 0(0 + 10)*11)*0(0 + 10)*1$$

As q_3 is the only final state, the regular expression corresponding to a given diagram is $1(1 + 0(0 + 10)*11)*0(0 + 10)*1$.

(f)   We get the following Equations:

$$q_1 = q_1a + q_2b + \varepsilon \qquad\qquad ...(1)$$
$$q_2 = q_1a + q_2b + q_3a \qquad\qquad ...(2)$$
$$q_3 = q_2a \qquad\qquad ...(3)$$

Substitute the value of q_3 from Equation (3) into Equation (2):

$$q_2 = q_1a + q_2b + q_2aa$$
$$= q_1a + q_2(b + aa)$$
$$= q_1a(b + aa)* \qquad\qquad ....(4) \quad \text{[by Arden's theorem]}$$

Now substituting the value of q_2 in Equation (1), we get

$$q_1 = q_1a + q_1a(b + aa)*b + \varepsilon$$
$$= q_1(a + a(b + aa)*b) + \varepsilon$$
$$= \varepsilon(a + a(b + aa)*b)* \qquad \text{[by Arden's theorem]}$$

Now substituting this value of q_1 in Equation (4) ,we get

$$q_2 = (a + a(b + aa)*b)*a(b + aa)*$$

Now substituting this value of q_2 in Equation (3), we get

$$q_3 = (a + a(b + aa)*b)*a(b + aa)*a$$

Since q_3 is a final state, therefore, the required regular expression is given by

$$(a + a(b + aa)*b)*a(b + aa)*a$$

(g)   We get the following Equations:

$$q_1 = q_10 + \varepsilon \qquad\qquad ...(1$$
$$q_2 = q_11 + q_21 \qquad\qquad ...(2$$
$$q_3 = q_20 + q_3(0 + 1) \qquad\qquad ...(3$$

Equation (1) can be written as

$$q_1 = \varepsilon0* = 0* \qquad \text{[by Arden's theorem]}$$

Now substituting $q_1 = 0*$ in Equation (2), we get

$$q_2 = 0*1 + q_21$$
$$= (0*1)1* \qquad \text{[by Arden's theorem]}$$

Since q_1 and q_2 are final states, we need not solve for q_3. Therefore, the required regular expression corresponding the given diagram is:

$$q_1 + q_2 = 0* + 0*(11*)$$
$$= 0*(\varepsilon + 11*)$$
$$= 0*1* \qquad [\text{ since } \varepsilon + pp* = p*]$$

19. (a) $\{a + b + c\}$

  (b) $a(aa)^*$

  (c) b^*ab^*

  (d) According to the question, string over $\{0, 1\}$ contains no 0's, or one 0's or two 0's, i.e., $1^* + 1^*01^* + 1^*001^*$

  (e) $aa(aaa)^*$

  (f) $(aa)^* + (aaa)^* + (aaaaa)^*$

  (g) $a(a + b)^*a$

  (h) $a^*(b + \varepsilon)a^*$

  (i) $(b + \varepsilon)(ab)^*(a + \varepsilon)$ or $(a + \varepsilon)(ab)^*(b + \varepsilon)$

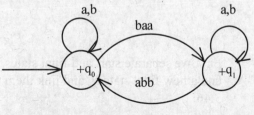

Fig. 3.41

20. (iv) Let the transition graph be M (see Figure 3.41):

First, we create a new start state q_2 and a new accepting state q_3 and link them to M (see Figure 3.42):

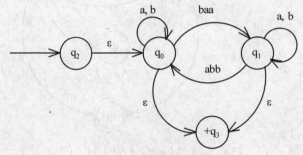

Fig. 3.42

Now, we remove state q_1, we get the TG (see Figure 3.43):

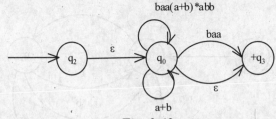

Fig. 3.43

Remove state q_0. Finally, we get the TG (see Figure 3.44):

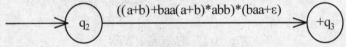

Fig. 3.44

Regular expression of the given transition graph is

$((a + b) + baa(a + b)^*abb)^*(baa + \varepsilon)$

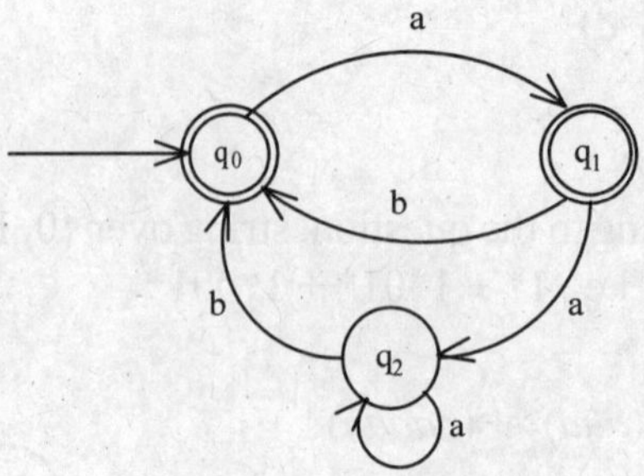

a

q_0 q_1

b

b   a

q_2

a

Fig. 3.45: NFA M

25. Let the NFA be M (see Figure 3.45):

First we separate start and final states. For this we create a new start state q_3 and a new final state q_4 and link them to M. We get NFA as shown in Figure 3.46.

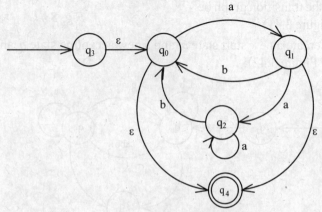

Fig. 3.46: Modified NFA M

Now, we remove state q_2. We get NFA as shown in Figure 3.47

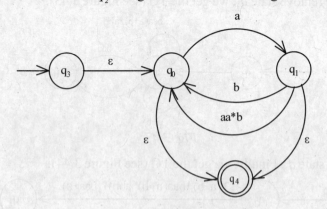

Fig. 3.47: Modified NFA M

Next, we remove state q_1. We get NFA as shown in Figure 3.48.

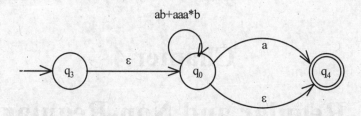

Fig. 3.48: Modified NFA M

Now, we remove state q_0. We get NFA as shown in Figure 3.49.

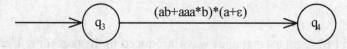

Fig. 3.49: Modified NFA M

The regular expression corresponding to the given non-deterministic finite automaton *M* is

$(ab + aaa*b)*(a + \varepsilon)$.

26. The following regular expression represents an identifier of the C language:

    (letter + _)(letter + digit + _)*

    where letter stands for $a + b + ... + z + A + B + ... + Z$ and digit stands for $0 + 1 + 2 + ... + 9$.

28. The following regular expression represents an identifier of the FORTRAN language:

    letter(letter + digit + ε)^5

    where letter stands for $A + B + ... + Z + \$$ and digit stands for $0 + 1 + 2 + ... + 9$.

29. The following regular expression represents an identifier of the FORTRAN language:

    letter(letter + digit + _) {3, 7}

    where letter stands for $a + b + ... + z + A + B + ... + Z$ and digit stands for $0 + 1 + 2 + ... + 9$ and $\alpha\{m, n\}$ means that the pattern α must occur at least *m* times and no more than *n* times.

Programming Problems

1. Write a program to simulate the transition graph.

2. Write a program to construct the finite automaton FA for the languages $L_1 \cup L_2$, $L_1 L_2$, L_1* and L_2*. L_1 and L_2 are the languages of the Finite Automata FA_1 and FA_2.

Chapter 4

Regular and Non-Regular Languages

The concept of regular languages was introduced in the preceding Chapters. The present Chapter explores the closure of the set of regular languages under various operations, Pigeonhole Principle and Pumping Lemma that provide the technique for proving non-regularity of some languages, decidability of Finite Automata and Regular languages and finally the relationship between regular languages and computers. The illustrative examples provide adequate emphasis on the clear understanding of the concepts.

Objectives

The objective of this Chapter is to identify the closure properties of regular languages and the methods for deciding whether a language is regular. After learning the contents of this Chapter, you will be able to:

1. Explain closure properties of regular languages,
2. Apply pumping lemma theorem for proving non regularity of some languages are regular and
3. Describe the decision properties of finite automata and regular languages.

4.1 Regular Languages

As explained earlier, a language that can be defined by a regular expression is called a regular language. By Kleene's theorem, a language is regular if and only if it can be accepted by a finite automaton. In the next section, we will discuss the closure properties of regular languages.

4.1.1 Closure Properties of Regular Languages

A closure property of a class of languages says that given languages in the class, the operation produces another language in the same class. Closure properties of regular languages are given as follows:

1. The union, concatenation and Kleene's closure of regular languages are regular language.

2. The intersection of regular languages is a regular language.

3. The transpose (reversal) of a regular language is regular.

4. The difference of two regular languages is a regular language.

5. A homomorphism of regular language is regular.

6. The inverse homomorphism of regular language is a regular language.

7. The complement of regular language is a regular language.

8. The quotient of regular languages is a regular.

Theorem 4.1: Class of regular languages is closed under union, concatenation, and Kleene closure. That is, If L_1 and L_2 are two regular languages, then $L_1 + L_2$, $L_1 L_2$ and L_1^* are also regular languages.

Proof: As we know $L_1 + L_2$ is the language of all words either in L_1 or L_2. $L_1 L_2$ is the language of all words formed by concatenating a word from L_1 with a word from L_2. L_1^* means words that are the concatenation of arbitrarily many factors from L_1.

If L_1 and L_2 are regular languages, then there exists regular expressions r_1 and r_2 that define these languages. Then $r_1 + r_2$ is a regular expression that defines the language $L_1 + L_2$. Since language defined by regular expression is regular, $L_1 + L_2$ is a regular language. Similarly, the language $L_1 L_2$ can be defined by the regular expression $r_1 r_2$. The language L_1^* can be defined by the regular expression $(r_1)^*$. Therefore, $L_1 L_2$ and L_1^* are definable by regular expressions, so $L_1 L_2$ and L_1^* are also regular languages.

Theorem 4.2: The class of regular languages is closed under complement. That is, if L is a regular language over the alphabet Σ, then $L' = \Sigma^* - L$ is also a regular language.

Proof: By Kleene's theorem, there exist some DFA M that accepts L. Define a DFA M' such that final states in M are non-final states in M' and non-final states in M are final states in M'. Clearly, the input string, which ends in a non-final state in M, will end in a final state in M' and vice-versa. M', therefore, accepts precisely those strings in Σ^* that are not accepted by M, i.e., L'. Because there is a DFA for it, we conclude L' is regular.

Theorem 4.3: The set of regular languages is closed under intersection. That is, if L_1 and L_2 are regular languages, then so is $L_1 \cap L_2$.

Proof: By De Morgan's law

$$L_1 \cap L_2 = (L_1' + L_2')'.$$

We already know that regular languages are closed under complement and union. Hence L_1' and L_2' and their union $L_1' + L_2'$ are regular languages. Again since $L_1' + L_2'$ is regular, $(L_1' + L_2')'$ is also regular. Consequently $L_1 \cap L_2$ is regular.

Theorem 4.4: The set of regular languages is closed under difference. In other words, if L_1 and L_2 are regular languages, then so is $L_1 - L_2$.

Proof: We know that $L_1 - L_2 = \{x | x \in L_1 \text{ and } x \notin L_2\} = L_1 \cap L_2'$. Since regular languages are closed under complement and intersection, $L_1 \cap L_2'$ is regular. In other words $L_1 - L_2$ is regular.

Theorem 4.5: The set of regular languages is closed under (reversal). In other words, if L is a regular language, then the language L^R, consisting of reversal of all strings in L, is also a regular language.

Proof: The reversal of a string $w = a_1 a_2 \ldots a_n \in L$ is the string $w^R = a_n a_{n-1} \ldots a_1 \in L^R$. Let L be recognized by a FA $M = (Q, \Sigma, \delta, q_0, F)$. We construct a FA M' by reversing the transition arrows in M, making q_0, the start state of M, the sole final state of M' and creating a new state p_0 which will be the start state with transitions to all final states in M. That is

$$M' = (Q \cup p_0, \Sigma, \delta', p_0, q_0)$$

such that for every $q \in Q$ and $a \in \Sigma$, $\delta'(q, a) = \{r \in Q : \delta(r, a) = q\}$ and $\delta'(p_0, \epsilon) F$.

Now, assume $q_0 q_1 \ldots q_n$ are the states in Q, that are followed on input w in M. Clearly, $p_0 q_n q_{n-1} \ldots q_1 q_0$ is a path on input w^R in M'. Since this path ends in the final state q_0, M' accepts w^R. Again, if $w \notin L$ then $w^R \notin L^R$. If there is an accepting path in M' on input w^R, reversing it we will get an accepting path for w in M. Since M does not accept w, there can be no accepting path in M' on input w^R. Therefore, M' is the FA that accepts L^R. Because there is a FA for it, we conclude L^R is regular.

Substitutions and Homomorphism

A *substitution* is a mapping f that maps symbols in alphabet Σ to languages, may be in a different alphabet Δ. That is for each $a \in \Sigma$, $f(a) = L_a$, $L_a \subset \Delta^*$.

The mapping f is extended to strings as follows:

(1) $f(\epsilon) = \epsilon$ (2) $f(xa) = f(x)f(a)$

where string $x \in L$

The mapping of f is extended to languages by defining

$$f(L) = \bigcup_{x \text{ in } L} f(x)$$

A *homomorphism* is a string substitution such that each letter is replaced by a string. That is, if Σ and Δ are alphabets then a function

$$h: \Sigma \to \Delta^*$$

is called a *homomorphism*.

The mapping h is extended to strings as follows: if $x = a_1 a_2 \dots a_n$ then $h(x) = h(a_1)h(a_2) \dots h(a_n)$.

Given a language L on Σ, $h(L) = \{h(w) : w \in L\}$ is called the *homomorphic image* of L. Inverse *homomorphic image* of a string w is defined as

$$h^{-1}(w) = \{x | h(x) = w\}$$

and the *inverse homomorphism image* of the language L is defined as

$$h^{-1}(L) = \{x | h(x) \in L\}$$

Example 4.1 : Let $f(0) = a$ and $f(1) = b^*$. That is, $f(0)$ is the language $\{a\}$ and $f(1)$ is the language of all strings of b's. Then $f(010) = f(0)f(1)f(0) = ab^*a$ is a language. If L is the language $0^*(0 + 1)1^*$, then $f(L) = f(0^*(0 + 1)1^*) = f(0^*)f(0 + 1)f(1^*) = a^*(a + b^*)(b^*)^* = a^*(a + b^*)b^*$.

Exercise 4.2: Let $\Sigma = \{a, b\}$, $\Delta = \{a, b, c\}$, and h is a homomorphism on Σ such that $h(a) = b$, $h(b) = ac$. If $L = \{aba, bba\}$ then $h(aba) = h(a)h(b)h(a) = bacb$ and $h(bba) = h(b)h(b)h(a) = acacb$. Hence the homomorphic image of language L is

$$h(L) = \{babc, acacb\}$$

Example 4.3 : Let $\Sigma = \{0, 1\}$ and $\Delta = \{a, b\}$ and h is a homomorphism on Σ such that $h(0) = aa$ and $h(1) = aba$ then $h(010) = h(0)h(1)h(0) = aaabaaa$. If L is the regular language denoted by

$$r = (01)^*$$

then $h(L) = (aaaba)^*$.

Example 4.4: Let $\Sigma = \{0, 1\}$ and $\Delta = ab$ and define h by

$$h(0) = aa$$
$$h(1) = aba$$

If L is the regular language defined by $(ab + ba)^*a$ i.e. $L = (ab + ba)^*a$. Find $h^{-1}(L)$.

Solution:

As we know that $h^{-1}(L) = \{x | h(x) \text{ is in } L\}$

Since both $h(0)$ and $h(1)$ begin with character a, each string $h(x)$ in L must begin with a. Thus if $h^{-1}(w)$ is non-empty and w is in L then w begins with a. Now either $w = a$, in which case $h^{-1}(w)$ surely employ or w is abw' for some w' in $(ab + ba)^*a$. We conclude that every word in $h^{-1}(w)$ begins with a 1, since $h(1) = aba$, w' must begin with a. If $w' = a$, we have $w = aba$ and $h^{-1}(w) = \{1\}$. However if $w' \neq a$, then $w' = abw''$ and hence $w = ababw''$. But no string x in $(0+1)^*$ has $h(x)$ beginning $abab$. Consequently we conclude that $h^{-1}(w)$ is empty in this case. Thus, the only string in L which has an inverse image h is aba, and therefore, $h^{-1}(L) = \{1\}$.

Theorem 4.6: The set of regular languages is closed under substitution. In other words, if the letters of a regular language are substituted by other regular languages, the result is still regular.

Proof: Let Σ and Δ be two alphabets. Let $R \subseteq \Sigma^*$ be a regular set and for each symbol a in Σ let $R_a \subseteq \Delta^*$ be a particular regular set. Let $f: \Sigma \to \Delta^*$ be the substitution defined by $f(a) = R_a$. Now replace each occurrence of the symbol a in the regular expression for R by the regular expression for R_a. To prove that the resulting regular expression describes $f(R)$, observe that the substitution of a union, product, or closure is the union, product, or closure of the substitution. To complete the proof we need induction on the number of operators in the regular expression.

Theorem 4.7: The set of regular languages is closed under homomorphism and inverse homomorphism. In other words, if L is a regular language and h is a homomorphism, then the homomorphic image $h(L)$ and inverse homomorphic image $h^{-1}(L)$ are also regular.

Proof: If L is regular, it can be represented using a regular expression R. Now exchange each symbol a in R by $h(a)$. The resulting regular expression describes $h(L)$. Since $h(L)$ is described with a regular expression, it is a regular language.

Let $M = (Q, \Sigma, \delta, q_0, F)$ be a DFA for L. We construct a DFA $M' = (Q, \Sigma, \delta', q_0, F)$ that accepts $h^{-1}(L)$. The transition functions of M' are such that for any input symbol a in Σ, M' will simulate $h(a)$ in M. Formally, $\delta'(q, a) = \delta(q, h(a))$ for q in Q. It can be easily proved by induction on $|x|$ for string x that $\delta'(q_0, x) = \delta(q_0, h(x))$ as follows:

Basis: $x = \varepsilon$

$$\delta'(q_0, \varepsilon) = q_0 \text{ and } \delta(q_0, h(\varepsilon)) = \delta(q_0, \varepsilon) = q_0$$

Induction: Let $x = x_1 a$

$$\delta'(q_0, x) = \delta'(\delta'(q_0, x_1)a)$$
$$= \delta'(\delta(q_0, h(x_1)a)$$
$$= \delta(\delta(q_0, h(x_1)), h(a))$$
$$= \delta(q_0, h(x_1)h(a))$$
$$= \delta(q_0, h(x_1 a))$$
$$= \delta(q_0, h(x))$$

Therefore, M' accepts x if and only if M accepts $h(x)$. That is $L(M') = h^{-1}(L)$. Because there is a FA for it, we conclude $h^{-1}(L)$ is regular.

4.2   Non-Regular Languages

A language that cannot be described by a regular expression is called a non-regular language. By Kleene's theorem, a non-regular language can also not be accepted by the FA or TG. Clearly, the language is either regular or non-regular but not both. In the following sections, we will discuss Pigeonhole principle and Pumping Lemma that can be used to prove that specific languages are non-regular.

4.2.1 Pigeonhole Principle

The term "pigeonhole principle" is used by mathematicians to refer to the following simple observation. If we put n pigeons (objects) into m pigeonholes (boxes) and if $n > m$, then at least one hole will have more than one pigeon.

Example 4.5: Show that the $L = \{a^n b^n : n \geq 0\}$ is not a regular language.

Solution:

We prove this by contradiction using pigeon hole principle. Assume L is regular. Then there is an FA $M = (Q, \Sigma, \delta', q_0, F)$ recognizing L. Considering all strings in a^* as pigeons and states in Q as holes. Assume pigeon a^n is put into hole $\delta(q_0, a^n)$ that is, the hole corresponding to the state that M reaches on input a^n. Now Q has only a finite number of states whereas there are infinitely many strings in a^*. Since number of holes is less than the number of pigeons, some holes must more than one pigeon in it. Let a^n and a^m, $n < m$, be in the same hole. That is $\delta(q_0, a^n) = \delta(q_0, a^m) = q$ with $n \neq m$.

But since M accepts $a^n b^n$, we must have $\delta(q, b^n) = q_f \in F$. Then

$$\delta(q, a^m b^n) = \delta(\delta(q_0, a^m), b^n)$$
$$= \delta(q, b^n)$$
$$= q_f$$

That is M accepts $a^m b^n$, $n \neq m$ which is not true. We conclude R is not regular.

4.2.2 Pumping Lemma for Regular Languages

Pumping Lemma was introduced by Yehoshua Bar-Hillel, Micha A. Perles, and Eliahu Shamin in 1961. It is a powerful tool that enables us to prove that a particular language is not in a given language class. However, it cannot be used to determine if a language is in a given class, since satisfying the pumping lemma is a necessary, but not sufficient condition for class membership.

The idea behind Pumping Lemma for regular languages is that a word can be "pumped" such that any string can be inserted into the middle of the word and the resulting word will be still in the language. This property is true of all regular languages. To prove that a language is not regular, we show that the Pumping Lemma does not hold. Although it is a theorem, it is called a "lemma" because, its main importance is as a tool in proving other results of more direct interest, namely proving that certain languages are non-regular.

Theorem 4.8 (Pumping Lemma)

Let L be a regular language. Then there exists a constant, such that if z is a string in L of length at least n, then z may be decomposed into three parts, $z = uvw$ (three substrings of z), satisfying the following conditions:

1. for each $i \geq 0$ $uv^i w \in L$.
2. $|v| > 0$, and

3. $|uv| \le n$

Proof: Let $M = (Q, \Sigma, \delta, q_0, F)$ be a DFA with n states that recognizes L. Let z be any string in L of length $m \ge n$, say $z = a_1a_2a_3 \ldots a_m$. Consider the path associated with z. Let for $i = 1, 2, 3 \ldots m$, $\delta(q_0, a_1a_2a_3 \ldots a_i) = q_i$. Since $|z| \ge n$, number of states on the path is at least $n + 1$. But there are only n different states in M. Therefore there must be a state that appears twice in the path. So there must be a loop. The path labeled $a_1a_2a_3 \ldots a_m$ in the transition diagram of M is shown in Figure 4.1. There are two integers j and k, $0 \le j < k \le n$, such that $q_j = q_k$. The path $q_j \ldots q_k$ forms a loop. Since $j < k$, the string $a_{j+1} \ldots a_k$ is of length at least 1, and since $k \le n$, its length is not more than n.

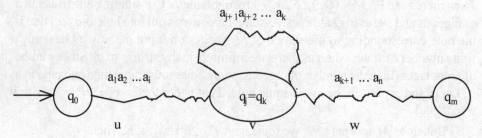

Fig. 4.1: String accepted by M

Now

$$\delta(q_0, a_1a_2a_3 \ldots a_j a_{k+1} a_{k+2} \ldots a_m) = \delta(\delta(q_0, a_1a_2a_3 \ldots a_j), a_{k+1} a_{k+2} \ldots a_m)$$
$$= \delta(q_j, a_{k+1}a_{k+2} \ldots a_m)$$
$$= \delta(q_k, a_{k+1}a_{k+2} \ldots a_m)$$
$$= q_m$$

Let $u = a_1a_2a_3 \ldots a_j$, $v = a_{j+1}a_{j+2} \ldots a_k$ and $w = a_{k+1}a_{k+2} \ldots a_m$

If $q_m \in F$, then $a_1a_2a_3 \ldots a_j a_{k+1} a_{k+2} \ldots a_m = uw = uv^0w \in L(M)$.

We can easily show that $\delta(q_0, a_1a_2a_3 \ldots a_j a_{j+1} a_{j+2} \ldots a_k a_{k+1} a_{k+2} \ldots a_m) = q_m$. Therefore, the string $a_1a_2a_3 \ldots a_{j+1}a_{j+2} \ldots a_k a_{k+1}a_{k+2} \ldots a_m = a_1a_2a_3 \ldots a_j(a_{j+1}a_{j+2} \ldots a_k)a_k$ $_{+1}a_{k+2} \ldots a_m = uvw \in L$. Similarly, we could go around the loop in the Figure 4.1 more than once, in fact, as many times as we like.

Thus, $a_1a_2a_3 \ldots a_j(a_{j+1}a_{j+2} \ldots a_k)^i a_{k+1}a_{k+2} \ldots a_m$ is in $L(M)$, i.e., $uv^iw \in L$ for any $i \ge 0$.

4.2.3   Application of Pumping Lemma

The steps to be followed for proving that a given set L is not regular using Pumping Lemma, are as under:

Step 1: Let L be a regular language and n be the number of states in the corresponding DFA.

Step 2: Select a string z in L. Break z into u, v and w with $|uv| \le n$ and $|v| > 0$.

Step 3: Find an integer i such that uv^iw is not in L. This contradicts our assumption. Hence L is not regular.

Example 4.6: Show that $L = \{a^i b^i | i \geq 1\}$ is not a regular language.

Solution:

Step 1: Let L be a regular language and n be the number of states in the finite automaton accepting L.

Step 2: Let $z = a^n b^n$. Then $|z| = 2n > n$. By pumping lemma, we can write $z = uvw$ with $|uv| \leq n$ and $|v| <> 0$

Step 3: The string v can be in one of the following forms:

case 1: v is composed of a's only, i.e., $v = a^k$ for some $k \geq 1$.

case 2: v is composed of b's only, i.e., $v = b^l$ for some $l \geq 1$.

case 3: v has both a's and b's, i.e., $v = a^k b^j$ for some $k, j \geq 1$.

In case 1, $z = a^n b^n = a^{n-k}(a^k) b^n = uvw$

Taking $i = 0$, $uv^i w = uw = a^{n-k} b^n \notin L$ as $k \geq 1$, $n - k \neq n$.

In case 2, $z = a^n b^n = a^n (b^l) b^{n-l} = uvw$

Taking $i = 0$, $uv^i w = uw = a^n b^{n-l} \notin L$ as $l \geq 1$, $n - 1 \neq n$.

In case 3, $z = a^{n-k} (a^k b^j) b^{n-j} = uvw$

Taking $i = 2$, $uv^i w = uvvw = a^{n-k} (a^k b^j)^2 b^{n-j}$
$$= a^{n-k} a^k b^j a^k b^j b^{n-j}$$

As $uv^i w$ is not of the form $a^i b^i$, $uv^2 w \notin L$. Thus in all cases we get a contradiction. Therefore, L is not regular.

Example 4.7: Show that $L = \{0^{i^2} \mid i$ is an integer, $i \geq 1\}$ is not a regular language.

Solution:

Step1: Let L be a regular language and n be the number of states in the finite automaton accepting L.

Step 2: Let $z = 0^{n^2}$. Then $|z| = n^2 > n$. By pumping lemma, we write $z = uvw$ with $|uv| \leq n$ and $|v| <> 0$ and $uv^i w$ is in L for all i.

Step 3: Let $i = 2$. $|uv^2 w| = |u| + 2|v| + |w| > |u| + |v| + |w|$ as $|v| > 0$.

This means that $n^2 = |uvw|$
$$= |u| + |v| + |w| < |uv^2 w|.$$ As $|uv| \leq n$, we have $|v| \leq n$. Therefore

$$|uv^2 w| = |u| + 2|v| + |w| < n^2 + n$$
$$\Rightarrow \quad n^2 < |uv^2 w| \leq n^2 + n$$
$$\Rightarrow \quad n^2 < |uv^2 w| < n^2 + n + n + 1$$
$$\Rightarrow \quad n^2 < |uv^2 w| < (n + 1)^2.$$

That is, the length of $uv^2 w$ strictly lies between n^2 and $(n + 1)^2$, and is thus not a perfect square and so not in L. But by Pumping Lemma $uv^2 w \in L$. This is a contradiction.

4.3 Decidability

A finite automaton is a rudimentary computer. Although certain parts and certain aspects of a computer obey the rules we have set up for FA's, we have not yet arrived at the mathematical model of a computer. Actually, a Finite Automaton receives input, and in response to that input produces the output "yes" or "no". A problem that can be answered yes or no is called a decision problem. *Computational problems* that can be solved by FA's are, therefore, limited to *decision problems*. A decision problem is *decidable* if and only if the answer to the question (problem) is yes. A decision problem is *undecidable* if and only if the answer to the question is no. In the next section, we will discuss the decision properties associated with regular languages and finite automata.

4.3.1 Decision Properties, Finite Automata and Regular Languages

The decision problems associated with finite automata and regular languages are as follows:

1. Given two regular expressions r_1 and r_2, do they define the same language?
2. Given a Finite Automaton M, does it accept any word? Alternatively, given an FA M, is $L(M) = \phi$?
3. Given a Finite Automaton M, is $L(M)$, the language defined by M, finite?
4. Given a Finite Automaton M, is $L(M)$, the language defined by M, is infinite?
5. Given two Finite Automata M_1 and M_2, are there any strings that are accepted by both?
6. Given two Finite Automata M_1 and M_2, do they accept the same language? In other words, is $L(M_1) = L(M_2)$?
7. Given two Finite Automata M_1 and M_2, is $L(M_1)$ a subset of $L(M_2)$?
8. Given a Finite Automaton M, is it a minimum-state Finite Automaton accepting the language $L(M)$?
9. Given a regular expression r and a string x, does x belong to the language corresponding to r?

Following are some of the decision algorithms for regular languages:

Theorem 4.9: Given a regular language L on alphabet Σ and any $w \in \Sigma^*$, there exists an algorithm for determining whether or not w is in L (Membership).

Proof: We represent the language by some DFA, and then test w to see if it is accepted by this DFA.

Theorem 4.10: Given a finite automaton, there exists an algorithm to determine whether or not finite automaton accepts any words.

Proof: We represent the language by some regular expression. As we know every regular expression defines some words. We can prove this by the algorithm. The algorithm is given in Algorithm 4.1.

Algorithm 4.1

Algorithm (To determine whether or not finite automation accepts anywords):

Step 1: Delete all stars.

Step2: For each +, we throw away the right half of the sum and the + sign itself.

Step 3: Remove the parentheses. Now, we have a concatenation of a's, b's and ε's. These taken together form a word.

Example 4.8: Show that the language defined by the regular expression $(a + b)^*a(a + b)^*$ represents at least one word.

Solution:

We will prove with the help of the following steps:

First we delete all *. We get,

$$(a + b)a(a + b)$$

Next, for each +, we throw away the right half of the sum and the + sign itself. We get,

$$(a)a(a)$$

Next, we remove the parentheses. We get,

aaa.

We have a concatenation of a's. We get a word *aaa*.

Theorem 4.11: There exists an algorithm for determining whether a regular language is empty, finite, or infinite.

Proof: First, we represent the language as a DFA. If there is a simple path from the initial vertex to any final vertex, then the language is not empty.

To determine whether or not a language is infinite, find all the vertices that are the base of some cycle. If any of these are on a path from the initial to a final vertex, the language is infinite. Otherwise, it is finite.

Theorem 4.12: Given two regular language L_1 and L_2, there exists an algorithm (Equality) to determine whether or not $L_1 = L_2$.

Proof: We define the language

$$L_3 = (L_1 \cap L_2') \cup (L_1' \cap L_2)$$

$$= (L_1' + L_2)' + (L_1 + L_2')'$$

[For sets L_1 and L_2, by De Morgan's law $L_1 L_2 = (L_1' + L_2')'$]

If $L_1 = L_2$ then $L_3 = \phi$. If $L_1 \neq L_2$, then $L_3 \neq \phi$.

4.4 Regular Languages and Programming Languages

It is quite natural to ask what relationship if any, exists between regular languages and programming languages. Is a programming language a regular language? The answer is obvious. Programming languages are not regular languages. In C programming language, the string main $\{^m\}^n$ is a valid program if and only if $m = n$. Using pumping lemma, it is very easy to prove that the set of valid programs is not regular.

Although regular languages and finite automata may be thought of similar to programming languages and their counterpart computers, there are a number of obvious differences. We have seen several examples of languages, such as $\{a^n b^n \mid n \geq 0]$, that no FA can recognize. But for $\{a^n b^n \mid n \geq 0\}$, program could be written and run on just about any computer. Clearly, Finite automata are less equipped to be computers. The significant differences having to do with memory, output capabilities, program mobility, and so on.

4.5   Applications and Limitations of FA

Some applications of finite automata we have already come across in Chapter 2. We will now discuss one application in detail.

Lexical Analyzers

A *token* is the smallest individual unit in a programming language. Tokens are almost always expressed as regular expressions. For example, C language identifiers, which are sequences of alphabets, digits and underscore character can be expressed as:

      letter(letter + digit + '_')*

where letter stands for $A + B + \ldots \ldots Z + a + b + \ldots z$ and digit stands for $0 + 1 + \ldots 9$.

Lexical analysis is the first phase in the compilation of a program. In this phase, a lexical analyzer takes source code as a string and outputs a sequence of tokens. The lexical analyzer, a fixed program used in a compiler as a module, is produced by the lexical analyzer generator.

A number of lexical analyzer generators take the sequence of regular expressions describing the tokens as input and output a single finite automaton recognizing any token. Generally this is done by converting the regular expression into an NFA with ε-transitions and then constructing the DFA directly without eliminating ε-transitions first. To occupy less space, the transition function of the FA is encoded differently than when transition table is represented as a two-dimensional array. The lexical analyzer interprets coded tables, together with particular table that represents the FA recognizing the tokens.

Limitations

The above examples give some idea about what finite automata can do. However, the main limitation of finite automata is their extremely limited memory, the memory being limited by the number of states. Due to the fact that FA cannot remember arbitrarily large amount of information, they cannot be used to solve the following types of problems:

    1.   Accept the language $a^n b^n$.

2. Recognize palindrome language.
3. Check arbitrarily nesting of balanced parenthesis.
4. Describe block structure in a programming language.

4.6 Summary

1. A language that can be defined by a regular expression or finite automaton or transition graph is called a regular language.
2. A language that cannot be defined in any of the three ways (regular expression or finite automaton or transition graph) is called a non-regular language.
3. Pumping Lemma was introduced by Yehoshua Bar-Hillel, Micha A. Perles, and Eliahu Shamin in 1961. It is a powerful tool that enables us to prove that a particular language is not a regular language.
4. A problem for which there exists an algorithm (i.e., a decision procedure) that gives the answer yes or no to the problem is called a decision problem.
5. A decision problem is decidable if and only if the answer to the question (problem) is yes.
6. A decision problem is undecidable if and only if the answer to the question is no.

4.7 Exercises

Objective Questions

1. The logic of pumping lemma is a good example of:
   (a) Pigeon hole principle
   (b) Induction principle
   (c) Recursion
   (d) Divide-and-conquer technique
2. If L_1 and L_2 be regular languages defined over the alphabet Σ, then:
   (a) $L_1 \cup L_2$ is regular
   (b) $L_1 \cup L_2$ is not regular
   (c) $-L_1$ is regular
   (d) Both (a) and (c)
3. If R_1 and R_2 be regular sets defined over the alphabet Σ, then
   (a) $R_1 \cap R_2$ is regular
   (b) R_1^T is regular
   (c) Homomorphism of R is regular
   (d) All of these
4. Pumping lemma is generally used for proving that:
   (a) Given language is regular
   (b) Given language is not regular
   (c) Whether two given regular expressions are equivalent
   (d) None of these
5. L_1 and L_2 be regular languages defined over the alphabet Σ. Which one is not true?
   (a) $\Sigma^* - L_2$ is regular
   (b) $L_1 - L_2$ is regular
   (c) L_1^T is regular
   (d) None of these

6.   Set of regular languages over a given alphabet is closed under:
     (a) Substitution   (b) Inverse Homomorphism
     (c) Transpose   (d) All of these

7. Which of the following regular expressions denotes a language comprising of all possible strings over Σ={*a*, *b*} of length *n* where *n* is multiple of 3.
     (a) (*a*+*b*+*aa*+*bb*+*aba*+*bba*)*   (b) (*aaa*+*bbb*)*
     (c) ((*a*+*b*)(*a*+*b*)(*a*+*b*))*   (d) (*aaa*+*ab*+*a*)+(*bbb*+*bb*+*a*)

8.   For which of the following application, regular expression cannot be used?
     (a) Describing tokens in programming language
     (b) Designing lexical analyzers
     (c) Developing editors
     (d) None of these

9.   Pumping Lemma is:
     (a) Theorem   (b) Lemma
     (c) Both (a) and (b)   (d) None of these

10. A problem is called decision problem if:
     (a) It has yes or no answer
     (b) It has an algorithm to solve the problem using finite amount of resources
     (c) It has an algorithm to solve the problem by using infinite resources
     (d) None of these

11. Let L_1 and L_2 be two regular languages, then:
     (a) $L_1 \cup L_2^T$ is a regular language   (b) $h(L_1)h^{-1}(L_2)$ is a regular language
     (c) $L_1 \cup L_2$ is a regular language   (d) All of these

12. A given language is not regular language if:
     (a) There is no FA exist   (b) There is no TG exist
     (c) There is no regular expression   (d) None of these

13. The class of regular sets is not closed under:
     (a) Union   (b) Quotient
     (c) Intersection   (d) None of these

14. Is family of regular languages closed under infinite intersection?
     (a) Yes   (b) No
     (c) Sometimes yes and sometimes no (d) None of these

Answers to Objective Questions

01.	(a)	02.	(d)	03.	(d)	04.	(b)	05.	(d)	06.	(d)
07.	(c)	08.	(d)	09.	(c)	10.	(a)	11.	(d)	12.	(d)
13.	(d)	14.	(b)								

Review Questions

1. What do you mean by closure properties of regular languages? State these properties.

2. Show that union, concatenation and Kleene's closure of regular languages are also regular.

A3. If L is a regular language, prove that the language $\{uv : u \in L, v \in L^R\}$ is also regular.

4. Prove that complement of a regular language is regular.

5. Show that intersection of two regular languages is regular.

6. Show that homomorphism of a regular language is regular.

A7. Prove that for any given w and any regular languages L_1 and L_2, there exists an algorithm to determine whether or not $w \in L_1 - L_2$.

8. Show that inverse homomorphism of a regular language is regular.

9. Prove that the transpose (reversal) of a regular language is regular.

A10. Consider the following finite automaton M. What is $L(M)$? Prove that $L(M)^T$ is regular.

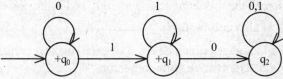

A11. Prove that for any regular languages L_1 and L_2, there exists an algorithm for determining if $L_1 \subseteq L_2$.

12. What do you mean by a decision problem? State six decision problems associated with regular languages/finite automata.

13. Show that there exists an algorithm to determine whether or not an FA accepts any word.

14. Show that the following regular expression defines at least one word
$$(a + \varepsilon)(ab^* + ba^*)^*(\varepsilon + b^*)^*$$

A15. Give suitable algorithm to show that the following finite automaton accepts no word:

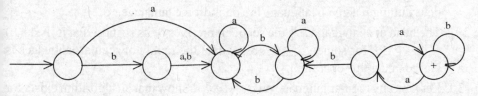

16. Show that for any regular languages L_1 and L_2, there is an algorithm to determine whether or not $L_1 = L_2$.

17. Show that there exists an algorithm for determining whether a regular language is empty, finite or infinite.

[A]18. The nor operation of two languages L_1 and L_2 is given by

$$\text{nor}(L_1, L_2) = \{x | x \notin L_1 \text{ and } x \notin L_2\}.$$

Show that the family of regular languages is closed under the nor operation.

19. Prove that the following languages are not regular:

   (i) $L = \{a^n b^l a^k : k \geq n + 1\}$ '   (ii) $L = \{a^p \mid p \text{ is a prime}\}$

   (iii) $L = \{w : n_a(w) \Longleftrightarrow n_b(w)\}$ (iv) $L = \{ww : w \in \{a, b\}^*\}$

   (v) $L = \{a^n b^l : n \leq l\}$ (vi) $L = \{a^{2n} \mid n \geq 1\}$

   (vii) $L = \{a^n b^{2n} \mid n > 0\}$ (viii) $L = \{wwww^R : w \in \{a, b\}^*\}$

   (ix) $L = \{a^n b^l a^k : n = l \text{ or } l \Longleftrightarrow k\}$

20. Determine if the following languages are regular:

   (i) $L = \{a^n : n \geq 2, n \text{ is a prime number}\}$

   (ii) $L = \{www^R u : u, v, w \in \{a, b\} +\}$

   (iii) $L = \{a^{2n} \mid n \geq 1\}$

   (iv) $L = \{a^n : n \text{ is not a prime number}\}$

[A]21. Show that the family of regular languages is closed under symmetric difference.

22. Prove or disprove the following statement: if L_1 and L_2 are non-regular languages, then $L_1 \cup L_2$ is also non-regular.

23. Consider the languages given below. For each, make a conjecture whether or not it is regular. Then prove your conjecture.

   (i) $L = \{a^n b^l a^k : n + 1 + k > 5\}$

   (ii) $L = \{a^n b^l a^k : n \geq 5, l > 3, k \leq l\}$

   (iii) $L = \{a^n b^l : n \text{ and } l \text{ are integer}\}$

24. If L is a regular language, prove that $L_1 = \{uv : u \in L, |v| = 2\}$ is also regular.

25. What is the relationship between regular languages and Finite automata?

26. Is regular languages subset of programming languages or vice-versa?

[A]27. The complementary (cor) of two languages is $\text{cor}(L_1, L_2) = \{w : w \in L_1^C \text{ or } w \in L_2^C\}$. Show that the family of regular languages is closed under the cor operation.

[A]28. A language is said to be a palindrome language if $L = L^R$. Find an algorithm for determining if a given language is a palindrome language.

29. The head of a language L is the set of all prefixes of its strings, that is, head(L) $= \{x : xy \in L \text{ for some } y \in \Sigma^*\}$. Show that the family of regular languages is closed under this operation.

[A]30. Let L be any regular language on $\Sigma = \{a, b\}$. Show that an algorithm exists for determining if L contains any strings of even length.

31. List the application of FA. Discuss any software design application of FA.

32. Explain one real world application of FA.

33. List the limitation of FA.

Answers/Hints for Selected Review Questions

3. L is a regular language. We know that regular languages are closed under reversal. Therefore, L^R is a regular language. We also know that the regular languages are closed under concatenation. Hence the language $\{uv : u \in L, v \in L^R\}$ is also a regular language.

7. Regular languages are closed under difference. So, $L_1 - L_2$ is a regular language. We know that there exists a membership algorithm determining whether or not $w \in L$. Hence there exists a membership algorithm for $L_1 - L_2$.

10. $L(M)$ is the language defined by M is given by the path values from initial to final states. Here, we can see that q_0 is initial as well as a final state and q_1 is also a final state. Therefore $L(M)$ consists of path values from q_0 to itself and from q_0 to q_1. As we can see that arrow do not come into q_0, the paths from q_0 to itself are self loops repeated any number of times. The corresponding path values are 0^i, $i \ge 0$. As no arrow comes from q_2 to q_0 or q_1, the path from q_0 to q_1 are of the form

$$q_0 \cdots \to q_0 \cdots \to q_1 \cdots q_1.$$

The corresponding path values are $0^i 1^j$, where $i \ge 0$ and $j \ge 1$. As the initial state q_0 is also a final state, $\varepsilon \in L(M)$. Thus $L(M) = \{0^i 1^j \mid i \ge 0, j \ge 0\}$. Hence $L(M)^T = \{1^j 0^i \mid i \ge 0, j \ge 0\}$. The construction of finite automaton M' corresponding to $L(M)^T$ is given as follows:

(i) The initial state of M' are q_0 and q_1

(ii) The (only) final state of M' is q_0

(iii) The direction of desired edges is reversed. M' is given in following Figure:

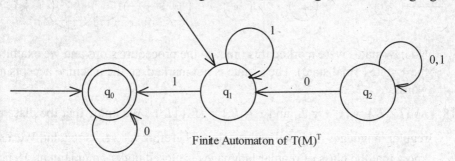

Finite Automaton of $T(M)^T$

From (i) & (iii), we can say that

$$T(M') = T(M)^T$$

Hence, $T(M)^T$ is regular.

11. If $L_1 \subseteq L_2$, then $L_1 \cup L_2 = L_2$. We know that there exists an algorithm to determine whether or not $L_1 = L_2$ provided both L_1 and L_2 are regular l. Since $L_1 \cup L_2$ is regular, then we have an algorithm for equality of sets $L_1 \cup L_2$ and L_2. Hence we also have an algorithm for $L_1 \subseteq L_2$.

15. **Step 1:** Mark the start state.

    Step 2: From every mark state follow each edge that leads out of it and mark the connecting state, then delete this edge from the machine.

    Step 3: Repeat step 2 until no new state is marked, then stop.

    Step 4: When the procedure has stopped, if any of the final states are marked, then the machine accepts some words and, if not, it does not.

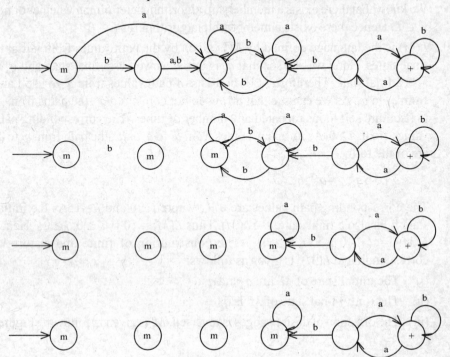

    No new states were marked this time, so the procedure stops and we examine the + state (final state). The + state is not marked, so the machine accepts no words.

18. $nor(L_1, L_2) = \{x \mid x \notin L_1 \text{ and } x \notin L_2\} = (L_1 \cup L_2)^c$. We know that the class of regular languages is closed under union. Therefore $L_1 \cup L_2$ is regular. We also know that the class of regular languages is closed under complement. Hence $(L_1 \cup L_2)^c$ is regular.

21. $L_1 \oplus L_2 = \{w \mid w \text{ is in } L_1 \text{ or } w \text{ is in } L_2 \text{ but } w \text{ is not in both } L_1 \And L_2\} = (L_1 \cup L_2) - (L_1 \cup L_2)^c$. We know that regular languages are closed under union, intersection, complement and difference. Therefore, $(L_1 \cup L_2) - (L_1 \cup L_2)^c$ is a regular language, i.e., $L_1 \oplus L_2$ is a regular language.

27. $cor(L_1, L_2) = \{w : w \in L_1^C \text{ or } w \in L_2^C\} = \{w : w \in L_1^C \cup L_2^C\} = L_1^C \cup L_2^C$

Regular languages are closed under union and complement operations. Therefore, $L_1^C \cup L_2^C$ is regular, that is, $cor(L_1, L_2)$ is regular.

28. First, we construct DFA for L and then from this DFA we can construct DFA for L^R. We know that if L_1 & L_2 are two regular languages then there exists an algorithm to determine whether or not $L_1 = L_2$. Hence there exists an algorithm for determining the equality of L & L^R.

30. Suppose if L contains no even strings, then $L \cap L((aa + ab + ba + bb)^*) = \phi$. We know that there exists an algorithm for determining whether a regular language is empty, finite or infinite language. The left hand side of the above equation is regular, so there exists an algorithm for determining if L contains any strings of even length.

Programming Problems

1. Write a program to find out whether a given word is member or not of a given regular language.

2. Write a program to determine whether a regular language is empty, finite or infinite.

3. Write a program to test whether or not two given regular languages L_1 and L_2 are equal.

Chapter 5

Context-Free Grammars and Languages

This Chapter introduces the concepts of Context-Free Grammar (CFG) and Regular Grammar (RG). We discuss derivation, derivation tree or parse tree and ambiguity in context-free grammar. We also explain how to simplify the context-free grammar. The concepts of Chomsky and Greibach normal forms, which are useful to prove many theorems, are explored next. The method for converting a context-free grammar into these normal forms concludes the Chapter.

Objectives: The aim of this Chapter is to introduce context-free grammar and language. After learning the contents of this Chapter, you will be able to:

1. Define and explain the concept of context-free grammars and regular grammars,
2. Describe derivation, derivation tree and ambiguous grammar,
3. Simplify the context-free grammar and
4. Explain Chomsky and Greibach Normal forms and convert CFG to these normal forms.

5.1 Context-Free Grammars (CFGs)

We are familiar with the word Grammar from our school days. As we all know, a grammar is a set of rules by which the valid sentences in a language are constructed. Determining how a sentence can be formed from the rules of grammars is called *sentence parsing*.

A *context-free grammar* is a simple recursive method of specifying rules (or productions) to generate patterns of strings. Although all possible languages cannot be generated by context-free grammars, they can generate all regular and some non-regular languages. In addition to this, context-free grammars are capable of specifying much of the syntax of high-level programming languages and other formal languages. Context-free grammars are generally used for describing arithmetic expressions, with arbitrary nesting of balanced parenthesis, and block structures in programming languages (i.e., begin and end pairs matched like parenthesis). Neither of these aspects of programming languages can be represented by regular expressions. Thus, context-free grammars present a much wider class of languages than do the regular expressions.

The original motivation for context-free grammar was the description of natural languages like English, which they can do only to a limited extent. For example, let us consider some of the rules of English language. The rules of English specify that a sentence is composed of a subject followed by a predicate. This is reflected in the first rule given below:

Rule 1:   <Sentence>   →   <subject> <predicate>

The other rules are:

Rule 2 :   <Subject>   →   <noun phrase>

Rule 3 :   <noun phrase>   →   <adjective> <noun phrase>

Rule 4 :   <noun phrase>   →   <article> <noun phrase>

Rule 5 :   <noun phrase>   →   <noun>

Rule 6 :   <noun phrase>   →   <preposition> <noun phrase>

Rule 7 :   <predicate>   →   <verb> <noun phrase>

Rule 8 :   <predicate>   →   <verb>

Rule 9 :   <noun>   →   bird, animal, boy, girl, rock, road

Rule 10: <adjective>   →   little, small, big, black

Rule 11: <article>   →   a, an, the

Rule 12: <preposition>   →   on, in, into, upon

Rule 13: <verb>   →   sits, runs, walks, sings, cries, likes

From the above rules of English grammar, we can construct various sentences like **'little bird sits on the black rock'**, **'small boy walks'**, **'girl sings'**, etc. Derivation of the sentence **'little bird sits on the black rock'**, using the above rules, is as follows:

sentence $\rightarrow$	\<subject> \<predicate>	by Rule
	\<noun phrase> \<predicate>	by Rule 2
	\<adjective> \<noun phrase> \<predicate>	by Rule 3
	\<adjective> \<noun > \<predicate>	by Rule 5
	\<adjective> \<noun> \<verb> \<noun phrase>	by Rule 7
	\<adjective> \<noun> \<verb> \<preposition> \<noun phrase>	by Rule 6
	\<adjective> \<noun> \<verb> \<preposition> \<article> \<noun phrase>	by Rule 4
	\<adjective> \<noun> \<verb> \<preposition> \<article> \<adjective> \<noun phrase>	by Rule 3
	\<adjective> \<noun> \<verb> \<preposition> \<article> \<adjective> \<noun>	by Rule 5
	little \<noun> \<verb> \<preposition> \<article> \<adjective> \<noun>	by Rule 10
	little bird \<verb> \<preposition> \<article> \<adjective> \<noun>	by Rule 9
	little bird sits \<preposition> \<article> \<adjective> \<noun >	by Rule 13
	little bird sits on \<article> \<adjective> \<noun>	by Rule 12
	little bird sits on the \<adjective> \<noun>	by Rule 11
	little bird sits on the black \<noun>	by rule 10
	little bird sits on the black rock	by Rule 9

which shows that the sentence '**little bird sits on the black rock**' is a valid sentence in English language. However, we can also derive the sentence '**rock sings**' as follows:

sentence $\rightarrow$	\<subject> \<predicate>	by Rule 1
	\<noun phrase> \<predicate>	by Rule 2
	\<noun> \<predicate>	by Rule 5
	\<noun> \<verb>	by Rule 7
	rock \<verb>	by Rule 9
	rock sings	by Rule 13

Clearly the sentence '**rock sings**' is meaningless. This shows that the sentence, although derived using grammar rules, may not be a valid sentence in English language. Therefore, some semantic information is necessary to rule out meaningless sentences like '**rock sings**'. However, this is exactly what a context-free grammar does not allow. Despite this, context-free grammars play an important role in computer linguistics.

5.1.1 Definition of CFG

A *context-free grammar* is a finite set of variables (also called *non-terminals* or *syntactic categories*) each of which represents a language. The languages represented by the variables are described recursively in terms of each other and *primitive symbols* called *terminals*.

The rules that relate the variables are called *productions*. Generally, the production tells that the language associated with a given variable contains strings that are formed by concatenating strings from the languages of certain other variables, possibly along with some terminals.

Formally, we can define a *context-free grammar* (CFG) G as a 4-tuple:

$$G = (V, T, P, S),$$

where

V is a finite set of non-terminal symbols, each of which represents a sub language of G.

T is a finite set of terminal symbols ($V \cap T = \phi$). Terminals are the basic symbols from which the strings are formed.

P is a finite set of productions of the form

$$A \to \alpha,$$

where A is a non-terminal and α is a string of terminals and non-terminals (α may be empty). A *production* is a replacement rule; that is, $A \to \alpha$ indicates that occurrences of the non-terminal A can be replaced by the string α .

S is a special non-terminal symbol, distinguished as the start state.

For example, $G = (\{S\}, \{a\}, P, S)$ where p consists of:

$$S \to aSb$$
$$S \to SS$$
$$S \to a$$

is a context-free grammar. The above productions, which all denote replacement for S, can be represented as

$$S \to aSb|SS \mid a$$

5.1.2 Derivations

The sequence of applications of productions, that produces the strings of terminals (word) from the start symbol, is called a *derivation* or a *generation* of the word/string.

We use $\overset{G}{\Rightarrow}$, $\overset{*}{\Rightarrow}$, and $\overset{i}{\Rightarrow}$ symbols to represent derivations. The symbol $\overset{G}{\Rightarrow}$ is used when a string is directly derived from the second string in one step, that is, by only one application of some production. For example, let α, β and γ are strings in $(V \cup T)^*$ and let $A \to \beta$ is a production in P. If this production is applied to the string α $A\gamma$, we get $\alpha\,\beta\,\gamma$. Since $\alpha\,A\,\gamma$ directly derives $\alpha\,\beta\,\gamma$ in grammar G, we write $\alpha A\,\gamma \overset{G}{\Rightarrow}$ $\alpha\,\beta\,\gamma$.

We write $\alpha \overset{*}{\Rightarrow} \beta$ if α derives β in zero or more steps (by application of zero or more productions). For example if $\alpha_1, \alpha_2, \dots \alpha_m$ are strings in $(V \cup T)^*$, $m \geq 1$, and

$$\alpha_1 \Rightarrow \alpha_2, \alpha_2 \Rightarrow \alpha_3, \dots \alpha_{m-1} \Rightarrow \alpha_m$$

then we can say that $\alpha_1 \xrightarrow{*} \alpha_m$ or α_1 derives α_m in grammar G. In the same way,

we can write $\alpha \xrightarrow{i} \beta$ if α derives β in exactly i steps.

Sentential Form

A *sentential form* is a string of terminals and variables α if $S \xrightarrow{*} \alpha$ where $S \in$

$V \& \alpha \in (V \bigcup T)^*$.

Leftmost and Rightmost Derivations

A derivation may involve sentential form with more than one variable. In such cases, we have a choice in the order in which variables are replaced. A derivation A

$\xrightarrow{*} w$ is said to be *leftmost* if in each step we apply a production to the leftmost

variable in the sentential form. A derivation $A \xrightarrow{*} w$ is said to be *rightmost* if in each

step we apply a production to the rightmost variable in the sentential form.

Let us consider a CFG G having productions $S \to aSb|SS|a$. The word *aaaba* can be derived from the grammar G by the leftmost derivation as well as by the rightmost derivation. The leftmost derivation of the word *aaaba* is as follows:

$$
\begin{aligned}
S &\Rightarrow SS && \text{[by application of the production } S \to SS] \\
&\Rightarrow aSbS && \text{[by application of the production } S \to aSb] \\
&\Rightarrow aSSbS && \text{[by application of the production } S \to SS] \\
&\Rightarrow aaSbS && \text{[by application of the production } S \to a] \\
&\Rightarrow aaabS && \text{[by application of the production } S \to a] \\
&\Rightarrow aaaba
\end{aligned}
$$

The rightmost derivation of the word *aaaba* is as follows:

$$
\begin{aligned}
S &\Rightarrow SS && \text{[by application of the production } S \to SS] \\
&\Rightarrow Sa && \text{[by application of the production } S \to a] \\
&\Rightarrow aSba && \text{[by application of the production } S \to aSb] \\
&\Rightarrow aSSba && \text{[by application of the production } S \to SS] \\
&\Rightarrow aaSba && \text{[by application of the production } S \to a] \\
&\Rightarrow aaaba && \text{[by application of the production } S \to a]
\end{aligned}
$$

5.1.3 Context-Free Languages (CFLs)

Let $G = (V, T, P, S)$ be a CFG. The language generated by G is

$$L(G) = \{w|w \text{ is in } T^* \text{ and } S \xrightarrow{*} w\}$$

A language L is a context-free language if there is a CFG G such that $L = L(G)$. A string is in $L(G)$ if the string consists solely of terminals and the string can be derived from S. Two grammars G_1 and G_2 are said to be equivalent if $L(G_1) = L(G_2)$.

Example 5.1: Consider the context-free grammar $G = (\{S\}, \{a, b\}, P, S)$ with productions

$$S \rightarrow aSb$$
$$S \rightarrow ab$$

Find the language generated by G.

Solution: We apply the first production $(n-1)$ times and then apply the second production:

$S \Rightarrow aSb$	[first production one time]
$\Rightarrow aaSbb$ or a^2Sb^2	[first production two times]
$\Rightarrow aaaSbbb$ or a^3Sb^3	[first production three times]
$\Rightarrow a^{n-1}Sb^{n-1}$	[first production $(n-1)$ times]
$\Rightarrow a^{n-1}abb^{n-1}$	[second production one time]
$\Rightarrow a^nb^n$	

It is clear from the derivation result, that, the only strings in $L(G)$ are a^nb^n for $n \geq 1$. Thus, the language generated by G is

$$L(G) = \{a^nb^n \mid n \geq 1\}$$

Example 5.2: Consider a context-free grammar $G = (V, T, P, S)$ where $V = \{S\}$, $T = \{a\}, P = \{S \rightarrow aS, S \rightarrow \varepsilon\}$ and S is the start symbol. Find the language generated by the grammar.

Solution: If we apply the first production once and then apply the second production, we get

$S \Rightarrow aS$ [by the application of first production]

$S \Rightarrow a$ [by the application of second production]

Similarly, if we apply the first production n times and then apply the second production, we get

$S \Rightarrow aS$	[first production one time]
$\Rightarrow aaS$	[first production two times]
$\Rightarrow aaaS$	[first production three times]
$\Rightarrow a^n$	[[first production n times]

The set of strings generated by the grammar is $\{\varepsilon, a, aa, \ldots a^n\}$. Thus, the language generated by this CFG is a^*.

A *context-free grammar* is called *context-free* because the substitution of the variable on the left of a production can be made anytime as a variable appears in a sentential form. It does not depend on the symbols in the rest of the sentential form (the context). This feature is the consequence of allowing a single variable on the left side of the production.

5.2 Derivation Trees and Ambiguity in Grammar
Derivation Trees

Derivation tree is a graphical representation of the derivation of a word from a given set of production rules. In other words, a derivation tree captures the grammatical structure of the string. It records that rules were applied to which variables during the string's derivation. Derivation tree is also called *parse tree, syntax tree, production tree* or *generation tree*. The vertices of a derivation tree are labeled with terminals, variables or ε. If an interior vertex is labeled A and its children are labeled $X_1, X_2 \ldots X_k$ from the left, then $A \rightarrow X_1|X_2| \ldots X_k$ must be the productions. Figure 5.1 shows the part of the derivation tree representing the productions:

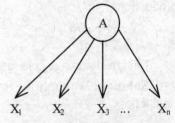

Fig. 5.1: Partial Derivation Tree

$$A \rightarrow X_1 | X_2 | \ldots X_k$$

A tree is a derivation tree for the context-free grammar $G = (V, T, P, S)$ if

(i)   The root of the parse tree is labeled S.

(ii)   Every vertex has a label from $V \cup T \cup \{\varepsilon\}$.

(iii)   Every interior vertex (a vertex that is not a leaf) has a label from V.

(iv)   Every leaf has a label from $T \cup \{\varepsilon\}$.

(v)   If a vertex A has n children $X_1, X_2 \ldots X_n$ from left to right, then
$$A \rightarrow X_1 | X_2 | \ldots X_k$$
must be productions in P.

(vi)   If a vertex has label ε, then it is a leaf, and it is the only child of its father.

Now, we will define and discuss some additional features of the derivation tree.

Yield of a derivation tree

The yield of a derivation tree is the concatenation of the labels of leaves form left to right.

Sub-tree of a derivation tree

A sub-tree of a derivation tree is also called partial derivation tree. A sub-tree of a derivation tree is a tree having the following properties:

(i)   The root of a sub-tree is any vertex with label A, where $A \in V$.

(ii)   Every leaf has a label from $V \cup T \cup \{\varepsilon\}$.

(iii)   The vertices of sub-tree are descendants of A, with their labels.

(iv)   The edges of sub-tree connect the descendants of A.

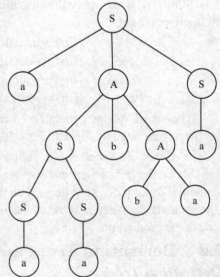

Fig. 5.2: Derivation trees

Example 5.3: Consider the grammar G, with productions

$$S \rightarrow aAS$$
$$S \rightarrow a$$
$$S \rightarrow SS$$
$$A \rightarrow SbA$$
$$A \rightarrow ba$$

Figure 5.2 shows the derivation tree for the above context-free grammar. Figure 5.3 shows partial derivation trees or sub-trees of the derivation tree shown in Figure 5.2.

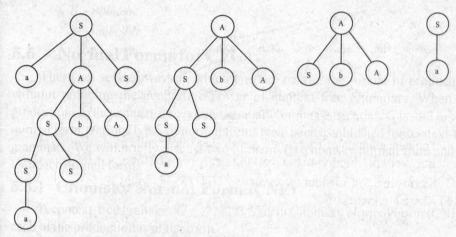

Fig. 5.3: Partial derivation trees of derivation tree given by Figure 5.2

The yield of derivation tree of Figure 5.2 is *aaabbaa* while strings *aaSbAS*, *aSbA*, *SbA* and *a* are the yields of the sub-trees of Figure 5.3. The strings *aaSbAS* and *a* are also sentential forms of $L(G)$.

A-tree

A sub-tree of a derivation tree is called *A*-tree if its root is labeled with variable *A*. Similarly, if there is a sub-tree whose root is labeled *B* then it is called a *B-tree*.

Working string

In a derivation process, the unfinished stages which are sentential forms are generally called working strings. The arrow symbol $\Rightarrow$ is employed between unfinished stages in the derivation of the word.

Total Language Tree

For a given CFG $G = (V, T, P, S)$, we define a tree whose root is the start symbol *S* and whose nodes are working strings of terminals and non-terminals. The descendants of each node are all the possible results of applying every production to the working string, one at a time. The terminal nodes are strings of all terminals. The resultant tree is called the *total language tree* of the CFG.

Example 5.4: Consider the Grammar $G = (\{S, X\}, \{a, b\}, P, \{S\})$, where *P* consists of

$S \rightarrow bX|aXX|aa$

$X \rightarrow ab|b$

The total language tree is given in Figure 5.4:

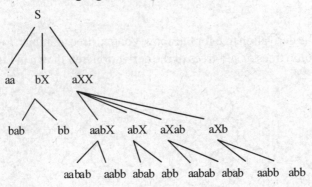

Fig. 5.4: Total language tree

The descendants of each node are all possible results of applying every production to the working string one at a time.

Example 5.5: Consider the Grammar $G = (\{S, X\}, \{a, b\}, P, S)$ where P consists of

$S \rightarrow X|a$

$X \rightarrow bX$

The total language tree is given as shown in Figure 5.5. It is clear from the Figure 5.5 that the language generated has only one word, i.e., a.

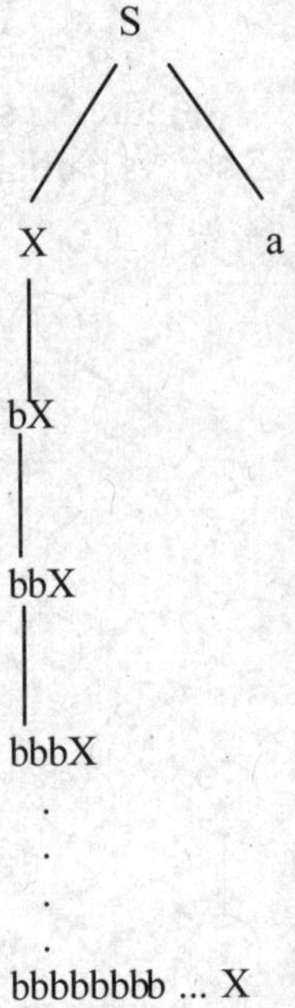

Fig. 5.5: Total language tree

Example 5.6: Consider the Grammar $G = (\{S, A, B\}, \{a, b\}, P, S)$ where P consists of

$S \rightarrow aB|bA$

$A \rightarrow a|aS|bAA$

$B \rightarrow b|bS|aBB$

For the word *aabbab* find:

(a) the leftmost derivation,

(b) the rightmost derivation, and

(c) the derivation tree.

Solution:

(a) $S \Rightarrow aB$ [by the application of the production $S \rightarrow aB$]

     $\Rightarrow aaBB$ [by the application of the production $B \rightarrow aBB$]

     $\Rightarrow aabB$ [by the application of the production $B \rightarrow b$]

     $\Rightarrow aabbS$ [by the application of the production $B \rightarrow bS$]

     $\Rightarrow aabbaB$ [by the application of the production $S \rightarrow aB$]

⇒ *aabbab*	[by the application of the production $B \to b$]
(b) $S \Rightarrow aB$	[by the application of the production $S \to aB$]
⇒ *aaBB*	[by the application of the production $B \to aBB$]
⇒ *aaBb*	[by the application of the production $B \to b$]
⇒ *aabSb*	[by the application of the production $B \to bS$]
⇒ *aabbAb*	[by the application of the production $S \to bA$]
⇒ *aabbab*	[by the application of the production $A \to a$]

(c)   The derivation tree is shown in Figure 5.6.

Ambiguity

If w is a word in the language defined by the Grammar $G = (V, T, P, S)$, then w has at least one parse tree. Each word defined by a parse tree has a unique leftmost and a unique rightmost derivation. If a word has more than one parse tree, then it has more than one rightmost or leftmost derivation. A context-free grammar $G = (V, T, P, S)$ is *ambiguous* if there is at least one word in the language having two or more parse trees (or equivalently, two or more leftmost/rightmost derivations).

Example 5.7: Show that $G = (\{S\}, \{a\}, P, S)$ where P consists of

$$S \to aS$$
$$S \to Sa$$
$$S \to a$$

is ambiguous grammar.

Fig. 5.6: Derivation tree

Solution:

The word a^3 can be derived by four different parse trees as shown in Figure 5.7.

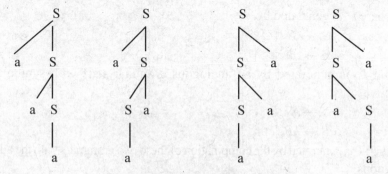

Fig. 5.7: Four different parse trees

The CFG has four parse trees for the word a^3. Therefore, it is ambiguous.

Example 5.8: Consider the grammar $G = (V, T, P, S)$ where

$V = \{S\}$

$T = \{a\}$ and P consists of

$S \rightarrow S + S$

$S \rightarrow S*S$

$S \rightarrow (S)$

$S \rightarrow a$

Show that grammar G is ambiguous.

Solution:

The word $a*a + a$ can be derived by two different parse trees. Figure 5.8 shows these parse trees.

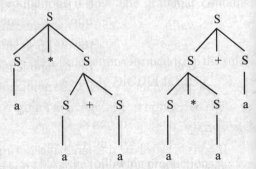

Fig. 5.8: Two parse trees for $a*a + a$

The word $a*a + a$ has two parse trees in grammar G. Therefore, grammar is ambiguous.

5.2.1 Inherent Ambiguous

A Language L is called unambiguous language if there exists an unambiguous grammar that generates L. If every grammar that generates L is ambiguous, then the language is said to be *inherently ambiguous*.

Example 5.9: Prove that the language

$$L = \{a^n b^n c^m\} \cup \{ a^n b^m c^m\} = a^n b^n c^n$$

where n and m are non-negative, is an inherently ambiguous CFL.

Solution:

We can write the language L as follows:

$$L = \{a^n b^n c^m\} \cup \{ a^n b^m c^m\}$$

$$= L_1 \cup L_2$$

where L_1 is generated by

$$S_1 \rightarrow S_1 c | A$$
$$A \rightarrow aAb | \varepsilon$$

and L_2 is generated by an analogous grammar start with symbol S_2 and productions

$$S_2 \rightarrow aS_2 | B$$
$$B \rightarrow bBc | \varepsilon$$

Then L is generated by the combination of these two grammars with the additional productions

$$S \rightarrow S_1 | S_2$$

The grammar is ambiguous since the string $a^n b^n c^n$ has two distinct derivations, one starting with $S \Rightarrow S_1$, the other with $S \Rightarrow S_2$. Still, we cannot say that L is inherently ambiguous as there might exist some other non-ambiguous grammar for it. But in some way L_1 and L_2 have conflicting requirements, the first putting a restriction on the number of a's and b's while the second does the same for b's and c's. However, it is impossible to combine these requirements in a single set of rules that cover the case $n = m$ uniquely.

5.3 Regular Grammars

As discussed in previous Chapters, finite automata and regular expressions are two equivalent ways of describing regular languages. A third way of describing regular languages is by means of certain simple grammars. Now, we define right linear, left linear and regular grammars.

Right-Linear Grammar

A context-free grammar $G = (V, T, P, S)$ is said to be *right-linear grammar* if each of its productions is one of the following forms:

$$A \rightarrow wB$$
or $\quad A \rightarrow w$

where $A, B \in V$ and $w \in T^*$.

Left-Linear Grammar

A context-free grammar $G = (V, T, P, S)$ is said to be *left-linear grammar* if each of its production is one of the following forms:

$$A \rightarrow Bw$$
or $\quad A \rightarrow w$

where $A, B \in V$ and $w \in T^*$.

Regular Grammar

A *regular grammar* is one that is either right-linear or left-linear grammar.

The following section explains how to convert the given FA into a context-free grammar. We will see that all the words accepted by the FA can be generated by the CFG and only the words accepted by the FA are generated by the CFG.

5.3.1 Conversion of FA into CFG

Let $M = (Q, \Sigma, \delta, q_0, F)$ is an FA. Every word accepted by M corresponds to a path from starting state to some of the final states. Every path has a step-by-step development sequence. Every development is a derivation in the CFG proposed. Therefore, every word accepted by the FA can be generated by the CFG. Keeping this in mind, we construct CFG G as follows:

$$G = (\{V_0, V_1, ...V_n\}, T, P, V_0)$$

where P is defined by the following rules.

i) For every transition from state q_i to $q_j \notin F$ labeled a ($a \in \Sigma$), we include the production

$$V_i \rightarrow aV_j \text{ in } P.$$

ii) For every transition from state q_i to q_j where $q_j \in F$ labeled a, we include the productions

$$V_i \rightarrow aV_j \text{ and } V_i \rightarrow a \text{ in } P.$$

We will show that $L(G) = L(M)$.

If w is a string in $L(G)$, then because of the form of the productions in G, the derivation must have the form

$$V_i \Rightarrow aV_j \qquad \text{iff } \delta(q_i, a) = q_j \notin F$$
$$V_i \Rightarrow a \qquad \text{iff } \delta(q_i, a) = q_j \in F$$

so,

$$V_0 \Rightarrow a_1 V_1 \qquad \text{iff } \delta(q_0, a_1) = q_1$$
$$\Rightarrow a_1 a_2 V_2 \qquad \text{iff } \delta(q_1, a_2) = q_2$$
$$\Rightarrow a_1 a_2 a_3 V_3 \qquad \text{iff } \delta(q_2, a_3) = q_3$$
$$\Rightarrow a_1 a_2 \ldots a_{k-1} V_{k-1}$$
$$\Rightarrow a_1 a_2 \ldots a_{k-1} a_k \qquad \text{iff } \delta(q_{k-1}, a_k) = q_n$$

This proves that $w = a_1 a_2 \ldots a_k \in L(G)$

iff $(q_0, a_1, \ldots a_k) = q_j \in F$, i.e., $w \in L(M)$

Example 5.10: Let us consider the FA (see Figure 5.9) which accepts the language of all words with double letters in them over the alphabet $\Sigma = \{a, b\}$ Construct a CFG corresponding to it.

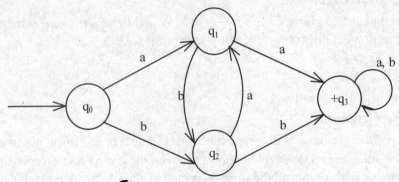

Fig. 5.9: Finite Automaton

Solution:

Number of variables must be equal to the number of states in the FA. Therefore Let $G = (\{V_0, V_1, V_2, V_3\}, \{a, b\}, P, V_0)$, where P includes the following productions

$V_0 \to aV_1$	since $\delta(q_0, a) = q_1$
$V_0 \to bV_2$	since $\delta(q_0, b) = q_2$
$V_1 \to bV_2$	since $\delta(q_1, b) = q_2$
$V_1 \to aV_3$	since $\delta(q_1, a) = q_3$ and q_3 in the final state
$V_1 \to a$	
$V_2 \to aV_1$	since $\delta(q_2, a) = q_1$
$V_2 \to bV_3$	since $\delta(q_2, b) = q_3$ and q_3 in the final state
$V_2 \to b$	
$V_3 \to a V_3$	since $\delta(q_3, a) = q_3$ and q_3 in the final state

$$V_3 \rightarrow b V_3 \qquad \text{since } \delta(q_3, b) = q_3 \text{ and } q_3 \text{ in the final state}$$
$$V_3 \rightarrow a$$
$$V_3 \rightarrow b$$

G is the required grammar.

Example 5.11: Construct a CFG corresponding to the finite automaton as shown in Figure 5.10.

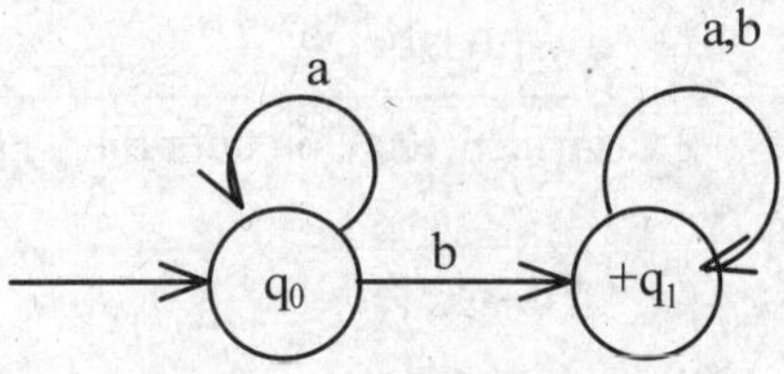

Fig. 5.10: Finite Automaton

Let $G = (\{V_0, V_1\}, \{a, b\}, P, V_0)$ where *P* is given as

$$V_0 \rightarrow aV_0 \qquad \text{since } \delta(q_0, a) = q_0$$
$$V_0 \rightarrow bV_1 \qquad \text{since } \delta(q_0, b) = q_1 \ \& \ q_1 \text{ is the final state}$$
$$V_0 \rightarrow b$$
$$V_1 \rightarrow aV_1 \qquad \text{since } \delta(q_1, a) = q_1 \ \& \ q_1 \text{ is the final state}$$
$$V_1 \rightarrow a$$
$$V_1 \rightarrow bV_1 \qquad \text{since } \delta(q_1, b) = q_1 \ \& \ q_1 \text{ is final state}$$
$$V_1 \rightarrow b$$

G is the required grammar.

5.3.2. Construction of FA from Regular Grammar

Let $G = (\{V_0, V_1, \ldots\ldots V_n\}, T, P, S)$ be a regular grammar. We construct a finite automaton whose:

(i)   States corresponds to variables in G

(ii) Initial state corresponds to V_0 and

(iii) Transitions in FA correspond to productions in *P*.

The algorithm given in Algorithm 5.1 converts a regular grammar into corresponding finite automaton.

Algorithm 5.1: Algorithm for Conversion of Regular grammar into Corresponding finite automaton

---

Algorithm (Conversion of Regular grammar into finite automaton): The steps to convert regular grammar $G = (\{V_0, V_1, \ldots\ldots V_n\}, T, P, V_0)$ into FA $M = (\{q_0, q_1, \ldots q_n\}, \{a, b\}, \delta, q_0, \{q_f\})$ are as follows:

Step 1: For each variable *Vi* in G, draw a small circle labeled q_i. Draw one extra circle, labeled q_f (final state).

Step 2: The state q_0 corresponding to the variable V_0 (Start symbol of the grammar) will be the start state of the Finite Automaton.

Step 3: For every production rule

$$V_i \rightarrow w_i V_j$$

include a transition from q_i to q_j with label w_i. (Draw a directed edge from state q_i to q_j and label it with the word w_i).

> **Step 4:** For every production of the form $V_k \to w_k$, include a transition from q_k to q_f with label w.

Example 5.12: Consider the CFG $G = (\{S, A, B\}, \{a, b\}, P, S)$ where P is given by

$$S \to aA | bB$$
$$A \to aS | a$$
$$B \to bS | b$$

Construct the equivalent Finite Automaton.

Solution: Let FA $M = (\{q_0, q_1, q_2, q_f\}, \{a, b\}, \delta, q_0, \{q_f\})$ where q_0, q_1 and q_2 correspond to S, A, and B, respectively. A new state q_f is introduced as the final state.

Step 1: Draw four small circles labeled q_0, q_1, q_2 and q_f, respectively as shown in Figure 5.11.

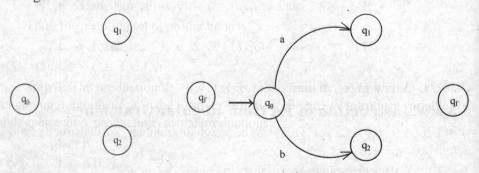

Fig. 5.11: Step 1 of construction   Fig. 5.12: Step 2 & Step 3 of construction
process   process

Step 2 & Step 3: Starting state of finite automation will be q_0. For each production of the form $V_i \to w_i V_j$, include a transition q_i to q_j with label w_i Therefore,

for $S \to aA | bB$, we get the Figure 5.12. For $A \to aS$ and $B \to bS$, we get the Automation as shown in Figure 5.13

Step 4:

For $A \to a$ and

$B \to b$,

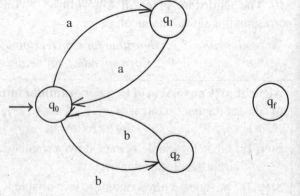

Fig. 5.13: Step 3 of construction process

Will will get a Transition Diagram of finite automation corresponding to CFG G as shown in Figure 5.14.

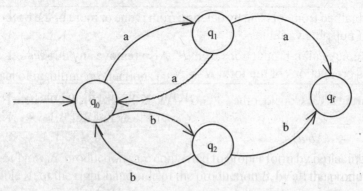

Fig. 5.14: Transition Diagram of Finite Automaton corresponding to CFG G

5.4 Simplification of Context-Free Grammars

Ambiguity is an undesirable property of a context-free grammar that we might wish to eliminate. The definition of a context-free grammar does not impose any restriction on the right side of a production. However, complete freedom is not necessary. In fact, it is a detriment in some cases. In many situations, it is even desirable to place more stringent restrictions on the grammar. The grammar may be reduced by eliminating certain types of productions. In the following section, simplification of CFG by removing ε-*productions*, *useless variables* and, finally *unit productions* without reducing the generative power of the grammar is considered.

5.4.1 Removing ε-productions

In a given *CFG*, a production of the form

$$N \rightarrow \varepsilon$$

where N is a variable, is called a ε-*production* and any variable N for which derivation

$$N \overset{*}{\Rightarrow} \varepsilon$$

is possible is called *nullable*.

A grammar G may generate a language $L(G)$ that may not contain ε, yet G may have some ε-productions or nullable variables. In such cases, the ε-productions can be removed.

The algorithm for removing ε-productions is given in Algorithm 5.2.

Algorithm 5.2: Algorithm for removing ε-production

Algorithm(Finding an Equivalent CFG with no ε-production): Given a CFG $G = (V, T, P, S)$ with ε-productions, construct a CFG $G' = (V, T, P', S)$ with no ε-*productions* as follows:

Step 1: If $N \rightarrow \varepsilon$ is a production, then N is nullable. If $M \rightarrow \alpha$ is a production and all symbols of α have been found nullable, then M is nullable.

Step 2: Repeat Step 1 until no more nullable symbols can be found.

Step 3: For every production $N \rightarrow \alpha$ in P, add to P' all productions that can be

> obtained from this one by deleting from α one or more of the occurrences of null able variables.
>
> **Step 4:** Remove all ε-productions from P'. Also remove any duplicates, as well as productions of the form $N \rightarrow N$.

Example 5.13: Consider the CFG $G = (\{S, X, Y\}, \{a, b\}, P, S)$ where P consists of

$$S \rightarrow a|Xb|aYa$$
$$X \rightarrow Y|\varepsilon$$
$$Y \rightarrow b|X$$

Remove ε-productions.

Solution:

By applying Step1 and Step 2 of the algorithm we get X and Y as nullable variables.

Step 3: For every production of the form $N \rightarrow \alpha$, we get:

Old productions with nullable	New productions formed from the rule
$S \rightarrow Xb$	$S \rightarrow b$
$S \rightarrow aYa$	$S \rightarrow aa$
$X \rightarrow Y$	nothing
$X \rightarrow \varepsilon$	nothing
$Y \rightarrow X$	nothing

Step 4: Delete ε- productions, i.e., $X \rightarrow \varepsilon$

Therefore, we get new CFG as follows:

$$S \rightarrow a|Xb|aYa|b|aa$$
$$X \rightarrow Y$$
$$Y \rightarrow b|X$$

Example 5.14: Find a CFG without ε-productions equivalent to the grammar defined by

$$S \rightarrow ABaC$$
$$A \rightarrow BC$$
$$B \rightarrow b|\varepsilon$$
$$C \rightarrow D|\varepsilon$$
$$D \rightarrow d$$

Solution:

By applying Step 1 and Step 2 of the algorithm we get B, C and A are nullable.

Step 3: For every production of the form $N \rightarrow \alpha$, we get:

Old productions with nullable	New productions without nullable
$S \rightarrow ABaC$	$S \rightarrow a|BaC|ABa|aC|Aa|Ba|AaC$
$A \rightarrow BC$	$A \rightarrow B, A \rightarrow C$

Step 4: Remove all ε-productions

i.e., $B \to \varepsilon \ \& \ C \to \varepsilon$

We get new CFG as follows:

$S \to ABaC|BaC|AaC|ABa|aC|Aa|Ba|a$

$A \to BC|B|C|$

$B \to b$

$C \to D$

$D \to d$

5.4.2 Removing Useless Variables/Symbols and Productions

Let $G = (V, T, P, S)$ be a context-free grammar. A variable $X \in V$ is useful if and only if there is at least one word w in T^* such that $S \overset{*}{\Rightarrow} \alpha X \beta \overset{*}{\Rightarrow} w$, with α, β in $(V \cup T)^*$. In other words, a variable is useful if and only if it occurs in at least one derivation. A variable that is not useful is called *useless*. A production is useless if it involves any useless variable. The algorithm for removing useless productions is given in Algorithm 5.3.

Algorithm 5.3: Algorithm for removing useless productions

Algorithm (Finding an Equivalent CFG with no useless production): Given a CFG $G = (V, T, P, S)$ with useless productions, construct a grammar $G' = (V', T', P', S)$ having no useless variable (symbols) or production. The steps in the algorithms are as follows:

Step1: First we construct an intermediate grammar $G_1 = (V_1, T, P_1, S)$ equivalent to grammar G, such that every variable in G_1 derives some terminal string in the following way:

    (i)   Set V_1 to ϕ.

    (ii) For every $A \in V$ for which P has a production of the form

        $A \to X_1 X_2 \ldots \ldots \ldots \ldots X_n$, with all X_i in $V_1 \cup T$, add A to V_1.

    (iii) Repeat the Step (ii) until no more variables are added to V_1.

    (iv) P_1 is constructed as follows:

        $P_1 = \{A \to \alpha \ | A, \alpha \in (V_1 \cup T)^*\}$ for each A.

Step 2: Now, we construct a grammar

    $G' = (V', T, P', S)$

Equivalent to $G_1 = (V_1, T, P_1, S)$ so that every symbol in G' appears in some sentential form of G' which is equivalent to G_1 and hence to G. G' is the required grammar having no useless variables or production.

    (i) $V_2 = \{S\}$ starting symbol of G'. For the production of the form

        $A \to \alpha$ with $A \in V_2$ and α containing the symbol $X \in V_1 \cup T$, add X

to V_2.

(ii) Repeat the Step (i) for all variables.

(iii) $V' = V_1 \cap V_2$

$T' = T \cap V_2$

$P' = \{A \to \alpha \mid A \in V_2\}$

Example 5.15: Consider the grammar $G = (V, T, P, S)$ where V, T, P, S are given as:

$V = \{S, A, B, C, E\}$

$T = \{a, b, c\}$

$S = \{S\}$ and

P consists of

$S \to AB$

$A \to a$

$B \to b$

$B \to C$

$E \to c$

Eliminate useless symbols and productions from the above grammar.

Solution:

Step 1: First, we construct an intermediate grammar $G_1 = (V_1, T, P_1, S)$ equivalent to grammar G so that each variable in G_1 derives some terminal strings.

(i) We start with $V_1 = \phi$.

(ii) The productions $A \to a, B \to b$ and $E \to c$ are of the form $A \to X_1 X_2 \dots X_n$, with all X_i in

$V_1 \cup T$, i.e., $(\{\phi\} \cup \{a, b, c\})$

Therefore, we add A, B & E to V_1, we get

$V_1 = \{A, B, E\}$

(iii) Next, the production $S \to AB$ is in the form is in the form $A \to X_1 X_2 \dots X_n$ with all $X_i \in V_1 \cup T$.

Therefore, the variable S is included in V_1. We get,

$V_1 = \{S, A, B, E\}$

(iv) Now, we construct P_1 as follows:

$S \to AB$ is added in P_1 since S, A and $B \in V_1 \cup T$.

Similarly, we add the productions $A \to a, B \to b$ and $E \to c$.

Thus P_1 consists of:

$S \to AB$

$$A \rightarrow a$$
$$B \rightarrow b$$
$$E \rightarrow c$$

Now $G_1 = (\{S, A, B, E\}, \{a, b, c\}, P_1, S)$

Step 2: (i) We begin with $V_2 = \{S\}$

The production $S \rightarrow AB$ is of the form $A \rightarrow \alpha$ with $A \in V_2$ and α containing the symbol $X \in V_1 \bigcup T$. Therefore A & B are added to V_2, that is

$$V_2 = \{S, A, B\}$$

(ii) The production $A \rightarrow a$ & $B \rightarrow b$ is of the form $A \rightarrow \alpha$ with $A \in V_2$ and α contains X, where $X \in V_1 \bigcup T$. Therefore a, b are added to V_2, that is

$$V_2 = \{S, A, B\} \bigcup \{a, b\}$$

(iii) Now, we construct

$$V' = V_1 \bigcap V_2$$
$$= \{S, A, B, E\} \bigcap \{S, A, B\}$$
$$= \{S, A, B\}$$
$$T' = T \bigcap V_2$$
$$= \{a, b, c\} \bigcap (\{S, A, B\} \bigcup \{a, b\})$$
$$= \{a, b\}$$

P' consists of:

$$S \rightarrow AB$$
$$A \rightarrow a$$
$$B \rightarrow b$$

Hence,

$$G' = (\{S, A, B\}, \{a, b\}, P', S) \text{ where } P' \text{ consists of}$$
$$S \rightarrow AB$$
$$A \rightarrow a$$
$$B \rightarrow b$$

is the required grammar.

Example 5.16: Eliminate useless symbols and productions from $G = (V, T, P, S)$, where $V = \{S, A, B, C\}$, $T = \{a, b\}$ and P consist of

$$S \rightarrow aS|A|C$$
$$A \rightarrow a$$
$$B \rightarrow aa$$
$$C \rightarrow aCb$$

Step 1: First, we construct an intermediate grammar $G_1 = (V_1, T, P_1, S)$ equivalent to grammar G so that each variable in G_1 derives some terminal string.

(i)   We start with $V_1 = \phi$.

(ii)   The productions $A \to a$ and $B \to bb$ are of the form

$$A \to X_1 X_2 \ldots\ldots\ldots X_n \text{ with all } X_i \text{ in } V_1 \cup T$$

Therefore, A, B variables are added to V_1. Therefore

$$V_1 = \{A, B\}$$

(iii) The production $S \to A$ is of the form

$$A \to X_1 X_2 \ldots\ldots\ldots X_n$$

So, S is added to V_1 and

$$V_1 = \{S, A, B\}$$

(iv) P_1 is constructed as follows: $P_1 = \{A \to \alpha | A, \alpha \in (V_1 \cup T)^*\}$ for each A. We get
the productions as

$$S \to aS|A$$
$$A \to a$$
$$B \to aa$$

Therefore, $G_1 = (\{S, A, B, \}, \{a, b\}, P_1, S)$

Step2: (i) We begin with $V_2 = \{S\}$

The production $S \to aS$ and $S \to A$ are of the form $A \to \alpha$, $A \in V_2$ and α
contains the symbol $X \in (V_1 \cup T)$. So, we add A to V_2. Hence $V_2 = \{S, A\}$.

(ii)   The production $A \to a$ is also in the above form. So a is added to V_2.

$$V_2 = \{S, A\} \cup \{a\}$$

(iii) Next

$$V' = V_1 \cap V_2$$
$$= \{S, A, B\} \cap (\{S, A\} \cup \{a\})$$
$$= \{S, A\}$$
$$T' = T \cap V_2$$
$$= \{a, b\} \cap (\{S, A\} \cup a\})$$
$$= \{a\}$$

Now, we construct P'. P' consists of $\{A \to \alpha | A \in V'\}$.

We get:

$$S \to aS|A$$
$$S \to aS|A$$
$$A \to a$$

Therefore,

$G' = (\{S, A\}, \{a\}, P', S)$ where P' consists of $S \to aS|A$, $A \to a$, is the required grammar.

5.4.3 Removing Unit Productions

A production of the form $A \to B$, where A and B are variables in CFG is called a *Unit Production*. The productions having single variable on both sides are also undesirable. To remove Unit productions, the following concepts are important:

i.   If $A \to B$ is a production then B is said to be *A-derivable*.

ii. If C is *A-derivable*, $C \to B$ is a production, $B \neq A$, then B is *A-derivable*.

iii. No other variables are *A-derivable*.

The algorithm for removing unit production is given in Algorithm 5.4.

Algorithm 5.4: Algorithm for removing unit productions

Algorithm (Construction of equivalent CFG with no Unit Productions): Given a context-free grammar $G = (V, T, P, S)$ with no ε–productions. We construct a grammar $G' = (V, T, P', S)$ from G having no unit productions as follows:

Step 1: Initialize P' to P.

Step 2: For each $A \in V$, find the set of A–derivable variables.

Step 3: For each pair (A, B) such that B is A–derivable, and for every non-unit production $B \to \alpha$, add the production $A \to \alpha$ to P' if it is not already present in P'.

Step 4: Remove all unit productions from P'.

Example 5.17: Consider the grammar $G = (\{S, A, B, C, D, E\}, \{a, b\}, P, S)$ where P consists of $S \to AB$, $A \to a$, $B \to C$, $B \to b$, $C \to D$, $D \to E$ and $E \to a$.

Step 1: Remove all unit productions.

After initialization of P' to P, We get

$S \to AB$

$A \to a$

$B \to C|b$

$C \to D$

$D \to E$ and

$E \to a$

Step 2: For each $A \in V$, we find the set of A–derivables as follows:

$S \to AB$	S-derivable	Nothing
$A \to a$	A-derivable	Nothing
$B \to C|b$	B-derivable	C, D, E
$C \to D$	C-derivable	D, E
$D \to E$	D-derivable	E
$E \to a$	E-derivable	Nothing

Step 3: For every pair (A, B) such that B is A-derivable, and for every non-unit production $B \to \alpha$, add $A \to \alpha$ to P' if it is not already present in P'. Therefore,

For (B, C) & no production	nothing to be added
For (B, D) & no production	nothing to be added
For (B, E) & $E \to a$	$B \to a$ to be added
For (C, D) & no production	nothing to be added
For (C, E) & $E \to a$	$C \to a$ to be added
For (D, E) & $E \to a$	$D \to a$ to be added

P' consists of: $S \to AB$

$A \to a$

$B \to C|b$

$C \to D$

$D \to E$ and $E \to a$

$B \to a$

$C \to a$

$D \to a$

Step 4: When unit productions are deleted, we are left with:

$S \to AB$

$A \to a$

$B \to a|b$

$E \to a$

$C \to a$

$D \to a$

Example 5.18: Remove all Unit Productions from

$S \to Aa|B$

$B \to A|bb$

$A \to a|bc|B$

Solution:

Step 1: First, we initialize P' to P. P' now consists of

$S \to Aa|B$

$B \to A|bb$

$A \to a|bc|B$

Step 2: Next, we find the set of A-derivable for each $A \in V$.

A, B are S-derivable.

B is A- derivable

A is B- derivable

Step3: For every pair (A, B) such that B is A-derivable, we add $A \to \alpha$ for every non-unit production of the form $B \to \alpha$. Therefore

For (S, A) & $A \to a|bc$	$S \to a|bc$ is added
For (S, B) & $B \to bb$	$S \to bb$ is added
For (A, B) & $B \to bb$	$A \to bb$ is added
For (B, A) & $A \to a|bb$	$B \to a|bc$ is added

Step4: When Unit Productions are deleted, we are left with:

$S \to Aa|a|bc|bb$

$B \to bb|a|bc$

$A \to a|bc|bb$

5.5 Normal Forms for CFGs

There are several ways in which one can restrict the format of productions without reducing the generative power of context-free grammars. When the productions in the context-free grammar satisfy certain restrictions, G is said to be in normal form. Various types of normal forms have been established for context-free grammars. We will briefly discuss two of them- (i) Chomsky normal form and (ii) Greibach normal form.

5.5.1 Chomsky Normal Form (CNF)

A context-free grammar $G = (V, T, P, S)$ is in Chomsky Normal Form (CNF) if each of the production is of the form

$A \to BC$

or $\quad A \to a$

where A, B and C are variables in V and a is in T.

The algorithm for converting CFG into CNF is given in Algorithm 5.5.

Algorithm 5.5: Algorithm for Converting CFG to CNF

Algorithm (Conversion from CFG to CNF): The following steps are used to convert the given CFG into CNF:

Step 1: If CFG has ε-productions and unit productions, remove them. After eliminating these, let $G = (V, T, P, S)$.

Step 2: Elimination of terminals on RHS: Construct grammar

$\quad G_1 = (V_1, T, P_1, S)$.

from G as follows:

(i) Consider from P all productions of the from

$\quad A \to x_1 x_2 \dots x_n$ ...(1)

where each x_i is a symbol either in V or T. If $n = 1$ then x_1 must be a terminal since P has no unit productions. Include this production in P_1 and A in V_1. If $n \geq 2$, introduce new variables B_a for each $a \in T$. For every production in P of the form (1), we include in P_1 the production:

$$A \to C_1 C_2 \ldots C_n,$$

where $C_i = x_i$ if x_i is in V, and $C_i = B_a$ if $x_i = a$.

For every B_a we also include the production $B_a \to a$ in P_1. We include every A and B_a in V_1.

At this state, we have removed all terminals from productions whose right side had more than one symbol, and replaced them with new variables. Now, we have a grammar G_1 whose every production is of the form

$$A \to a \qquad \qquad \ldots (2)$$

or $\quad A \to C_1 C_2 \ldots\ldots\ldots\ldots C_n, \qquad \qquad \ldots (3)$

where $C_i \in V_1$.

Step 3: Restricting the number of variables on the right hand side of the productions. We construct $G_2 = (V_2, T, P_2, S)$ from G_1 as follows:

(i)   First, we include all productions of the form (2) as well as all productions of the form (3) with $n = 2$ in P_2. All variables in V_1 are added to V_2.

(iii) We introduce additional variables, wherever necessary, to reduce the length of the right hand sides of the productions. For $n > 2$, we introduce new variables $D_1, D_2 \ldots$ and put in P_2 the productions

$$A \to C_1 D_1$$
$$D_1 \to C_2 D_2$$

.

.

.

$$D_{n-2} \to C_{n-1} C_{n-2} \; C_n.$$

We also include the new variables $D_1, D_2 \ldots D_n$ in V_2. Thus, we get G_2 which is in CNF.

Example 5.19: Reduce the grammar G with following productions to CNF:

$S \to ASA | bA$

$A \to B|S$

$B \to c$

Step 1: Eliminate unit productions as follows:

Initialize P' to P. Then P' consists of

$S \to ASA | bA$

$A \to B|S$

$B \to c$

Next, for each $A \in V$, we find the set of A-derivable. Obviously B and S are A-derivable. For every pair (A, B) such that B is A-derivable, we add $A \to \alpha$ for every non-unit production of the form $B \rightarrow \alpha$. Hence

      For (A, B) & $B \rightarrow c$ $A \rightarrow c$ is added

      For (A, S) & $S \rightarrow ASA|bA$ $A \rightarrow ASA|bA$ are added

Now P_1 consists of

      $S \rightarrow ASA|bA$

      $A \rightarrow B|S$

      $A \rightarrow ASA|bA$

      $B \rightarrow c$

      $A \rightarrow c$

After removing unit productions, we get

      $S \rightarrow ASA|bA$

      $A \rightarrow ASA|bA|c$

      $B \rightarrow c$

Step 2: Eliminate terminals from RHS:

      The productions $S \rightarrow ASA$

      $A \rightarrow ASA$, $A \rightarrow C$ and

      $B \rightarrow c$

are in proper form. We have to modify $S \rightarrow bA$ and $A \rightarrow bA$.

We replace $S \rightarrow bA$ by $S \rightarrow C_b A$ and $C_b \rightarrow b$ and

          $A \rightarrow bA$ by $A \rightarrow C_b A$

So, $G_2 = (\{S, A, B, C_b\}, \{b, c\}, P_2, S)$ where P_2 consists of

      $S \rightarrow ASA|C_b A$

      $S \rightarrow ASA|c|C_b A$

      $B \rightarrow c$

      $C_b \rightarrow b$

Step 3: Restructure the number of variables on RHS

      $S \rightarrow ASA$ is replaced by $S \rightarrow AD, D \rightarrow SA$

      $A \rightarrow ASA$ is replaced by $A \rightarrow AE, E \rightarrow SA$

So, the equivalent grammar in CNF is

      $G_3 = (\{S, A, B, C_b, D, E\}, \{b, c\}, P_3, S)$

where P_3 consists of:

      $S \rightarrow C_b A|AD$

      $A \rightarrow C_b A|AE|c$

      $B \rightarrow c, C_b \rightarrow b, D \rightarrow SA, E \rightarrow SA$

Example 5.20 : Reduce the following grammar G to CNF.

      $S \rightarrow AACD$

      $A \rightarrow aAb|\varepsilon$

$C \rightarrow aC|a$

$D \rightarrow aDa|bDb|\varepsilon$

Step1: We, first eliminate ε-productions if any. The grammar contains ε-productions. So, we eliminate ε-productions as follows:

Since A and D nullable variables hence we have

Old productions with nullable	New productions formed from the rule
$S \rightarrow AACD$	$S \rightarrow ACD|CD|AAC|AC|C$
$A \rightarrow aAb$	$A \rightarrow ab$
$D \rightarrow aDa$	$D \rightarrow aa$
$D \rightarrow bDb$	$D \rightarrow bb$

After removing all ε-productions, we have the following productions:

$S \rightarrow AACD|ACD|AAC|AC|CD|C$

$A \rightarrow aAb|ab$

$C \rightarrow aC|a$

$D \rightarrow aDa|bDb|aa|bb$

Step 2: Next eliminate unit productions:

C is S - derivable. Therefore

For (S, C) & $C \rightarrow aC|a$ we *add* $S \rightarrow aC|a$

After deleting unit productions, we get

$S \rightarrow AACD|ACD|AAC|AC|CD|aC|a$

$A \rightarrow aAb|ab$

$C \rightarrow aC|a$

$D \rightarrow aDa|bDb|aa|bb$

Step 3: Elimination of terminals in RHS

We have to modify $S \rightarrow aC$ by $S \rightarrow R_aC, R_a \rightarrow a$

$A \rightarrow aAb$ by $A \rightarrow R_aAR_b, R_b \rightarrow b, R_a \rightarrow a$

$A \rightarrow ab$ by $A \rightarrow R_aR_b$

$C \rightarrow aC$ by $C \rightarrow R_aC$

$D \rightarrow aDa$ by $D \rightarrow R_aDR_a$

$D \rightarrow bDb$ by $D \rightarrow R_bDR_b$

$D \rightarrow aa$ by $D \rightarrow R_aR_a$

$D \rightarrow bb$ by $D \rightarrow R_bR_b$

P_2 consists of:

$S \rightarrow AACD|ACD|AAC|AC|CD|R_aC|a$

$A \rightarrow R_aAR_b|R_aR_b$

$C \rightarrow R_aC|a$

$D \rightarrow R_aDR_a|R_bDR_b|R_aR_a|R_bR_b$

$$R_a \rightarrow a$$
$$R_b \rightarrow b$$

Step 4: Restrict the number of variables in RHS.

$S \rightarrow AACD$ is replaced by $S \rightarrow AE, E \rightarrow ACD$, now $E \rightarrow ACD$ is replaced by $E \rightarrow AF, F \rightarrow CD$.

$S \rightarrow ACD$ is replaced by $S \rightarrow AG, G \rightarrow CD$

$S \rightarrow AAC$ is replaced by $S \rightarrow AH, H \rightarrow AC$

$A \rightarrow R_a AR_b$ is replaced by $A \rightarrow R_a I, I \rightarrow AR_b$

$D \rightarrow R_a DR_a$ is replaced by $D \rightarrow R_a J, J \rightarrow DR_a$

$D \rightarrow R_b DR_b$ is replaced by $D \rightarrow R_b K, K \rightarrow DR_b$

So, the equivalent grammar in CNF is $G = (\{S, A, E, F, C, D, G, H, I, J, K\}, T, P, S)$ where P consists of

$$S \rightarrow AE,$$
$$E \rightarrow AF,$$
$$F \rightarrow CD$$
$$S \rightarrow AG,$$
$$G \rightarrow CD$$
$$S \rightarrow AH,$$
$$H \rightarrow AC$$
$$A \rightarrow R_a I,$$
$$I \rightarrow AR_b$$
$$D \rightarrow R_a J,$$
$$J \rightarrow DR_a$$
$$D \rightarrow R_b K,$$
$$K \rightarrow DR_b,$$

5.5.2 Greibach Normal Form (GNF)

Greibach Normal Form (GNF) is another very important normal form. It has many theoretical and practical consequences. *GNF* is useful for proving the equivalence of CFG and NPDA. A context-free grammar $G = (V, T, P, S)$ is said to be in GNF if every production in G is of the form

$$A \rightarrow a\alpha$$

where $a \in T$ and $A \in V$, $\alpha \in V^*$. The right hand side of each production of GNF always starts with a terminal symbol perhaps followed by some variables. Therefore, we can say that productions in GNF are a natural generalization of a regular grammar. In a regular grammar, the productions are of the form $A \rightarrow a\alpha$, where $a \in T$, and $\alpha \in V \bigcup \{\varepsilon\}$. A context-free grammar can be converted into GNF by using the following two Lemmas:

Lemma 5.1: A production is to be said A-production if and only if variable A is on the left side of production. Let $G = (V, T, P, S)$ be a CFG. Let $A \to \alpha_1 B \alpha_2$ be a production in P and $B \to \beta_1 | \beta_2 | \ldots \beta_r$ be the set of all B-productions. Let $G_1 = (V, T, P_1, S)$ be obtained from G by deleting the productions $A \to \alpha_1 B \alpha_2$ from P and adding the productions

$$A \to \alpha_1 \beta_1 \alpha_2 | \alpha_1 \beta_2 \alpha_2 | \ldots \ldots \ldots \ldots \ldots \ldots \alpha_1 \beta_r \alpha_2.$$

Then $L(G) = L(G_1)$.

Proof: Obviously $L(G_1) \subseteq L(G)$, since if $A \to \alpha_1 \beta_i \alpha_2$ is used in a derivation of G_1, then $A \Rightarrow \alpha_1 \beta_1 \alpha_2 \Rightarrow \alpha_1 \beta_i \alpha_2$ can be used in G. To show $L(G) \subseteq L(G_1)$. The production $A \to \alpha_1 B \alpha_2$ is the only production in G that is not in G_1. Whenever $A \to \alpha_1 B \alpha_2$ is used in the derivation by G, the variable B must be rewritten at some later step using a production of the form and $B \to \beta_i$. These two steps can be replaced by a single step $A \Rightarrow \alpha_1 \beta_i \alpha_2$.

Lemma 5.2: Let $G = (V, T, P, S)$ be a CFG. Let $A \to A\alpha_1 | A\alpha_2 | \ldots A\alpha_r$ be the set of A-productions for which A is the leftmost symbol of the RHS Let $A \to \beta_1 | \beta_2 | \ldots \ldots$ β_s be the remaining A productions. Let $G_1 = (V \cup \{B\}, T, P_1, S)$ be the CFG formed by adding the variable B to V and replacing all the A-productions by the productions:

(1) $A \to \beta_i$

$A \to \beta_i B$ where $1 \le i \le s$

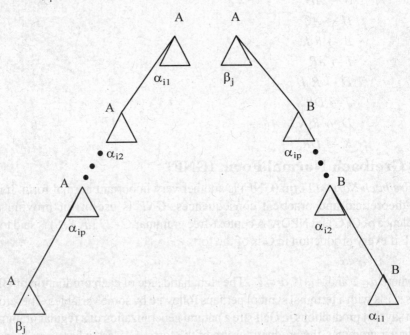

Fig. 5.15: Transformation of Lemma 5.2 by the derivation tree

(2) $B \to \alpha_i$

   $B \to \alpha_i B$ where $1 \le i \le r$

   Then $L(G_I) = L(G)$.

   Proof: A sequence of productions of the form $A \to A\alpha_i$ must end with a production $A \to \beta_j$ in a leftmost derivation. The sequence of replacements $A \to A\alpha_{i_j} \Rightarrow A\alpha_{i_2} A\alpha_{i_1}$ $\ldots \Rightarrow A\alpha_{i_p} A\alpha_{i_{p-1}} \ldots \alpha_{i_1} \Rightarrow \beta_j \alpha_{i_p} \alpha_{i_{p-1}} \ldots \ldots \ldots \alpha_{i_1}$ in G can be replaced in G_I by $A \to \beta_j B \Rightarrow \beta_j^i \alpha_{i_p} B \Rightarrow \beta_j \alpha_{i_p} \alpha_{i_{p-1}} B \Rightarrow \ldots \ldots \ldots \Rightarrow \beta_j \alpha_{i_p} \alpha_{i_{p-1}} \ldots \ldots \ldots \alpha_{i_2} B \Rightarrow \beta_j \alpha_{i_p} \alpha_{i_{p-1}} \ldots \ldots \ldots \ldots \ldots \alpha_{i_2} \alpha_{i_1}$. The reverse transformation can also be made. Thus, $L(G)$ $= L(G_I)$. This transformation can also be visualized from the derivation tree given in Figure 5.15.

   The algorithm of conversion from CFG to GNF is given in Algorithm 5.6.

   Algorithm 5.6: Algorithm of conversion from CFG to GNF

Algorithm (Construction of GNF from CFG) : Every CFL without ε can be generated by a CFG in GNF. The following steps are used to construct GNF from given CFG $G = (V, T, P, S)$:

Step 1: We eliminate ε-productions if any in the CFG and then construct a grammar in CNF generating language L. We rename the variables as $A_1, A_2 \ldots A_n$ with $S = A_1$. We get

$$G = (\{A_1, A_2, \ldots A_n\}, T, P, A_1)$$

Step 2: Convert the A_i-productions to the form $A_i \to A_j \gamma$ such that $j > i$. If suppose $A_k \to A_j \gamma$ is a production with $j < k$, we generate a new set of productions by substituting for A_j the right-hand side of each A_j production according to Lemma 5.1. By repeating the process $k-1$ times at most, we obtain productions of the form

$$A_k \to A_l \gamma, l \ge k.$$

Step 3: The productions of the form $A_k \to A_l \gamma$ with $l = k$ is then replaced according to Lemma 5.2, introducing a new variable B_k. Now we get:

   $A_i \to A_j \gamma, \ j > i,$

   $A_i \to a\gamma, \ a$ in T,

   $B_i \to \gamma, \gamma$ in $(V \cup \{B_1, B_2 \ldots B_{i-1}\})^*$

Step 4: For all productions of the form $A_{m-1} \to A_m \gamma$, we generate new productions by replacing A_m according to Lemma 5.1.

Step 5: We repeat the Step 4 for each production $A_{m-2} \ldots A_2, A_1$ until the right side of each production for A_i starts with a terminal symbol.

Step 6: We convert $B_1, B_2 \ldots \ldots B_m$ into GNF by substituting the value of proper A_i.

Example 5.21: Construct a grammar in Greibach normal form equivalent to the grammar

$S \to AA|a$

$A \to SS|b$

Solution:

Step 1: The given grammar is in CNF and does not contain ε-productions. S and A are renamed as A_1 and A_2, respectively. We get productions as follows:

$A_1 \to A_2A_2|a$

$A_2 \to A_1A_1|b$

Step 2: Now, we convert the A_i productions to the form $A_i \to A_j\gamma$ such that $j \geq i$. $A_1 \to A_2A_2$, $A_1 \to a$ and the production $A_2 \to b$ are in the required form. But the production $A_2 \to A_1A_1$ is not in the required form. So, we take the production $A_2 \to A_1A_1$ and substitute the string $A_2A_2|a$ for left most A_1. We get

$A_2 \to A_2A_2A_1$

$A_2 \to aA_1$

Thus, the resulting set of productions is:

$A_1 \to A_2A_2|a$

$A_2 \to A_2A_2A_1|aA_1|b$

Step 3: The production $A_2 \to A_2A_2A_1$ is in the form $A_k \to A_l\gamma$ with $l = k$. And remaining A_2 productions in the form $A_2 \to \beta_1 \beta_2 \ldots \beta_s$. So, we introduce variable B and replace all A-productions by the productions:

$\left.\begin{array}{l} A \to \beta_i \\ A \to \beta_iB \end{array}\right\} \quad 1 \leq i \leq s$

$\left.\begin{array}{l} B \to \alpha_i \\ B \to \alpha_iB \end{array}\right\} \quad 1 \leq i \leq r$ by the lemma.

Therefore, variable B_2 is introduced and production $A_2 \to A_2A_2A_1$ is replaced by

$A_2 \to aA_1$

$A_2 \to aA_1B_2$

$A_2 \to b$

$A_2 \to bB_2$

$B_2 \to A_2A_1$

$B_2 \to A_2A_1B_2$

The resulting set is:

$A_1 \to A_2A_2|a$

$A_2 \to aA_1B_2|bB_2|aA_1|b$

$B_2 \to A_2A_1|A_2A_1B_2$

Step 4: The production $A_1 \to A_2A_2A_1$ is in the form $A_{m-1} \to A_m\gamma$. So, we replace the variable A_2 of the above production by all of the A_2 productions. We get:

$A_1 \to aA_1B_2A_2$

$$A_1 \to bB_2A_2$$
$$A_1 \to aA_1A_2$$
$$A_1 \to bA_2$$

The set of resulting productions is:

$$A_1 \to a|aA_1A_2|bA_2|aA_1B_2A_2|bB_2A_2$$
$$A_2 \to aA_1B_2|bB_2|aA_1|b$$
$$B_2 \to A_2A_1|A_2A_1B_2$$

Step 5: Now, B_2 productions are converted to proper form by replacing the left-most variable A_2 of the right-hand side of the production B_2 by all the productions of A_2. We get:

$$B_2 \to aA_1B_2A_1 \qquad\qquad B_2 \to aA_1B_2A_1B_2$$
$$B_2 \to bB_2A_1 \qquad\qquad B_2 \to bB_2A_1B_2$$
$$B_2 \to bA_1 \qquad\qquad B_2 \to bA_1B_2$$
$$B_2 \to aA_1A_1 \qquad\qquad B_2 \to aA_1A_1B_2$$

Hence the equivalence grammar is:

$$G = (\{A_1, A_2, B_2\}, \{a, b\}, P_1, A_1)$$

where P_1 consists of:

$$A_1 \to a|aA_1A_2|bA_2|aA_1B_2A_2|bB_2A_2$$
$$A_2 \to aA_1B_2|bB_2|aA_1|b$$
$$B_2 \to aA_1B_2A_1|bB_2A_1|aA_1A_1|bA_1$$
$$B_2 \to aA_1B_2A_1B_2|bB_2A_1B_2|aA_1A_1B_2|bA_1B_2$$

5.6 Summary

1. A context-free grammar is a simple recursive method of specifying rules (or productions) to generate patterns of strings. Although all possible languages cannot be generated by context-free grammars, they can generate all regular and some non-regular languages.

2. A context-free grammar is a finite set of variables (also called non-terminals or syntactic categories) each of which represents a language. The languages represented by the variables are described recursively in terms of each other and primitive symbols called terminals.

3. The sequence of applications of productions, that produces the strings of terminals (word) from the start symbol, is called a derivation or a generation of the word/ string.

4. A sentential form is a string of terminals and variables α if $S \overset{*}{\Rightarrow} \alpha$ where $S \in V$ & $\alpha \in (V \cup T)^*$.

5. A derivation $A \overset{*}{\Rightarrow} w$ is said to be left most if in each step, we apply a production to the leftmost variable in the sentential form. A derivation $A \overset{*}{\Rightarrow} w$ is said to be

rightmost if in each step we apply a production to the rightmost variable in the sentential form.

6. Derivation tree is a graphical representation of the derivation of a word from a given set of production rules. In other words, a derivation tree captures the grammatical structure of the string.

7. The yield of a derivation tree is the concatenation of the labels of leaves form left to right.

8. In a derivation process, the unfinished stages which are sentential forms are generally called working strings.

9. A context-free grammar is ambiguous if there is at least one word in the language having two or more parse trees (or equivalently, two or more leftmost/rightmost derivations).

10. A regular grammar is one that is either right linear or left linear grammar.

11. In a given CFG, a production of the form

$$N \rightarrow \varepsilon$$

where N is a variable, is called a ε-production and any variable N for which derivation

$$N \overset{*}{\Rightarrow} \varepsilon$$

is possible is called nullable.

12. A variable is useful if and only if it occurs in at least one derivation. A variable that is not useful is called useless. A production is useless if it involves any useless variable.

13. A production of the form $A \rightarrow B$, where A and B are variables in CFG is called a Unit Production.

14. When the productions in the context-free grammar satisfy certain restrictions, G is said to be in normal form. Various types of normal forms have been established for context-free grammars.

15. A context-free grammar $G = (V, T, P, S)$ is in Chomsky Normal Form (CNF) if each of the production is of the form

$$A \rightarrow BC$$

or $A \rightarrow a$

where A, B and C are variables in V and a is in T.

16. Greibach Normal Form (GNF) is another important normal form. It has many theoretical and practical consequences.

5.7   Exercises

Objective Questions

1. Which of the following statements is false?

    (a) A context-free grammar can be viewed as a language generator

(b) Context-free grammars are a more powerful method of describing languages than regular languages.

(c) The original motivation for context-free grammar was the description of natural languages

(d) None of these

2. Which of the following context-free grammar cannot be simulated by a finite state machine?

(a) $S \rightarrow Sa|a$ (b) $S \rightarrow abX, X \rightarrow CY, Y \rightarrow a|aX$

(c) $S \rightarrow aSb|ab$ (d) None of these

3. A regular grammar can be recognized by:

(a) Finite state machine   (b) Push down automaton

(c) 2-way linear bounded automata   (d) All of above

4. Which of the following statements is false?

(a) A derivation tree is called parse tree

(b) A derivation tree is called syntax tree

(c) A derivation tree is called generation tree

(d) None of these

5. A given grammar is said to be ambiguous if:

(a) There is at least one word in the language having two or more derivation trees

(b) There is at least two words in the language having two or more derivation trees

(c) Two or more productions have the same non-terminal on the left hand side

(d) A derivation tree has more than one associated word

6. Which of the following statements is false?

(a) A grammar is ambiguous if it has more than one leftmost derivation of at least one word in the language

(b) A grammar is ambiguous if it has more than one rightmost derivation of at least one word in the language

(c) A context-free grammar can be viewed as a language generators

(d) The original motivation for context-free grammar was the description of programming languages

7. The context-free grammar $G = (\{S\}, \{a, b\}, P, S)$ with productions
$S \rightarrow S|bS|a|b,$
is equivalent to regular expression:

(a) $(a + b)$ (b) $(a + b)(a + b)$

(c) $(a + b)(a + b)*$ (d) All of these

8. A context-free grammar is called right-linear grammar if each of its production is one of the form:

(a) $A \to wB|w$ where $A, B \in V$ and $w \in T^*$

(b) $A \to Bw|w$ where $A, B \in V$ and $w \in T^*$

(c) $A \to BC|w$ where $A, B, C \in V$ and $w \in T^*$

(d) $A \to a\alpha$ where $\alpha \in V^*, a \in T$

9.   A context-free grammar can be recognized by:

(a) Finite state machine   (b) Push down automaton

(c) 2-way linear bounded automata   (d) Both (b) and (c)

10. A context-free grammar is called left-linear grammar if each production is one of the two form:

(a) $A \to wB|w$ where $A, B \in V$ and $w \in T^*$

(b) $A \to Bw|w$ where $A, B \in V$ and $w \in T^*$

(c) $A \to BC|w$ where $A, B, C \in V$ and $w \in T^*$

(d) $A \to a\alpha$ where $\alpha \in V^*, a \in T$

11. A string w is in sentential form if:

(a) $S \xrightarrow{*} w$, where S is the starting symbol of grammar and $w \in (V \bigcup T)^*$

(b) $A \xrightarrow{*} w$, where $A \in V$ and $w \in (V \bigcup T)^*$

(c) Both (a) and (b)

(d) None of these

12. A context-free grammar G is said to be ambiguous if:

(a) It has two or more leftmost derivations for some word $\in L(G)$

(b) It has two or more rightmost derivations for some word $\in L(G)$

(c) Neither (a) nor (b) is true

(d) Both (a) and (b) are true

13. Which of the following statements is false?

(a) A CFG is said to be a right-linear grammar if each production is one of the two forms $A \to wB|w$ where $A, B \in V$ and $w \in T^*$

(b) A CFG is said to be a left-linear grammar if each production is one of the two forms $A \to Bw|w$ where $A, B \in V$ and $w \in T^*$

(c) A CFG is said to be a linear grammar if each production is of the form $A \to xBw|w$, where $A, B \in V$ and $x, w \in T^*$

(d) None of these

14. A context-free grammar having productions $A \to a\alpha$ where $A \in V, a \in T$ and $\alpha \in V^*$ is in:

(a) Chomsky normal form   (b) Greibach normal form

(c) Both (a) and (b)   (d) Neither (a) nor (b)

15. A context-free grammar having productions $A \to wB|w$ where $A, B \in V, w \in T^*$ is in:

(a) Chomsky normal form   (b) Greibach normal form

(c) Both (a) and (b)   (d) Neither (a) nor (b)

16. In a context-free grammar:

(a) ε can not be the right-hand side of any production

(b) Terminal symbols can not be present in the left hand side of any production

(c) The number of grammar symbols in the left hand side is not greater than The number of grammar symbols in the right hand side

(d) All of these

17. Consider the following grammar $G = (\{S\}, \{a, b\}, P, S)$ with P given as

$S \to abS|a$.

Which of the following regular expressions corresponds to the grammar G?

(a) $(ab)*$ (b) $(ab)*a$

(c) $a(ab)*$ (d) $b(ab)*$

18. Consider the following grammar $G = (\{S, A, B, C, D\}, \{a, b\}, P, S)$ with P given as

$S \to Aab$,

$A \to Aab|B$

$B \to a$

Which of the following regular expressions corresponds to the grammar?

(a) $aa(ab)*$ (b) $aabb(ab)*a$

(c) $aab(ab)*$ (d) None of these

19. Which one is false for the regular grammar?

(a) A right linear grammar is a regular grammar.

(b) A left linear grammar is a regular grammar

(c) A regular grammar is always linear.

(d) All linear grammars are regular.

20. Which of the following statements is false?

(a) Any regular language has an equivalent context-free grammar.

(b) All languages can be generated by context-free grammar

(c) Some non-regular languages can't be generated by any context-free grammar

(d) A right-linear grammar is a regular grammar

21. Every context-free grammar can be converted into an equivalent:

(a) Chomsky normal form   (b) Greibach normal form

(c) Either (a) or (b)   (d) None of these

22. Consider the context-free grammar $G = (\{S, A, B, C\}, \{a, b\}, P, S)$ with productions

$S \to BC$,

$B \rightarrow AB|\varepsilon$

$A \rightarrow abb|b$

$C \rightarrow DC|\varepsilon,$

$D \rightarrow ab$

which of the following regular expressions corresponds to the grammar G?

(a) $(abb + a)*(ab)*$ (b) $(abb + b)*(ba)*$

(c) $(b + ab)*(ab)*$ (d) $(abb + b)*(ab)*$

23. Which of the following context-free grammars can not be simulated by a finite automaton?

(a) $S \rightarrow Sa|ab$ (b) $S \rightarrow abX$

                                     $X \rightarrow cY$

                                     $Y \rightarrow d|aX$

(c) $S \rightarrow abSb|ab$ (d) None of these

24. Consider the grammar:

$S \rightarrow SABa|SB|ASab$

$A \rightarrow a$

$B \rightarrow b$

to get a string of n terminals, the number of productions to be used is:

(a) n^2 (b) $n + 1$

(c) $2n$ (d) $2n - 1$

25. The language $L = \{a^n b^n | n \geq 1\}$ is generated by CFG:

(a) $S \rightarrow aS|bS|\varepsilon$ (b) $S \rightarrow aSb|ab$

(c) Both (a) & (b)   (d) None of these

26. A language L is accepted by a finite automaton if and only if it is:

(a) Right-linear grammar   (b) Context-free grammar

(c) Recursive grammar   (d) Context-sensitive grammar

27. A language L is accepted by a finite automaton if and only if it is:

(a) Context-free grammar   (b) Left-linear grammar

(c) Recursive grammar   (d) Context-sensitive grammar

28. A language L is accepted by a finite automaton if and only if:

(a) L is a regular language

(b) L is defined by regular grammar

(c) L is defined by left-linear grammar

(d) All of these

29. Productions in GNF are a natural generalization of:

(a) CFG   (b) Regular grammar

(c) Context-sensitive grammar   (d) None of these

Answers to Objective Questions

01.	(d)	02.	(c)	03.	(a)	04.	(d)	05.	(d)	06.	(d)
07.	(c)	08.	(c)	09.	(d)	10.	(b)	11.	(a)	12.	(d)
13.	(d)	14.	(b)	15.	(d)	16.	(d)	17.	(b)	18.	(c)
19.	(d)	20.	(b)	21.	(c)	22.	(d)	23.	(c)	24.	(d)
25.	(b)	26.	(a)	27.	(b)	28.	(d)	29.	(b)		

Review Questions

1. Why is CFG not considered adequate for describing natural language? Explain with suitable example.

^2. The context-free grammars, like regular languages, can be viewed as language generators. Justify.

3. What is the derivation? List the properties of derivation.

4. What do you mean by partial derivation tree?

5. What are left most and right most derivations? Explain with suitable example.

6. Explain the following terms with suitable examples:
   (i)   Derivation tree
   (ii) Yield of derivation tree
   (iii) Subtree of derivation tree
   (iv) A-tree
   (v)   Working string
   (vi) Total language tree

^7. What do you mean by ambiguity of the grammar? Show that the following grammar is ambiguous.

$$S \rightarrow aSbS|bSaS|\varepsilon$$

^8. Prove or disprove that regular expressions can be ambiguous.

^9. Prove that the language $L = \{a^n b^n | n \geq 1\}$ is a context-free language.

^10. Show that the following grammar is ambiguous:

$$S \rightarrow AB|aaB$$
$$A \rightarrow a|Aa$$
$$B \rightarrow b$$

11. Consider the CFG $G = (\{\text{Statement, Expression}\}, \{\text{if, else, fun1}(), \text{fun2}(), \text{exp}, (,)\}, P, S)$

   where P consists of

   Statement $\rightarrow$ if (expression) statement
   $\rightarrow$ if (expression) statement else statement
   $\rightarrow$ fun1()
   $\rightarrow$ fun2()
   expression $\rightarrow$ expression 1
   $\rightarrow$ expression 2

   Show that the context-free grammar G is ambiguous.

12. Show that the grammar:

    $S \rightarrow a|abSb|aAb$

    $A \rightarrow bS|aAAb$

    is ambiguous.

^13. Why is ambiguity a problem for context-free grammar? Explain with taking suitable example.

^14. Construct a CFG of the following finite Automaton (see Figure 5.16):

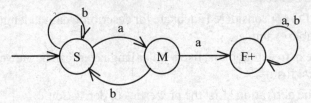

Fig. 5.16

15. Define regular grammar. Write an algorithm to convert regular grammar to the finite automaton.

16. Construct the TG or Transaction system M accepting the regular language L(G), for regular grammar given by the production:

    (a) $S \rightarrow aaS|bbS|abX|baX|\varepsilon$

      $X \rightarrow aaX|bbX|abS|baS$

    (b) $G = (\{S, A\}, \{a, b\}, P, S)$

      $S \rightarrow aA, A \rightarrow bA, A \rightarrow a, A \rightarrow bS, S \rightarrow aS|a$

^17. Prove that the language of even-length palindromes, i.e., $L = \{ww^R \,|w \in \{a, b\}^*\}$ is a context-free language but not a regular language.

^18. Prove that $\{w \in \{a, b\} \,| \#a(w) = \#b(w)\}$ is not a regular but it is a context-free language.

19. What is inherently ambiguous grammar? Discuss with suitable example.

20. What is ε-production? Write an algorithm to remove the ε-production.

21. What is useless production? Write an algorithm to remove the useless production.

22. What is unit production? Write an algorithm to remove unit production.

23. What is CNF? Write an algorithm to convert a given CFG into CNF.

24. What is GNF? State the relationship between GNF and Regular grammar.

25. Show that the two CFGs

    $S \rightarrow abAb|ba$ $A \rightarrow aaa$

    $B \rightarrow aA|bb$

    and

    $S \rightarrow abAaA|abAbb|ba$ $A \rightarrow aaa$

    are equivalent.

26. Eliminate all ε-productions from the following grammars:

(a) $S \to AaB|aaB$ $A \to \varepsilon$
  $B \to bbA|\varepsilon$

(b) $S \to XY$ $Z \to AB$
  $Y \to Zb$ $W \to Z$
  $Y \to bW$ $A \to aA|bA|\varepsilon$
  $B \to Ba|Bb|\varepsilon$

(c) $S \to Xa$ $X \to aX|bX|\varepsilon$

7. Eliminate all useless productions from the following grammar:

  $S \to aS|AB$
  $A \to ba$
  $B \to AA$

What language does this grammar generate?

8. Eliminate useless productions from the following grammars:

(i) $S \to a|aA|B|C$
  $A \to aB|\varepsilon$
  $B \to Aa$
  $C \to cCD$
  $D \to ddd$

(ii) $S \to AB|CA$
  $B \to BC|AB$
  $A \to a$
  $C \to aB|b$

(iii) $S \to aAa$
  $A \to SB|bCC|DaA$
  $C \to abb|DD$
  $E \to aC$
  $D \to aDA$

9. Remove all Unit Productions from the following grammar:

  $S \to Aa|B$ $B \to A|bb$
  $A \to a|bc|B$

0. Remove all unit productions, all useless productions and all ε-productions from the grammar.

  $S \to aA|aBB$
  $A \to aaA|\varepsilon$
  $B \to bB|bbC$
  $C \to B$

What language does this grammar generate?

31. Give an example of a situation in which the removal of ε-productions introduced previously non-existent unit productions.

32. Convert the following grammars into Chomsky normal form:
    (a) $S \rightarrow aSb|ab$
    (b) $S \rightarrow aSaA|A$, $S \rightarrow abA|b$
    (c) $S \rightarrow abAB$, $A \rightarrow bAB|\varepsilon$
        $B \rightarrow Baa|A|\varepsilon$
    (d) $S \rightarrow AB|aB$, $A \rightarrow aab|\varepsilon$
        $B \rightarrow bbA$
    (e) $S \rightarrow aACa$, $A \rightarrow B|a$
        $B \rightarrow C|c$ $C \rightarrow cC|\varepsilon$

33. Show that for every CFG $= (V, T, P, S)$ there is an equivalent one in which all productions have the form

    $$A \rightarrow aBC \text{ or } A \rightarrow \varepsilon \text{ where } a \in T \cup \{\lambda\}\ A, B, C \in V$$

34. Convert the following grammars into Greibach normal form:
    (a) $S \rightarrow aSb|bSa|a|b$
    (b) $S \rightarrow aSb|ab$
    (c) $S \rightarrow ab|aS|aaS$
    (d) $S \rightarrow ABb|a$, $A \rightarrow aaA|B$
        $B \rightarrow bAb$

Answers/Hints for Selected Review Questions

2. Let us take a regular expression $a(a^* + b^*)b$. The description of how to generate a string in accordance with this expression is as follows:

   First output a. Then do one of the following two things: Either output a number of a's or output a number of b's. Final output is ab.

   The language associated with this language generator is the set of all strings that can be produced by the process just described. Thus, we can say that regular expressions serve as language generators in such a way that strings in the language can be produced from left to right, i.e., each symbol of the generated string to be output as it is determined. However, the context-free grammars are more complex sorts of language generators, which are based on a more complex understanding of the structure of the strings belonging to the language.

7. The word *abbaab* can be derived by two different parse tree as shown in Figure 5.17.

   There are two derivation trees for the word *abbaab*. Therefore, Grammar G is ambiguous.

8. Regular expression can be ambiguous. Let us take a regular language over $\Sigma = \{a, b\}$ which is defined as follows:

   $$L = \{w \mid w \text{ contains at least one } a\}$$

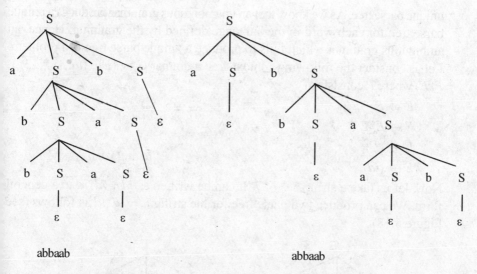

Fig. 5.17: Two parse trees for the word abbaab

A language can be defined by the regular expression as follows:

$$(a + b)^*a(a + b)^*$$

We can generate the string *aaa* in two ways as follows:

We can take first *a* from $(a + b)^*$, then

> take second *a* from $(a + b)^*$, then
>
> take third *a* from *a*, then
>
> take ε from $(a + b)^*$. We get string *aaa*.

or

We can take ε from $(a + b)^*$, then

> take first *a* from *a*, then
>
> take second *a* from $(a + b)^*$, then
>
> take third *a* from $(a + b)^*$. We get string *aaa*.

9. The language $L = \{a^n b^n | n \ge 1\}$ is a context-free language since it can be generated by the grammar $G = (\{S\}, \{a, b\}, P, S)$ where P consists of $S \to aSb | \varepsilon$.

10. There are two leftmost derivations for $w = aab$.

$$S \Rightarrow aaB \qquad\qquad S \Rightarrow AB$$
$$\Rightarrow aab \qquad\qquad\quad \Rightarrow AaB$$
$$\qquad\qquad\qquad\quad \Rightarrow aaB$$
$$\qquad\qquad\qquad\quad \Rightarrow aab$$

The word *aab* can be derived by two different parse trees.

13. A context-free grammar defines a context-free language. We generally need internal structure of the context-free language. For this, we assign meaning to a given string $w \in L$. It is usually difficult to assign a unique meaning without a

unique parse tree. As we know that an unambiguous grammar produces a unique parse tree for each word in the language defined by the grammar. Hence, an ambiguous grammar which fails to produce a unique parse tree is a problem. Let us consider the following context-free grammar $G = (\{E\}, \{id, +, *, (,) \},$ $P, E)$ where P consists of

$$E \rightarrow E + E$$
$$E \rightarrow E*E$$
$$E \rightarrow (E)$$
$$E \rightarrow (id)$$

Now, let us take a string 5 + 6*7. It can be written as $id + id*id$ in a general form. We can produce two parse tree for the string $id + id*id$ as follows (see Figure 5.18).

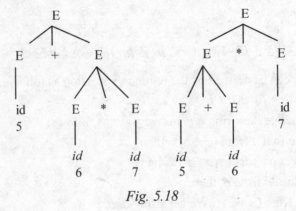

Fig. 5.18

From first parse tree, we get the value of expression 47 but from the second parse tree 77.

14. Let $G = (\{S, M, F\}, \{a, b\}, P, S)$

Where P is given by

$$S \rightarrow b\,S$$
$$S \rightarrow a\,M$$
$$M \rightarrow b\,S$$
$$M \rightarrow a\,F$$
$$M \rightarrow a$$
$$F \rightarrow a\,F$$
$$F \rightarrow b\,F$$
$$F \rightarrow a$$
$$F \rightarrow b$$

G is the required grammar.

17. The language $L = \{ww^R \mid w \in \{a, b\}^*\}$ is a context-free language since it can be generated by the grammar $G = (\{S\}, \{a, b\}, P, S)$ where P consists of $S \rightarrow aSa \mid bSb \mid \varepsilon$.

18. The language $L = \{w \in \{a, b\} \mid \#a(w) = \#b(w)\}$ is a context-free language since it can be generated by the grammar $G = (\{S\}, \{a, b\}, P, S)$ where P consists of $S \rightarrow aSb|bSa|SS|\varepsilon$.

Programming Problems

1. Write a program to convert a given regular grammar into DFA.

2. Write a program to convert a given DFA into regular grammar.

3. Write a program to simplify a given CFG by removing
    (i) ε-productions
    (ii) Useless productions
    (iii) Unit productions

4. Write a program to convert a given CFG into CNF.

5. Write a program to convert a given CFG into GNF.

Chapter 6

Pushdown Automata

The present Chapter deals with Pushdown Automata (PDA), a computational model more powerful than finite automata and strongly related to context-free languages. Methods of converting CFG to PDA and vice-versa are discussed in this Chapter. PDA is a non-deterministic device and its deterministic version describes a subset of a context-free language, called deterministic context-free language. The Chapter ends with a description of 2-stack pushdown automata.

Objectives: The aim of this Chapter is to explore a powerful computational model, called Pushdown Automata. After learning the contents of this Chapter, you will be able to:

1. Explain working of pushdown automata and the language they define,
2. Convert pushdown automaton into given context-free language and vice-versa and
3. Define and explain 2-Stack PDA.

6.1 Pushdown Automata (PDA) and their Description

Pushdown Automata (PDA) are similar to *Non-Deterministic Automata* except that they have a stack as an extra component. The stack, called *pushdown stack*, is a place where input letters can be stored until we wish to refer to them again.

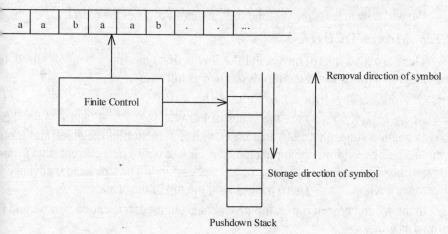

Fig. 6.1 : *Block Diagram of a Pushdown Automaton*

The stack provides additional memory beyond the finite amount available in the control. This additional memory allows Pushdown Automata to accept or define context-free languages. Context-free languages have pushdown automata as language acceptors just as regular languages have finite automata as language acceptors. Figure 6.1 shows the block diagram of a Pushdown Automaton.

Pushdown Automata have an input tape, finite control and pushdown stack. A stack is an *LIFO* (Last In First Out) or *FILO* (First In Last Out) list into which a symbol may be entered or deleted at one end only, called the top of the list. When a symbol is entered at the top (pushed to the stack), the symbol previously at the top becomes second from the top, the symbol previously second from the top becomes third and so on. In the same way, when a symbol is removed from the top of the stack (popped from the stack), the symbol previously second from the top becomes the top symbol, the symbol previously third from the top becomes second, and so on.

Pushdown automata were proposed by Anthony Goettinger in 1961 and Marcelp. Schutzenberger in 1963 and were further studied by Robert J. Evey, also in 1963.

6.1.1 Definition of PDA

A (non-deterministic) *pushdown automaton* is a seven-tuple $P = (Q, \Sigma, \Gamma, \delta, q_0, Z_0, F)$, where

Q is a non-empty finite set of states,

Σ is the input alphabet,

Γ is a non-empty finite set of symbols called the stack alphabet,

δ is the state transition function, that is, $\delta: Q \times (\Sigma \cup \{\varepsilon\}) \times \Gamma \rightarrow$ the set of finite subsets of $Q \times \Gamma*$.

$q_0 \in Q$ is the initial state,

$Z_0 \in \Gamma$ is the stack start symbol (bottom of the stack),

$F \subseteq Q$ is the set of final states,

We will now discuss moves, and instantaneous description of PDA.

6.1.2 Moves in PDA

There are two types of moves in PDA. In the first type, input symbol is used. In this case move (transition function) is defined as follows:

$$\delta(q, a, Z) = \{(p_1, y_1), (p_2, y_2), \dots (p_n, y_n)\} \qquad \dots (1$$

where $q, p_i (1 \le i \le n)$ are the states of PDA, $a \in \Sigma$, $Z \in \Gamma$ and $y_i \in \Gamma*$. The above equation states that PDA in state q with Z at the top of the stack and input symbol a being read from the input tape, may choose both a new current state p_i and a new string of symbols y_i to replace the top stack symbol. The tape head is advanced. The transition $\delta(q, a, \varepsilon) = (p, a)$ pushes a on the top of the stack.

In the second type of move, input symbol is not used. It is called ε-move and is defined as follows:

$$\delta(q, \varepsilon, Z) = \{(p_1, y_1), (p_2, y_2), \dots (p_n, y_n)\} \qquad \dots (2$$

where $q, p_i(1 \le i \le n) \in Q, a \in \Sigma, Z \in \Gamma, y \in \Gamma*$. Equation (2) states that the pushdown automata in state q, independent of input symbol being scanned and with Z at the top of the stack may enter state p_i and replace Z by y_i. In this case, the input head does not move. The transition $\delta(q, a, a) = (p, \varepsilon)$ pops a from the top of the stack.

6.1.3 Instantaneous Description of PDA

As with finite automata, the portion of the input string already scanned has no effect on the subsequent operation of the PDA. The instantaneous description (or the current configuration) of the PDA is given by a triple (q, w, y), where q is the current state of the device, w is the portion of the input string yet to be read and y is the current stack contents. The current configuration is, therefore, a member of $Q \times \Sigma \times \Gamma*$.

If $M = (Q, \Sigma, \Gamma, \delta, q_0, Z_0, F)$ is a PDA, we define

$$(q, aw, Z\alpha) \vdash^M (p, w, \beta\alpha) \text{ if } \delta(q, a, Z) = (p, \beta)$$

which means the ordered pair (p, β) from the set specified by $\delta(q, a, Z)$ can cause a move in the PDA M from the configuration $(q, aw, Z\alpha)$ to the configuration $(p, w, \beta\alpha)$. The symbol $\vdash^M$ describes the transitions between configurations. The symbol $\vdash^*$ is used to describe a sequence of successive moves.

A *computation* of Pushdown Automaton M is a finite sequence of configurations $C_0, C_1, \dots C_n$ such that $C_i \vdash^M C_{i+1}$ for $0 \le i < n - 1$. C_0 is the initial configuration which is represented by $C_0 = (q_0, w, Z_0)$. C_n is the final configuration which is represented by $C_n = (p, \varepsilon, y)$ where $p \in F$, $y \in \Gamma^*$or $C_n = (p, \varepsilon, \varepsilon)$ where $p \in Q$, $y \in \Gamma^*$.

6.1.4 Transition Diagram of PDA

Like a finite automaton, Pushdown Automaton is also represented by directed graph, called the *Transition Diagram of Pushdown Automaton*. Algorithm 6.1 shows the algorithm for the construction of the Transition Diagram.

Algorithm 6.1: Algorithm for construction of the Transition Diagram of PDA

Algorithm (Construction of the Transition diagram of PDA): Let $M = (Q, \Sigma, \Gamma, \delta, q_0, Z_0, F)$ be a Pushdown automaton. The following steps are used to construct transition diagram:

Step 1: Draw small circles corresponding to each state with the name of the state written inside the circle.

Step 2: Indicate start state by an incoming arrow or labeling with word "start" or symbol "–".

Step 3: Indicate final state by double circle or labeling with word "final" or symbol " + ".

Step 4: Draw an arc from circle q to circle p labeled $a|Z|y$ if there is a transition function $\delta (q, a, Z) = \{(p, y)$.

6.1.5 The Language of PDA

Acceptance of an input string by pushdown automata can be defined in two ways, that is, after the entire string is scanned, the stack is empty or the automaton is in the final state.

6.1.5.1 *Acceptance by Empty Stack*

For the PDA $M = (Q, \Sigma, \Gamma, \delta, q_0, Z_0, F)$, the language $L(M)$ accepted by the device via empty stack, is, therefore, the set of all words accepted by the empty stack condition. Formally,

$$L(M) = \{w \mid (q_0, w, Z_0) \vdash^* (p, \varepsilon, \varepsilon), p \in Q \}$$

6.1.5.2 *Acceptance by Final State*

For the PDA $M = (Q, \Sigma,, \delta, q_0, Z_0, F)$, the language $N(M)$, accepted by M via final state, is the set of all words accepted by the final state criterion. Formally,

$$N(M) = \{w \mid (q_0, w, Z_0) \vdash^* (p, \varepsilon, y), p \in F \text{ and } y \in \Gamma^* \}$$

When acceptance is by empty stack, the set of final states is irrelevant. In case of acceptance is by a final state, the final stack content y is irrelevant.

Example 6.1: Consider the Pushdown Automaton $M = (Q, \Sigma, \Gamma, \delta, q_0, Z_0, F)$, where

$$Q = \{q_0, q_1, q_2\}$$
$$\Sigma = \{a, b, c\}$$
$$\Gamma = \{a, b, z_0\}$$

$$q_o = \{ q_o \}$$
$$Z_o = \{ z_o \}$$

$F = (q_2)$ and δ is defined as

$$\delta(q_o, a, z_o) = (q_o, az_o)$$
$$\delta(q_o, b, z_o) = (q_o, bz_o)$$
$$\delta(q_o, a, a) = (q_o, aa)$$
$$\delta(q_o, b, a) = (q_o, ba)$$
$$\delta(q_o, a, b) = (q_o, ab)$$
$$\delta(q_o, b, b) = (q_o, bb)$$
$$\delta(q_o, c, a) = (q_1, a)$$
$$\delta(q_o, c, b) = (q_1, b)$$
$$\delta(q_o, c, z_o) = (q_1, z_o)$$
$$\delta(q_1, a, a) = \delta(q_1, b, b) = (q_1, \varepsilon)$$
$$\delta(q_1, \varepsilon, z_o) = (q_2, z_o)$$

Draw transition diagram and transition table of PDA, *M*. What will happen when the string *bacab* is input to *M*? Illustrate the operation of this machine on the input string *bacab*.

Solution:

The Figure 6.2 and Table 6.1 show the transition diagram and transition table of PDA, respectively.

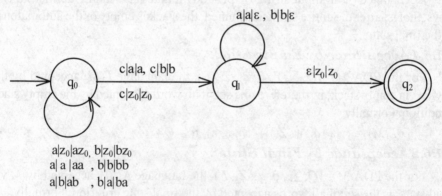

Fig. 6.2: Transition diagram

Table 6.1: Transition Table

Input	a			b			c			ε		
Stack	z_0	a	b	z_0	a	b	z_0	a	b	z_0	a	b
States												
q_0	(q_0, az_0)	(q_0, aa)	(q_0, ab)	(q_0, bz_0)	(q_0, ba)	(q_0, bb)	(q_1, z_0)	(q_1, a)	(q_1, b)			
q_1		(q_1, ε)	(q_1, ε)							(q_2, z_0)		
q_2												

The initial configuration of M is $(q_o, bacab, z_o)$

$$(q_o, bacab, z_o) \vdash (q_o, acab, bz_o)$$
$$\vdash (q_o, cab, abz_o)$$
$$\vdash (q_1, ab, abz_o)$$
$$\vdash (q_1, b, bz_o)$$
$$\vdash (q_1, \varepsilon, z_o)$$
$$\vdash (q_2, \varepsilon, z_o)$$

As M reaches the final state after the input is exhausted, the input is accepted by the PDA.

Example 6.2: Design a PDA that accepts the language $\{w|w$ has the equal number of a's and b's, $w \in \{a, b\}^*\}$ via final state and also draw the transition diagram.

Solution:

Let $M = (Q, \Sigma, \Gamma, \delta, q_0, Z_0, F)$ be the PDA. The machine starts in state q_0. It stores a symbol of the input string in the stack and continues storing it until a different symbol occurs. That is, if the input symbol is a and the top symbol of the stack is a or z_o, then a is pushed to the stack. In case top is neither a nor z_o then top symbol is popped from the stack. Similarly, if input symbol read is b and the symbol on top of the stack is b or z_o, then the symbol b is pushed on the stack but if top symbol is different then it is popped from the stack. The following moves will implement the working of PDA:

$$\delta (q_o, a, z_o) = (q_o, az_o)$$
$$\delta (q_o, b, z_o) = (q_o, bz_o)$$
$$\delta (q_o, a, a) = (q_o, aa)$$
$$\delta (q_o, b, b) = (q_o, bb)$$
$$\delta (q_o, b, a) = (q_o, \varepsilon)$$
$$\delta (q_o, a, b) = (q_o, \varepsilon)$$

When the input string becomes empty, and the top of the stack is z_o, then PDA moves to the final state q_1 indicating that it has read equal number of a's and b's. We include the following one more move:

$$\delta(q_o, \varepsilon, z_o) = (q_1, z_o)$$

When the input string is exhausted, three possible situations about the stack contents may arise.

1. The stack contains a's only,
2. The stack contains b's only,
3. The stack contains z_o (topmost symbol of a stack).

A stack of a's indicates the excess of a's over b's in the given input string. A stack of b's indicates the excess of b's over a's in the given input string. A stack of z_o

indicates the equal number of a's and b's in the given string. The required PDA is given as follows:

$$M = (Q, \Sigma,, \delta, q_0, Z_0, F)$$
$$Q = \{q_o, q_1\}$$
$$\Sigma = \{a, b\}$$
$$\Gamma = \{a, b, z_o\}$$
$$q_o = \{q_o\}$$
$$Z_o = \{z_o\}$$

$F = \{q_1\}$ and δ consists of :

$$\delta(q_o, a, z_o) = (q_o, az_o)$$
$$\delta(q_o, b, z_o) = (q_o, bz_o)$$
$$\delta(q_o, a, a) = (q_o, aa)$$
$$\delta(q_o, b, b) = (q_o, bb)$$
$$\delta(q_o, b, a) = (q_o, \varepsilon)$$
$$\delta(q_o, a, b) = (q_o, \varepsilon)$$
$$\delta(q_o, \varepsilon, z_o) = (q_1, z_o)$$

Figure 6.3 shows the transition diagram of the PDA.

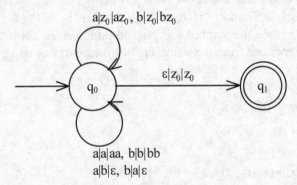

Fig. 6.3: Transition diagram

Example 6.3: Construct a Pushdown Automaton to accept the language $\{ww^R : w \in \{a, b\}^*\}$ and also draw the transition diagram.

Solution:

To design the machine, we need to know the midpoint of the string that is, when w ends and w^R starts. The non-deterministic pushdown automaton correctly guesses where the middle of the string is and switches states at that point.

The required PDA is given as follows:

$$M = (Q, \Sigma, \Gamma, \delta, q_0, Z_0, F) \text{ where}$$
$$Q = \{q_o, q_1, q_2\}$$
$$\Sigma = \{a, b\}$$

$$\Gamma = \{a, b, z_o\}$$
$$q_o = \{q_o\}$$
$$Z_o = \{z_o\}$$

$F = \{q_2\}$ and δ consists of :

$$\delta(q_o, a, z_o) = (q_o, az_o)$$
$$\delta(q_o, b, z_o) = (q_o, bz_o)$$
$$\delta(q_o, a, a) = (q_o, aa)$$
$$\delta(q_o, b, a) = (q_o, ba)$$
$$\delta(q_o, a, b) = (q_o, ab)$$
$$\delta(q_o, b, b) = (q_o, bb)$$
$$\delta(q_o, \varepsilon, a) = (q_1, a)$$
$$\delta(q_o, \varepsilon, b) = (q_1, b)$$
$$\delta(q_1, a, a) = (q_1, \varepsilon)$$
$$\delta(q_1, b, b) = (q_1, \varepsilon)$$
$$\delta(q_1, \varepsilon, z_o) = (q_2, z_0)$$

The moves $\delta(q_o, \varepsilon, a) = (q_1, a)$ and $\delta(q_o, \varepsilon, b) = (q_1, b)$ guess the middle of the string. The moves $\delta(q_1, a, a) = (q_1, \varepsilon)$ and $\delta(q_1, b, b) = (q_1, \varepsilon)$ match w^R against the contents of the stack. Figure 6.4 represents the transition diagram of the machine.

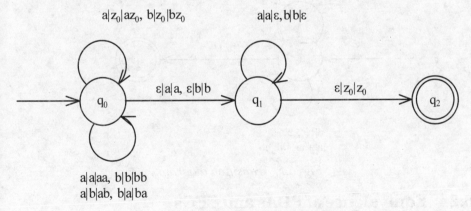

Fig. 6.4: Transition diagram

Example 6.4: Design a PDA to accept the language $\{x \in \{a, b\}^* \mid n_a(x) > n_b(x)\}$.

Solution:

As explained in Example 6.2 above, PDA starts by storing a symbol of the input string and continues storing it until a different symbol occurs. If the top of the stack is z_o or same as the input symbol then input symbol is pushed to the stack otherwise the top of the stack is popped from the stack. When a string is exhausted and stack contains a, then input string has more a's than b's. The following PDA accepts the desired language:

$M = (Q, \Sigma, \Gamma, \delta, q_0, Z_0, F)$ where

$Q = \{q_o, q_1\}$

$\Sigma = \{a, b\}$

$\Gamma = \{a, b, z_o\}$

$q_o = \{q_o\}$

$Z_o = \{z_o\}$

$F = \{q_1\}$

$(q_o, a, z_o) = (q_o, az_o)$

$(q_o, a, a) = (q_o, aa)$

$(q_o, b, z_o) = (q_o, bz_o)$

$(q_o, b, b) = (q_o, bb)$

$(q_o, a, b) = (q_o, \varepsilon)$

$(q_o, b, a) = (q_o, \varepsilon)$

$(q_o, \varepsilon, a) = (q_1, a)$

Figure 6.5 represents the transition diagram.

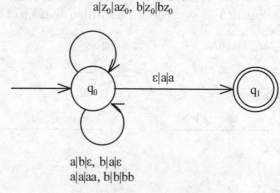

Fig. 6.5: Transition diagram

6.2   Equivalence of PDAs and CFGs

In this section, it will be shown that if language L is accepted by the PDA, then L can be generated by a CFG, and, conversely, every context-free language can be recognized by a PDA.

6.2.1   CFG to PDA Conversion

Each Pushdown automata corresponds to a context-free grammar. The Algorithm 6.2 is used to convert a given context-free grammar to PDA.

Algorithm 6.2: Algorithm for Conversion of CFG into PDA

Algorithm (Conversion of CFG into PDA): Let $G = (V, T, P, S)$ be a context-free grammar. We construct PDA $M = (Q, \Sigma, \Gamma, \delta, q_0, Z_0, F)$, as follows:

Step 1: $Q = \{ q_0, q_1, q_2 \}$, $F = \{q_2\}$

$\Gamma = \{V \cup T \cup Z_0\}$ where $Z_0 \notin V \cup \Sigma$

$\Sigma = T$.

Step 2: The initial move of PDA M is to place S on the stack and move to state q_1. This move (δ) is given by

$$\delta (q_0, \varepsilon, z_0) = (q_1, SZ_0)$$

Step 3: (a) If grammar is not in Greibach Normal form then

    (i)   For every $X \in V$, we include the transition function $\delta(q_1, \varepsilon, X)$ $= \{(q_1, \alpha) | X \to \alpha$ is a production in $G\}$

    (ii)   For every $a \in \Sigma$, we include the transition function $\delta(q_1, a, a)$ $= (q_1, \varepsilon)$.

(b) If grammar is in Greibach Normal form then

    (i)   For every $X \in V$, we include the transition function $\delta(q_1, a, X)$ $= \{(q_1, \alpha) | X \to a\alpha$ is a production in $G\}$

Step 4: When the input string becomes ε, and the machine is in the state q_1 then it moves to the final accepting state q_2. This move is given by

$(q_1, \varepsilon, Z_0) = (q_2, Z_0)$

Example 6.5: Consider the grammar:

$S \to aA$

$A \to aABC \,|\, bB \,|\, a$

$B \to b$

$C \to c$

Construct PDA corresponding to this grammar. Also provide moves of the PDA and the leftmost derivation for any string in the language defined by the grammar.

Solution:

Let PDA $M = (Q, \Sigma, \Gamma, \delta, q_0, Z_0, F)$

Step 1: We define Q, F, and T as follows:

$Q = \{q_0, q_1, q_2\}$

$F = \{q_2\}$

$Z_0 = \{z_0\}$

$\Gamma = \{V \cup T \cup z_0 \}$

$= \{S, A, B, C, a, b, z_0 \}$

$T = \{a, b\}$

Step 2: The initial move of PDA M is to place S on the stack and move to state q_1. The move (δ) is given by $(q_0, \varepsilon, z_o) = (q_1, Sz_o)$

Step 3: For every variable $X \in V$, we include the following moves:

$\delta(q_1, a, X) = \{(q_1, \alpha)|X \to a\alpha$ is a production $\}$

Therefore, we get the following moves:

$(q_1, a, S) = (q_1, A)$ since $S \to aA$

$(q_1, a, A) = (q_1, ABC)$ since $A \to aABC$

$(q_1, b, A) = (q_1, \varepsilon)$ since $A \to b$

$(q_1, a, A) = (q_1, \varepsilon)$ since $A \to a$

$(q_1, b, B) = (q_1, \varepsilon)$ since $B \to b$

$(q_1, c, C) = (q_1, \varepsilon)$ since $C \to c$

$(q_1, \varepsilon, z_o) = (q_2, z_o)$

We consider the string $x = aaabc \in L$ and compare the moves made by M in accepting x with a leftmost derivation of x in the grammar. The moves and derivatives as follow:

$(q_0, aaabc, z_o) \vdash (q_1, aaabc, Sz_o)$ S

$\vdash (q_1, aabc, Az_o)$ $S \Rightarrow aA$

$\vdash (q_1, abc, ABCz_o)$ $S \Rightarrow aaABC$

$\vdash (q_1, bc, BCz_o)$ $S \Rightarrow aaaBC$

$\vdash (q_1, c, Cz_o)$ $S \Rightarrow aaabC$

$\vdash (q_1, \varepsilon, z_o)$ $S \Rightarrow aaabc$

$\vdash (q_2, \varepsilon, z_o)$

6.2.2 PDA to CFG Conversion

The algorithm for constructing a CFG for the given PDA is given in Algorithm 6.3.

Algorithm. 6.3: Algorithm (Conversion from PDA to Grammar)

Algorithm (Conversion from PDA to CFG): Let $M = (Q, \Sigma, \Gamma, \delta, q_0, Z_0, \emptyset)$ be a PDA accepting a language L by empty stack. Then there is a CFG G with $L(G) = L(M)$. We construct $G = (V, T, P, S)$ using the following steps:

Step 1: We define V and T as follows:

$$V = \{S\} \bigcup \{ [q, A, p]|A \in \Gamma, p, q \in Q\}, T = \Sigma$$

Step2: P is the set of productions as follows:

   (i)   For every $q \in Q$, then we include production $S \to [q_0, Z_o, q]$ in P.

   (ii)   For every $q, q_1 \in Q, a \in \Sigma \bigcup \{\varepsilon\}$, and $A \in \Gamma$, if $\delta(q, a, A) = (q_1, \varepsilon)$, then we include the production $[q, A, q_1] \to a$ in P.

> (iii) For every $q, q_1 \in Q, a \in \Sigma \cup \{\varepsilon\}, A \in \Gamma$ and $m \geq 1$, if $\delta(q, a, A) = (q_1, B_1 B_2 \ldots \ldots \ldots B_m)$ for some $B_1, B_2 \ldots B_m \in \Gamma$, then for every choice of $q_2, q_3, \ldots q_{m+1} \in Q$, the production
>
> $[q, A, q_{m+1}] \to a[q_1, B_1, q_2][q_2, B_2, q_3] \ldots \ldots \ldots [q_m, B_m, q_{m+1}]$
> is in P.

Example 6.6: Consider PDA $M = (\{q_o, q_1\}, \{0, 1\}, \{X, Z_o\}, \delta, q_o, Z_o, \phi)$ where is given by

$$\delta(q_o, 0, Z_o) = (q_o, XZ_o)$$
$$\delta(q_o, 0, X) = (q_o, XX)$$
$$\delta(q_o, 1, X) = (q_1, \varepsilon)$$
$$\delta(q_1, 1, X) = (q_1, \varepsilon)$$
$$\delta(q_1, \varepsilon, X) = (q_1, \varepsilon)$$
$$\delta(q_1, \varepsilon, Z_o) = (q_1, \varepsilon)$$

Construct a CFG $G = (V, T, P, S)$ generating $N(M)$.

Solution:

Given $\Gamma = \{X, Z_o\}, T = \{0, 1\}, Q = \{q_o, q_1\}$

Step 1: $V = \{S\} \cup \{[q, A, p] | A \in \Gamma, p, q \in Q\}$

$V = \{S, [q_o, X, q_o], [q_o, X, q_1], [q_o, Z_o, q_o], [q_o, Z_o, q_1], [q_1, X, q_o], [q_1, X, q_1],$

$[q_1, Z_o, q_o], [q_1, Z_o, q_1]\}$

Step 2: For every $q \in Q$, the production $S \to [q_o, Z_o, q]$ is in P.

So, $S \to [q_o, Z_o, q_o]$ and
$S \to [q_o, Z_o, q_1]$ are in P.

Next for every $q, q_1 \in Q, a \in \Sigma \cup \{\varepsilon\}$, and $A \in \Gamma$, if $\delta(q, a, A) = (q_1, \varepsilon)$ then the production $[q, A, q_1] \to a$ is in P.

So, if $\delta(q_0, 1, X) = (q_1, \varepsilon)$
then $[q_0, X, q_1] \to 1$ is in P.
Similarly

if $\delta(q_1, 1, X) = (q_1, \varepsilon)$
$[q_1, X, q_1] \to 1$ is in P.

if $\delta(q_1, \varepsilon, X) = (q_1, \varepsilon)$
$[q_1, X, q_1] \to \varepsilon$ is in P.

if $\delta(q_1, \varepsilon, Z_o) = (q_1, \varepsilon)$
$[q_1, Z_o, q_1] \to \varepsilon$ is in P.

Step 3: if $\delta(q_1, a, A) = (q_1, B_1 B_2 \ldots \ldots B_m)$. Then, for every q, q_1 the production
$[q, A, q_{m+1}] \to a[q_1, B_1, q_2][q_2, B_2, q_3] \ldots [q_m, B_m, q_{m+1}]$ is in P.

Now $\delta(q_o, 0, Z_o) = (q_o, XZ_o)$

then $[q_o, Z_o, q_o] \to 0[q_o, X, q_o][q_o, Z_o, q_o]$

$[q_o, Z_o, q_o] \to 0[q_o, X, q_1][q_1, Z_o, q_o]$

$[q_o, Z_o, q_1] \to 0[q_o, X, q_o][q_o, Z_o, q_1]$

$[q_o, Z_o, q_1] \to 0[q_o, X, q_1][q_1, Z_o, q_1]$

$\delta(q_o, 0, X) = (q_o, XX)$ is in the form $[\delta(q_o, 0, A) = (q_o, B_1B_2)]$. So, we include the following productions in P:

$[q_o, X, q_o] \to 0 [q_o, X, q_o][q_o, X, q_o]$

$[q_o, X, q_o] \to 0 [q_o, X, q_1][q_1, X, q_o]$

$[q_o, X, q_1] \to 0 [q_o, X, q_o][q_o, X, q_1]$

$[q_o, X, q_1] \to 0 [q_o, X, q_1][q_1, X, q_1]$

We get the following CFG $G = (V, T, P, S)$ where

$V = \{S, [q_o, X, q_o], [q_o, X, q_1], [q_o, Z_o, q_o], [q_o, Z_o, q_1], [q_1, X, q_o], [q_1, X,$
$q_1], [q_1, Z_o, q_o], [q_1, Z_o, q_1]\}$

$T = \{0, 1\}$ and P consists of

$S \to [q_o, Z_o, q_o] \mid [q_o, Z_o, q_1]$

$[q_o, X, q_1] \to 1$

$[q_1, X, q_1] \to 1$

$[q_1, X, q_1] \to \varepsilon$

$[q_1, Z_o, q_1] \to \varepsilon$

$[q_o, Z_o, q_o] \to 0[q_o, X, q_o][q_o, Z_o, q_o]$

$[q_o, Z_o, q_o] \to 0[q_o, X, q_1][q_1, Z_o, q_o]$

$[q_o, Z_o, q_1] \to 0[q_o, X, q_o][q_o, Z_o, q_1]$

$[q_o, Z_o, q_1] \to 0[q_o, X, q_o][q_o, Z_o, q_1]$

$[q_o, X, q_o] \to 0[q_o, X, q_o][q_o, X, q_o]$

$[q_o, X, q_o] \to 0[q_o, X, q_1][q_1, X, q_o]$

$[q_o, X, q_1] \to 0[q_o, X, q_o][q_o, X, q_1]$

$[q_o, X, q_1] \to 0[q_o, X, q_1][q_1, X, q_1]$

In the above grammar, we can see that there are no productions for the variables $[q_1, X, q_o]$ and $[q_1, Z_o, q_o]$. We can also see that all productions for $[q_o, X, q_o]$ and $[q_o, Z_o, q_o]$ have $[q_1, X, q_o]$ or $[q_1, Z_o, q_o]$ on the right, no terminal strings can be derived from $[q_o, X, q_o]$ or $[q_o, Z_o, q_o]$ either. Deleting all the productions involving one of these four variables on either the right or the left, finally we get the following productions:

$S \to [q_o, Z_o, q_1]$

$[q_o, X, q_1] \to 1$

$[q_1, X, q_1] \to 1$

$[q_1, X, q_1] \to \varepsilon$

$$[q_1, Z_o, q_1] \to \varepsilon$$
$$[q_o, Z_o, q_1] \to 0[q_o, X, q_1] [q_1, Z_o, q_1]$$
$$[q_1, X, q_1] \to 0[q_o, X, q_1] [q_1, X, q_1]$$

Example 6.7: Design a PDA to accept the language $\{a^n b^m a^n \mid m, n \geq 1\}$ by empty stack. Construct context free grammar that accepts the same set.

Solution:

PDA starts by storing a and continues storing until a different symbol occurs. If the input symbol is b and top of the stack symbol is a then, there is no change in the content of the stack and the PDA goes to state q_1. On the subsequent input of b, there will be no change in the state of PDA and also there will be no change in the contents of the stack. Once all b's in the input string are exhausted, the remaining a's are compared with top of the stack contents, if match found, then top of the stack is popped. When input becomes empty, and top of the stack is Z_o, then Z_0 is popped. The following PDA accepts the desired language:

$$M = (\{q_o, q_1\}, \{a, b\}, \{a, Z_o\}, \delta, q_o, Z_o, \emptyset)$$ where is define by
$$\delta(q_o, a, Z_o) = (q_o, aZ_o)$$
$$\delta(q_o, a, a) = (q_1, aa)$$
$$\delta(q_o, b, a) = (q_1, a)$$
$$\delta(q_1, b, a) = (q_1, a)$$
$$\delta(q_1, a, a) = (q_1)$$
$$\delta(q_1, Z_o) = (q_1)$$

Now, we construct the grammar as follows:

Step 1: Define the grammar $G = (V, T, P, S)$, where $T = \{a, b\}$ and
$$V = \{S, [q_o, Z_0, q_o], [q_o, Z_0, q_1], [q_1, Z_0, q_o], [q_1, Z_0, q_1], [q_o, a, q_o],$$
$$[q_o, a, q_1], [q_1, a, q_o], [q_1, a, q_1]\}$$

Step 2: For every $q \in Q$ the production
$$S \to [q_o, Z_o, q_o]$$

So,
$$S \to [q_o, Z_o, q_o] \text{ and }$$
$$S \to [q_o, Z_o, q_1] \text{ are in } P.$$

Next $q, q_1 \in Q$ $a \in T \cup \{\varepsilon\}$

$A \in \Gamma$ if $\delta(q, a, A) = (q_1, \varepsilon)$ then the production

$[q, A, q_1] \to a$ is in P.

If $\delta(q_1, a, a) = (q_1, \varepsilon)$

then $[q_1, a, q_1] \to a$

If $\delta(q_1, \varepsilon, Z_o) (q, \varepsilon)$

then $[q_1, Z_o, q_1] \to \varepsilon$

Step 3: If $\delta(q_o, a, Z_o) \to (q_o, aZ_o)$ then

$$[q_o, Z_o, q_o] \to a [q_o, a, q_o] [q_o, Z_o, q_o]$$

$[q_o, Z_o, q_o] \rightarrow a[q_o, a, q_1] [q_1, Z_o, q_o]$

$[q_o, Z_o, q_1] \rightarrow a[q_o, a, q_o] [q_o, Z_o, q_1]$

$[q_o, Z_o, q_1] \rightarrow \text{a}[q_o, a, q_1] [q_1, Z_o, q_1]$

If $\delta(q_o, a, a) \rightarrow (q_o, aa)$ then

$[q_o, a, q_o] \rightarrow a[q_o, a, q_o] [q_o, a, q_o]$

$[q_o, a, q_o] \rightarrow a[q_o, a, q_1] [q_1, a, q_o]$

$[q_o, a, q_1] \rightarrow a[q_o, a, q_o] [q_o, a, q_1]$

$[q_o, a, q_1] \rightarrow a[q_o, a, q_1] [q_1, a, q_1]$

If $\delta(q_o, b, a) \rightarrow (q_1, a)$ then

$[q_o, a, q_o] \rightarrow b[q_1, a, q_o]$

$[q_o, a, q_1] \rightarrow b[q_1, a, q_1]$

If $\delta(q_1, b, a) \rightarrow (q_1, a)$ then

$[q_1, a, q_o] \rightarrow b[q_1, a, q_o]$

$[q_1, a, q_1] \rightarrow b[q_1, a, q_1]$

Now, we can get the following grammar $G = (V, T, P, S)$ where

$V = \{S, [q_o, Z_o, q_o], [q_o, Z_o, q_1], [q_1, Z_o, q_o], [q_1, Z_o, q_1], [q_o, a, q_o],$
$[q_o, a, q_1], [q_1, a, q_o], [q_1, a, q_1]\}$

$T = \{a, b\}$

$S = \{S\}$

and P consists of

$S \rightarrow [q_o, Z_o, q_o]$

$S \rightarrow [q_o, Z_o, q_1]$

$[q_1, a, q_1] \rightarrow a$

$[q_1, Z_o, q_1] \rightarrow \varepsilon$

$[q_o, a, q_o] \rightarrow b[q_1, a, q_o]$

$[q_o, a, q_1] \rightarrow b[q_1, a, q_1]$

$[q_1, a, q_o] \rightarrow b[q_1, a, q_o]$

$[q_1, a, q_1] \rightarrow b[q_1, a, q_1]$

$[q_o, Z_o, q_o] \rightarrow a[q_o, a, q_o] [q_o, Z_o, q_o]$

$[q_o, Z_o, q_o] \rightarrow a[q_o, a, q_1] [q_1, Z_o, q_o]$

$[q_o, Z_o, q_1] \rightarrow a[q_o, a, q_o] [q_o, Z_o, q_1]$

$[q_o, Z_o, q_1] \rightarrow a[q_o, a, q_1] [q_1, Z_o, q_1]$

$[q_o, a, q_o] \rightarrow a[q_o, a, q_o] [q_o, a, q_o]$

$[q_o, a, q_o] \rightarrow a[q_o, a, q_1] [q_1, a, q_o]$

$[q_o, a, q_1] \rightarrow a[q_o, a, q_o] [q_o, a, q_1]$

$[q_o, a, q_1] \rightarrow a[q_o, a, q_1] [q_1, a, q_1]$

6.3 Deterministic Pushdown Automata and Deterministic Context-free Languages

A *Deterministic Pushdown Automaton* (DPDA) is a pushdown automaton that has at most one move from any *configuration* (ID). A Pushdown automaton $M = (Q, \Sigma, \Gamma, \delta, q_0, Z_0, F)$ is deterministic if:

1. For every $q \in Q$, $a \in \Sigma \cup \{\varepsilon\}$ and $Z \in \Gamma$, the transition function $\delta(q, a, Z)$ contains at most one element,

2. For every $q \in Q$ and $Z \in \Gamma$, whenever $\delta(q, \varepsilon, Z) \neq \phi$, then $\delta(q, a, Z) = \phi$ for every $a \in \Sigma$.

The condition 1 states that for any given input symbol and any top of stack symbol, at most one move can be made. The condition 2 states that if a ε-move is possible for some configuration, then move involving input symbol will not be possible. A language L is deterministic context-free language if and only if there exists a deterministic pushdown automaton M such that $L = L(M)$.

Example 6.8: Prove that the language $L = \{a^n b^{2n} | n \geq 0\}$ is a deterministic context-free language.

Solution:

The language $L = \{a^n b^{2n} | n \geq 0\}$ is a deterministic context-free language if there exists a DPDA that defines it. The following DPDA accepts the language by pushing two a's onto the stack for every a in the input string and by popping single a for each input b. That is

$$\delta(q_0, \varepsilon, Z_0) = (q_0, \varepsilon)$$
$$\delta(q_0, a, Z_0) = (q_0, aaZ_0)$$
$$\delta(q_0, a, a) = (q_1, aaa)$$
$$\delta(q_0, b, a) = (q_1, \varepsilon)$$
$$\delta(q_1, b, a) = (q_1, \varepsilon)$$
$$\delta(q_1, \varepsilon, Z_0) = (q_1, \varepsilon)$$

The Figure 6.6 shows the transition diagram of the DPDA.

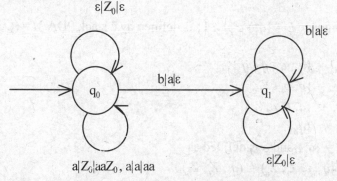

Fig. 6.6: Transition diagram

6.4   2-stack PDA

A *2-stack Pushdown Automaton* is similar to a Pushdown Automaton except that it has two pushdown stacks instead of one. Formally, a 2-stack PDA *M* is a 7-tuple $(Q, \Sigma, \Gamma, \delta, q_0, Z_0, F)$, where

Q is a non-empty finite set of states,

Σ is the input alphabet,

Γ is a finite set of symbols called the stack alphabet. We assume both stacks use the same alphabet,

δ is a transition function mapping from $Q \times (\Sigma \cup \{\varepsilon\}) \times \Gamma \times \Gamma$ to finite symbols of $(Q \times \Gamma^* \times \Gamma^*)$,

$q_0 \in Q$ is the start state,

$Z_0 \in \Gamma$ is the start top symbol of both the stacks, and

$F \subseteq Q$ is the set of final states.

The configuration of 2-stack PDA is a 4-tuple (q, α, y_1, y_2), where q is the current state, α the portion of the input that is still to be read, and y_1 and y_2 are the contents of the two stacks. For the 2-stack PDA $M = (Q, \Sigma, \Gamma, \delta, q_0, Z_0, F)$ we can define the transition between configurations as follows:

$$(q, aw, x\gamma_1, y\gamma_2) \vdash (p, w, \alpha\gamma_1, \beta\gamma_2) \text{ if } \delta(q, a, x, y) = (p, \alpha, \beta), \text{ where } a \in \Sigma,$$
$x, y \in \Gamma^*$ and $\gamma_1, \gamma_2 \in \Gamma^*$.

A computation of 2-stack PDA on input w is a finite sequence of configurations $C_0, C_1, \dots C_n$ such that:

(i) C_0 is an initial (start) configuration (q_0, w, Z_0, Z_0),

(ii) C_n is the final configuration $(p, \varepsilon, y_1, y_2)$ for some $p \in F$ and $y_1, y_2 \in \Gamma^*$.

(iii) $C_i \vdash C_{i+1}$ for all $0 \le i \le n-1$.

The *language* accepted by the 2-stack PDA is the set of all strings $w \in \Sigma^*$ such that $(q_0, w, Z_0, Z_0) \vdash (p, \varepsilon, y_1, y_2)$ for some $p \in F$ and $y_1, y_2 \in \Gamma^*$.

Example 6.9: Design a 2-Stack PDA for the non-context free language $L = \{a^n b^n c^n | n \ge 1\}$.

Solution:

The language $L = \{a^n b^n c^n | n \ge 1\}$ is defined by 2 stack PDA $M = (Q, \Sigma, \Gamma, \delta, q_0, Z_0, F)$ where

$\qquad Q = \{q_0, q_1, q_2, q_3\}$,

$\qquad \Sigma = \{a, b, c\}$,

$\qquad \Gamma = \{a, b, c, Z_0\}$,

$\qquad q_0 = \{q_0\}$.

$\qquad F = \{q_3\}$ and δ is defined as

$$\delta(q_0, \varepsilon, Z_0, Z_0) = (q_3, Z_0, Z_0)$$
$$\delta(q_0, a, Z_0, Z_0) = (q_0, aZ_0, Z_0)$$
$$\delta(q_0, a, a, Z_0) = (q_0, aa, Z_0)$$

$$\delta(q_0, b, a, Z_0) = (q_1, a, bZ_0)$$
$$\delta(q_1, b, a, b) = (q_1, a, bb)$$
$$\delta(q_1, c, a, b) = (q_2, \varepsilon, \varepsilon)$$
$$\delta(q_2, c, a, b) = (q_2, \varepsilon, \varepsilon)$$
$$\delta(q_2, \varepsilon, Z_0, Z_0) = (q_3, Z_0, Z_0)$$

2-stack PDA starts by storing a symbol of the input string on the first stack and continues storing until a different symbol occurs. That is if the symbol read is a and symbol on the top of the first stack is Z_0 or a then symbol a is pushed on the first stack, and the PDA remains in the same state q_0. If the symbol read is b and symbol on the top of the second stack is Z_0 then b is pushed on the second stack, and the machine goes to the state q_1. On subsequent inputs of b, the machine continues pushing b on the second stack until different symbol occurs. If the input symbol is c and top of the first and the second stack are a and b, respectively, then the machine pops from both the stacks and goes to the state q_2 and continues popping from both the stacks on the subsequent input symbol c. When the input string is exhausted, and the top symbols of both the stack are Z_0, then the PDA goes to state q_3. The state q_3 is a final state. If the input string is exhausted and current state of the machine is q_3, then input string is accepted by 2-stack PDA.

6.5   Summary

1.   Pushdown Automata were proposed by Anthony Goettinger in 1961 and Marcelp. Schutzenberger in 1963 and were further studied by Robert J. Evey, also in 1963.

2.   A Pushdown Automaton is a finite state non-deterministic machine. It defines context-free languages and its deterministic version defines deterministic context-free languages which accept proper subsets of the context-free language. A Pushdown automaton can be used in parser design.

3.   The components of pushdown automata are input tape (infinite in one direction), finite control and stack. The stack of pushdown automaton is called pushdown stack.

4.   Acceptance of a language by pushdown automaton can be defined in two ways, that is, by the final state or by the empty stack in contrast to the Finite Automaton and Turing machine where it is defined by the final states.

5.   A Two-Stack Pushdown Automaton is similar to the Pushdown Automaton except that it has two pushdown stacks instead of one. It is more powerful than pushdown automata. Further, it is equivalent to Turing machine in terms of power.

6.6   Exercises

Objective Questions

1.   Which is true for the subsequent operation of the PDA?
      (a)   It depends upon the input already scanned

    (b)   It does not depend upon the input already scanned

    (c)   It occasionally depends upon the input already scanned

    (d)   None of these

2.   Which of the following is true for PDA?

    (a)   It is a deterministic machine.

    (b)   It is a non-deterministic machine.

    (c)   It does not define CFL.

    (d)   None of these

3.   Which of the following is not true for 2-stack PDA?

    (a)   2-stack PDA is more powerful than PDA.

    (b)   2-stack PDA is equivalent in power in terms of acceptability of language to Turing machine.

    (c)   n-stack PDA is more powerful than 2-stack PDA

    (d)   None of these

4.   Which of the following languages over {a, b, c} is accepted by DPDA?

    (a) $\{ww^R|w \in \{a, b\}^*\}$ (b) $\{a^n b^{2n}|n \geq 0\}$

    (c) $\{a^n b^n|n \geq 0\}$ (d)   All of these

5.   The number of auxiliary memory required for PDA to behave like a TM is A:

    (a)   2   (b)   1

    (c)   0   (d)   4

6.   As far as acceptability is concerned, which of the following statements is false?

    (a)   Non-deterministic push down automata are equivalent to deterministic push down automata

    (b)   Non-deterministic Finite Automata are equivalent to Deterministic Finite Automata

    (c)   Multitape Turing machines are equivalent to single-tape turing machines.

    (d)   None of these

7.   The acceptance of the input words by a PDA can be defined in terms of:

    (a)   Only final state   (b)   Only empty state

    (c)   Only null store   (d)   All of these

8.   The number of auxiliary memory required for a PDA to behave like a finite automaton is:

    (a)   1   (b)   2

    (c)   4   (d)   0

9.   Which of the following languages over $\{a, b, c\}$ is accepted by 2-stack PDA?

    (a) $a^n b^n a^n b^n$ (b) $a^n b^n c^n$

    (c) $a^n b^n a^{2n}$ (d)   All of these

10. The Instantaneous description (ID) of PDA shows:

[A](ii) $L = \{a^i b^j c^k : i = j \text{ or } j = k\}$

(iii) $L = \{a^i b^j : 2i = 3j + 1\}$

(iv) $L = \{w \in \{a, b\}^* \mid \#_a(w) = 2\#_b(w)\}$

(v) $L = \{w \in \{a, b\}^* \mid$ every prefix of w has at least as many a's as b's$\}$

(vi) $L = \{a^m b^n c^p d^q : m, n, p, q \geq 0 \text{ and } m + n = p + q\}$

(vii) $\{b_i \# b_i + 1^R : b_i$ is the binary representation of some integer $i, i \geq 0$, without leading zeros $\mid$ (For instance $101\#011 \in L)$

(viii) $\{x^R \# y : x, y \in \{0, 1\}^* \text{ and } x \text{ is a substring of } y\}$

(ix) L_1^*, where $L_1 = \{xx^R : x \in \{a, b\}^*\}$

[A]7. Is it possible to find a DFA that accepts the same language as the PDA $M = (\{q_0, q_1\}, \{a, b\}, \{z\}, q_0, \{q_1\})$, with $\delta(q_0, a, z) = \{(q_1, z)\}$

$$\delta(q_0, b, z) = \{(q_0, z)\}$$
$$\delta(q_1, a, z) = \{(q_1, z)\}$$
$$\delta(q_1, b, z) = \{(q_0, z)\}$$

8. Define DPDA. Give formal definition of DPDA configuration and the language accepted by such automaton by the final state.

[A]9. What language is accepted by the PDA $M = (\{q_0, q_1, q_2\}, \{a, b\}, \{a, b, z\}, \delta, q_0, z, \{q_2\})$ with following transitions:

$$\delta(q_0, a, z) = \{(q_1, a)\}, (q_2, \varepsilon)\},$$
$$\delta(q_1, b, a) = \{(q_1, b)\}$$
$$\delta(q_1, b, b) = \{(q_1, b)\}$$
$$\delta(q_1, a, b) = \{(q_2, \varepsilon)\}$$

[A]10. Find a PDA with no more than two internal states that accepts the language $L = \{aa^*ba^*\}$.

[A]11. Construct a PDA that accepts the language generated by the grammar $S \rightarrow aSbb|aab$.

[A]12. Construct a PDA that accepts the language generated by the grammar $S \rightarrow aSSS|ab$.

[A]13. Construct a PDA M equivalent to the following grammar $S \rightarrow aAA, A \rightarrow aS|bS|a$. Also test whether $abaaaa$ is in the language generated by the grammar.

14. What is a 2-stack PDA? Design a 2-stack PDA accepting the language $L = \{a^n b^{2n} a^n b^n | n \geq 0\}$.

15. Construct a 2-stack PDA for the following languages:

(i) $a^n b^n c^n d^n | n \geq 0$

(ii) $a^n b^n c^m d^n | m, n \geq 0$

(iii) $a^n b^n a^n b^{3n} | n \geq 0$

(iv) $a^n b^n a^{2n} | n \geq 0$

[A](v) $a^n b^n a^n b^n | n \geq 0$

16. Construct a PDA for language generated by the following grammars:

(i) $S \rightarrow aSa \mid A \mid C$

$A \rightarrow aAa \mid bAb \mid a \mid b \mid \varepsilon$

(ii) $S \to aA \mid \varepsilon$

$A \to bB$

$B \to cS$

$^{A}17.$ Construct a PDA to accept the language $\{wcw^{R} \mid w \in \{a, b\}^{*}\}$ by the final state. Also draw a transition diagram.

Answers/Hints for Selected Review Questions

6.   (i) $L = \{a^{n}b^{m} \mid n \leq m \leq 3n\}$

$Q = \{q_{0}, q_{1}, q_{2}\}, \Gamma = \{a, b, Z_{0}\}, q_{0} = \{q_{0}\},$

$F = \{q_{2}\}$ and $Z_{0} = \{Z_{0}\},$

δ consists of:

$\delta (q_{0}, a, Z_{0}) = (q_{0}, aZ_{0})$

$\delta (q_{0}, a, Z_{0}) = (q_{0}, aaZ_{0})$

$\delta (q_{0}, a, Z_{0}) = (q_{0}, aaa\, Z_{0})$

$\delta (q_{0}, a, a) = (q_{0}, aa)$

$\delta (q_{0}, a, a) = (q_{0}, aaa)$

$\delta (q_{0}, a, a) = (q_{0}, aaaa)$

$\delta (q_{0}, b, a) = (q_{1}, \varepsilon)$

$\delta (q_{1}, b, a) = (q_{1}, \varepsilon)$

$\delta (q_{1}, \varepsilon, Z_{0}) = (q_{2}, \varepsilon)$

As long as PDA sees a's, it stays in state q_{0} and pushes 1 a's or 2 a's or 3 a's. When it reads b, it pops a single a and moves to state q_{1}. This process is continued for subsequent b's. When the string becomes empty, the machine moves to state q_{2} which is a final state.

(ii) $L = \{a^{i}b^{j}c^{k} : i = j \text{ or } j = k\}$

The PDA $M = (Q, \Sigma, \Gamma, \delta, q_{0}, Z_{0}, F)$ where

$Q = \{q_{0}, q_{1}, q_{2}, q_{3}, q_{4}, q_{5}, q_{6}\}$

$\Sigma = \{a, b, c\}$

$\Gamma = \{a, b, Z_{0}\}$

$q_{0} = \{q_{0}\}$

$Z_{0} = \{Z_{0}\}$

$F = \{q_{1}, q_{3}\}$

$\delta(q_{0}, \varepsilon, Z_{0}) = (q_{1}, Z_{0})$

$\delta(q_{0}, \varepsilon, Z_{0}) = (q_{2}, Z_{0})$

$\delta(q_{0}, \varepsilon, Z_{0}) = (q_{3}, Z_{0})$

$\delta(q_{2}, b, a) = (q_{4}, \varepsilon)$

$\delta(q_{4}, b, a) = (q_{4}, \varepsilon)$

$\delta(q_{4}, \varepsilon, Z_{0}) = (q_{1}, Z_{0})$

$\delta(q_{1}, c, Z_{0}) = (q_{1}, Z_{0})$

$$\delta(q_3, a, Z_0) = (q_3, Z_0)$$
$$\delta(q_3, b, Z_0) = (q_5, bZ_0)$$
$$\delta(q_5, b, b) = (q_5, bb)$$
$$\delta(q_5, c, b) = (q_6, \varepsilon)$$
$$\delta(q_6, c, b) = (q_6, \varepsilon)$$
$$\delta(q_6, \varepsilon, Z_0) = (q_3, Z_0)$$

accepts L.

7. The given PDA does not use the stack during its working. That is why it is equivalent to finite automaton. The transition function of finite automaton can be directly derived by the PDA as follows:

$$\delta(q_0, a, Z) = (q_1, Z) \Rightarrow \delta(q_0, a) = q_1,$$
$$\delta(q_0, b, Z) = (q_0, Z) \Rightarrow \delta(q_0, b) = q_0,$$
$$\delta(q_1, a, Z) = (q_1, Z) \Rightarrow \delta(q_1, a) = q_1,$$
$$\delta(q_1, b, Z) = (q_0, Z) \Rightarrow \delta(q_1, b) = q_0.$$

9. First we draw the transition diagram of the given PDA as given below:

We can observe from the above figure that there is a transition from q_0 to q_2 with input a. The transition from state q_0 to q_1 on input a, followed by one or more b's and terminated by an a. We can conclude that the language accepted by the PDA is $L = \{a\} \cup \{abb^*a\}$.

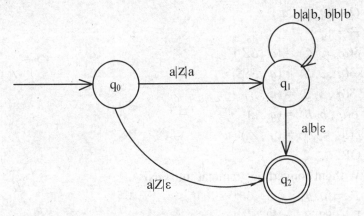

10. The PDA $M = (\{q_0, q_1\}, \{a, b\}, \{a, b, Z_0\}, \delta, q_0, Z_0, \{q_1\})$ where δ is defined by

$$\delta(q_0, a, Z_0) = (q_0, XZ_0),$$
$$\delta(q_0, a, X) = (q_0, X),$$
$$\delta(q_0, b, X) = (q_0, Y),$$
$$\delta(q_0, a, Y) = (q_0, Y),$$
$$\delta(q_0, \varepsilon, Y) = (q_1, Y).$$

represents the language $L(aa^*ba^*)$ by the final state.

We have only two states, the initial state q_0 and the accepting state q_1.

11. $T = \{a, b\}$

$\Gamma = \{V \bigcup T \bigcup Z_0\}$

$= \{S, Z_0, a, b\}$

$Q = \{q_0, q_1, q_2\}$

$\delta(q_0, \varepsilon, Z_0) = (q_1, SZ_0)$

$\delta(q_1, \varepsilon, S) = (q_1, aSbb)$

$\delta(q_1, \varepsilon, S) = (q_1, aab)$

$\delta(q_1, a, a) = (q_1, \varepsilon)$

$\delta(q_1, b, b) = (q_1, \varepsilon)$

$\delta(q_1, \varepsilon, Z_0) = (q_2, Z_0)$

12. We can construct PDA in two ways:

   (i)   First, we convert the grammar in GNF. We get

   $S \rightarrow aSSS$

   $S \rightarrow aB$

   $B \rightarrow b$

   $T = \{a, b\}$

   $\Gamma = \{V \bigcup T \bigcup Z_0\}$

   $= \{S, Z_0, a, b, B\}$

   $Q = \{q_0, q_1, q_2\}$

   $F = \{q_2\}$

   $\delta(q_0, \varepsilon, Z_0) = (q_1, SZ_0)$

   $\delta(q_1, a, S) = (q_1, SSS)$

   $\delta(q_1, a, S) = (q_1, B)$

   $\delta(q_1, b, B) = (q_1, \varepsilon)$

   $\delta(q_1, \varepsilon, Z_0) = (q_2, Z_0)$

   OR

   (ii) Without converting grammar into GNF.

   $T = \{a, b\}$

   $\Gamma = \{S, Z_0, a, b\}$

   $Q = \{q_0, q_1, q_2\}$

   $F = \{q_2\}$

   $\delta(q_0, \varepsilon, Z_0) = (q_1, SZ_0)$

   $\delta(q_1, \varepsilon, S) = (q_1, aSSS)$

   $\delta(q_1, \varepsilon, S) = (q_1, ab)$

   $\delta(q_1, a, a) = (q_1, \varepsilon)$

   $\delta(q_1, b, b) = (q_1, \varepsilon)$

$$\delta(q_1, \varepsilon, Z_0) = (q_2, Z_0)$$

13. $T = \{a, b\}$

$\Gamma = \{V \cup T \cup Z_0\}$

$\quad = \{a, b, A, S, Z_0\}$

$Q = \{q_0, q_1, q_2\}$

$\delta(q_0, \varepsilon, Z_0) = (q_1, SZ_0)$

$\delta(q_1, \varepsilon, S) = (q_1, aAA)$

$\delta(q_1, \varepsilon, A) = (q_1, aS)$

$\delta(q_1, \varepsilon, A) = (q_1, bS)$

$\delta(q_1, \varepsilon, A) = (q_1, a)$

$\delta(q_1, a, a) = (q_1, \varepsilon)$

$\delta(q_1, b, b) = (q_1, \varepsilon)$

$\delta(q_1, \varepsilon, Z_0) = (q_2, Z_0).$

$(q_0, abaaaa, Z_0) \vdash (q_1, abaaaa, SZ_0)$

$\qquad\qquad\qquad \vdash (q_1, abaaaa, aAAZ_0)$

$\qquad\qquad\qquad \vdash (q_1, baaaa, AAZ_0)$

$\qquad\qquad\qquad \vdash (q_1, abaaa, bSAZ_0)$

$\qquad\qquad\qquad \vdash (q_1, aaaa, SAZ_0)$

$\qquad\qquad\qquad \vdash (q_1, aaaa, aAAAZ_0)$

$\qquad\qquad\qquad \vdash (q_1, aaa, AAAZ_0)$

$\qquad\qquad\qquad \vdash (q_1, aaa, aAAZ_0)$

$\qquad\qquad\qquad \vdash (q_1, aa, AAZ_0)$

$\qquad\qquad\qquad \vdash (q_1, aa, aAZ_0)$

$\qquad\qquad\qquad \vdash (q_1, a, aZ_0)$

$\qquad\qquad\qquad \vdash (q_1, \varepsilon, Z_0)$

15. (v) $\Sigma = \{a, b\}$

$\Gamma = \{a, b, z_0\}$

$Q = \{q_0, q_1, q_2, q_3, q_4\}$

$\delta(q_0, a, Z_0, Z_0) = (q_0, aZ_0, Z_0)$

$\delta(q_0, a, a, Z_0) = (q_0, aa, Z_0)$

$\delta(q_0, b, a, Z_0) = (q_1, a, bZ_0)$

$\delta(q_1, b, a, b) = (q_1, a, bb)$

$\delta(q_1, a, a, b) = (q_2, \varepsilon, b)$

$\delta(q_2, a, a, b) = (q_2, \varepsilon, b)$

$\delta(q_2, b, Z_0, b) = (q_3, Z_0, \varepsilon)$

$$\delta(q_3, b, Z_0, b) = (q_3, Z_0, \varepsilon)$$
$$\delta(q_3, \varepsilon, Z_0, Z_0) = (q_4, Z_0, Z_0)$$

17. The input alphabet c divides the input string in two equal parts. We also know that the symbols are retrieved from a stack in the reverse order of their insertion.

    As PDA reads the first part of the input string, it pushes symbols on the stack and remains in its initial state. When it reads c, it moves to state q_1 and replace top symbol by top symbol. Next, as PDA reads the second part, it pops the top symbol on the stack, compare it with current input symbol.

    If the input symbol does not match the top symbol on the stack, no further operation is possible. Since symbols are retrieved from the stack in reverse of the order in which they were inserted, a complete match will be achieved if and only if the input is of the form wcw^R. The following PDAs accept the language:
    $L = \{wcw^R : w \in \{a, b\}^*\}$

    $$M = (Q, \Sigma, \Gamma, \delta, q_0, Z_0, F)$$
    $$Q = \{q_0, q_1, q_2\}$$
    $$\Sigma = \{a, b, c\}$$
    $$\Gamma = \{a, b, z_0\}$$
    $$q_0 = \{q_0\}$$
    $$Z_0 = \{z_0\}$$

    $F = \{q_2\}$ and δ consists of

    $$\delta(q_0, a, z_0) = (q_0, az_0)$$
    $$\delta(q_0, b, z_0) = (q_0, bz_0)$$
    $$\delta(q_0, a, a) = (q_0, aa)$$
    $$\delta(q_0, b, b) = (q_0, bb)$$
    $$\delta(q_0, a, b) = (q_0, ab)$$
    $$\delta(q_0, b, a) = (q_0, ba)$$
    $$\delta(q_0, c, z_0) = (q_1, z_0)$$
    $$\delta(q_0, c, a) = (q_1, a)$$
    $$\delta(q_0, c, b) = (q_1, b)$$
    $$\delta(q_1, a, a) = (q_1, \varepsilon)$$
    $$\delta(q_1, b, b) = (q_1, \varepsilon)$$
    $$\delta(q_1, \varepsilon, z_0) = (q_2, z_0)$$

    We get the following transition diagram:

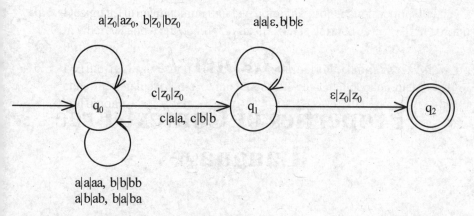

Programming Problems

. Write a program to design the PDA for the given context-free language.

. Write a program to convert a given CFG to PDA.

. Write a program to convert a given PDA to equivalent context-free grammar.

. Write a program to design 2-stack PDA for the non-context free language.

Chapter 7

Properties of Context-Free Languages

The present Chapter focuses primarily on pumping lemma for context-free languages. Closure and decision properties of context-free languages and grammars are also discussed.

Objectives: The objective of this Chapter is to explore the closure and decision properties of context-free languages and how to prove that a given language is not a context-free language. After learning the contents of this Chapter, you will be able to:

1. Use pumping lemma to prove that certain languages are non-context-free languages,

2. Explain closure and decision properties of context-free languages.

7.1 Pumping Lemma for Context-Free Languages (CFLs)

Context-free languages occupy a very important place in the hierarchy of formal languages. A given language is context-free if there exists a context-free grammar or pushdown automaton that defines the language.

Recall the pumping lemma has been discussed earlier. It states that a sufficiently long input string contains a short substring, which can be pumped as often as we like, and the resulting string will be still in the regular set. This fact enables us to prove that certain languages are not regular. Here, we introduce a similar lemma for context-free languages. The lemma for context-free languages states that there are always two short substrings, close together, that can be pumped as many times as we like (both to be pumped same number of times).

Theorem 7.1 (The pumping lemma for context-free languages): Let L be a context-free language. Then there is a constant n, depending only on L, such that if Z is in L and $|Z| \geq n$ then we can break Z into five substrings, that is

$Z = uvwxy$ such that

1. $|vx| \geq 1$
2. $|vwx| \leq n$ and
3. uv^iwx^iy is in L for all $i \geq 0$

Proof: If the parse tree of the word, generated by a CNF grammar G, contains no path of length greater than i, then the word cannot be of length greater than 2^{i-1}. This can be easily proved by induction on i as follows:

For the basis $i = 1$, the parse tree is shown in Figure 7.1(a). Obviously the basis is trivial.

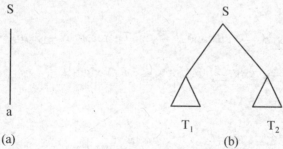

Fig. 7.1: Parse tree

For $i > 1$, the tree with root S and subtrees T_1 and T_2, is shown in Figure 7.1. If neither T_1 nor T_2 contains any path of length greater than $i - 1$, then both generate words of length not greater than 2^{i-2}. The entire tree, therefore, generates word of 2^{i-1} or fewer symbols. Let G have k variables and let $n = 2^k$. If Z is in $L(G)$ and $|Z| \geq n$, that is $|Z| \geq 2^k$, then any parse tree for Z must have a path of length at least $k + 1$. Clearly such a path has at least $k + 2$ vertices and all of these, except the last, are labeled by variables. Thus there must be some variable that appears twice on the path. These variables will be appearing twice near the bottom of the path.

Let p be a path that is as long as or longer than the path in the tree. Then there must be two vertices v_1 and v_2 on the path satisfying the following conditions:

(i)   The vertices v_1 and v_2 both have the same label, say B.

(ii) Vertex v_1 is closer to the root than vertex v_2.

(iii) The portion of the path from v_1 to the leaf is of length at most $k+1$.

Now let T_1 and T_2 be the subtrees with V_1 and V_2 as roots. Let Z_1 and Z_2 be the yield of sub trees T_1 and T_2, respectively. $|Z_1| \leq 2^k$ since Z_1 is the yield of T_1 (There can be no path in T_1 of length greater than $k+1$, since p was a path of longest length in the entire tree.)

To better understand, let us consider the grammar whose productions are given as follow:

$$S \rightarrow AB$$
$$A \rightarrow aB|a$$
$$B \rightarrow bA|b$$

We illustrate the construction of subtrees T_1 and T_2 for the above grammar. The construction is given in Figure 7.2.

In Figure path $P = S \rightarrow A \rightarrow B \rightarrow A \rightarrow B \rightarrow b$

$$Z = a\ b\ a\ b\ b,\ Z_1 = bab,\ Z_2 = b$$

As we know that T_2 is the subtree generated by vertex V_2 and Z_2 is the yield of subtree T_2 then, we can write $Z_1 = Z_3 Z_2 Z_4$. Furthermore, Z_3 and Z_4 can both be ε, since the first production used in the derivation of Z_1 must be of the form $B \rightarrow bA$ for some variable A. The subtree T_2 must be completely within either the subtree generated by A or the subtree generate by B.

$$Z_1 = b\ a\ b$$

We know that

$S \overset{*}{\Rightarrow} uBy$ and $B \overset{*}{\Rightarrow} vBx$ and $B \overset{*}{\Rightarrow} w$. Therefore, $S \overset{*}{\Rightarrow} uBy \rightarrow uwy, uv^0wx^0y$

$\in L$. For $k \geq 1$, $S \overset{*}{\Rightarrow} uBy \overset{*}{\Rightarrow} uv^kBx^ky \overset{*}{\Rightarrow} uv^kwx^ky \in L$.

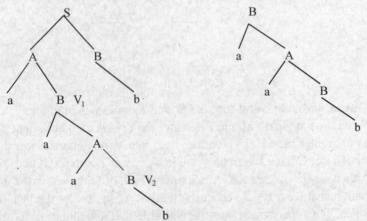

Fig. 7.2: Tree and its Subtrees T_1 and T_2

7.1.1 Application of Pumping Lemma

Pumping lemma can be used to show that a language does not belong to the family of context-free languages. In other words, it can be used to prove that certain languages are not context-free. The following steps are used to prove that a given language is not a CFL:

Step 1: We assume L is a context-free language. Let n be the constant.

Step 2: Select $Z \in L$ so that $|Z| \geq n$. We write $Z = uvwxy$ using the pumping lemma.

Step 3: Find a suitable i so that $uv^iwx^iy \notin L$. This is a contradiction. So, L is not CFL.

Example 7.1: Show that the language $L = \{a^nb^na^n | n \geq 1\}$ is not context-free.

Solution:

Step 1: Assume L is a context-free language. Let n be the constant.

Step 2: Let $Z = a^nb^na^n$, then $|Z| = 3n > n$. Write $Z = uvwxy$, where $|vx| \geq 1$, i.e., at least one of v or x is not ε.

Step 3: As $|vx| \geq 1$ and $|vwx| \leq n$. The v or x cannot contain all the three symbols. All words in a^nb^n have exactly one occurrence of the substring ab or ba no matter what the n has a value. Therefore v or x can be in any of the following form:

(i)   Either v or x has the substring ab.

(ii) Either v or x has the substring ba.

(iii) v and x has all a's, all b's.

Case 1: If $v = ab$ or $x = ab$ then uv^2wx^2y will have more than one substring of ab. So, $uv^2wx^2y \notin L$.

Case 2: If $v = ba$ or $x = ba$ then uv^2wx^2y will have more than one substring of ba. So, $uv^2wx^2y \notin L$.

Case 3: If $v = a^i$ or $x = b^j$ then we can write $Z = a^{n-i} a^i b^{n-j} b^j a^n$.

Now $uv^2wx^2y = a^{n-i} (a^i)^2 b^{n-j} (b^j)^2 a^n$

$$= a^{n-i} a^{2i} b^{n-j} b^{2j} a^n$$

$$= a^{n+i} b^{n+j} a^n$$

As $i > 1$ & $j > 1$, $n + i \neq n$ and $n + j \neq n$

So, $uv^2wx^2y \notin L$

Thus in all the cases we get a contradiction. Therefore, L is not context-free language.

7.2   Closure Properties of CFLs

In this section, we will discuss some closure properties of context-free languages. The context-free languages are closed under certain operations. The operations are not only useful to prove or construct that certain languages are context-free. But are also useful in proving that certain languages are not to be context-free. How will we use the closure properties of context-free languages to prove that certain languages are not context-free? A given language L can be shown not to be context-free using only operations preserving context-free languages by constructing from L a language that is not context-free. Some of the *closure properties* of context-free languages are as follows:

1. Context-free languages are closed under union.
2. Context-free languages are closed under product.
3. Context-free languages are closed under kleene star.
4. The intersection of context-free languages may or may not be a context-free language.
5. The complement of context-free languages may or may not be a context-free language.
6. Context-free languages are not closed under difference.
7. Context-free languages are closed under difference with regular languages.
8. Context-free languages are closed under substitution.
9. Context-free languages are closed under homomorphism.

Theorem 7.2: If L_1 and L_2 are context-free languages, then their union $L_1 + L_2$, is also a context-free language. In other words, the context-free languages are closed under union.

Proof: Let L_1 and L_2 be context-free languages generated by context-free grammars $G_1 = (V_1, T_1, P_1, S_1)$ and $G_2 = (V_2, T_2, P_2, S_2)$, respectively. As we know, we may rename variables without changing the language generated. Let us assume that V_1 and V_2 are distinct. Now we build a new CFG $G_3 = (V_1 \cup V_2 \cup \{S_3\}, T_1 \cup T_2, P_3, S_3)$ where P_3 consists of

$$P_3 = P_1 \cup P_2 \text{ and } S_3 \to S_1 | S_2 \text{ for } L_1 \cup L_2.$$

If w is in L_1, then derivation $S_3 \Rightarrow S_1 \overset{*}{\Rightarrow} w$ is a derivation in G_3 as every production of G_1 is a production of G_3. Similarly, every word in L_2 has a derivation in G_3 begins with $S_3 \Rightarrow S_2$. Therefore, we can say that all words from both languages can obviously be generated by G_3 as we have created a CFG that generates the language $L_1 \cup L_2$ or $(L_1 + L_2)$. Thus, $L_1 \cup L_2 \subseteq L(G_3)$. For the converse, let w be in $L(G_3)$. Then the derivation $S_3 \overset{*}{\Rightarrow} w$ begins with either $S_3 \overset{*}{\Rightarrow} S_1 \overset{*}{\Rightarrow} w$ or $S_3 \overset{*}{\Rightarrow} S_2 \overset{*}{\Rightarrow} w$. Suppose derivation starts with $S_3 \Rightarrow S_1$, as V_1 and V_2 are disjoint, only symbols of G_1 may appear in the derivation $S_3 \Rightarrow w$. As the only productions of P_3 that involve only symbols of G_1 are those from P_1. We conclude that only productions of P_1 are used in the derivation $S_1 \overset{*}{\Rightarrow} w$. Thus, $S_1 \overset{*}{\Rightarrow} w$ and w is L_1. Hence $L(G_3) \subseteq L_1 \cup L_2$. So, $L(G_3) = L_1 \cup L_2$.

Theorem 7.3: If L_1 and L_2 are context-free languages, then so is $L_1 L_2$. In other words, the context-free languages are closed under product.

Proof: Let $G_1 = (V_1, T_1, P_1, S_1)$ and $G_2 = (V_2, T_2, P_2, S_2)$ are the context-free grammar for the languages L_1 and L_2. We build new CFG, $G_3 = (V_1 \cup V_2 \cup \{S_3\}, T_1 \cup T_2, P_3, S_3)$ where P consists of $P_3 = P_1 \cup P_2$ and $S_3 \to S_1 S_2$ for $L_1 L_2$. Any word generated by G_3 has a front part derived from S_1, and a rear part derived from S_2. The two sets of products cannot cross over and interact with each other because V_1 and V_2 are disjoint, i.e, $V_1 \cap V_2 = \Phi$. Therefore, the words are in the language $L_1 L_2$.

If w is a word in $L_1 L_2$, then $w = w_1 w_2$ where w_1 is in L_1 and w_2 is in L_2. We can also generate w from the grammar G_3 as follows:

$$S_3 \Rightarrow S_1 S_2$$
$$\Rightarrow w_1 w_2 \; [S_1 \overset{*}{\Rightarrow} w_1 \; \& \; S_2 \overset{*}{\Rightarrow} w_2]$$
$$\Rightarrow w$$

The above derivation shows that w_1 is in L_1 and w_2 is in L_2. Adversely if w can be derived from S_3, then the first step of a derivation must be $S_3 \to S_1 S_2$ and w must be derivable from $S_3 \overset{*}{\Rightarrow} w$. Therefore, $w = w_1 w_2$, where w_1 must be derived from S_1 and w_2 must be derived from S_2. Thus, $w = w_1 w_2$ shows that the concatenation of two context-free languages is also context-free language.

Theorem 7.4: If L is a context-free language, then L^* is one too. In other words, the context-free languages are closed under Kleene star.

Proof: Let $G = (V, T, P, S)$ is the context-free grammar for the language L. Now, we define a grammar $G_1 = (\{V \cup S_1\}, T, P_1, S)$ where P_1 consists of

$$P \cup \{S \to S_1 S | \varepsilon\} \text{ for the language } L^*.$$

Now we repeat the productions $S \to S_1 S$ i times and followed by $S \to \varepsilon$, we get

$$S \Rightarrow S_1 S \qquad \text{application of the production } S \to S_1 S \text{ one time}$$
$$\Rightarrow S_1 S_1 S \qquad \text{application of the production } S \to S_1 S \text{ two times}$$

.

.

.

$$\Rightarrow S_1 S_1 S_1 \ldots S_i S \qquad \text{application of the production } S \to S_1 S \text{ i times}$$
$$\Rightarrow S_1 S_1 S_1 \ldots S_i \qquad \text{application of the production } S \to \varepsilon$$

We can see from the above derivation that we can form any word in L^* made up of i concatenation of words form L. Each of these S_1's is the root of a distinct branch of the tree do not effect those on another. Similarly, any word in L^* can be generated by starting with enough copies of S_1.

Theorem 7.5: The intersection of two context-free languages may or may not be context-free.

Proof: we can break the proof into two parts: may and may not.

May: As we already know that all regular languages are context-free. The intersection of two regular languages is regular. Therefore, if L_1 and L_2 are regular and context-free then $L_1 \cap L_2$ is both regular and context-free.

May Not: Let Language be $L_1 = \{a^n b^n a^m |$ where $n \geq 0$, $m \geq 0\}$

$$= \{aba, abaa, aabba, aabbaa, aabbaaa, ...\}$$

To prove this language is context-free, we have to give grammar that generates it. The following grammar generates the language L_1.

$$S \rightarrow XA$$
$$X \rightarrow aXb|ab$$
$$A \rightarrow aA|a$$

Alternatively, we can also say that L_1 is a context-free language because it can be obtained by the concatenation of (product of) the context-free language $a^n b^n$ and regular language aa^*.

Let $L_2 = \{a^n b^m a^m |n \geq 0, m \geq 0\}$ be the context-free language. To prove L_2 is a context-free, we have to give grammar that generates it. The following grammar generates L_2.

$$S \rightarrow AX$$
$$X \rightarrow aXb|ab$$
$$A \rightarrow aA|a$$

Alternatively, we can also observe that the L_2 is the product of a regular language aa^* and context-free language $\{b^n a^n\}$.

L_1 and L_2 are context-free, but their intersection is the language

$$L_3 = L_1 \cap L_2 = \{a^n b^n a^n : \text{where } n \geq 0\}$$

But we know that $a^n b^n a^n$ is not a context-free language. Thus, the context-free languages are not closed under intersection.

Theorem 7.6: The complement of a context-free language may or may not be context-free.

Proof: The proof of the theorem has two parts.

May: if L is regular, then L' is also regular. Therefore, if L_1 is regular and context-free then L_1' is also regular and context-free.

May Not: Suppose the complement of every context-free is context-free. If L_1 and L_2 are two context-free languages than their complements L_1 and L_2 are also context-free. Furthermore,

$$L_1' + L_2' \qquad \text{[Union of two context-free language is also context-free]}$$

$$\Rightarrow (L_1' + L_2')' \qquad \text{[The complement of context-free language is also context-free]}$$

$$\Rightarrow L_1 \cap L_2$$

$L_1 \cap L_2$ must be context-free. But L_1 and L_2 are any arbitrary context-free languages, a contradiction. Therefore, not all context-free languages have context-free complements.

Theorem 7.7: Context-free languages are not closed under difference.

Proof: The complement of a language L is defined as follows:

$$L^C = \Sigma^* - L$$

Σ^* is context-free. So, if languages were closed under difference, the complement of any context-free language must be the context-free language. But we know that CFLs are not closed under complement. This is a contradiction. Hence, context-free languages are not closed under difference.

Theorem 7.8: Context-free languages are closed under difference with Regular languages.

Proof: The difference between two languages L_1 and L_2 can be defined as follows:

$$L_1 - L_2 = L_1 \cap L_2^C$$

Suppose if L_2 is regular, the L_2^C is also regular, since regular languages are closed under complement. We know that the CFLs are closed under intersection with regular languages. Therefore, $L_1 - L_2$ is a context-free language. Thus, context-free languages are closed under difference with regular languages.

7.3 Decision Properties of CFLs

There are a number of the questions about context-free languages. Some of questions have an answer for which there exist an algorithm. However, there are certain un-answerable questions. There are no algorithms exist to solve them. No algorithms have been found because no such algorithms exist anywhere ever. Following are some of the un-answerable questions about context-free language given as follows.

- Whether or not two different context-free grammars are equivalent.
- Whether or not a context-free language is cofinite.
- Whether or not the complement of a given context-free language is also a context-free language.
- Whether or not given context-free grammar is ambiguous.
- Whether or not a given context-free grammar have an equivalent DPDA.
- Whether or not the intersection of two context-free languages is also context-free?
- Whether or not there are any words that a given context-free grammar does not generate.
- Whether or not there is a different context-free grammar from a given ambiguous context-free grammar that generates the same language.

Following are the solvable problems about context-free grammars that we can answer:

- Whether a given context-free grammar is empty. This is a question of emptiness.
- Whether a given context-free language is finite. This is a question of finiteness.
- Whether a given context-free language is infinite. This is a question of infiniteness
- Whether a given word is in a given context-free language? This is the question of memberships.

7.3.1 Emptiness

Theorem 7.9: Given any context-free grammar, there is an algorithm (decision) to determine whether or not it can generate any words.

Proof: Let us assume that the ε is not a word generated by a context-free grammar. Now, we are able to convert context-free grammar to Chomsky Normal Form preserving the entire language. If there is a production of form

$$S \rightarrow t$$

Where t is a terminal, then t is a word in the language. If there are no such productions, the Algorithm 7.1 is used to determine whether or not a given CFG generate any word.

Algorithm 7.1: Determining whether or not a given CFG generate any word

---

Algorithm(Determine whether or not a given CFG generate any word): Let Grammar G is in CNF. The steps are as follows:

Step 1: For every variable A that has some productions of the form

$$A \rightarrow t$$

Where $t \in T^*$. We chose one of these productions and throw out all other productions for which A is on the left side. We then replace A by t in all the productions in which A is on the right side. This process elements the non-terminal altogether.

Step 2: Repeat **Step 1** until it elements S or it elements no new non-terminals. if S has been eliminated, then CFG produces same words, if not it does not.

The above algorithm is obviously finite, since it cannot run Step 1 more times than there are variables in the original CNF. If Step 2 makes us stop while we still have not replaced S, then we can show that no words are generated by this CFG.

Example 7.3: Show that $G = (V, T, P, S)$ where $V = \{S, X, Y, A, B\}$, $T = \{a, b\}$, $S = \{S\}$ and P consist of

$$S \rightarrow XY$$
$$X \rightarrow AX|AA$$
$$A \rightarrow a$$
$$Y \rightarrow BY|BB$$
$$B \rightarrow b$$

generates at least one word.

Solution:

Step 1: The variable A and B are in the form $A \to t$ where $t \in T^*$. So, we replace all A's by a and all B's by b. We get:

$S \to XY,$

$X \to aX|aa,$

$Y \to bY|bb.$

Now, we can also see that X and Y are in the form $A \to t$. So, we replace all X's by aa and all Y's by bb. We get $S \to aabb$.

Now we can see that the variable S is in the form

$S \to t$

So, replace all S's by aabb.

Step 2: Step 1 is terminated and found that S has been eliminated.

Therefore, the CFG produces at least one word.

7.3.2 Finiteness

Theorem 7.10: There is an algorithm to decide whether a given CFG generates an infinite language or a finite language as defined in Algorithm 7.2:

Algorithm 7.2: To find out whether a given CFG generates an infinite or finite language

---

Algorithm (To find out whether a given CFG generates an infinite or finite language):

Step 1: Eliminate useless variables and useless productions.

Step 2: If the languages are infinite, then there must be some words long enough so that pumping lemma applies to them. The essence of the pumping lemma was to find a self-embedded non-terminal X, that is, one such that some derivation trace starting at X leads to another X.

Step 3: To test variable A is self-embedded or not. We do the steps from Step 4 to Step 7.

Step 4: Change all A's on the left side of productions into the variable that is not given in V, such as R_1. We leave all the A's on the right side of productions alone.

Step 5: Mark all A's to *.

Step 6: If B is any non-terminal that is the left side of any productions with same * on the right side, then mark all B's to *.

Step 7: Repeat Step 5 until nothing new is marked *.

Step 8: If R_1 is *, the A is self-embedded. If not, not.

Step 9: If any one of the variable is self-embedded, the language generated is infinite. If not the language is finite.

Step 10: If we found self-embedded variable, we stop, otherwise we repeat the steps from Step 2 to Step 7 for each variable.

Example 7.4: Consider the grammar $G = (V, T, P, S)$ where $V = \{S, A, B, X, Z\}$, $T = \{a, b\}$, $S = \{S\}$ and P consists of:

$S \rightarrow ABa|bAZ|b$

$A \rightarrow Xb|bZa$

$B \rightarrow bAA$

$X \rightarrow aZa|bA|aaa$

$Z \rightarrow ZAbA$

Step1: After removing useless variable, we get:

$S \rightarrow ABa|b$

$A \rightarrow Xb$

$B \rightarrow bAA$

$X \rightarrow bA|aaa$

Step 2: We test to see if X is self-embedded.

Step 3: $S \rightarrow ABa|b$

$A \rightarrow Xb$

$B \rightarrow bAA$

$R_1 \rightarrow bA|aaa$

Step 4: Mark all X's to *.

Step 5: $A \rightarrow Xb$, so A is marked as *.   [since X is marked]

$R_1 \rightarrow bA$, so R_1 is marked as *   [since A is marked]

$B \rightarrow A$, so B is marked as *.   [since A is marked]

$S \rightarrow ABa$, so S is marked as *.   [since A is marked]

R_1 is marked as *, so the language are generated by this CFG is infinite.

7.3.3 Memberships

Theorem 7.11: There is an algorithm to decide whether a given word is in a given CFL.

Algorithm 7.3: To determine whether a given word is in a given CFL

Membership Algorithm for CFG(CYK Algorithm): The CYK algorithm was discovered by J. Cocke, D.H. Younger, and T. Kasami. The algorithm works only if the grammar is in CNF. It begins by breaking one problem into a sequence of smaller once. Given a CFG and a word w in the same alphabet, we can decide whether or not w can be generated by the CFG.

Step 1: Make a list of all the variables. These will be the column heading of the table. The row of the table will be the length of the strings generated by each variable.

Step 2: We write single letter terminal (word of length 1) under each symbol that they can generate. It can be obtained by looking $A \rightarrow t$ production for each variable.

Step 3: We list for each variable all the words of length 2 that it generates. The second row of the table contains the word of length 2 generated by each variable. The variable at row 2 must have a production of the form $X \to YZ$ where Y generates a word of length 1 and Z also generates a word of length of 1. For each production of the form $X \to YZ$, we multiply the set of words of length 1 that Y generates (already in the table) by the set of words of length 1 that Z generates.

Step 4: In the next row, we write the word of length 3. The third row of the table contains the word length 3.

Step 5: We continue this table until we have all words of lengths up to the length (w) generated by each variable.

Step 6: If w is among those words generated by S. then w is a word generated by the grammar.

Example 7.5: Determine whether the string $w = baaba$ is in the language generated by the following grammar:

$S \to AB|BC$
$A \to BA|a$
$B \to CC|b$
$C \to AB|a$

Solution: By applying Steps 1, 2 and 3, we get the Table 7.1.

Table 7.1

S	A	B	C	Word length
	a	b	a	1
ab ba	ba	aa	ab	2
aaa, bab bab, aaa	bba, aaa	aab, aba	aaa, bab	3

Next, we eliminate duplication it exists. We can also see that our target word does not contain *aaa*, so retaining that possibility cannot helps us form w. So, we eliminate this from column S, A, and C. We get the Table 7.2:

Table 7.2

S	A	B	C	Word length
	a	b	a	1
ab, ba	ba	aa	ab	2
bab	bba	aab, aba	bab	3

Now, we generate the word of length four (4). We get the Table 7.3.

S	A	B	C	Word length
	a	b	a	1
ab, ba	aa	aa	ab	2
bab	bba	aab, aba	bab	3
aaab,aaba baaa, bbab bbab, aaab aaba, abaa	bbba aaba aaba abaa	abab	aaba aaab baaa bbab	4

After deletion of duplicate, we generate the world of length fire. We will get the following Table 7.4.

S	A	B	C	Word length
	a	b	a	1
ab,ba	ba	aa	ab	2
bab	bba	aab, aba	bab	3
aaab,aaba baaa, bbab abaa	bbba, aaba abaa	abab	aaba, aaab, baaa, bbab	4
aabab, baaab baaba, bbaaa bbbab, aabab abaab, baaba baaab, bbaaa bbbab, aabab aabab, abaab ababa	-	-	-	5

We can see the word *baaba* is among the word of length 5 generate by *S*. So, *w* = *baaba* is in the language generated by the grammer.

7.4   Summary

1. A context-free language is very important in the hierarchy of formal languages. A language is a context-free language if there is a context-free grammar or pushdown automaton.

2. Pumping lemma theorem is used to prove that some of the languages are not context-free languages. Pumping lemma states that there are always two substrings in a sufficiently long input string of CFL close together that can be pumped, as many times as you wish.

3. The context-free languages are closed under union, product, Kleene star, substitution and also homomorphism. But context-free languages are not closed under difference. In addition to this, context-free languages may or may not be closed under intersection and complement.

4. There are certain unanswerable questions (undecidable/unsolvable) for which no algorithm exist to solve them. There are also certain answerable questions (decidable/solvable problems) for which algorithms exist that solve them.

7.5   Exercises

Objective Questions

1. The class of context-free language is not closed under:
   - (a) Complement
   - (b) Homomorphism
   - (c) Substitution
   - (d) Product

2. Which of the following is decidable (solvable) problem about CFG?
   - (a) Whether or not a given context-free grammar is ambiguous
   - (b) Whether or not two given context-free grammars are equivalent
   - (c) Whether or not there are any words that a given CFG does not generate
   - (d) Whether or not a given CFG generates any word

3. If L_1 and L_2 are context free languages and R a regular set, which one of the languages below is not necessarily a context-free language?
   - (a) $L_1 L_2$
   - (b) $L_1 \cup L_2$
   - (c) $L_1 \cap L_2$
   - (d) $L_1 R$

4. The class of context-free language is not closed under:
   - (a) Concatenation
   - (b) Intersection
   - (c) Union
   - (d) Substitution

5. Context free languages are closed under:
   - (a) Union, complement
   - (b) Product, intersection
   - (c) Substitution, homomorphism
   - (d) Kleene star, complement

6. Which of the following is a decidable problem of CFG?
   - (a) Whether a given CFG is empty
   - (b) Whether a given CFG is finite
   - (c) Whether a given CFG is infinite
   - (d) All of the above

7. Which of the following is a technique to show that a language is context-free?
   - (a) By exhibiting a CFG
   - (b) By exhibiting a PDA
   - (c) By pumping theorem
   - (d) All of the above

8. Which of the following statements is true?
   (a) Ogden's Lemma is used to show that a language is not context-free
   (b) Ogden's Lemma is a generalization of the pumping theorem
   (c) Pumping theorem is a tool for showing that a language is not context-free
   (d) All of the above

9. Which of the following statements is not true?
   (a) Any regular language has an equivalent context-free grammar
   (b) Some non-regular languages cannot be generated by any context-free grammar
   (c) Intersection of CFL and a RL is always CF
   (d) All languages can be generated by context-free grammar

10. A class of language that is closed under:
    (a) Union and intersection has to be closed under complement
    (b) Intersection and complement has to be closed under union
    (c) Union and complement has to be closed under intersection
    (d) Both (b) and (c)

11. Which of the following statements is false?
    (a) The intersection of context-free languages may or may not be CFL
    (b) The complement of CFLs may or may not be CFL
    (c) Every DCFL has an unambiguous grammar
    (d) None of the above

12. Which of the following is a false statement?
    (a) The DCFLs are closed under complement
    (b) The DCFLs are closed under union
    (c) Every regular language is DCFL
    (d) Every DCFL has an unambiguous grammar

13. Which of the following is true?
    (a) The DCFLs are not closed under intersection.
    (b) The DCFLs are not closed under union
    (c) Both (a) and (b)
    (d) None of these

14. Which one is Parikh's theorem?
    (a) Every context-free language is letter-equivalent to some regular language.
    (b) Any context-free language over a single-character alphabet is regular
    (c) For every DCFL there exists an unambiguous grammar
    (d) None of these

15. Which one is a decidable problem about CFLs?

(a)   Given two deterministic context-free languages L_1 and L_2, is $L_1 = L_2$?

(b)   Given a CFG G, is G ambiguous?

(c)   Given two context-free languages L_1 and L_2, is $L_1 L_2 = \Phi$?

(d)   Given a CFL L, is $L = \Sigma^*$?

16.   Which one is undecidable problem about CFLs/CFGs?

(a)   Given a CFL L, is $L = \Phi$?

(b)   Given a CFL L, is $L = \Sigma^*$?

(c)   Given a CFL L, is L infinite?

(d)   Given two DCFLs L_1 and L_2, is $L_1 = L_2$?

Answers to Objective Questions

01.	(a)	02.	(d)	03.	(b)	04.	(b)	05.	(c)	06.	(d)
07.	(d)	08.	(d)	09.	(d)	10.	(d)	11.	(d)	12.	(b)
13.	(c)	14.	(a)	15.	(a)	16.	(b)				

Review Questions

1.   States the Pumping Lemma for a context-free language.

2.   Determine whether or not the following languages are in context-free:

^{A}(a) $L = \{a^p \,|\, p$ is a prime$\}$

(b) $L = \{w_1 \subset w_2 : w_1, w_2 \in \{a, b\}^*, w_1 \neq w_2\}$

^{A}(c) $L = \{a^m b^m c^n \,|\, m \leq n \leq 2m\}$

^{A}(d) $L = \{a^{n^2} \,|\, n \geq 1\}$

(e) $L = \{wcw \,|\, w \in \{a, b\}^*\}$

^{A}(f) $L = \{w \,|\, n_a(w) = n_b(w) = n_c(w)\}$

^{A}(g) $L = \{ww \,|\, w \in \{a, b\}^*\}$

(h) $L = \{a^n b^i \,|\, n = j^2\}$

(i) $L = \{ww^R w : w \in \{a, b\}^*\}$

(j) $L = \{a^n b^i : n \leq j^2\}$

^{A}(k) $L = \{a^n b^n c^n \,|\, n > 1, \Sigma = \{a, b, c\}\}$

.   Show that the family of context-free languages is closed under union.

.   Show that the family of context-free languages is closed under product.

.   Show that the family of context-free languages is closed under Kleene Star.

.   Show that the family of context-free languages is closed under reversal.

.   Show that the family of context-free languages may or may not be closed under intersection.

.   Show that the family of context-free languages is closed under complement.

.   Show that the family of context-free languages is closed under homomorphism.

0.   Show that the family of context-free languages is closed under substitution.

1.   Show that context-free languages are closed under difference with the regular languages.

12. Show that the family of DCFLs is closed under complement.
13. Show that the family of DCFLs is not closed under union.
14. Show that the family of DCFLs is closed under difference.
15. Show that $G = (V, T, P, S)$ where $V = \{S, X, Y, A, B\}$, $T = \{a, b\}$, $S = \{S\}$ and P consist of $S \to XY$

$X \to AX$

$A \to a$

$Y \to BY|BB$

$B \to b$

generates at least one word.
16. Show that $G = (V, T, P, S)$ where $V = \{S, X, Y, A, B, Z\}$, $T = \{a, b\}$, $S = \{S\}$ and P consist of

$S \to XY$ $\quad B \to b$

$X \to ZX$ $\quad A \to XA$

$Z \to a$

$Y \to AX|ZZ$

$Y \to BB$

generates at least one word.
17. Consider the grammar $G = \{S, X, Y, Z\}, \{a, b\}, P, S\}$ where P consists of

$S \to XS|b$

$X \to YZ$

$Z \to XY$

$Y \to ab$

Prove that whether the language generated by the CFG is finite or infinite.
18. Prove that whether the language generated by the following CFG is finite or infinite.

(i) $S \to XS|b$

$X \to YZ$

$Z \to XY$

$X \to ab$

(ii) $S \to XY|bb$

$X \to YX$

$Y \to XY|SS$

(iii) $S \to AB|bb$

$A \to BB$

$B \to AB|SS$

(iii) $X \to A$

$Y \to B$

$A \to C$

$B \to D$

$C \to E$

(iv) $S \to AB$

$A \to CC|AB|b$

$C \to DE$

$D \to CE$

$E \to DC$

$B \to a$

19. Using Cock, Younger and Kasami algorithm decide whether word *babaa* can be generated by the following CFG or not:

$$S \rightarrow XY$$
$$X \rightarrow XA|a|b$$
$$Y \rightarrow AY|a$$
$$A \rightarrow a$$

Give only the tabular form and your conclusion. No explanations are needed. The capital letters denote non-terminals.

Answers/Hints for Selected Review Questions

2. (a) **Step 1:** Let us assume that $L = \{a^p \,|p \text{ is prime}\}$ is a context-free language. Let n be a natural number constant.

   Step 2: Let p be a prime number greater than n. $Z = a^p \in L$. We write $z = uvwxy$.

   Step 3: $a^p = uvwxy$. By pumping lemma, $uv^0wx^0y = uwy \in L$. So $|uwy|$ is a prime number, say m. Let $|vx| = q$. Then $|uv^mwx^my| = m + mq = m(1 + q)$ is not a prime. Thus, $uv^mwx^my \notin L$. This is a contradiction. Therefore, L is not a context-free language.

   (d) **Step 1:** Let us assume that $L = \{ a^{n^2} \mid n \geq 1 \}$ is a context-free language. Let n be a natural number constant.

   Step 2: Let $z = a^{n^2}$. $z = uvwxy$ where $1 \leq vx \leq n$.

   Step 3: Let $|vx| = m$, $m \leq n$. By pumping lemma uv^2wx^2y is in L. As $|uv^2wx^2y| > n^2$, $|uv^2wx^2y| = k^2$, where $k \geq n + 1$. But $|uv^2wx^2y| = n^2 + m < n^2 + 2n + 1$. So, $|uv^2wx^2y|$ must be lies between n^2 and $(n + 1)^2$ which means $uv^2wx^2y \notin L$, a contradiction. Hence, $L = \{ a^{n^2} \mid n \geq 1 \}$ is not a context-free language.

   (f) Let us assume $L = \{w|n_a(w) = n_b(w) = n_c(w) \text{ and } w \in \{a, b, c\}\}$ is a context-free language. Then $L \cap L(a*b*c*) = \{a^nb^nc^n : n \geq 0\}$ would also be context-free. But we know that $a^nb^nc^n$ is not so. This is a contradiction. Therefore, L is not context-free.

   (g) Let $L = \{ww : w \in \{a, b\}*\}$ is a context-free language. Then $L(a*b*a*b*) = \{a^kb^ka^kb^k : k \geq 0\}$ would also be context-free. But we can prove that $a^kb^ka^kb^k$ is not a CFL.

   Step 1: Let $L = a^kb^ka^kb^k$ is a CFL. Let k is a constant.

   Step 2: $z = uvwxy = a^kb^ka^kb^k$

   Case 1: if either $v = a^ib^j$ or $x = a^ib^j$ for some i, j such that $i + j \leq k$

   Case 2: if either $v = b^ia^j$ or $x = b^ia^j$ for some i, j such that $i + j \leq k$

   Case 3: if either $v = a^i$ or $x = a^i$ for some i, j such that $i + j \leq k$

Case 4: if either $v = b^i$ or $x = b^i$ for some i such that $i \leq k$

when v or x is of the form $a^i b^j$, $v^2 = a^i b^j a^i b^j$(or $x^2 = a^i b^j a^i b^j$). Since v^2 is a substring of $uv^2 wx^2 y$, then $uv^2 wx^2 y$ will not be in the form $a^k b^k a^k b^k$. So $uv^2 wx^2 y \notin L$. Similarly we can show for the Case 2, 3 and 4. Thus for any choice of v or x, we get a contradiction. Therefore L, is not a context free.

2.   (k)   **Step 1:** Suppose L is context-free. Let n be the constant.

Step 2: Let $Z = a^n b^n c^n$. $|Z| = 3n > n$. Write $Z = uvwxy$, where $|vx| \geq 1$, $|vwx| \leq n$ by the pumping lemma.

Step 3: All the words in $a^n b^n a^n$ have only one substrings ab and only one substring of bc, no matter what n has a value. The v or x may be said blocks of a's, b's, or c's or ε. As $|vwx| \leq n$, so v or x cannot be contained the three symbols a, b, c. therefore v or x can be any of the following form:

(i)   Either v or x has the substring ab.

(ii)   Either v or x has the substring bc.

(iii) v and x have all a's, all b's or c's or $x = a^i b^j (b^i c^j)$ or ε.

(iv)   Either v or x is of the form $a^i b^j$ (or $b^i c^j$) for some i, j such that $i + j \leq n$.

Case 1: If $v = ab$ or $x = ab$ then $uv^2 wx^2 y$ will have more than one substring of ab. So, $uv^2 wx^2 y \notin L$.

Case 2: If $v = bc$ or $x = bc$ then $uv^2 wx^2 y$ will have more than one substring of bc. So, $uv^2 wx^2 y \notin L$.

Case 3: If $v = a^i$ or $x = b^j$ then we can write $Z = uvwxy = a^{n-i} a^i b^{n-j} b^j c^n$.

Now $uv^2 wx^2 y = a^{n-i} (a^i)^2 b^{n-j} (b^j)^2 c^n$

$$= a^{n-i} a^{2i} b^{n-j} b^{2j} c^n$$

$$= a^{n+i} b^{n+j} c^n$$

As $i > 1, j > 1$, $n + i \neq n$ and $n + j \neq n$, So, $uv^2 wx^2 y \notin L$

Case 4: If $v = a^i b^j$ or $x = b^k c^l$ then we can write $Z = uvwxy = a^{n-i} a^i b^j b^{n-j-k} b^k c^l c^{n-l}$.

Now $uv^2 wx^2 y = a^{n-i} (a^i b^j)^2 b^{n-j-k} (b^k c^l)^2 c^{n-l}$

$$= a^{n-i} a^{2i} b^{2j} b^{n-j-k} b^{2k} c^{2l} c^{n-l}$$

$$= a^{n+i} b^{n+j+k} c^{n+l}$$

As $i > 1, j > 1, l > 1$ $n + i \neq n$ and $n + j + k \neq n$, $n + l \neq 1$

So, $uv^2 wx^2 y \notin L$

Thus in all the cases we get a contradiction. Therefore, L is not context-free language.

Programming Problems

1.   Write a program to determine whether or not a given word is a member of the language defined by the given context-free grammar.

2.   Write a program to determine the given CFG generates finite words, infinite words or no word.

Chapter 8

Turing Machines

This Chapter presents Turing machine, the ultimate mathematical model of a Computer. The Chapter considers basic Turing model, the different ways to represent the Turing machine and the modifications of Turing machine. We then present a thorough discussion of use of Turing machine as a computer of integer functions. The Chapter also includes Linear Bounded Automata, a special type of Turing machine. Church's thesis concludes the Chapter.

Objectives: The objective of this Chapter is to explore Turing machine, the widely accepted general model of computation. After learning the contents of this Chapter, you will be able to:

1. Define basic Turing model and its working,
2. Describe various representations of Turing machine,
3. Describe variants of Turing machine,
4. Construct Turing machine,
5. Define LBA and UTM and their working.

8.1   Basic Model of Turing Machine (TM)

Turing machines and their theory were developed by Alan Mathison Turing and Emil Post in 1930s and 1940s. A Turing machine is an automaton which consists of a finite control, tape and head. The tape is divided into cells. Each cell may contain exactly one tape symbol. The tape has a leftmost cell but is infinite on the right. Tape head reads and writes one symbol of the tape at a time and moves one cell left or right. The basic model of Turing machine is shown in Figure 8.1.

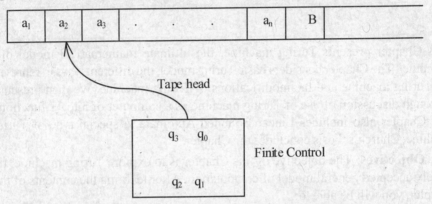

Fig. 8.1: The Basic Model of Turing machine

In one move, the Turing machine scans the symbol pointed by the tape head. Depending upon the present state of finite control and scanned symbol, it must

(i)   Change state,

(ii)   Write a new symbol on the tape cell, and

(iii)   Move the head one cell left or right.

8.1.1 Definition

Formally, A Turing machine (Standard Turing machine) M is a 7-tuple $(Q, \Sigma,$ $\Gamma, \delta, q_0, B, F)$ where

Q is the finite set of states,

$\Sigma \subset \Gamma$ is a finite set of input symbols called input alphabet and $B \notin \Sigma$,

Γ is the finite set of tape symbols called the tape alphabet,

$B \in \Gamma$ is the blank symbol,

δ is the transition function (next move function), a mapping from $Q \times \Gamma$ to $Q \times \Gamma \times \{L, R\}$. δ may not be defined for same element $Q \times \Gamma$,

$q_0 \in Q$ is the start state,

$F \subseteq Q$ is the set of final states.

8.2   Representation of Turing Machines

Turing machine can be represented by various ways. In this section, we will see the representation of Turing machine by Instantaneous description, Transition table and Transition diagram.

8.2.1 Instantaneous Description (ID)

Instantaneous description represents the configuration of Turing machine at any instant of time. Configuration is determined by the current state of the machine, the contents of the tape, and the position of the tape head. ID of Turing machine M can be represented by

$$\alpha_1 q \alpha_2 \text{ or } x_1 x_2 x_3 \ldots x_{k-1} q x_k x_{k+1} \ldots x_n$$

where $q \in Q$ is the current state of M and $\alpha_1 \alpha_2$ is a string in Γ^*, $\alpha_1 = x_1 x_2 x_3 \ldots x_{k-1}$ and $\alpha_2 = x_k x_{k+1} \ldots x_n$.

Figure 8.2 shows the ID of Turing machine. The string $\alpha_1 \alpha_2$ shows the contents of the tape, whereas q defines the state of the control unit. We assume that the tape head is at the cell containing the symbol immediately following q.

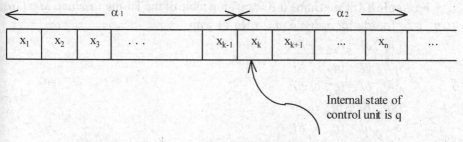

Fig. 8.2: Instantaneous Description of Turing Machine

Let $M = (Q, \Sigma, \Gamma, \delta, q_0, B, F)$ be a Turing machine, and $x_1 x_2 x_3 \ldots x_{k-1} q_i x_k x_{k+1} \ldots x_n$ with $x_i \in \Gamma$ and $q_i \in Q$, is an ID of M. We define move (transition between configurations) as follows:

A move $x_1 x_2 x_3 \ldots x_{k-1} q_1 x_k x_{k+1} \ldots x_n \vdash x_1 x_2 x_3 \ldots x_{k-1} y q_2 x_{k+1} \ldots x_n$ is possible if $\delta(q_1, x_k) = (q_2, y, R)$. A move $x_1 x_2 x_3 \ldots x_{k-1} q_1 x_k x_{k+1} \ldots x_n \vdash x_1 x_2 x_3 \ldots q_2 x_{k-1} y x_{k+1} \ldots x_n$ is possible if $\delta(q_1, x_k) = (q_2, y, L)$.

A *Computation* of Turing machine M on the input w is a finite sequence of configurations $C_0, C_1, \ldots C_n$ such that :

(i) C_0 is an initial configuration $q_0 w$, $w \in \Sigma^*$

(ii) C_n is halt state $\alpha_1 q \alpha_2$ where $q \in F$

(iii) $C_i \vdash C_{i+1}$ for all $0 \geq i < n - 1$

8.2.2 Transition Table

A Turing machine can be represented by a transition table. The *transition table* is a tabular representation of transition function. Algorithm 8.1 is used to construct the transition table of Turing machine.

Algorithm 8.1: Algorithm for Construction of Transition Table

---

Algorithm(Construction of Transition Table): Let $M = (Q, \Sigma, \Gamma, \delta, q_0, B, F)$ be a Turing machine. Following steps are used to construct the Transition Table:

Step 1: Draw a table in which number of rows indicates the number of states in TM and number of columns indicates the number of symbols in Σ.

Step 2: Start state is preceded by "−" and final states are preceded by " + ".

Step 3: Label the rows with the state names and the columns with the symbols in Σ.

Step 4: For each transition function $\delta(q, a) = (p, y, R)$ or $\delta(q, a) = (p, y, L)$ put pyR or pyL in the cell (q, a).

Example 8.1: Determine the Transition table of the Turing machine $M = (\{q_0, q_1, q_2, q_3\}, \{a, b\}, \{a, b, B\}, \delta, q_0, B, \{q_3\})$ with

$$\delta(q_0, a) = (q_1, a, R)$$
$$\delta(q_0, b) = (q_2, b, R)$$
$$\delta(q_1, b) = (q_1, b, R)$$
$$\delta(q_1, B) = (q_3, B, R)$$
$$\delta(q_2, a) = (q_3, a, R)$$
$$\delta(q_2, b) = (q_2, b, R)$$

Solution:

We draw four rows and three columns in the transition table since the Turing machine has four states and three symbols in Γ. The start state and the final state are $\{q_0\}$ and $\{q_3\}$, respectively, so we put − and + sign before the row labelled q_0 and q_3. For each transition function $\delta(q, a) = (p, y, R)$ or $\delta(q, a) = (p, y, L)$ we are to put pyR or pyL in the cell (q, a). Since $\delta(q_0, a) = (q_1, a, R)$, we put q_1aR in the cell (q_0, a). Similarly, we put q_2bR, q_1bR, q_3BR, q_3aR and q_2bR in the cell(q_0, b), cell(q_1, b), cell(q_1, B), cell(q_2, a) and cell(q_2, b), respectively. We get the Transition table as summarized in Table 8.1.

Table 8.1: Transition Table

Present State	Tape Input Symbol		
	a	b	B
$-q_0$	q_1aR	q_2bR	-
q_1	-	q_1bR	q_3BR
q_2	q_3aR	q_2bR	-
$+q_3$	-	-	-

Example 8.2: Determine when presented with the inputs *aba* and *aaabbbb*, what the following Turing machine does $M = (\{q_0, q_1, q_2, q_3, q_4\}, \{a, b\}, \{a, b, x, y, B\}, \delta, q_0, B, \{q_4\})$ with

$$\delta(q_0, a) = (q_1, x, R)$$

$$\delta(q_1, a) = (q_1, a, R)$$
$$\delta(q_1, y) = (q_1, y, R)$$
$$\delta(q_1, b) = (q_2, y, L)$$
$$\delta(q_2, y) = (q_2, y, L)$$
$$\delta(q_2, a) = (q_2, a, L)$$
$$\delta(q_2, x) = (q_0, x, R)$$
$$\delta(q_0, y) = (q_3, y, R)$$
$$\delta(q_3, y) = (q_3, y, R)$$
$$\delta(q_3, B) = (q_4, B, R)$$

Solution:

When the input *aba* is fed to the Turing machine, it starts with the initial configuration $q_0 aba$. We get the following sequence of Instantaneous Description:

$q_0 aba \vdash xq_1 ba \vdash q_2 xya \vdash xq_0 ya \vdash xyq_3 a$. At this state, no transition is defined. So, machine halts. However, q_3 is not a final state. Hence the input string *aba* is not accepted by the machine.

For the input *aaabbb*, we get the following sequence of instantaneous descriptions:

$(q_0 aaabbb) \vdash xq_1 aabbb \vdash xaq_1 abbb \vdash xaaq_1 bbb \vdash xaq_2 aybb \vdash xq_2 aaybb \vdash q_2 xaaybb \vdash xq_0 aaybb \vdash xxq_1 aybb \mid xxaq_1 ybb \vdash xxayq_1 bb \vdash xxaq_2 yyb \vdash xxq_2 ayyb \vdash xq_2 xayyb \vdash xxq_0 ayyb \vdash xxxq_1 yyb \vdash xxxyq_1 yb \; xxxyyq_1 b \vdash xxxyq_2 yy \vdash xxxq_2 yyy \vdash xxq_2 xyyy \vdash xxxq_0 yyy \vdash xxxyq_3 yy \vdash xxxyyq_3 y \vdash xxxyyyq_3 B \vdash xxxyyyBq_4 B$

Machine halts in the state q_4 which is a final state. Therefore, input *aaabbb* is accepted by *M*.

Note: The move of a Turing machine can be expressed as a pair of instantaneous descriptions, separated by "$\vdash$", as we define the relation $\vdash$ between ID'.

8.2.3 Transition Diagram

Like finite automata and Pushdown Automata, Turing machine can also be represented by a directed graph called *Transition diagram*. States are represented by vertices and transitions between states are represented by directed edges. Labels are triples of the form (α, β, γ) where $\alpha \in \Gamma$, $\beta \in \Gamma$ and $\gamma \in \{L, R\}$. Algorithm 8.2 is used to construct the transition diagram of Turing machine.

Algorithm 8.2: Algorithm for the Construction of Transition Diagram

---

Algorithm (Construction of Transition Diagram): Let $M = (Q, \Sigma, \Gamma, \delta, q_0, B, F)$ be a Turing machine. Following steps are used to construct the Transition Diagram.

Step 1: Draw small circles for each state with the name of the state written inside the circle.

Step 2: Indicate the start state by an incoming arrow or labeling with word "start" or "−".

Step 3: Indicate final states by double circles or labeling by the word "Final" or "+".

Step 4: Draw an arc labeled with (α, β, γ) from the circle q_i to circle q_j if there is a transition $\delta(q_i, \alpha) = (q_j, \beta, \gamma)$.

Step 5: Repeat the Step 4 for each transition.

Example 8.3: Draw the transition diagram of Turing machine given in Example 8.1.

Solution:

First, we draw small circles, one for each state q_0, q_1, q_2 and q_3 with the name of the state written inside the circle. Start state q_0 is indicated by an incoming arrow and final state q_3 is indicated by '+'. Next, we draw an arc from state q_0 to q_1 with label (a, a, R) corresponding to the transition $\delta(q_0, a) = (q_1, a, R)$. Similarly, we draw the arcs for each transition. We get the transition diagram as shown in Figure 8.3.

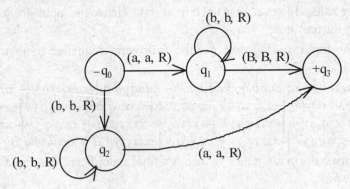

Fig. 8.3: Transition Diagram

8.3 Language Acceptability of Turing Machines

Let $M = (Q, \Sigma, \Gamma, \delta, q_0, B, F)$ be a Turing machine. The language accepted by M is $L(M) = \{w \mid w \text{ in } \Sigma^* \text{ and } q_0 w * \alpha_1 p \alpha_2 \text{ for some } p \in F, \alpha_1, \alpha_2 \in \Gamma^*\}$

Note: The reflexive-transitive closure of will $\vdash$ be denoted by $\vdash^*$.

Example 8.4: Design a Turing machine that accepts $L = \{a^n b^n \mid n \geq 1\}$

Solution: Turing machine M will work on an input string w as follows:

Step 1: M starts with state q_0. It searches for the leftmost a. If it finds, M replaces a with symbol X and moves to the right and enters a state q_1. Instead of a if M finds Y, M skips it and moves to the right. M enters the state q_3.

Step 2: In state q_1, M skips the rest of a's and Y's and looks for the leftmost b. If M reads b, replaces it with symbol Y and moves to the left. M enters state q_2. If M reads anything else, it crashes.

Step 3: In state q_2, M skips over a's and Y's, moving left until X occurs. If M reads X, M replaces it with the same symbol and moves right. M enters the state q_0.

Step 4: In state q_3, M skips over Y's, moving right until B occurs. If M reads B, M replaces it with the same symbol and moves right. M enters the state q_4 which is a final state.

Based on the above discussion, the formal description of Turing machine M is as follows:

$$M = (Q, \Sigma, \Gamma, \delta, q_0, B, F) \text{ where}$$
$$Q = \{q_0, q_1, q_2, q_3, q_4\},$$
$$\Sigma = \{a, b\},$$
$$\Gamma = \{a, b, X, Y, B\},$$
$$q_0 = \{q_0\} \text{ and}$$
$$F = \{q_4\}.$$

Figure 8.7 shows the transition diagram.

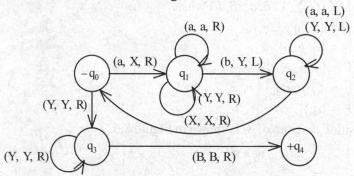

Fig. 8.4: Transition Diagram of M

For the input string $aabb$, the computation sequence is given as:

$$q_0 aabb \vdash Xq_1 abb \vdash Xaq_1 bb \vdash Xq_2 aYb \vdash q_2 XaYb \vdash Xq_0 aYb \vdash XXq_1 Yb$$
$$\vdash XXYq_1 b \vdash XXq_2 YY \vdash Xq_2 XYY \vdash XXq_0 YY \vdash XXYq_3 Y \vdash XXYYq_3 B \vdash XXYYBq_4.$$

Example 8.5: Design a Turing machine M that accepts $L = \{a^n b^n c^n | n \geq 0\}$. Construct the computation sequence for the input string aabbcc.

Solution:

Turing machine M will work on an input string w as follows:

Step1: M starts with state q_0. If M reads a, replaces it with symbol A and moves to the right. M enters state q_1. If M reads B(blank), replaces it with symbol B and moves to the right. M enters state q_8 that is a final state. If M reads anything else, M crashes.

Step 2: In state q_1, M skips over a's, moving right until b occurs. If M reads b, M replaces it with symbol b and moves to the right. M enters state q_2.

Step 3: In state q_2, M skips over b's, moving right until c occurs. If M reads c, M replaces it with c and moves to the left. M enters state q_3.

Step 4: In state q_3, if M reads b, M replaces it with symbol c and moves to the right. M enters state q_4.

Step 5: In state q_4, M skips over c's, moving right until B (Blank) occurs. If M reads B, M replaces it with B and moves to the left. M enters state q_5.

Step 6: In state q_5, M reads c, replaces it with B and moves to the left. M enters state q_6.

Step 7: In state q_6, M reads c, replaces it with B and moves to the left. M enters state q_7.

Step 8: In state q_7, M skips over a's and b's, moving left until A occurs. If M reads A, replaces it with A and moves to the right. M enters state q_0.

Keeping above steps in mind, we give the formal description of Turing machine M as follows:

$$M = (Q, \Sigma, \Gamma, \delta, q_0, B, F) \text{ where}$$
$$Q = \{q_0, q_1, ...q_8\},$$
$$\Sigma = \{a, b, c\},$$
$$\Gamma = \{a, b, A, B\},$$
$$q_0 = \{q_0\} \text{ and}$$
$$F = \{q_8\}.$$

Transition diagram of M is shown in Figure 8.5.

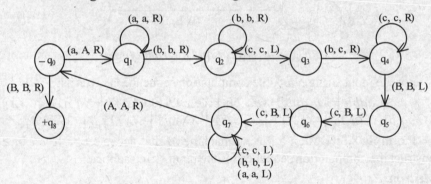

Fig. 8.5: Transition Diagram of M

For the input string aabbcc, the computation sequence is given as:

$q_0aabbcc \vdash Aq_1abbcc \vdash Aaq_1bbcc \vdash Aabq_2bcc \vdash Aabbq_2cc \vdash Aabq_3bcc \vdash Aabcq_4cc \vdash Aabccq_4c \vdash Aabcccq_4B \vdash Aabccq_5c \vdash Aabcq_6cB \vdash Aabq_7c \vdash Aaq_7bc \vdash Aq_7abc \vdash q_7Aabc \vdash Aq_0abc \vdash AAq_1bc \vdash AAbq_2c \vdash AAq_3bc \vdash AAcq_4c \vdash AAccq_4B \vdash AAcq_5c \vdash AAq_6c \vdash Aq_7A \vdash AAq_0B \vdash AABq_8.$

Example 8.6: Design a TM to recognize the language $L = (a + b)b(a + b)*\}$

Solution: The Turing machine M will work on an input string w as follows:

Step 1: The Turing machine M starts with state-q_0 as shown in Figure 8.6. If M reads a or b, M replaces it with the same symbol and moves to the right. M enters state q_1. If M reads anything else, it crashes.

Step 2: In state q_1, M reads b, replaces it with symbol b and moves to the right. M enters the state q_2.

Step 3: In state q_2, M skips a's and b's, moving right until B occurs. If M reads B, M replaces it with B and moves to the right. M enters the state q_3 which is a final state.

Based on the above discussion, we can design Turing machine $M = (Q, \Sigma, \Gamma, \delta, q_0, B, F)$ as shown in Figure 8.6.

$$Q = \{q_0, q_1, q_2, q_3\},$$
$$\Sigma = \{a, b\},$$
$$\Gamma = \{a, b, B\},$$
$$q_0 = \{q_0\} \text{ and}$$
$$F = \{q_3\}.$$

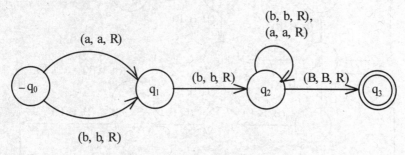

Fig. 8.6: Transition Diagram of M

Example 8.7: Design a Turing machine to accept the language $L = \{w \mid w = w^R$ and $w \in \{a, b\}^*\}$.

Solution:

Turing machine M will work on an input string w as follows:

Step 1: The Turing machine M starts with state-q_0 as shown in Figure 8.7. If M reads a, M replaces it with symbol B and moves to the right. M enters state q_1. If M reads b, M replaces it with symbol B and moves to the right and enters state q_4. If M reads B, M replaces it with symbol B and moves to the right. M enters state q_7.

Step 2: In states q_1 and q_4, moving right M skips over a's and b's, until Blank symbol occurs. If M reads B at state q_1 or state q_4, M replaces it with symbol B and moves to the left. M enters state q_2 or q_5 depending upon previous states q_1 or q_4.

Step 3: If M reads a at state q_2 or b at state q_5, M replaces it with B and moves to the left and enters state q_3 or q_5, respectively.

Step 4: In states q_3 and q_6, if M reads B, M replaces it with B and moves to the right. M goes to state q_0.

Based on the above steps, we now give formal description of Turing machine M as depicted in Figure 8.7.

$M = (Q, \Sigma, \Gamma, \delta, q_0, B, F)$ where

$Q = \{q_0, q_1, ..., q_7\}$,

$\Sigma = \{a, b, B\}$,

$\Gamma = \{a, b, B\}$,

$q_0 = \{q_0\}$,

$F = \{q_7\}$.

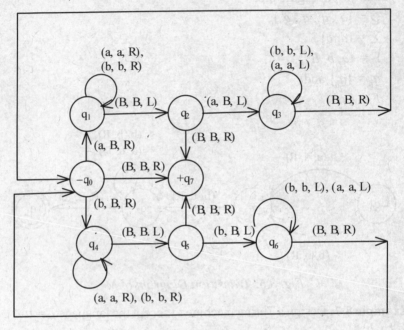

Fig. 8.7: Transition Diagram of M

Example 8.8: Let us consider the following Turing machine:

$M = (Q, \Sigma, \Gamma, \delta, q_0, B, F)$ where

$Q = \{q_0, q_1, q_2, q_3\}$,

$\Sigma = \{a, b\}$,

$q_0 = \{q_0\}$,

$F = \{q_3\}$ and δ is defined as:

$\delta(q_0, a) = (q_1, a, R)$,

$\delta(q_0, b) = (q_0, b, R)$,

$\delta(q_1, a) = (q_2, a, R)$,

$\delta(q_1, b) = (q_0, b, L)$,

$\delta(q_2, a) = (q_2, a, R)$,

$\delta(q_2, \backslash b) = (q_2, b, R)$,

$\delta(q_2, B) = (q_3, B, R)$.

From the above definition, we get the transition diagram as shown in Figure 8.8 of the Turing machine.

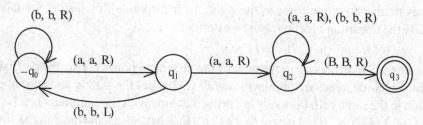

Fig. 8.8: Transition Diagram

This Turing machine accepts the language of all strings that have double a, that is, substring aa in them. To see how the machine behaves with other strings, consider the string $w = ba$. The machine M starts with initial state q_0. It reads b, replaces it with b and moves to the right. M remains in the same state q_0. Now, M reads a, replaces it with a and moves to the right. M enters the state q_1. Next, M reads B (Blank symbol) and since no action is defined for this case, M crashes. Now consider the string $w = ab$. In this case M starts with the initial state q_0. It reads a, replaces it with a and moves to the right. M goes to state q_1. M reads b, replaces it with b and moves to the left. M enters state q_0. Now M is back exactly in the original state q_0, and the above sequence of moves starts again. Thus, M moves back and forth between q_0 and q_1. With this specific input, Turing machine does not halt. Taking an analogy from programming terminology, it can be said that Turing machine is in an infinite loop.

From the above discussion, we can conclude that when input is fed into the machine, one of the following three situations may arise: machine is in the halt state (acceptance) or reject state(crash) or may loop forever. In other words, we can say that every Turing machine M over the alphabet Σ divides the set of strings Σ^* into three classes:

(1) Class Accept(M) is the set of all strings leading to a halt state (final state). This set is called the language accepted by M.

(2) Class Reject(M) is the set of all strings that lead to the machine crash while execution.

(3) Class Loop(M) is the set of all strings that lead the machine to loop forever.

8.4 Techniques for TM Construction

In the previous section, we have seen designing of Turing machine by writing complete set of states and transitions. To describe complicated Turing machines, we need some high-level description. The advantage of this is that it reduces complexity and increases understandability. In this section, we will discuss some high-level conceptual tools.

8.4.1 Turing Machine with Stationary Head

In some situation it may be required that for some input symbol, Turing machine moves neither to the left nor to the right. To incorporate this feature we have to modify the transition function. Now we define:

$$\delta(q, a) = (p, y, S)$$

where S indicates no movement of the tape head pointer. This means that the Turing machine, reads a, it replaces a with y, changes the state q and continues to remain in the same cell. Formally, a Turing machine with the stationary head is a 7-tuple $(Q, \Sigma, \Gamma, \delta, q_0, B, F)$ where $Q, \Sigma, \Gamma, q_0, B, F$ have the same meaning as for the standard Turing machine except δ, which is defined as $Q \times \Gamma$ to $Q \times \Gamma \times \{L, R, S\}$. In terms of ID, we can define the move (transitions between configurations) as follows:

$x_1 x_2 \dots x_{k-1} q x_k x_{k+1} \dots x_n \vdash x_1 x_2 \dots x_{k-1} p y x_{k+1} \dots x_n$ is possible if and only if $\delta(q, x_k) = (p, y, S)$.

8.4.2 Storage in Finite Control

We know that we store finite amount of information in the state of Finite Automata as well as that of Pushdown Automata. We can also write the state as a pair of elements in which first element is a state and second is a symbol. Now state becomes an element of $Q \times \Gamma$.

Example 8.9: Design a Turing machine M, which recognizes the language ab^* $+ ba^*$ by the concept of storage in the finite control.

Solution:

We have to design a Turing machine M that records the first symbol in its finite control and checks that this symbol does not appear again in the input string. The following Turing machine M will work on the input string $w \in ab^* + ba^*$:

$M = (Q, \Sigma, \Gamma, \delta, q_0, B, F)$ where
$Q = \{\{q_0, q_1\} \times \{a, b, B\} = \{[q_0, a], [q_0, b], [q_0, B], [q_1, a], [q_1, b],$
    $[q_1, B]\},$
$\Sigma = \{a, b\},$
$\Gamma = \{a, b, B\},$
$q_0 = \{q_0, B\}$ and
$F = [q_1, B].$

Now, the Turing machine has storage facility in the finite control. That is, first component of state controls the action whereas the second component remembers the symbol. The transition function δ is defined as follows:

$$\delta([q_0, B], a) = ([q_1, a], a, R) \qquad \text{... (i)}$$
$$\delta([q_0, B], b) = ([q_1, b], b, R) \qquad \text{... (ii)}$$
$$\delta([q_1, a], b) = ([q_1, a], b, R) \qquad \text{...(iii)}$$
$$\delta([q_1, b], a) = ([q_1, b], a, R) \qquad \text{...(iv)}$$
$$\delta([q_1, a], B) = ([q_1, B], a, L) \qquad \text{...(v)}$$

$$\delta([q_1, b], B) = ([q_1, B], a, L) \qquad ...(vi)$$

The transitions (i) and (ii) are responsible for storing the first symbol scanned into the second component. The machine moves to the state (q_1, a) or (q_1, b). Machine remains in the state (q_1, a) or (q_1, b) and continues to move to the right when it has stored a and sees b or vice-versa. Machine halts when it reaches the blank symbol without getting the second copy of the stored symbol. This is achieved by the transitions (v) and (vi).

8.4.3 Multiple Tracks

In *Multiple Track Turing machines*, the tape is divided into k tracks where $k \geq 2$. The symbol on the tape is considered to be a k-tuple, one component for each track. Thus in standard Turing machine tape symbol is an element of Γ whereas in the multiple track machines the tape symbol is an element of Γ^k. However, this view does not extend the definition of standard Turing machine. Figure 8.9 shows 4-track Turing machine.

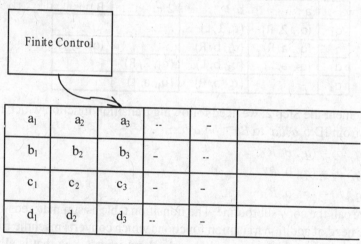

Fig. 8.9 : 4-track Turing machine

8.4.4 Subroutines

A Turing machine can simulate subroutine call or recursive procedure or parameter passing mechanisms. The *subroutine* has an initial state and return state. The return state is temporary halt state. To design a Turing machine that calls the subroutine, a new set of states are introduced and the move from the return state is specified. The call is affected by entering the initial state for the subroutine, and the return is affected by the move from the return state.

Example 8.10: Design a Turing machine which implements the total recursive function "multiplication".

Solution:

We assume the Turing machine takes the input string in the form of $a^m b a^n$ and leaves on the tape Ba^{mn}. The Turing machine will work on the input string w as follows:

Step 1: Put the symbol b after the input string $a^m ba^n$.

Step 2: The leftmost a is erased.

Step 3: Copy the block of n a's onto the right end m times.

Step 4: Repeat the Steps 2 and 3 m times. At the end, we get the string $a^n\$a^{mn}$ on the tape.

Step 5: The prefix $ba^n\$$ of $ba^n\$a^{mn}$ is erased. We get a^{mn} on the tape.

The Turing machine uses the subroutine copy which has initial state q_1 and final state q_5. The work of this subroutine is to copy the block of n a's on to the right end m times, i.e., Step 3 of the algorithm. Table 8.2 shows the transition functions of subroutine copy.

Table 8.2: Transition table of subroutine copy

	a	b	2	B
q_1	$(q_2, 2, R)$	$(q_4 1, L)$		
q_2	(q_2, a, R)	(q_2, b, R)		(q_3, a, L)
q_3	(q_3, a, L)	(q_3, b, L)	$(q_1, 2, R)$	
q_4		(q_5, a, R)	(q_4, a, L)	

To implement the Step 2, we need following transition function which moves the machine from ID $q_0 a^m ba^n$ to $Ba^{m-1}bq_1 a^n b$.

$$\delta(q_0, a) = (q_6, B, R)$$
$$\delta(q_6, a) = (q_6, 0, R)$$
$$\delta(q_6, b) = (q_1, b, R)$$

Now, we call the copy subroutine. The transition table as summarized in Table 8.3 fulfils the need of addition transition functions which converts machine from ID $B^i a^{m-i}bq_5 a^n ba^{ni}$ to $B^{i+1}a^{m-i-1}q_1 a^n ba^{ni}$ and also check whether $i = m$, that is all m a's have been erased. In case of $i = m$, the leading $ba^n b$ is erased and computation halts in state q_{12}.

Table 8.3: Addition transition table

	a	b	2	B
q_5	(q_7, a, L)			
q_7		(q_8, b, L)		
q_8	(q_9, a, L)			(q_{10}, B, R)
q_9	(q_9, a, L)			(q_{10}, B, R)
q_{10}		(q_{11}, B, R)		
q_{11}	(q_{11}, B, R)	(q_{12}, B, R)		

8.5 Variants of TM

In this section, we will study various modified versions of Turing machine that intend to increase the computing power. However, we will see that modifications from standard Turing machine do not provide increased power.

8.5.1 Two-way Infinite tape

A *two-way infinite tape Turing machine* is similar to Standard Turing machine with one exception that the tape is infinite to the left as well as to the right. The initial ID is $q_0 w$. The ID of two-way infinite tape Turing machine is given as $\alpha_1 q \alpha_2$ with the assumption that there are infinite blank cells both to the left and right of the current non-blank portion of the tape. α_1, α_2 and q are same as in the case of standard Turing machine.

A *two-way infinite tape Turing machine* is, just like a Standard Turing machine, a 7-tuple $(Q, \Sigma, \Gamma, \delta, q_0, B, F)$. The difference is in the notions of configurations (IDs) and in the definition of the yield relation $\vdash M$ which relates two ID's. The Figure 8.10 shows the block diagram of the two-way infinite tape Turing machine.

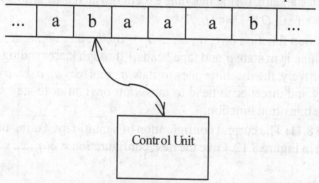

Fig. 8.10: Two-way infinite tape Turing machine

The difference in the moves between the two-way infinite tape Turing machine and the standard Turing machine is as follows:

(i) In two-way infinite tape Turing machine $qX\alpha \vdash pBY\alpha$ if and only if $\delta(q, X) = (p, Y, L)$ but in the standard Turing machine no such move could be made.

(ii) In two-way infinite tape Turing machine $qX\alpha \vdash p\alpha$ if and only if $\delta(q, X) = (p, B, R)$ but in the standard Turing machine B would appear to the left of p.

Is the two-way infinite Turing machine more powerful than the standard Turing machine? Of course not. Any function that is computed or language that is decided or accepted by a Turing machine with a two-way infinite tape is also computed, decided or accepted, respectively by a standard Turing machine.

8.5.2 Multi-tape Turing machine

A *Multi-tape Turing machine* is like a standard Turing machine consisting of several (one-way infinite) tapes. Each tape has its own independent read/write head. A diagram of k-tape Turing machine is shown in Figure 8.11:

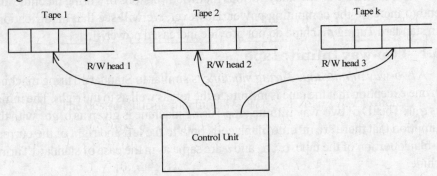

Fig. 8.11: k-tape Turing machine

Formally, we can define k-tape Turing machine as follows:

A *k-tape Turing machine* is a 7-tuple $(Q, \Sigma, \Gamma, \delta, q_0, B, F)$ where $Q, \Sigma, \Gamma, q_0, B,$ F are same as in standard Turing machine except δ which is as follows:

$$\delta: Q \times \Gamma^k \text{ to } Q \times \Gamma^k \times \{L, R\}^k$$

The transition function $\delta(q_i, a_1, a_2, \ldots a_k) = (q_j, b_1, b_2, \ldots b_k, L, R, \ldots, L)$ means that if the machine is in state q_i and tape heads, 1 through k, are reading symbols $a_1,$ $a_2, \ldots a_k$, respectively, the machine goes to state q_j, replaces $a_1, a_2, \ldots a_k$ by $b_1, b_2, \ldots$ b_k, respectively and direct each head to move left or right or to stay stationary as specified in the transition function.

Example 8.11: The current configuration of a multi-tape Turing machine with $k = 3$, is shown in Figure 8.12. Give the next configuration if $\delta(q_0, x_1, y_3, z_2) = (q_1, a,$ $b, c, R. L, R)$.

Solution:

Machine is in state q_0. The first head points to x_1, second head points to y_3 and third head points to z_2. The symbol on the first tape is replaced by a and the tape head moves to right. Meanwhile, the second head scans the symbol y_3, replaces it with b and then moves to left. At the same time third head reads z_2 replaces it with c and then moves to right. After the movements of all the heads, the machine goes to the state q_1.

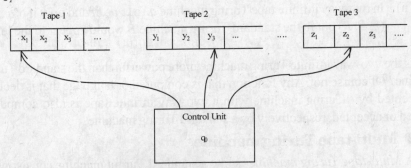

Fig. 8.12: 3-tape Turing machine

8.5.3 Non-deterministic Turing Machine (NTM)

A *Non-deterministic Turing Machine (NTM)* is a 7-tuple $M = (Q, \Sigma, \Gamma, \delta, q_0, B, F)$ where

Q is the finite set of states,

$\Sigma \subset \Gamma$ is a finite set of input symbols, called input alphabet and $B \notin \Sigma$,

Γ is the finite set of tape symbols called the tape alphabet,

$B \in \Gamma$ is the blank symbol,

δ is the transition function (next move function), a mapping from $Q \times \Gamma$ to $2^{Q \times \Gamma \times \{L, R\}}$,

$q_0 \in Q$ is the start state,

$F \subseteq Q$ is the set of final states,

If $\delta(q, x) = \{(q_1, y_1, L/R), (q_2, y_2, L/R) \ldots (q_n, y_n, L/R)\}$ then the *Non-deterministic Turing machine* chooses any one of the actions defined by $(q_i, y_i, L/R)$ for $i = 1, 2, 3, \ldots$.

A *move* (transition between configurations) is defined as follows:

$$x_1 x_2 \ldots x_{k-1} q x_k x_{k+1} \ldots x_n \vdash x_1 x_2 \ldots x_{k-1} y_1 q_1 x_{k+1} \ldots x_n$$

or $$x_1 x_2 \ldots x_{k-1} q x_k x_{k+1} \ldots x_n \vdash x_1 x_2 \ldots x_{k-2} q_2 x_{k-1} y_2 x_k \ldots x_n$$

or $$x_1 x_2 \ldots x_{k-1} q x_k x_{k+1} \ldots x_n \vdash x_1 x_2 \ldots x_{k-2} q_3 x_{k-1} y_3 x_k \ldots x_n$$

if and only if $\delta(q, x_k) = \{(q_1, y_1, R), (q_2, y_2, L), (q_3, y_3, L)\}$

8.5.4 Multidimensional Turing Machine

A *multidimensional Turing machine* is like a standard Turing machine in which tape consists of k-dimensional array of cells infinite in all *2k* directions, for some fixed k. The Figure 8.13 shows the diagram of a two-dimensional Turing machine.

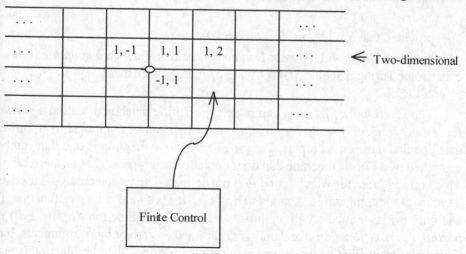

Fig. 8.13: Two-dimensional Turing machine

Formally, we can define *two-dimensional Turing machine* as follows:

Two dimensional Turing machine is a7 tuple $M = (Q, \Sigma, \Gamma, \delta, q_0, B, F)$ where $Q, \Sigma, \Gamma, \delta, q_0, B, F$ have same meaning as in the Standard Turing machine, except δ which is as below:

$$\delta: Q \times \Gamma \rightarrow Q \times \Gamma \times \{L, R, U, D\}$$

where U and D indicate the movement of the read-write head Up and Down, respectively.

8.5.5 Multihead Turing Machine

Multihead Turing machine consists of k-heads instead of 1-head, numbered 1 through k. The move of the machine depends on the current state and input symbols scanned by each head. In one move, the machine reads all symbols pointed by the k-heads and moves independently left, right or remain stationary.

8.5.6 Offline Turing machine

Offline Turing machine is a *multi-tape Turing machine* consisting of read-only tapes. The input tape is generally surrounded by end markers, £ left and $ on the right. Turing machine is not allowed to move the input tape head off the region between £ and $. This type of Turing machine is useful when we limit the amount of storage space to less than the input length.

8.6   Turing Machine as a Computer of Integer Functions

The computer acts as a transducer since it transforms the input into output. Turing machine is to be studied not only as a language accepter but also as an abstract model of the digital computer. In this sense, Turing machine may act as a transducer. In other words, we may view TM M as a computer of integer functions that implements a function f defined by

$$w' = f(w)$$

provided that $q_0 w \vdash^*_M p w'$ for some final state p.

A *function f(w)* with *domain D* is *computable* or *Turing computable* if there exists some Turing machine $M = (Q, \Sigma, \Gamma, \delta, q_0, B, F)$ such that $q_0 w \vdash^* p \in f(w), p \in F$ for all $w \in D$.

The *function $f(a_1, a_2, ...a_n)$* computed by a Turing machine is called a *partial recursive function*. A *recursive function* is one that can be computed by a Turing machine that halts on all inputs. The *partial recursive* function is one that can be computed by a Turing machine that does not halt on all inputs. That is, there exists a loop on any input for which function is not defined. The term recursive is used as a synonym for computable. A *function $f(a_1, a_2, ...a_n)$* is a total recursive function, if and only if f is defined on all arguments $a_1, a_2, ... a_n$. A function $f(a_1, a_2, ...a_n)$ is *partial recursive function* if and only if f is defined on zero or more arguments, but not all arguments that is, there exist some arguments on which the function is not defined. In the next chapter, we will study in detail the recursive function. The *total recursive functions* correspond to the *recursive language* which is computed by a

Turing machine that always halts corresponds to recursive language whereas the partial recursive functions corresponds to the recursive *enumerable language*.

To construct a Turing machine for a function $f(i_1, i_2 \dots i_n)$, where arguments are separated by b, we will use unary notation to represent positive integers. Positive integer is represented by a string $a*$. For constructing a Turing machine for a function $f(i_1, i_2 \dots i_n)$, we place the arguments, $i_1, i_2 \dots i_n$ on the tape as $a^{i1}ba^{i2}\dots a^{in}$ initially. When the Turing machine halts with a tape consisting of a^m, then the function $f(i_1, i_2 \dots i_n) = m$ is computed by a Turing machine. In other words, we can say that the function $f(i_1, i_2 \dots i_n) = m$ is Turing computable function if there exists some Turing machine $M = (Q, \Sigma, \Gamma, \delta, q_0, B, F)$ such that $q_0 a^{i1}ba^{i2} \dots a^{in} \vdash^* pa^m$ or $a^m p, p \in F$.

Example 8.11: Design a Turing machine to compute zero function, i.e., $f(x) = 0$ for all $x \geq 0$.

Solution:

To design a Turing machine to compute zero function, i.e., $f(x) = 0$ for all $x \geq 0$, we initially keep input x in the form $a*$ which represents the integer (ε-B, a-1, aa-2, aaa-3, ...). At the end of the computation, the tape contains only blank symbol which represents zero.

The following Turing machine $M = (Q, \Sigma, \Gamma, \delta, q_0, B, F)$ represents the zero function:

$Q = \{q_0, q_1\}$,

$\Sigma = \{a\}$,

$\Gamma = \{a, B\}$,

$q_0 = \{q_0\}$,

$F = \{q_1\}$ and δ is summarized in the Table 8.4.

Table 8.4

	a	B
$-q_0$	q_0BR	q_1BR
$+q_1$		

We get the following transition diagram as shown in Figure 8.14:

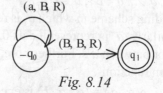

Fig. 8.14

8.7 Universal Turing Machine (UTM)

Digital computers are general purpose machines. They can be programmed to perform different type of computations at different times. On the other hand, a Turing machine is a special purpose computer. That is, it is designed to execute a particular type of computation. To perform different type of computations, we need different Turing machines. Due to this limitation, Turing machine cannot be considered equivalent to general purpose digital computers.

A *Universal Turing machine* overcomes the limitation of Turing machine. It is a reprogrammable Turing machine. It is called universal because it is capable of simulating the action of any Turing machine on any input by giving description of that Turing machine. The Universal Turing machine was designed by Alan Turing in 1936.

A *Universal Turing machine* is an automaton that simulates the computation of M (given arbitrary Turing machine) on w (any input string). The Figure 8.15 shows the block diagram of *UTM*.

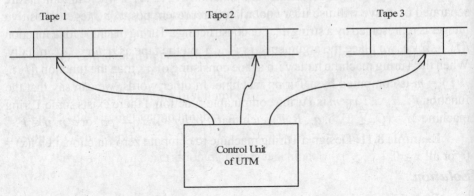

Tape 1   Tape 2   Tape 3

Control Unit
of UTM

Fig 8.15: Block Diagram of UTM

The Universal Turing machine M_u will use three tapes to simulate the execution of M on w. Tape 1 will contain an encoded definition of M, Tape 2 will keep the Tape contents of M, Tape 3 will contain the internal state of M at any instant of time. We may think that Tape 3 acts as a program counter of a digital computer. M_u looks first at the contents of Tape 2 and Tape 3 to determine the configuration of M. It then consults Tape 1 to see what M would do in this configuration. Finally, Tape 2 and Tape 3 will be modified to reflect the result of the move.

Let $M_u = (Q, \Sigma, \Gamma, \delta, q_0, B, F)$ be a Universal Turing machine with $\Sigma = \{0, 1\}$, $\Gamma = \{q_1, q_2, \dots q_m, B\}$, $q_0 = \{q_1\}$, $F = \{q_2\}$, $Q = \{q_1, q_2, \dots q_n\}$. In a *UTM*, we select an encoding scheme in which q_1 is represented by 0, q_2 is represented by 00 and so on. Similarly, a_1 is represented as 0, a_2 as 00, etc. The symbol 1 will be used as a separator between a's. Furthermore, L is encoded as 0 and R is encoded as 00. The transition function

$$\delta(q_i, a_j) = (q_k, a_p, L) \text{ is encoded by a binary string } 0^i 10^j 10^k 10^l 10.$$

8.8   Linear Bounded Automata (LBA)

In Section 8.5, we discussed various modifications of Turing machine that aim at increasing its power. Unfortunately, we did not get any machine that shows greater power. Thus, we can say that, while it is possible to limit the power of Turing machine by restricting the way in which the tape can be used, it is not possible to enhance its power by complicating the tape structure.

A *Linear Bounded Automaton(LBA)* is a *Non-Deterministic Turing machine* which has an unbounded tape, but how much of the tape can be used is a function of the input. Its input alphabet includes two special symbols, the left-end marker(£) and the right-end marker($). In addition to this, LBA has no move to the left from £ or to right from $, nor it may print any other symbol over £ or $. Formally, A *Linear Bounded Automaton* is a non-deterministic Turing machine $M = (Q, \Sigma, \Gamma, \delta, q_0, B,$

F) subject to the restriction that Σ must contain two special symbol £ and \$, such that $\delta(q_i, £) = (q_j, £, R)$ and $\delta(q_i, \$) = (q_j, \$, L)$.

The language accepted by *M* is $\{w \mid w \{£, \$\}^* \text{ and } q_0 £w\$ \vdash^* \alpha q \beta \text{ for some } q \text{ in } F \& \alpha, \beta \in \Gamma^*\}$. A language *L* is *context-sensitive* if and only if there exists an *LBA*.

8.9 Church's Thesis

To say that a Turing machine is a general model of computation is simply to say that any algorithmic procedure that can be carried out at all (by a human, a team of humans, or computer) can be carried out by a TM. This statement was first formulated by Alonzo Church, a logician, in 1930s, and is usually referred to as Church's thesis. It is not a mathematically precise statement as we do not have a precise definition of the term algorithmic procedure. Therefore, Church's thesis is not something that we can prove. However, provable or not, *Church's thesis* is generally accepted to be true.

Church's original statement was little different because his thesis was presented slightly before Turing invented his machines. *Church* actually said that any machine that can do a certain list of operations will be able to perform all conceivable algorithms.

Church's thesis is, also known as the *Church-Turing* thesis, because of the combined research of Alonzo church and Alan Turing which appeared in the American Journal of Mathematics in 1936. The Church-Turing thesis states that all possible models of computation, if they are sufficiently broad, must be equivalent. Various computational models have been proposed in the literature. Some are as follows:

(i)   Post System

(ii) λ-Calculus

(iii) Godel-Herbrand-Kleene equational calculus

(iv) Unlimited register machine

(v)   Markov algorithms

(vi) One-dimensional cellular automata

(vii) Various theoretical models of DeoxyriboNucleic Acid or DNA-based computing

(viii) Partial recursive function

All of the above models have been shown to be equivalent to Turing machine.

8.10 Summary

1.   Turing machines and their theory were developed by Alan Mathison Turing and Emil Post in the 1930s and 1940s. Turing machine (most powerful of all models of computation), is the ultimate mathematical model of a digital computer.

2.   A Turing machine is an automaton that consists of a tape (infinite in one direction), a finite control and head. The three common ways to represent Turing machine are: Instantaneous description, transition table and transition diagram.

3.   Turing machine is also called transducer like computer since it transforms the

input into output. Turing machine is studied not only as a language accepter but also for the class of functions it computes.

4. A function is computable or Turing-computable if there exists a Turing machine that computes the function.

5. A function is called total recursive function if it is defined on all arguments. A function is called partial recursive function if it is defined on zero or more arguments but not all arguments.

6. A function computed by a Turing machine that does not halt on all inputs is called a partial recursive function. A partial recursive function corresponds to the recursive enumerable language.

7. A function computed by a Turing machine that halts on all inputs is called recursive language.

8. The Universal Turing machine overcomes the limitation of Turing machine. It is a reprogrammable Turing machine. Universal Turing machine is capable of simulating the action of any Turing machine on any input.

9. A Linear Bounded Automaton(LBA) is a non-deterministic Turing machine which has an unbounded tape, but how much of the tape can be used is a function of the input. A language is context-sensitive iff there exist an LBA.

8.11 Exercises

Objective Questions

1. A Turing machine:
    (a) Is a simple mathematical model of a computer
    (b) Is equivalent in computing power to the digital computer
    (c) Is the most general mathematical notions of computation
    (d) All of the above

2. A Turing machine is:
    (a) A mathematical model of special purpose digital computer
    (b) A mathematical model of general purpose digital computer
    (c) Not a mathematical model of special purpose digital computer
    (d) None of the above

3. An ID of a Turing machine can be defined in terms of:
    (a) Current state and contents of tape
    (b) Current state, contents of the tape and the position of the tape head
    (c) Current state only
    (d) Input string only

4. The number of symbols necessary to simulate a Turing machine with m symbols and n states is:
    (a) $4mn + m$ (b) mn

(c) $2n(m + n)$ (d) $8mn + 4n$

5.   A Finite Automaton can be considered to be a Turing machine of finite tape length and:

(a)   With rewinding capability and bidirectional tape movement

(b)   Without rewinding capability and bidirectional tape movement

(c)   Without rewinding capability and unidirectional tape movement

(d)   With rewinding capacity, and unidirectional tape movement

6.   A Universal Turing machine:

(a)   Is equivalent to special purpose digital computer

(b)   Is equivalent to general purpose computer

(c)   Is not equivalent to general purpose computer

(d)   None of the above

7.   Turing machine is more powerful than Finite Automaton because:

(a)   Tape movement is confined to one direction

(b)   It has no finite state

(c)   It has the capability to remember arbitrarily long sequences of input symbols

(d)   None of the above

8.   Universal Turing machine influenced the concept of:

(a)   Stored program concept

(b)   Interpretative implementation of programming language

(c)   Computability

(d)   All of these

9.   The statement "A TM can not solve halting problem" is:

(a)   True   (b)   False

(c)   Still an open question   (d)   All of these

10.   Number of external states of a UTM should be at least:

(a)   1   (b)   2

(c)   3   (d)   4

11.   When input string is fed into Turing machine, then which one is true?

(a)   It may be in halt state   (b)   It may be in reject state

(c)   It may be in loop forever   (d)   All of the above

12.   Which of the following statements is false?

(a)   Any language accepted by Non-deterministic Turing machine is accepted by a Deterministic Turing machine

(b)   Any language accepted by NPDA is accepted by a DPDA

(c)   Any language accepted by NFA is accepted by DFA.

(d)   None of the above

13. A Liner Bounded Automaton is:
    (a) NTM with restriction that Σ must contain two special symbol £ and $\$$ such that $\delta(q_i, £) = (q_j, £, L)$ and $\delta(q_i, \$) = (q_j, \$, R)$
    (b) DTM with restriction that Σ must contain two special symbol £ and $\$$ such that $\delta(q_i, £) = (q_j, £, L)$ and $\delta(q_i, \$) = (q_j, \$, R)$
    (c) UTM with restriction that Σ must contain two special symbol £ and $\$$ such that $\delta(q_i, £) = (q_j, £, L)$ and $\delta(q_i, \$) = (q_j, \$, R)$
    (d) None of the above

14. If there exists a TM which when applied to any problem in the class, terminates if correct answer is yes and may or may not be terminated otherwise is called:
    (a) Partially solvable   (b) Stable
    (c) Unsolable   (d) Unstable

15. A pushdown automaton behaves like a Turing machine when the number of auxiliary memory it has is:
    (a) 0   (b) 1 or more
    (c) 2 or more   (d) None of the above

16. For any solvable decision problem, there is a way to encode instances of the problem so that the corresponding language can be recognized by a TM with time complexity:
    (a) Polynomial   (b) Linear
    (c) Exponential   (d) None of the above

Answers to Objective Questions

01. (d)   02. (a)   03. (b)   04. (a)   05. (c)   06.   (b)
07. (c)   08. (d)   09. (a)   10. (b)   11. (d)   12.   (b)
13. (a)   14. (a)   15. (c)   16. (b)

Review Questions

1. Give a formal definition of Turing machine, ID, computation and the languages accepted by the Turing machine.

2. What is Turing machine? Discuss and explain the Basic Turing machine model.

^3. Differentiate the purpose of the study of Turing machine with Finite Automata/ Pushdown Automata.

4. Consider the Turing machine $M = (Q, \Sigma, \Gamma, \delta, q_0, B, F)$ where

    $Q = (q_0, q_1, q_2, q_3, q_4, q_5)$,
    $\Sigma = \{a, b\}$,
    $\Gamma = \{a, b, B\}$,
    $q_0 = \{q_0\}$,
    $F = \{q_5\}$.

    and δ is given by the Table 8.5:

Table 8.5

Present state	Tape input symbol				
	a	b	B	x	y
$-q_0$	q_1xR	-	q_5BR	-	-
q_1	q_1aR	q_3yL			q_1yR
q_2	-			q_4xR	q_2yL
q_3	q_3aL			q_0xR	
q_4	-		q_5BR		q_4yR

Trace the computation of M starting from the configuration (q_0, *aabb*).

5. Differentiate between Standard Turing machine and two-way infinite tape Turing machine.

6. Write a procedure for constructing Transition Table and Transition diagram of Turing machine.

A7. What are the differences in the roles of tape and tape head of finite automata, pushdown automata and Turing machine?

8. What is Turing-computable function? Define recursive, partial recursive and total recursive functions.

9. What is Universal Turing Machine (UTM)? How UTM overcomes the limitation of Turing machine? Define UTM. Also discuss the working of UTM.

10. Write short notes on the following:
    (a) Storage in Finite control
    (b) Multiple track Turing machine
    (c) Turing machine as a subroutine
    (d) Turing machine with stationary head
    (e) Church's thesis

11. Define multi-tape (k-tape) Turing machine. Discuss the yields in one step relation $\vdash_M$ between configurations of such a machine with the help of the diagram.

12. Explain and discuss on the following:
    (a) Turing machine with two-way infinite tape
    (b) Multi-tape Turing machine
    (c) Non-deterministic Turing machine
    (d) Multidimensional Turing machine
    (e) Multihead Turing machine
    (f) Offline Turing machine

13. Formally define:
    (a) M accepts L, where M is a two-way infinite tape Turing machine.
    (b) M computes f, where M is a k-tape Turing and f is a function from strings to strings

14. Formally define:

(a) A Non-deterministic Turing machine

(b) A configuration of such a machine

(c) The yields in one step relation $\vdash_{M}$ between configurations of such a machine

15. What is Linear Bounded Automaton? Give formal definition and language accepted by the LBA.

A16. Construct a Turing machine that can accept the strings over $\{0, 1\}$ containing even number of 1's.

17. Design Turing machine which performs the addition of two positive integers n and m. What is the time complexity of this machine?

A18. Present a Turing machine that inserts symbol # in the beginning of a string on the Turing tape. Assume $\Sigma = \{a, b\}$.

19. Give a Turing Machine to recognize strings of matched parenthesis.

20. Design a Turing machine to recognize the language $\{a^n b^n c^m \mid n, m \geq 1\}$.

21. Construct a Turing machine that can accept the set of all even palindrome over $\{0, 1\}$.

22. Design a Turing machine that reads string in the language given by the expression $(0, 1)^*$ and replaces the right-most symbol by a blank (#).

A23. Design a Turing machine that can compute proper subtraction, i.e., $m \to n$, where m and n are positive integers, mn is defined as $m-n$ if $m > n$ and 0 if $m \geq n$.

24. Construct Turing machines that will accept the following languages:

A(a) $L = L\{aba^*b\}$

(b) $L = L\{w \mid \mid w \mid$ is multiple of 3, $w \in \{a, b\}^*\}$

(c) $L = L\{a^n b^{2n} \mid n \geq 1\}$

A(d) $L = \{0^{2^n} \mid n \geq 0\}$

A(e) $L = \{w\#w \mid w\{a, b\}^*\}$

(f) $L = \{a^i b^j c^k \mid i \times j = k$ and $i, j, k \geq 1\}$

(g) $L = \{\#a_1 \#a_2 \# \ldots \#a_i \mid$ each $a_i \in \{a, b\}^*$ and $a_i \neq a_j$ for each $i \neq j\}$

A(i) $L = \{w \mid w$ contains an equal numbers of a's and b's$\}$

(j) $L = \{w \mid w$ contains twice as many a's as b's$\}$

(k) $L = \{w \mid w$ does not contain twice as many a's as b's$\}$

(l) $L = \{a^*ba^*b\}$

For each problem write down δ in complete detail, then check your answers by tracing several test examples.

A25. Design a TM that reads binary strings and performs the following actions: if the input represents an odd number, subtracts one to the number, if the input represents an even number, add one to the number. For example, for input "101" the output should be "100" and for input "1010" the output should be "1011".

26. Design a Turing machine with = $\{0, 1, B\}$ that when started on any cell containing a blank or a 1, will halt if and only if its tape has a 0 some where on it.

27. Design a Turing machine that reads binary strings and counts the number of 1's in the sequence. The output is 0 if the number of 1's in the string is even and 1 if the number of 1's is odd.

28. Design a Turing machine to compute the following functions for x and y positive integers represented in unary.
    (a) $f(x) = 3x$
    (b) $f(x, y) = 2x + 3y$
    (c) $f(x) = x/2$, if x is even
       $= x + 1/2$, if x is odd
    ^(d) $f(x, y) = x + y$
    (e) $f(x) = x \bmod 5$
    (f) $f(x) = x + 1$ for all $x \geq 0$
    (g) $f(x, y) = x.y$
    (h) $f(n) = 2^n$ where n is a non-zero positive integer.

^29. Give a Turing machine that copies strings of 1's. More precisely, find a machine that performs the computation $q_0 w \vdash^* q_f www$ for any $w \in \{1\}^+$.

30. Design a Turing machine to recognize the language $\{w|w \in \Sigma^*$ and $|w|$ is odd$\}$. Assume $\Sigma = \{a\}$.

31. Present a Turing machine to recognize the language $\{w|w$ contains at least one a and $w \in \Sigma^*\}$. Assume $\Sigma = \{a, b\}$.

32. Design a TM that adds 1 to a number represented in binary possibly with leading zeros.

33. Design a Turing machine for the function $f(w) = www$, where w is a string over $\{a, b\}^*$.

^34. Give a Turing machine that subtract 1 from a number represented in binary form.

35. Present a Turing machine for the function MAX(x, y) which is equal to the larger of the two non-negative integers x and y.

36. Design a Turing machine for the "i^{th} of n" selector function.

^37. Design a Turing machine that adds two numbers presented in binary notation and leaves the answer on the tape in binary form.

Answers/Hints for Selected Review Questions

3. The finite automata and pushdown automata were used as accepting devices where as Turing machine is studied for three basic purposes: first, as a class of language it defines (recursively enumerable and recursive language) second, as a computer of integer functions and third as a accepting device similar to finite automata and pushdown automata.

7. The following are differences between role of tape /tape head of Finite Automata and Turing machine:

    (i)   The contents of tape of a Finite Automata and Pushdown Automata are only read/scanned but are never changed/written into, while the contents of tape of a TM are not only read/scanned but changed/written also.

    (ii) The tape head of FA or a PDA always moves from left to right whereas the tape head of a Turing machine can move in both directions that is to left as well as to right.

    (iii) The contents of tape already scanned do not play any role in future moves of the automaton whereas in TM, the already scanned symbol plays a role in deciding future moves. The consequence of this leads to the slightly different definition of Instantaneous configuration in Turing machine.

16. The required Turing machine $M = (Q, \Sigma, \Gamma, \delta, q_0, B, F)$ where

    $Q = (q_0, q_1, q_2)$,

    $\Sigma = \{0, 1\}$,

    $\Gamma = \{0, 1, B\}$,

    $q_0 = \{q_0\}$,

    $F = \{q_2\}$.

    Figure 8.16 depicts the transition diagram of Turing machine M:

    The Turing machine M will work on a input string w as follows:

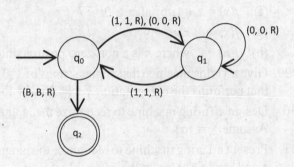

Fig. 8.16

Step 1: The Turing machine M starts with state q_0 (initial state). If 1 is read, M replaces it with symbol 1 and moves to the right and enters state q_1. If 0 is read, M replaces it with symbol 0 and moves to the right and enters state q_1. If M reads B, M replaces it with symbol B and moves to the right and enters state q_2.

Step 2: In state q_1, if M read 1, M replaces it with symbol 1 and moves to the right and M enters state q_0. q_0 is initial as well as final state. If M reads 0, M replaces it with symbol 0 and moves to the right. Then M remains in the same state q_1.

18. The desired Turing machine $M = (Q, \Sigma, \Gamma, \delta, q_0, B, F)$ where

    $Q = (q_0, q_1, q_2 \dots q_5)$,

    $\Sigma = \{a, b\}$,

    $\Gamma = \{a, b, \#\}$,

    $q_0 = \{q_0\}$,

    $F = \{q_5\}$ is given in Figure 8.17.

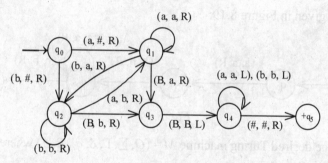

Fig. 8.17

23. We will use unary notation in which positive number is represented by $w(x) \in \{a\}^*$, such that

$$|w(x)| = x, \{a^x\} = x$$

The number m and n are placed on the tape initially as follows:

$w(m)w(n)$, i.e., $a^m b a^n$.

After the computation, tape ends up with $w(m-n)$, i.e., a^{m-n}. The required Turing machine $M = (Q, \Sigma, \Gamma, \delta, q_0, B, F)$ where

$$Q = (q_0, q_1, q_2 \ldots q_{11}),$$
$$\Sigma = \{a, b\},$$
$$\Gamma = \{a, b, A, B\},$$
$$q_0 = \{q_0\},$$
$$F = \{q_{11}\}$$

is given in Figure 8.18.

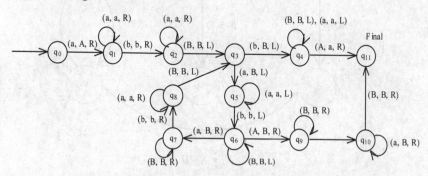

Fig. 8.18

4. (a) The required Turing machine $M = (Q, \Sigma, \Gamma, \delta, q_0, B, F)$ where

$$Q = (q_0, q_1, q_2, q_3),$$
$$\Sigma = \{a, b\},$$
$$\Gamma = \{a, b, B\},$$
$$q_0 = \{q_0\},$$
$$F = \{q_3\}$$

is given in Figure 8.19.

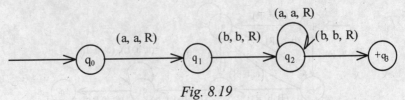

Fig. 8.19

(d)   The desired Turing machine $M = (Q, \Sigma, \Gamma, \delta, q_0, B, F)$ where

$Q = (q_0, q_1, q_2 \dots q_6),$
$\Sigma = \{0\},$
$\Gamma = \{0, x, *, B\},$
$q_0 = \{q_0\},$
$F = \{q_5\}$

is given in Figure 8.20.

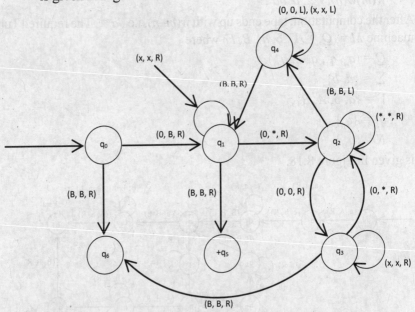

Fig. 8.20

(e)   The desired Turing machine $M = (Q, \Sigma, \Gamma, \delta, q_0, B, F)$ where

$Q = (q_0, q_1, q_2 \dots q_8),$
$\Sigma = \{a, b, \#\}$
$\Gamma = \{a, b, \#, A, B\}$
$q_0 = \{q_0\},$
$F = \{q_2\}$

is given in Figure 8.21.

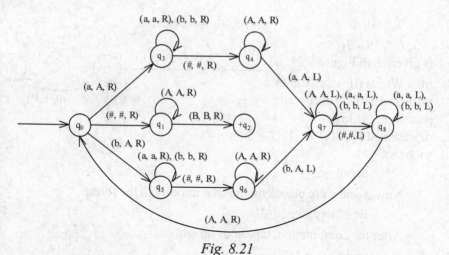

Fig. 8.21

(i) The desired Turing machine $M = (Q, \Sigma, \Gamma, \delta, q_0, B, F)$ where

$Q = (q_0, q_1, q_2 \dots q_5)$,

$\Sigma = \{a, b\}$

$\Gamma = \{a, b, x, y, B\}$

$q_0 = \{q_0\}$,

$F = \{q_5\}$

is given as Figure 8.22.

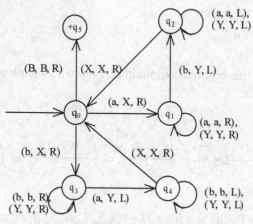

Fig. 8.22

25. We know that a number is even when in the binary representation right most bit must be 0, otherwise number will be odd. The desired Turing machine $M = (Q, \Sigma, \Gamma, \delta, q_0, B, F)$ where

$Q = (q_0, q_1, q_2)$,

$\Sigma = \{0, 1\}$

$\Gamma = \{0, 1, B\}$

$q_0 = \{q_0\}$,

$F = \{q_2, q_3\}$

is given as in Figure 8.23:

28 (d) We will use unary notation in which any positive integer x is represented by $w(x) \in \{1\}^+$, such that

$$|w(x)| = x, \ |1^x| = x$$

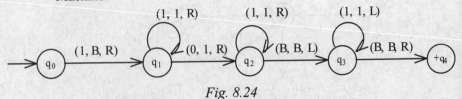

Fig. 8.23

Now, x and y are placed on the tape initially in the form:

$w(x)0w(y)$, i.e., 1^x01^y

After the computation, tape ends up with

$w(x + y)$ or 1^{x+y}.

Therefore, we want to design a Turing machine for performing the computation

$$q_0 1^x 0 1^y \vdash q_f 1^{x+y}$$

where q_0 is the initial state and q_f is final state. The following Turing machine $M = (Q, \Sigma, \Gamma, \delta, q_0, B, F)$ where

$Q = (q_0, q_1, q_2, q_3, q_4)$,

$\Sigma = \{0, 1\}$

$\Gamma = \{0, 1, B\}$

$q_0 = \{q_0\}$,

$F = \{q_4\}$

performs the required computation. Figure 8.24 depicts the desired Turing Machine.

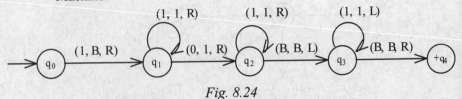

Fig. 8.24

29. The following Turing machine $M = (Q, \Sigma, \Gamma, \delta, q_0, B, F)$ where

$Q = (q_0, q_1, q_2, q_3, q_4)$,

$\Sigma = \{1\}$

$\Gamma = \{1, \#, B\}$

$q_0 = \{q_0\}$,

$F = \{q_7\}$

performs the required computation. Figure 8.25 represents the required Turing Machine.

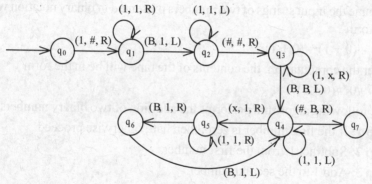

Fig. 8.25

34. Assume that the input string presented in binary notation will be of the form

   #(0 + 1)*#

   After the computation, the contents of the tape will be in the form

   #(0 + 1)*

   We also assume that the number is not 0. Therefore, we have to design a Turing machine for performing the computation q_0#(0 + 1)*# q_f(0 + 1)*. The following algorithm performs the desired operations.

   Step 1: First, we take the one's complement of the number.

   Step 2: Add 1 to number

   Step 3: Take the one's complement of the number.

   The following Turing machine $M = (Q, \Sigma, \Gamma, \delta, q_0, B, F)$ where

   $$Q = (q_0, q_1, q_2, q_3, q_4, q_5),$$
   $$\Sigma = \{0, 1\}$$
   $$\Gamma = \{0, 1, \#, B\}$$
   $$q_0 = \{q_0\},$$
   $$F = \{q_5\}$$

   performs the required computation. Figure 8.26 shows the desired Turing Machine.

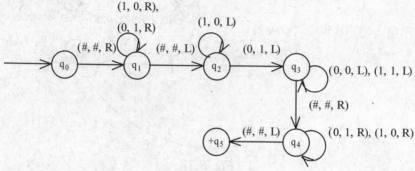

Fig. 8.26

37. Assume the input strings of two numbers presented in binary notation will be of the form

    #(0 + 1)*#(0 + 1)*

    After the computation, the contents of the tape will be in the form

    #0*#(0 + 1)*

    The following algorithm performs the addition of two binary numbers:

    Step 1: If the first number is zero, then halt, otherwise proceed.

    Step 2: Subtract 1 from the first number.

    Step 3: Add 1 to the second number.

    Step 4: Go to Step 1.

    Now, we give formal description of Turing machine $M = (Q, \Sigma, \Gamma, \delta, q_0, B, F)$ where

    $$Q = (q_0, q_1, q_2, q_3, \ldots\ldots q_{11}),$$
    $$\Sigma = \{0, 1\}$$
    $$\Gamma = \{0, 1, \#, B\}$$
    $$q_0 = \{q_0\},$$
    $$F = \{q_{11}\}$$

    performs the required computation. Figure 8.27 represents the desired Turing Machine.

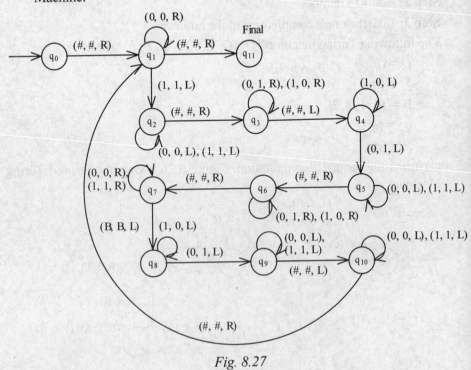

Fig. 8.27

Programming Problems

1. Write a program to simulate following Turing machine:

   (a) $f(w) = w^R$ where $w \in \{0, 1\}^+$.

   (b) $f(x, y) = x + y - 1$ where x and y are positive integer.

   (c) $L = \{a^n b^m a^{n+m} : n \geq 0, m \geq 1\}$.

   (d) $L = \{ww : w \in \{a, b\}^+\}$.

   (e) $L = n^2$.

   (f) factorial n.

Chapter 9

Recursively Enumerable Languages and Decidability

The present Chapter introduces recursively enumerable languages and decidability. Types of grammars and Chomsky Hierarchy of grammar are discussed. Decidable and Undecidable problems are presented. The Chapter also covers Turing halting problem, PCP, modified PCP and recursive function. Finally, the Chapter ends with Tractable and Intractable problems.

Objectives: The objective of this Chapter is to explore recursively enumerable languages and decidability. After learning the contents of this Chapter, you will be able to:

1. Understand languages defined by Turing machine,
2. Describe Chomsky hierarchy of grammars,
3. Explain decidable and undecidable problems,
4. Show that a given function is primitive recursive,
5. State and explain PCP and MPCP.

9.1 Recursive and Recursively Enumerable Languages

We have already seen that when we fed input strings from some alphabet to Turing machine, we break the set of all finite strings over Σ into three disjoint sets: $\Sigma^* = \text{Accept}(M) + \text{Loop}(M) + \text{Reject}(M)$. This leads to two possible definitions of languages recognized by a Turing machine.

Recursively Enumerable Language

A Language L on alphabet Σ is called recursively enumerable if there exists a Turing machine M that accepts it. In more details, a language L on the alphabet Σ is called recursively enumerable if there is a Turing machine M that accepts every word in L and either rejects or loops for every word in the language L^C, the complement of L (every word in Σ^*, not in L). That is

$$L = \text{Accept}(M)$$
$$L^C = \text{Reject}(M) + \text{Loop}(M)$$

The word enumerable is derived from the fact that the strings of a language can be enumerated (listed) by a Turing machine. The class of recursively enumerable languages is very broad and includes the CFLs.

Recursive language

A language on alphabet Σ is called recursive if there exists a Turing machine that accepts every word in L and rejects every word in L^C. In other words, the language is recursive iff there exists a membership algorithm for it. That is

$$L = \text{Accept}(M)$$
$$L^C = \text{Reject}(M)$$
$$\Phi = \text{Loop}(M)$$

Some closure properties of recursively enumerable languages and recursive languages are as follows:

1. The complement of a recursive language is recursive.
2. The union of two recursive languages is recursive.
3. The intersection of two recursive languages is recursive.
4. The union of two recursively enumerable languages is recursive enumerable.
5. The intersection of two recursively enumerable languages is recursive enumerable.
6. If a language L and its complement L^C are both recursively enumerable, then L (and hence L^C) is recursive.

Theorem 9.1: The complement of a recursive language is recursive.

Proof: If L is a recursive language then there exists a Turing machine M that accepts every word in L and rejects every word in L^C. We construct a Turing machine M' from the Turing machine M as follows: if M enters a final state on input w, then M' halts without accepting w. If M halts without accepting w, M' enters a final state.

Obviously, M' is the complement of L since it accepts all words that are rejected by M and rejects all words that are accepted by M. We conclude that the complement of L is a recursive language. Figure 9.1 shows the construction of M' from M.

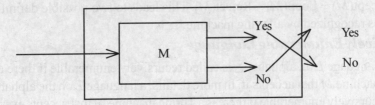

Fig. 9.1: Construction of M'

Theorem 9.2: The union of two recursive languages is recursive.

Proof: Let L_1 and L_2 are the recursive languages accepted by the Turing machines M_1 and M_2, respectively. We construct a Turing machine M that accepts the language $L_1 \cup L_2$ as follows: First M simulates on M_1. If M_1 rejects, then M simulates M_2. If M_2 accepts then M accepts otherwise rejects. The construction causes M to accepts iff any one of the machines M_1 or M_2 accepts otherwise rejects. Obviously, the language accepted by M is $L_1 \cup L_2$. The construction of Turing machine M is given in Figure 9.2.

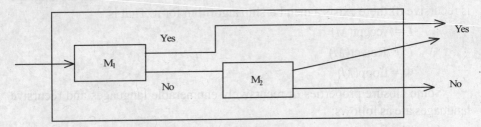

Fig. 9.2: Construction of M

Theorem 9.3: The union of two recursively enumerable languages is recursively enumerable.

Proof: Let L_1 and L_2 are the recursively enumerable languages accepted by the Turing machines M_1 and M_2, respectively. The construction of the Turing machine M that accepts the language $L_1 \cup L_2$ is as follows. We simulate M_1 and M_2 simultaneously on separate tapes. The construction causes M to accept iff at least one of the two machines M_1 and M_2 accepts. So we conclude that M accepts the language $L_1 \cup L_2$. The construction of Turing machine M is given in Figure 9.3.

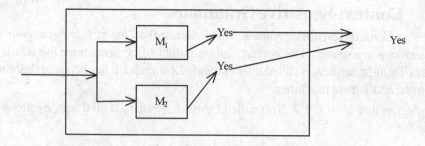

Fig. 9.3: Construction of M

Theorem 9.4: If a language L and its complement L^c are both recursively enumerable, then L (and hence L^c) is recursive.

Proof: Let M_1 and M_2 are the Turing machines accepting languages L and L^C, respectively. Now we construct the composite machine M as follows. The Turing machine M accepts the word w if M_1 accepts w. M does not accept the word if M_2 accepts. Since the word is in either L or L^C, any one of M_1 or M_2 will accept the word. Therefore, M always halts, i.e., either accepts or does not accept the word. This is possible only when the language is recursive.

The construction of M is shown in Figure 9.4.

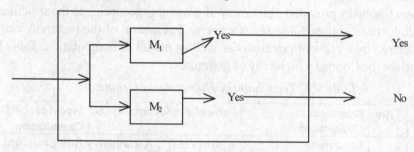

Fig. 9.4: Construction of M

9.2 Unrestricted Grammars

A Grammar $G = (V, T, P, S)$ is called *unrestricted, type 0, phrase structure* or *semi-Thue* if all the productions P are of the form

$$A \to B$$

where $A, B \in (V \cup T)^*$ and A contains at least one variable. In addition to this, V and T are disjoint sets of variables and terminals, respectively. $S \in V$ is called the start symbol. The unrestricted grammar is the largest family of grammars in the Chomsky hierarchy. The language generated by unrestricted grammar is called *recursively enumerable*. The corresponding model of computation is called Turing machine.

9.3   Context-Sensitive Grammars

The *Context-Sensitive grammar* lies between the *Unrestricted grammar* and *Context-free grammars*. The corresponding model of computation, the restricted class of Turing machines, is called *linear bounded Automata*. It lies between Pushdown automata and Turing machines.

A grammar $G = (V, T, P, S)$ is called *Context-sensitive* if all the productions are of the form

$A \rightarrow B$ with $|A| \leq |B|$ where $A, B \in (V \bigcup T)^*$ and A contains at least one variable.

Some closure properties of Context-sensitive languages are as follows:

1.   Context-sensitive languages are closed under union operation.
2.   Context-sensitive languages are closed under concatenation operation.
3.   Context-sensitive languages are closed under Kleene Star operation.
4.   Context-sensitive languages are closed under intersection operation.
5.   Context-sensitive languages are closed under complement operation.

9.4   Chomsky Hierarchy

The Noam Chomsky was the founder of the formal language theory. In 1959, the Noam Chomsky provided a hierarchy of grammars according to the structure of their productions, called *Chomsky Hierarchy*. Each level of the hierarchy can be characterized by a class of grammars as well as model of computation. Table 9.1 summarizes the Chomsky hierarchy of grammars.

Table 9.1: The Chomsky Hierarchy of Grammars

S.No.	Type	Languages (Grammars)	Form of productions A B	Model of Computation
1.	0	Recursively enumerable (unrestricted or phrase structure)	$A, B \in (V \bigcup T)^*$, A contains at least one Variable	Turing machine
2.	1	Context-sensitive	$A, B \in (V \bigcup T)^*$, $|A| \leq |B|$, A contains at least one variable	LBA (Linear Bounded Automata)
3.	2	Context-free	$A \in V$, $B \in (V \bigcup T)^*$	PDA (Pushdown Automata)
4.	3	Regular	$A \in V$, B=tN or B=t, $t \in T$, N $\in V$	Finite Automata

The six classes of languages are shown in Figure 9.5.

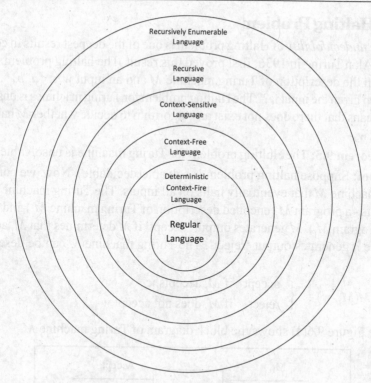

Fig. 9.5: Six classes of language

The hierarchical relationship of these six languages is as follows:

Regular language $\subset$ Deterministic Context-Free Language $\subset$ Context-Free Language $\subset$ Context-Sensitive Language $\subset$ Recusive language $\subset$ Recursively Enumerable Language.

9.5 Introduction to Decidable and Undecidable Problems

A problem is *decidable* iff there exists an algorithm that takes as input an instance of the problem and determines the answer to that instance as "yes" or "no". Otherwise, the problem is *undecidable*. In other words, a problem whose language is recursive is said to be decidable. We must know the domain of the problem for stating *decidability* or *undecidability* of the problem since this affects the conclusion. The problem may be decidable on some domain but not on another. Generally, a single instance of the problem is always decidable, since the answer is either true or false. In the first case Turing machine always give the answer "yes" while in the second case it always gives the answer "no". There is a large number of problems for which no computer that exists or will exist or even be dreamed of, can solve. Nevertheless, the number of problems that can be solved computationally is much less than the number of problems that can never be solved computationally. *Undecidable* does not mean that we do not know the solution of the problem today but might find the solution tomorrow. It means that whatever resources or time may be available, we can never find an algorithm to solve the problem.

9.6   Halting Problem

The *undecidability* of Halting problem is one of the deepest results in computer science. Alan Turing in 1936, first proved this result. The halting problem is stated as "Given the description of Turing machine M and an input $w \in \{a, b\}^*$, does M halts when given the input w?" The Halting problem for Turing machines is unsolvable, which means that there does not exist any algorithm to decide whether M halts given the input w.

Theorem 9.5: The Halting problem for Turing machine is unsolvable.

Proof: Suppose halting problem is solvable(decidable). Now, we construct a Turing machine M that eventually halts on all inputs. The Turing machine M takes two inputs - a program M_1(encoded description of Turing machine M_1) and w (input for the program M_1). M generates output 'accept' if M determines that M_1 accepts w otherwise it generates output 'reject'. The Turing machine M can be described as follows.

$$M(M_1, w) = \begin{cases} \text{accept} & \text{if } M_1 \text{ accepts } w \\ \text{reject} & \text{if } M_1 \text{ does not accept } w \end{cases}$$

The Figure 9.6(a) shows the block diagram of Turing machine M.

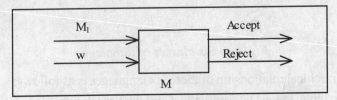

Fig. 9.6 (a) : Block diagram of Turing Machine M

Let us construct a new Turing machine K with M as subroutine. Turing machine K calls M to determine what M_1 does when it receives the input $<M_1>$(since M_1 is a program). The Turing machine K generates the outputs "reject" if M outputs "accept" (M_1 accept $<M_1>$)and "accept" if M outputs "reject" (M_1 does not accept $<M_1>$). The machine K will output the opposite of M's output. The Figure 9.6(b) shows the Turing machine K.

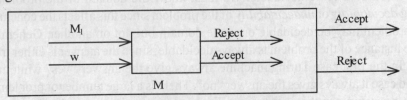

Fig. 9.6 (b) : Block diagram of Turing Machine K

The working of Turing machine can be described as:

$$K(M_1, <M_1>) = \begin{cases} \text{accept} & \text{if } M_1 \text{ does not accept } <M_1> \\ \text{reject} & \text{if } M_1 \text{ accepts } <M_1> \end{cases}$$

Let us see the action of Turing machine K on the input K (encoded description of K as a string) as shown in Figure 9.6(c).

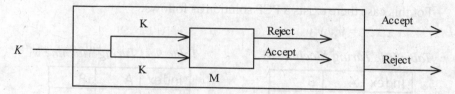

Fig. 9.6 (c): Block diagram of Turing Machine K

If M outputs "reject" (K does not accept $<K>$) then K "accepts" and if M outputs "accept" (K accepts $<K>$) then K "rejects". That is

$$K(K, <K>) = \begin{cases} \text{accept} & \text{if } K \text{ does not accept } <K> \\ \text{reject} & \text{if } K \text{ accepts } <K> \end{cases}$$

This means that in either case Turing machine K gives the wrong answer, which is a contradiction. Hence, the Halting problem is undecidable.

9.7 Undecidable Problems about Turing Machine

The following are undecidable problems about Turing machines:

(i)   Given a Turing machine M and a string w, does M halt on w?

(ii) Given a Turing machine M and a string w, does M not halt on w?

(iii) Given a Turing machine M, does M halt on the empty tape?

(iv) Given a Turing machine M, is there any string on which M halts?

(v)   Given a Turing machine M, does M accept all strings?

(vi) Given Turing machines M_1 and M_2, do they accept the same language?

(vii) Given a Turing machine M, is the language that M accepts regular?

(viii) Given a Turing machine M, is the language that M accepts context-free?

(ix) Given a Turing machine M, is the language that M accepts decidable?

9.8 Post Correspondence Problem (PCP)

The *Post Correspondence Problem* (PCP) was introduced by Email Post in 1946. The halting problem of Turing machine can be used to show other problems, especially in the area of context-free languages, are unsolvable. In some situations, it is difficult to use halting problem directly. In such cases, it is convenient to use Post Correspondence Problem which acts as an intermediate result. It fills the gap between the halting problem and other problems. The *Post Correspondence Problem* is stated as follows:

Given two sequences of n strings $A = x_1, x_2 \ldots x_n$ and $B = y_1, y_2 \ldots y_n$ over some alphabet Σ. The PCP is to determine whether or not there exists a non-empty sequence of integers $i_1, i_2, \ldots i_m$, with $m \geq 1$, such that $x_{i_1} x_{i_2} \ldots x_{i_m} = y_{i_1} y_{i_2} \ldots y_{i_m}$.

The sequence $i_1, i_2, \ldots i_m$ is a solution of PCP.

Example 9.1: Let $\Sigma = \{0, 1\}$. Let A and B are two sequences of 4 strings over Σ is defined in Table 9.1.

For this case there exists a PCP solution as follows:

$$x_2 x_1 x_3 x_4 = y_2 y_1 y_3 y_4$$

Table 9.1: Turing Machine M_1

Index	A	B
I	X_i	W_i
1	11	01
2	100	10
3	11	11111
4	100	00

Table 9.2: Turing Machine M_1

Index	A	B
I	X_i	Y_i
1	10	110
2	011	01
3	101	1011
4.	10	01

Let A and B be sequences of 4 strings as shown in Table 9.2.

Then this instance of PCP has no solution because any string composed by B will be longer than the corresponding string from A.

9.9 Modified Post Correspondence Problem (MPCP)

The *Modified Post Correspondence Problem* (MPCP) is stated as follows:

Given two sequences of k strings $x = x_1, x_2, \dots x_k$ and $B = y_1, y_2, \dots y_k$ each from some alphabet Σ^*. The modified PCP has a solution if there exists a sequence of integers $i_1, i_2, \dots i_r$ such that

$$x_1 x_{i_1} x_{i_2} \dots x_{i_r} = y_1 y_{i_1} y_{i_2} \dots y_{i_r}.$$

An MPCP solution must start with the first string on each sequence.

9.10 Other Models of Computation

We have seen that Turing machine is the most powerful model of computation. In the literature, various models of computation have been proposed which are equivalent to Turing machine in power. The Church's thesis tells us that all possible models of computation if they are sufficiently broad must be equivalent. We have already seen that some of the problems cannot be computed by any Turing machine. The Church's thesis is also significant in this case. We should not expect to find some other reasonable computation model in which those same problems can be solved.

9.10.1 Lambda Calculus

The *lambda calculus* was developed by Alonzo Church. It is a way to formalize the notion of an algorithm. The lambda calculus is the basis for modern functional programming languages like Lisp, scheme, ML and Haskell.

The lambda calculus is an *expression language*. Each expression defines a function of a single argument. The single argument is written as a variable bound by the operator λ (lambda). For instance, the following lambda calculus expression defines the successor function $f(x) = x + 1$:

$(\lambda x.\ x + 1)$.

The function can be applied to arguments by binding each argument to a formal parameter. Therefore, $(\lambda x.\ x + 1)5$ is evaluated by binding 5 to x and computing the result 6. Functions may be arguments to other functions and the value that is computed by a function may be another function. For instance, we can define a function to multiply two numbers by the following lambda calculus expression $(\lambda x.\lambda y.\ x*y)$.

Suppose we want to multiply 5 by 4. So $(\lambda x.\lambda y.\ x*y)\ 5\ 4$ is evaluated by binding 5 to x to create a new function $(\lambda y.\ 5*y)$, which is then applied to 4 to return 20. The lambda calculus can be shown to be equivalent in power to the TM. We can also say that, the set of functions that can be defined as lambda calculus is equal to the set of functions that can be computed by a TM. Due to this equivalence, any problem that is undecidable for Turing machine is also undecidable for the lambda calculus.

9.10.2 Post System

Post system is equivalent in power to Turing machine. Formally, A *Post System* (Π) is a 4-tuple (C, V, A, P) where

C is a finite set of constants, consisting of two disjoint sets C_N, called the non-terminal constants, and C_T, the set of terminal constants,

V is a finite set of variables,

A is a finite set from C^*, called the axioms,

P is a finite set of productions. The productions in a Post system must satisfy certain restrictions. Each production is of the form

$$x_1 V_1 x_2 \dots\ V_n x_{n+1} \rightarrow y_1 W_1 y_2 \dots\ W_m y_{m+1}$$

where $x_i, y_i \in C^*$, and $V_i, W_i \in V$, subject to the requirement that any variable can appear at most once on the left, so that

$$V_i \neq V_j \text{ for } i = j$$

and that each variable on the right must appear on the left, that is

$$\bigcup_{i=1}^{m} W_i \subseteq V \bigcup_{i=1}^{n} V_i$$

The language generated by the Post System $\Pi = (C, V, A, P)$ is

$$L(\Pi) = \{w \in C_T \cdot \underset{\Longrightarrow}{*}\ \text{for some } w_0 \in A\}$$

9.11 Introduction to Recursive Function Theory

A *function* is a mapping of an element of one set, called domain of the function to a unique element in another set, called range of the function. A recursive function is one that can be computed by a Turing machine that halts on all inputs. A *partial recursive function* is one that can be computed by some Turing machine (but one that may loop if there are any inputs on which the function is undefined). The word recursive is misnomer. The word makes sense if we think of recursive as a synonym for computable.

9.11.1 Primitive Recursive Function

Primitive recursive functions are a subclass of *partial recursive functions*. The Turing machine is viewed as a mathematical model of partial recursive function. A partial function f from A to B is a rule which assigns every element of A at most to one element of B. A *total function* f from A to B is a rule which assigns every element of A to a unique element of B. A *partial* or *total function* f from x_k to x is called a function of k variables and denoted by $f(x_1, x_2, ...x_k)$.

We will discuss the primitive functions of one or two variables. The domain will be either I or $I \times I$ and range will be I, where I is the set of all non-negative integers. The primitive recursive functions are defined by three basic primitive recursive functions and two combining rules (Composition and Primitive recursion).

Basic Primitive Functions

1. The *zero function* $z(x) = 0$, for all $x \in I$.
2. The *successor function* $s(x) = x + 1$, for all $x \in I$.
3. The *projector function* $p_k(x_1, x_2) = x_k, k = 1, 2$

Composition and Primitive Recursion

1. The *composition of* h with g_1 and g_2

    $h(g_1(x, y), g_2(x, y))$
2. The primitive recursion of f in terms of g_1, g_2 and h

    $f(x, 0) = g_1(x)$

    $f(x, y + 1) = h(g_2(x, y), f(x, y))$

A given function is called *primitive recursive function* if and only if it can be obtained from the *basic primitive functions* by some sequence of operations of composition and primitive recursion. A *total function* is called primitive recursive if and only if either it is any one of the basic primitive functions or it can be constructed by applying composition and recursion a finite number of times to the primitive functions. Thus, every primitive recursive function is a total function. Every primitive function is *computable*, but reverse is not true.

Example 9.2: Show that the function add(x, y) is primitive recursive function

Solution: The function add (x, y) with two variables x and y can be constructed by primitive recursion as follows:

   add$(x, 0) = x$

   add$(x, y + 1) =$ add$(x, y) + 1$

Thus, add(x, y) is a primitive.

Example 9.3: Show that the function mul(x, y) is primitive recursion.

Solution: The function mul(x, y) is a primitive recursive function because it can be constructed by repeated addition as follows:

$$\text{mul}(x, 0) = 0 = g(x) = z(x)$$
$$\text{mul}(x, y + 1) = \text{add}(x, \text{mul}(x, y))$$
$$= \text{add}(P_1(x, y, \text{mul}(x, y)), P_3(x, y, \text{mul}(x, y)))$$
$$= \text{add}(p_1(x, y, z), p_3(x, y, z))$$
$$= h(x, y, z)$$

We shown that $\text{mul}(x, y)$ is defined by recursion and $g(x)$ and $h(x, y, z)$ are primitive recursive. Therefore, $\text{mul}(x, y)$ is a primitive recursive.

9.11.2 Ackermann's Function

Ackermann's function is total and computable but not a primitive recursive function. It is a function from $I \times I$ to I, defined by

$$A(0, y) = y + 1,$$
$$A(x, 0) = A(x - 1, 1),$$
$$A(x, y + 1) = A(x - 1, A(x, y)).$$

$A(x, y)$ can be computed for every (x, y). Therefore, $A(x, y)$ is total.

9.11.3 μ-recursive Function

The minimization f of a function g with $k + 1$ arguments is a function of k arguments defined as follows:

$f(n_1, n_2 ... n_k) = $ the smallest m such that $g(n_1, n_2, ... n_k, m) = 1$ if there is such an m otherwise 0.

We can observe that given any total function g and any set of k arguments to it, here either is at least one value m such that $g(n_1, n_2, ... n_k, m) = 1$ or there is not. If g is computable then there exists a Turing machine that computes g.

A function is μ-recursive if it can be constructed from the basic functions by a equence of applications of the minimization function and the operations of omposition and primitive recursion. A function is μ-recursive if and only if it is omputable.

9.12 Rice's Theorem

R is a *trivial property* of recursively enumerable languages if it is satisfied by ll such languages or by none of them. R is a *non-trivial* property if it is satisfied by ome but not all recursively enumerable languages.

Rice's theorem is stated as follows:

If R is a non-trivial property of recursively enumerable languages then the ecision problem;

Given a Turing Machine T, does $L(T)$ have property R is unsolvable.

Rice theorem can also be stated as:

Any non-trivial property about the language recognized by a Turing machine is ndecidable.

The property is non-trivial if there is at least one Turing machine that has the roperty, and at least one that has not.

Rice theorem cannot be applied if the property R is trivial.

The following decision problems are all unsolvable:

1. AcceptsSomething: Give a TM T, is $L(T)$ non-empty?
2. AcceptsEverything: Give a TM T, with input alphabet Σ, is $L(T) = \Sigma*$?
3. Subset: Given two TMs T_1 and T_2, is $L(T_1) \subseteq L(T_2)$?
4. WritesSymbol: Given a TM T, and a symbol a in its tape alphabet, does T ever write a if it is started with a blank symbol?
5. AcceptsTwo: Given a TM T, does T accepts at least two strings?
6. AcceptsRecursive: Given a TM T, is the language accepted by T recursive?

9.13   Tractable and Intractable Problems

A problem is called *non-computable* if no algorithm exists that can solve it. However, a problem may be *computationally* solvable only in principle and not in practice as the solution may require huge amount of computation time and memory.

A computable problem is often called *computationally tractable* if there exists an algorithm of *polynomial complexity* to solve it. Examples of tractable problems are sorting, searching, string editing, etc. Conversely, a computable problem will be called *intractable or computationally hard* if the algorithm to solve it cannot solve all of its instances in polynomial time. Examples of intractable problems are Traveling Salesman problem, Graph Coloring problem, Hamilton cycle problem, Satisfiability problem, etc.

9.13.1 P and NP Problem

Class P is the set of all decision problems that are solvable by *deterministic algorithms* in *polynomial time*. The *Class NP* consists of all those decision problems whose solutions can be verified in polynomial time or equivalently that are solvable by *non-deterministic algorithms* in *polynomial time*.

In terms of TM, the *class P* consists of all those decision problems that can be solved by a *deterministic* TM in polynomial time complexity $T(n)$, n being the size of the input and *class NP* is the set of all decision problems solvable on a *non-deterministic* TM of polynomial time complexity. Clearly, $P \subseteq NP$.

The most famous unsolved problem in theoretical computer science is:

Is P equal to NP?

9.13.2 NP-Complete Problem

In order to approach the above problem, the concept of *NP-completeness* is very useful. A decision problem is *NP-complete* if it is in *NP* and all other *NP problems* are *polynomial-time* reducible to it. A consequence of this definition is that if any of the *NP-complete* problems was to be solved in *polynomial time* then all *NP problems* can be solved in *polynomial time*.

A problem is NP-hard if all NP problems can be reduced to it in polynomial time. Therefore, an NP-hard problem is at least as hard as the hardest problem in

NP, although, it might, in fact, be harder. NP-hard problems need not be in NP. Note that all *NP-complete problems* are also *NP-hard*.

The relationship among P, NP, NP-complete and NP-hard, as generally seen, is represented in the Figure 9.7.

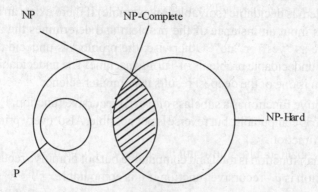

Fig. 9.7: Relationship among P, NP, NP-complete and NP-hard

If an *NP-problem* can be solved in polynomial time, all other *NP-problems* can also be solved in polynomial time. However if an *NP-hard problem* can be solved in polynomial time then all *NP-complete problems* can also be solved in polynomial time. No polynomial-time algorithms have ever been found that solve any of *NP-complete problems*, and determining whether these problems are tractable or intractable remains one of the most important question in computer science.

Some NP-Complete problems: Following is the list of some NP-Complete problems:

1. The Traveling Salesman Problem
    2. The Satisfiability problem
    3. The Vertex Cover Problem
    4. The Hamilton Circuit Problem
    5. The Integer Linear Programming
    6. The Exact Cover Problem
    7. The Partition Problem
    8. The Chromatic Number Problem

9.14 Summary

1. A given language is called a recursively enumerable language if there exists a Turing machine that accepts all words in the language and rejects or loops the words that are not in the language.

2. A given language is called a recursive language if there exists a Turing machine that accepts all words in the language and rejects the words that are not in the language.

3. The recursive languages are closed under union, intersection and complement whereas recursively enumerable languages are closed under union.

4. Noam Chomsky was the founder of formal languages. He presented the hierarchy of grammars according to the structure of their productions in 1959.

5. A problem is decidable (solvable/Answerable) if there exists an algorithm that takes as input an instance of the problem and determines the answer to that instance as "yes" or "no". Otherwise, the problem is undecidable. There are various undecidable problems of Turing machine. The undecidability of Halting problem is one of the deepest results in computer science.

6. A primitive function is a subclass of partial recursive function. Every primitive function is computable, but reverse is not possible. Also, every primitive function is total function.

7. Ackerman function is total and computable but not primitive recursive function. A function is μ –recursive function if it is computable.

9.15 Exercises

Objective Questions

1. Which of the following is not primitive recursive but partially recursive?
   (a) Carnot's function   (b) Ricmann function
   (c) Bonded function   (d) Ackermann's function

2. Which of the following instances of the post correspondence problem have a viable sequence?
   (a) $\{(b, bb), (bb, bab), (bab, abb), (abb, babb)\}$
   (b) $\{(ab, aba), (bab, aa), (aba, baa)\}$
   (c) $\{(ab, abb), (ba, aaa), (aa, a)\}$
   (d) None of these

3. Which of the following statement(s) is (are) correct?
   (a) Recursive languages are closed under complement
   (b) If language and its complement are both regular, the language is recursive.
   (c) Set of recursively enumerable languages is closed under union
   (d) All of these

4. Recursively enumerable languages are not closed under:
   (a) Union   (b) Intersection
   (c) Complementation   (d) Concatenation

5. Recursive languages are:
   (a) A proper super set of CFL   (b) Always recognizable by PDA
   (c) Recognizable by TM   (d) Both (a) and (c)

6. Correct hierarchical relationship among context-free, right-linear, and context-sensitive language is:

   (a) Context-free $\subset$ right linear $\subset$ context-sensitive
   (b) Context-free $\subset$ context-sensitive $\subset$ right linear
   (c) Context-sensitive $\subset$ right linear $\subset$ context-free
   (d) Right linear $\subset$ context-free $\subset$ context-sensitive

7. Which of the following statements is false?
    (a) Halting problem of Turing machine is undecidable
    (b) Determining whether a CFG is ambiguous is undecidable
    (c) Given two arbitrary CFGs G_1, G_2 and it is undecidable whether $L(G_1) = L(G_2)$.
    (d) Given two regular grammars G_1, G_2 and it is undecidable whether $L(G_1) = L(G_2)$

8. If there exists a language L, for which there exists a Turing machine, T, that accepts every word in L and either rejects or loops for every word that is not in L, is called:
    (a) Recursive   (b) Recursive enumerable
    (c) Both (a) and (b)   (d) None of these

9. Which of the following statements is true?
    (a) $L = \{a^n b^n a^n \mid n \geq 1\}$ is recursively enumerable}
    (b) Recursively enumerable languages are closed under union
    (c) Every recursive language is closed under union
    (d) All of above

10. The statement "A Turing machine can't solve halting problem" is:
    (a) True   (b) False
    (c) Still at open question   (d) All of these

11. If there exists a Turing machine which when applied to any problem in the class terminates, if correct answer is yes and may or may not terminate is called:
    (a) Stable   (b) Unsolvable
    (c) Partially solvable   (d) Unstable

12. A total recursive function is also a:
    (a) Partial recursive function   (b) Primitive recursive function
    (c) Both (a) and (b)   (d) None of these

13. If there exists a TM that accepts every word in L and rejects every word in L^c(complement of L). The language L is called:
    (a) Recursive   (b) Recursively enumerable
    (c) Both (a) and (b)   (d) None of these

14. If a language L and its complement L^C, both are recursively enumerable language, then both L and L^C are:
    (a) Regular language

(b)   Recursive language

(c)   Recursively enumerable language

(d)   None of these

15.   If all of the productions of the grammar G, are in the form $\alpha \to \beta$, where $\alpha, \beta \in$ $(V \cup T)^*$ and α contains at least one variable, then G is called:

(a)   Context-free grammar   (b)   Context-sensitive grammar

(c)   Unrestricted grammar   (d)   None of the above

16.   The other name of unrestricted grammar is:

(a)   Type 0   (b)   Phrase structure

(c)   Semi-Thue   (d)   All of the above

17.   Noam Chomsky provided a hierarchy of grammars according to the:

(a)   Structure of their productions   (b)   Language they accept

(c)   Model of computation   (d)   None of these

18.   Lamda calculus was developed by:

(a)   Alan Turing   (b)   Alonzo Church

(c)   Claude Shannon   (d)   None of the above

19.   Lamda calculus is basis for:

(a)   C#   (b)   Java language

(c)   C++   (d)   Haskell language

Answers to Objective Questions

01.	(d)	02.	(c)	03.	(d)	04.	(c)	05.	(d)	06.	(d)
07.	(d)	08	(b)	09.	(d)	10.	(a)	11.	(c)	12.	(d)
13.	(a)	14.	(b)	15.	(c)	16.	(d)	17.	(a)	18.	(b)
19.	(d)										

Review Questions

1.   Show that the following are primitive functions:

(i) $f(x, y) = xy$

^{A}(ii) The predecessor function $p(x)$ defined by $p(x) = x - 1$ if $x <> 0, p(x) = 0$ $x = 0$

(iii) The proper substraction function defined by

$xy = x - y$ if $x \geq y$ and $xy = 0$ if $x < y$

(iv) $\min(x, y)$, i.e., minimum of x and y.

(v)   The absolute value function $| |$ given by

$$|x| = x \text{ if } x \geq 0$$
$$|x| = -x \text{ if } x < 0$$

(vi) $f(x, y) = x$ if $x \neq y$
$$= 0 \text{ if } x = y$$

^{A}(vii) $f(x_1, x_2, \ldots x_n) = 6$

(viii) equals $(x, y) = 1$ if $x = y$

$= 0$ if $x \ne y$

^{A}(ix) $f(x, y) = x^3y^5 + 9xy^4 + 5x^6$

(x) $f(n) = 2^n$

^{A}(xi) $f(x, y) = x^y$

2. Present Chomsky hierarchy of grammar in tabular form gives grammar type, production restriction, the acceptor machine and the name of the language generated.

3. Define recursive and recursively enumerable languages. Show by construction that recursive languages are closed under complementation and union.

4. Define primitive recursive functions over integers. Show that the addition and multiplication of integers can be written in a recursive form using these primitive functions.

5. Give some examples of undecidable problems. Show that Halting problem is Turing undecidable.

6. Write short notes on the following:
   (i) Halting problem
   (ii) PCP
   (iii) Lambda Calculus
   (iv) Post System
   (v) Primitive Recursive Function
   (vi) μ–recursive function

7. Differentiate between PCP and MPCP. Prove that the PCP with $\Sigma = \{0, 1, 2\}$ two lists $A = \{0, 1, 2\}$ and $B = \{00, 11, 22\}$ has no solution.

8. What is Modified Post Correspondence Problem? Show that the PCP with $\Sigma = \{a, b\}$ and two lists $A = \{ba, abb, bab\}$ and $B = (bab, bb, abb\}$ has a no solution.

^{A}9. Prove or disprove that the following Post Correspondence Problem with Σ and two lists A and B have a solution.
   (i) $\Sigma = \{0, 1\}$, $A = \{1, 101^3, 10\}$, $B = (1^3, 10, 0)$
   (ii) $\Sigma = \{a, b\}$, $A = \{ab, b, b\}$, $B = \{ab^2, ba, b\}$

^{A}10. Show that the function subtr (x, y) is primitive recursive.

11. Integer division can be defined by two functions div and rem:

$$div(x, y) = n,$$

where n is the largest integer such that $x \ge ny$, and

$$rem(x, y) = x - ny$$

Show that the functions div and rem are primitive recursive.

^A12. Compute the following for the Ackermann function:

   (i) $A(1, 1)$

   (ii) $A(2, 1)$

13.. Prove the following for the Ackermann function:

   ^A(a) $A(1, y) = y + 2$

   ^A(b) $A(2, y) = 2y + 3$

   (c) $A(3, y) = 2^{y+3} - 3$

^A14. Define the function

$$greater(x, y) = 1 \text{ if } x > y$$
$$= 0 \text{ if } \leq y$$

Show that this function is primitive recursive.

^A15. If $f(x_1, x_2)$ is primitive recursive, show that $g(x_1, x_2, x_3) = f(x_1, x_3)$ is primitive recursive.

^A16. If (x, y) is primitive recursive, show that $g(x, y) = f(8, y)$ is primitive recursive.

17. Define trivial and non-trivial property. State Rice's theorem.

18. Discuss tractable and intractable problem. Draw commonly believed relationship between class P, NP, NP-complete and NP-hard.

19. Define P, NP, NP-complete problems. Also list NP-complete problems.

Answers/Hints for Selected Review Questions

1.   (ii) $pred(0) = 0$

        $pred(x + 1) = P_1(x, P(x))$

              $= x$

      So, $pred(x)$ is a primitive recursive.

   (vii) $6 = s^6(0)$

          $= s^6(z(x_1))$

          $= s^6(z(P_1^n(x_1, x_2, ...x_n)))$

          $= f(x_1, x_2, ... x_n)$

      Since f is constructed from basic primitive functions, f is primitive recursive.

   (ix) Since $f_1(x, y) = x + y$ is primitive recursive, we have to show that operands are primitive recursive. $x^3 y^5 = P_1(x, y) \times P_1(x, y) \times P_1(x, y) \times P_2(x, y) \times P_2(x, y) \times P_2(x, y) \times P_2(x, y) \times P_2(x, y)$. Since multiplication is primitive recursive, therefore, $f_2(x, y) = x^2 y^4$ is primitive recursive. Similarly, we can show that xy^4 is primitive recursive and therefore, $9xy^4 = xy^4 + xy^4 + ...$ xy^4 is primitive recursive. In the same way, we can also show that $5x^6$ is primitive recursive.

   (xi) We define $f(x, y) = x^0 = 1$

        $f(x, y + 1) = x \times f(x, y)$

$$= P_1(x, y, f(x, y)) \times P_3(x, y, f(x, y))$$

Therefore $f(x, y)$ is primitive recursive.

9. (i) We have to determine whether or not there exists a sequence of substrings of A such that the string formed by this sequence and the string formed by the sequence of corresponding substrings of B are identical. The required sequence is given by

$i_1 = 2, i_2 = 1, i_3 = 1, i_4 = 3$ i.e. (2, 1, 1, 3) and $m = 4$. The corresponding strings are 1013 11 10 = 1013130, i.e., $A_2 A_1 A_1 A_3 = B_2 B_1 B_1 B_3$. Thus, the PCP has a solution.

(ii) For each substring $A_i \in A$ and $B_i \in B$, we have $\{A_i| < |B_i|$ for all i. Hence the string generated by a sequence of substrings of A is shorter than the string generated by the sequence of corresponding substrings of B. Therefore, PCP has no solution.

10. $\mathrm{subtr}(x, 0) = x$

$\qquad = g(x)$

$\qquad = z(x)$

$\mathrm{subtr}(x, y + 1) = \mathrm{pred}(\mathrm{subtr}(x, y))$

$\qquad = \mathrm{pred}(p_3(x, y, \mathrm{subtr}(x, y)))$

$\qquad = p_3(x, y, \mathrm{pred}(p_3(x, y, \mathrm{subtr}(x, y))))$

12. (i) $A(1, 1) = A(0, A(1, 0))$

$\qquad = A(0, A(0, 1))$

$\qquad = A(0, 2)$

$\qquad = 3$

(ii) $A(2, 1) = A(1, A(2, 0))$

$\qquad = A(1, A(1, 1))$

$\qquad = A(1, A(0, A(1, 0))$

$\qquad = A(1, A(0, A(0,1))$

$\qquad = A(1, A(0, 2))$

$\qquad = A(1, 3)$

$\qquad = A(0, A(1, 2))$

$\qquad = A(0, A(0, A(1, 1)))$

$\qquad = A(0, A(0, A(0, A(1, 0)))))$

$\qquad = A(0, A(0, A(0, A(0,1))))$

$\qquad = A(0, A(0, A(0, 2))))$

$\qquad = A(0, A(0, 3))$

$\qquad = A(0, 4)$

$\qquad = 5$

13. (a) $A(1, y) = A(0, A(1, y - 1))$

$$= A(1, y-1) + 1$$
$$= A(1, y-2) + 2$$

$$\vdots$$

$$= A(1, 0) + y$$
$$= y + 2$$

(b)   Assume that for $y = 1, 2, \ldots n-1$

We have $A(2, y) = 2y + 3$

Then $A(2, n) = A(1, A(2, n-1))$

$$= A(1, 2n+1)$$

$$= 2n + 3 \text{ since } A(2, 0) = A(1, 1) = 3$$

14.   greater $(x, y) = \text{subtr}(1, \text{subtr}(1, \text{subtr}(x, y)))$

15. $g(x_1, x_2, x_3) = f(x_1, x_3)$

$$= f(\ p_1^3(x_1, x_2, x_3),\ p_3^3(x_1, x_2, x_3))$$

since p_1^3 and P_3^3 both are basic primitive functions, therefore, primitive recursive. Function g is obtained by applying composition to primitive recursive functions. Thus, g is primitive recursive.

16.   Let $f_1(x, y) = 8$

$$= s^8(0)$$
$$= s^8(z(x))$$
$$= s^8(z(p_1(x, y)))$$

f_1 is a composition of basic primitive function. Hence f_1 is primitive recursive.

$$g(x, y) = f(8, y)$$
$$= f(f_1(x, y), P_1(x, y))$$

Since f is a primitive recursive, therefore, $g(x, y)$ is primitive.

References

1. J.E.Hopcraft and J.D. Ullman, 1994, Introduction to Automata theory, Languages and Computation, Narosa Publishing House.
2. J.C. Martin, Introduction to Languages and the Theory of Computation, 3rd Edition, Tata McGraw Hill.
3. H.R. Lewis and C.H. Papadimitriou, Elements and Theory of Computation, PHI.
4. P. Linz, An Introduction to Formal Languages and Automata, 3rd Edition, Narosa Publishing House.
5. K.L.P. Mishra & N. Chandrasekaran, Theory of Computer Science: Automata, Languages and Computation, 3rd edition, PHI.
6. D.I.A. Cohen, Introduction to Computer Theory, 2nd edition, John Wiley & Sons, Inc.
7. M. Sipser, Theory of Computation, Cengage Learning.

Model Paper-I

Time : 03 Hours   *Total Marks : 100*

Note : (1) Attempt **ALL** questions.

(2) All questions carry equal marks.

(3) Notations/Symbols/Abbreviations used have usual meaning.

(4) Make suitable assumptions, wherever required.

1. Attempt any **four** parts of the following: (5 × 4 = 20)

   a. What are the major areas in theory of computation? Discuss them briefly.

   b. Define Finite Automata. Give any five real world examples of a FA and explain one of them.

   c. Suppose δ is the transition function of a DFA. If $\delta(q, x) = \delta(q, y)$, prove that $\delta(q, xz) = \delta(q, yz)$ for all strings z in Σ^+.

   d. Consider the following NFA with ε-transition.

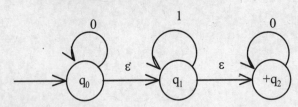

Compute $\hat{\delta}(q_0, 1)$ & $\hat{\delta}(q_2, 0)$.

   e. What is the regular expression? Give recursive definition of the regular expression.

   f. Describe in English, as briefly as possible, the language defined by each of these regular expressions:

     (a) $(b + ba)(b + a)^*(ab + b)$

     (b) $(1 + \varepsilon)(00^*1)^*0^*$

2. Attempt any **four** parts of the following: (5 × 4 = 20)

   a. Consider the problem of determining whether a string is a legal password. Suppose that we require that all passwords meet the following requirements:

     (i)   A password must begin with a letter

     (ii) A password may contain only letters, numbers and the underscore characters and

      (iii) A password must contain at least four characters and no more than eight characters

      Write a regular expression to describe the language of legal password.

b.   Why is CFG not considered adequate for describing natural language? Explain with suitable example.

c.   Explain the following terms with suitable examples:

      (i)   A-tree

      (ii) Total language tree

d.   Give a formal definition of PDA, configurations, computations and the language accepted by the PDA.

e.   What is ε-production? Write an algorithm to remove the ε-production.

f.   Show that the family of context-free languages is closed under reversal.

3.   Attempt any **Two** parts of the following: (10 × 2 = 20)

a.   Define and explain NFA. Convert the NFA($\{p, q, r, s\}$, $\{0,1\}$, δ, p, $\{s\}$) to equivalent DFA. δ is given by the following table:

Input States	0	1
p	p	p
q	q	r
r	r	-
s	s	s

b.   Define Moore machine. Construct a Moore machine that determines whether an input string contains an even or odd number of 1s. The machine should give 'E' as output if an even number of 1s are in the string and 'O' otherwise.

c.   Define regular grammar. Write an algorithm to convert regular grammar to the finite automaton. Construct a CFG of the following finite Automaton:

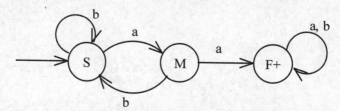

4.   Attempt any **Two** parts of the following: (10 × 2 = 20)

a.   Define Chomsky Normal Form. Convert the following grammar into Chomsky normal form:

      $S \rightarrow aSb | ab$

b.   Define language accepted by PDA. Construct PDA that accepts the following language on $\Sigma = \{a, b\}$ by final state.

      (i) $L = \{a^n b^m : n \le m \le 3n\}$

c.   Explain 2-stack PDA. Construct a 2-stack PDA for the following language:

(i) $a^n b^n c^n d^n | n \geq 0$

5.   Attempt any **Two** parts of the following: $(10 \times 2 = 20)$

a.   States the Pumping Lemma for a context-free language. Determine whether or not the following language is in context-free:

(i) $L = \{a^n b^j : n \leq j^2\}$

b.   Present a Turing machine that inserts symbol # in the beginning of a string on the Turing tape. Assume $\Sigma = \{a, b\}$.

c.   Present Chomsky hierarchy of grammar in tabular form giving grammar type, production restriction, the acceptor machine and the name of the language generated.

Model Paper-II

Time : 03 Hours

Total Marks : 100

Note : (1) Attempt **ALL** questions.

      (2) All questions carry equal marks.

      (3) Notations/Symbols/Abbreviations used have usual meaning.

      (4) Make suitable assumptions, wherever required.

1. Attempt any **four** parts of the following: $(5 \times 4 = 20)$

    a. What do you mean by ε-closure of a state in a finite automaton?

    b. Define DFA. List three household applications of finite Automata.

    c. Design deterministic finite automaton accepting the following languages over the alphabet {0,1}:

      (i) The set of all words that have exactly four 1s.

      (ii) The set of all words that end with 0.

    d. A student walks into a class room and sees on the black-board a diagram of a transition graph with two states that accepts only the word ε. The student reverses the direction of exactly one edge learning all other edges and all labels and all +'s and −'s the same. But now the new transition graph accepts the language a*. What was the original machine?

    e. The following grammar generates the language of regular expression 0*1(0 + 1)*:

$$S \rightarrow A1B$$
$$A \rightarrow I0A \mid \varepsilon$$
$$B \rightarrow I0B \mid 1B \mid \varepsilon$$

    f. States and proof distinguishability lemma.

2. Attempt any **four** parts of the following: $(5 \times 4 = 20)$

    a. What is the relationship between regular languages and Finite automata?

    b. The context-free grammars, like regular languages, can be viewed as language generators. Justify.

    c. What do you mean by ambiguity of the grammar? Show that below grammar is ambiguous.

$$G = (V, T, E, P) \ V = \{E, I\}, T = \{a, b, c, +, *, (,)\} \text{ and productions}$$
$$E \rightarrow I$$

$$E \rightarrow E + E$$
$$E \rightarrow E*E$$
$$E \rightarrow (E)$$
$$I \rightarrow a|b|c$$

d. State the difference between PDA and the FA.

e. What is useless production? Write an algorithm to remove the useless production.

f. Show that the family of context-free languages is closed under union.

3. Attempt any **Two** parts of the following: (10 x 2 = 20)

a. Define and explain NFA with ε-transition. Convert the NFA ($\{q_0, q_1, q_2, q_3, q_4\}, \{0, 1\}, \delta, q_0, \{q_4\}$) to equivalent DFA. δ is given by the following table:

Input States	0	1
q_0	$\{q_1, q_3\}$	q_0
q_1	$\emptyset$	q_2
q_2	q_2	q_2
q_3	q_4	$\emptyset$
q_4	q_4	q_4

b. Design a Moore machine for incrementing a given binary number by 1.

c. Eliminate all ε-productions from the following grammars:

$$S \rightarrow AaB \mid aaB \qquad A \rightarrow \varepsilon$$
$$B \rightarrow bbA \mid \varepsilon$$

4. Attempt any **Two** parts of the following: (10 × 2 = 20)

a. List the applications of Chomsky Normal Form(CNF). Convert the following grammar into CNF:

$$S \rightarrow aSaA \mid A, \qquad S \rightarrow abA|b$$

b. Construct PDA that accepts the following language on $\Sigma = \{a, b\}$ by final state:

$$L = \{a^i b^j c^k : i = j \text{ or } j = k\}$$

c. Construct a 2-stack PDA for the following language:

$$a^n b^n c^m d^n \mid m, n \geq 0$$

5. Attempt any **Two** parts of the following: (10 × 2 = 20)

a. Show that $G = (V, T, P, S)$ where $V = \{S, X, Y, A, B\}$, $T = \{a, b\}$, $S = \{S\}$ and P consist of $S \rightarrow XY$

$$X \rightarrow AX$$
$$A \rightarrow a$$
$$Y \rightarrow BY|BB$$
$$B \rightarrow b$$

generates at least one word.

b. Design a Turing machine that can compute proper subtraction, i.e., $m \rightarrow n$, where m and n are positive integers, mn is defined as $m - n$ if $m > n$ and 0 if $m \leq n$.

c. Define recursive and recursively enumerable languages. Show by construction that recursive languages are closed under complementation and union.

Model Paper-III

Time : 03 Hours   *Total Marks : 100*

Note : (1) Attempt **ALL** questions.

      (2) All questions carry equal marks.

      (3) Notations/Symbols/Abbreviations used have usual meaning.

      (4) Make suitable assumptions, wherever required.

1. Attempt any **four** parts of the following: $(5 \times 4 = 20)$

   a. Give formal definition of DFA with a suitable example, also differentiate DFA with NFA.

   b. What do you mean by the extended transition function of DFA? Is it necessary to use a different symbol for the extended transition function than that of the transition function? Give the reason for your answer.

   c. Design deterministic finite automaton accepting the following languages over the alphabet $\{0,1\}$:

       (i) $L = \{w| \ |w| \bmod 4 = 0\}$

       (ii) $L = \{w| \ |w| \bmod 4 > 1\}$

   d. Find the regular grammar for the language

       $L = \{a^n b^m \mid n + m \text{ is even}\}$

   e. Construct a regular expression defining each of the following languages over the alphabet $\Sigma = \{a, b\}$.

       (i) All words with double a within.

       (ii) All words that have different first and last letters.

   f. Show that union of regular languages is also regular.

2. Attempt any **four** parts of the following: $(5 \times 4 = 20)$

   a. The complementary (cor) of two languages is $\mathrm{cor}(L_1, L_2) = \{w : w \in L_1^C$ or $w \, L_2^C \}$. Show that the family of regular languages is closed under the cor operation.

   b. What is the derivation? List the properties of derivation.

   c. Prove that the language $L = \{a^n b^n \mid n \geq 1\}$ is a context-free language.

   d. Give a formal definition of 2-stack pushdown automaton, configurations, computations and the language accepted by such automaton.

e. What is unit production? Write an algorithm to remove unit production.

f. Formally define:

    (i) A configuration of NFA

    (ii) The yields in one step relation $\vdash_M$ between configurations of such a machine

3. Attempt any **Two** parts of the following: $(10 \times 2 = 20)$

a. Draw a Mealy machine equivalent to the following circuit.

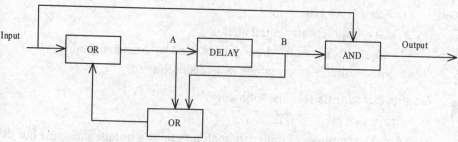

b. What is Arden's theorem? Give an algorithm to convert the DFA into a regular expression.

c. Define ε-production. Eliminate all ε-productions from the following grammar:

$$S \to Xa \qquad X \to aX \mid bX \mid \varepsilon$$

4. Attempt any **Two** parts of the following: $(10 \times 2 = 20)$

a. Define Greibach normal form. Convert the following grammars into Greibach normal form:

$$S \to aSb \mid ab$$

b. Construct PDA that accepts the following languages on $\Sigma = \{a, b\}$ by final state.

$$L = \{a^m b^n c^p d^q : m, \text{n}, p, q \geq 0 \text{ and } m + n = p + q\}$$

c. Construct a 2-Stack PDA for the following languages:

$$a^n b^n a^n b^{3n} \mid n \geq 0$$

5. Attempt any **Two** parts of the following: $(10 \times 2 = 20)$

a. Prove that whether the language generated by the following CFG is finite or infinite.

$$S \to AB \mid bb$$
$$A \to BB$$
$$B \to AB \mid SS$$

b. Define TM. Construct. Turing machine that computes the integer function f defined as follows: $f(n) = 3^n$ where n is integer and $n \geq 0$.

c. Give some examples of undecidable problems. Show that Halting problem is Turing undecidable.

Model Paper-IV

Time : 03 Hours   *Total Marks : 100*

Note : (1) Attempt **ALL** questions.

       (2) All questions carry equal marks.

       (3) Notations/Symbols/Abbreviations used have usual meaning.

       (4) Make suitable assumptions, wherever required.

1. Attempt any **four** parts of the following: $(5 \times 4 = 20)$

   a. Prove that NFA = DFA.

   b. Any Deterministic Finite Automaton defines a unique language but the converse is not true. Justify it with the help of a suitable example.

   c. Design deterministic finite automaton accepting the following languages over the alphabet $\{0, 1\}$:

      (i) The set of all words that ends up in either 00 or 11.

      (ii) The set of all words with no more than three 1's.

   d. What is the limitation of FA? Differentiate between the Moore and Mealy machines with examples.

   e. State Pumping Lemma theorem for regular language.

   f. Prove that the following language is not regular.

      (i) $L = \{a^n b^l a^k : k >= n + 1\}$

2. Attempt any **four** parts of the following: $(5 \times 4 = 20)$

   a. List the application of FA. Discuss any software design application of FA.

   b. What are left most and right most derivations? Explain with suitable example.

   c. Define PDA. Discuss the moves of PDA.

   d. Prove that the language of even-length palindromes, i.e., $L = \{ww^R \mid w \in \{a, b\}^*\}$ is a context-free language but not a regular language.

   e. Show the derivation tree for string '*aabbbb*' with the following grammar:

$$S \rightarrow AB|\varepsilon$$
$$A \rightarrow aB$$
$$B \rightarrow SB$$

   f. Write short notes on the Church's thesis.

3. Attempt any **Two** parts of the following: $(10 \times 2 = 20)$

   a. Minimize the states in the DFA depicted in the following diagram:

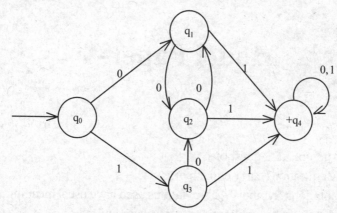

b. Design an NFA that accepts the language $L = \{bb^*(a + b))$.

c. Construct a Mealy machine that scans sequences of 0s and 1s and generates output '*A*' if the input string terminates in 00, output '*B*' if the string terminates in 11 and output '*C*' otherwise.

4. Attempt any **Two** parts of the following: $(10 \times 2 = 20)$

a. Define useless variable and production. Eliminate all useless productions from the following grammar:

$$S \rightarrow aS \,|\, AB$$
$$A \rightarrow ba$$
$$B \rightarrow AA$$

What language does this grammar generate?

b. Construct a PDA that accepts the language generated by the grammar $S \rightarrow aSbb \,|\, aab$

c. Construct a 2-stack PDA for the following language:

(i) $a^n b^n a^{2n} \,|\, n \geq 0$

5. Attempt any **Two** parts of the following:

a. Using Cock, Younger and Kasami algorithm decide whether word *babaa* can be generated by the following CFG or not:

$$S \rightarrow XY$$
$$X \rightarrow XA \,|\, a \,|\, b$$
$$Y \rightarrow AY \,|\, a$$
$$A \rightarrow a$$

b. Explain basic TM model. Construct Turing machines that will accept the following languages:

[A](b) $L = L\{w| \,|w|$ is multiple of 3, $w \in \{a, b\}^*\}$

c. (i) Prove that if a language L and Complement of L both are recursively enumerable then L is recursive.

(ii) Give a example of a language that is recursively enumerable but not recursive. Justify your answers.

Model Paper-V

Time : 03 Hours   *Total Marks : 100*

Note : (1) Attempt **ALL** questions.

(2) All questions carry equal marks.

(3) Notations/Symbols/Abbreviations used have usual meaning.

(4) Make suitable assumptions, wherever required.

1. Attempt any **four** parts of the following: $(5 \times 4 = 20)$

    a.   Differentiate between Mealy and Moore machine with example.

    b.   Suppose δ is the transition function of a DFA. Prove that for any input strings x and y, $\delta(q, xy) = \delta(\delta(q, x), y)$.

    c.   Design deterministic finite automaton accepting the following languages over the alphabet $\{0, 1\}$:

    (i)   The set of all words that either begin with 01 or end with 01.

    (ii) The set of all words that have different first and last symbols.

    d.   What is the reason of calling the language defined by Finite Automata a regular language?

    e.   Show that Kleene's closure of regular language is also regular.

    f.   State and proof Myhill-Nerode Theorem.

2. Attempt any **four** parts of the following: $(5 \times 4 = 20)$

    a.   Design NFA to recognize the following sets of string, abc, abd and aacd. Assume $\Sigma = \{a, b, c, d\}$.

    b.   What do you mean by partial derivation tree?

    c.   Prove that $\{w \in \{a, b\} \mid \#a(w) = \#b(w)\}$ is not a regular but it is a context-free language.

    d.   Show that the predecessor function $p(x)$ defined by $p(x) = x - 1$ if $x \diamondsuit 0$, $p(x) = 0$ if $x = 0$ is a primitive function.

    e.   Differentiate the purpose of the study of Turing machine with Finite Automata/Pushdown Automata.

    f.   How UTM overcomes the limitation of Turing machine? Define UTM.

3. Attempt any **Two** parts of the following: $(10 \times 2 = 20)$

    a.   Consider the Deterministic Finite Automata M_1 and M_2 as pictured in the following figures which recognize the languages L_1 and L_2, respectively.

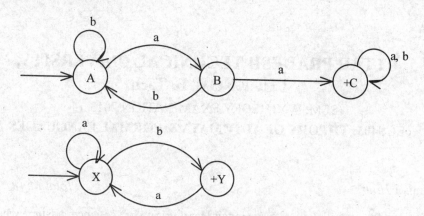

Draw Deterministic Finite Automaton recognizing the following languages:

(i) $L_1 \cup L_2$

(ii) $L_1 L_2$

b. Prove that if L is accepted by a DFA, then L is represented by a regular expression.

c. define Unit production. Remove all Unit Productions from the following grammar:

$$S \to Aa \mid B \qquad\qquad B \to A \mid bb$$
$$A \to a \mid bc \mid B$$

4. Attempt any **Two** parts of the following: (10 x 2 = 20)

a. Define Greibach normal form. Convert the following grammars into Greibach normal form:

$$S \to aSb \mid bSa \mid a \mid b$$

b. Construct a PDA M equivalent to the following grammar $S \to aAA, A \to aS\mid bS\mid a$. Also test whether abaaaa is in the language generated by the grammar.

c. Discuss in detail 2-stack PDA .

5. Attempt any **Two** parts of the following: (10 x 2 = 20)

a. Construct Turing machines that will accept the following language:

(i) $L = \{a^n b^{2n} \mid n > 0\}$

(ii) $L = \{a^n b^n c^n \mid n > 1\}$

b. There exists a recursively enumerable language whose complement is not recursively enumerable. Prove it.

c. Differentiate between PCP and MPCP. Prove that the PCP with $\Sigma = \{0, 1, 2\}$ two lists $A = \{0, 1, 2\}$ and $B = \{00, 11, 22\}$ has no solution.

UTTAR PRADESH TECHNICAL UNIVERSITY, LUCKNOW B. Tech.

(SEM. IV) THEORY EXAMINATION 2013-14
ECS403: THEORY OF AUTOMATA & FORMAL LANGUAGES

Time: 3 Hours   *Total Marks: 100*

Note: Attempt all the questions in fair Handwriting in Sequence. Assume where required and Mention it.

1. Attempt any **four parts** of the following:

    (a) Write Regular expressions for each of the following languages over the alphabet (0,1):

         (i)   The set of all strings in which every pair of adjacent zero's appears before any pair of adjacent one's.

         (ii) The set of all strings not containing 101 as substring.

    (b) Draw DFA of following language over {0, 1} :

         (i)   All strings with even no. of 0's and even no. of 1's.

         (ii) All strings of length at most 5.

    (c) Convert following NFA to equivalent DFA:

$\rightarrow$ p	{q, s}	{q}
*q	{r}	{q, r}
r	{s}	{p}
*s	$\emptyset$	{p}

    (d) Show that every context-free language is context-sensitive.

    (e) Draw DFA for following over set $\Sigma = \{0, 1\}$

         (i) $L = \{w : |w| \bmod 3 = 0\}$

         (ii) $L = \{w : |w| \bmod 3 > 1\}$

         |w| represents length of string w.

    (f) Find the regular grammar for the language

         $L = \{a^n b^m \mid n + m \text{ is even}\}$.

2. Attempt any **four parts** of the following : $(5 \times 4 = 20)$

    (a) Convert the given grammar in Chomsky Normal form (CNF)

         $S \rightarrow ABa$ $A \rightarrow aab$ $B \rightarrow Ac$.

    (b) Following Grammar generates language of Regular Expression: 0*1(0 + 1)*

         $S \rightarrow SA1B$ $A \rightarrow 0A/\varepsilon$ $B \rightarrow 0B \mid 1B \mid \varepsilon$

         Give leftmost and rightmost derivation of strings 00101.

    (c) Show the below grammar is ambiguous:

$$G = (V, T, EP), \ V = (E, I), \ T = \{a, b, c, +, *, (.....)\}$$
$$P \Rightarrow EI \quad E E + E \quad E E * E \quad E (E) \quad I a \mid b \mid c.$$

(d) Find context-free grammar for following languages with ($n \geq 0, m \geq 0, k \geq 0$):

  (i) $L = \{a^n b^n c^k \mid k \geq 3\}$

  (ii) $L = \{a^m b^n c^k \mid n = m \text{ or } m \leq k\}$

(e) Given context-free Grammar, how do you determine that grammar as:

  (i) Empty or non-empty

  (ii) Finite or non-finite

  (iii) Whether a string x belongs to language of grammar.

(f) Design a NFA to recognize following set of strings 0101, 101 and 011. Alphabet set is $\{0, 1\}$. Find the equivalent Regular expression.

3. Attempt any **two parts** of the following: $(10 \times 2 = 20)$

(a) Construct PDA for following:
$$L = \{a^n c b^{2n} \mid n \geq 1\}$$
over alphabet $\Sigma = \{a, b, c\}$. Specify the acceptance state.

(b) Prove that following are not Regular Languages:

  (i) $\{0^n \mid n \text{ is perfect square}\}$.

  (ii) The set of strings of form $0^i 1^j$ such that the greatest common divisor of i and j is 1.

(c) (i) For given CFG, find equivalent CFG with no useless variables:

$$S \rightarrow AB \mid AC \qquad A \rightarrow aAb \mid bAa \mid a \qquad B \rightarrow bbA \mid aaB \mid AB$$
$$C \rightarrow abCa \mid aDb \qquad D \rightarrow bD \mid aC$$

  (ii) Explain Chomsky Normal form and Greibach Normal form. Convert following CFG to equivalent Greibach Normal form:
$$S \rightarrow AA, \quad A \rightarrow SS \ S \rightarrow a, \ A \rightarrow b$$

4. Attempt any **two parts** of the following: $(10 \times 2 = 20)$

(a) Consider given PDA:
$$\text{PDA } M = (\{q_0\}, \{0, 1\}, \{a, b, z_0\}, d, q_0, z_0, \emptyset)$$
d is defined as :
$$d(q_0, a, z_0) = \{(q_0, az_0)\}$$
$$d(q_0, 1, z_0) = \{(q_0, bz_0)\}$$
$$d(q_0, 0, a) = \{(q_0, aa)\}$$
$$d(q_0, 1, b) = \{(q_0, bb)\}$$
$$d(q_0, 0, b) = \{(q_0, \varepsilon)\}$$
$$d(q_0, 1, a) = \{(q_0, \varepsilon)\}$$
$$d(q_0, \varepsilon, z_0) = \{(q_0, \varepsilon)\}$$
Convert given PDA M to corresponding CFG.

(b) Prove the Lemma that language recognized by final state PDA machine and vice-versa, i.e., $L(M) = N(M)$

where $L(M) \rightarrow$ Language by Final State PDA machine.

$N(M) \rightarrow$ Language by Empty Stack PDA machine.

(c) Prove that language L_1 and L_2 are closed under Intersection and complementation if they are regular, but not closed under the above said two properties if they are context-free lzanguages.

5. Attempt any **two parts** of the following: $(10 \times 2 = 20)$

(a) Design a Turing machine that can compute proper substraction i.e. $m \& n$, where m and n are positive integers, $m \& n$ is defened as $m - n$ if $m > n$ and o it $m \leq n$.

(b) State True/False with reason:

(i) Every language described by Regular Expression can be recognized by DFA.

(ii) Every R.E.L. can be generated by CFL.

(iii) The Halting of TM is decidable.

(iv) Every CFL can be recognized by TM.

(c) Design a Transducer (Mealy or Moore) machine to compute multiplication of two n-bit binary numbers.

Index